SAA/LU 6.2
Distributed
Networks and
Applications

J. Ranade Series on Computer Communications

ISBN	AUTHOR	TITLE
0-07-054418-2	Sackett	*IBM's Token-Ring Networking Handbook*
0-07-004128-8	Bates	*Disaster Recovery Planning: Networks, Telecommunications, and Data Communications*
0-07-005075-9	Berson	*APPC: Introduction to LU 6.2*
0-07-012926-6	Cooper	*Computer and Communications Security*
0-07-016189-5	Dayton	*Telecommunications*
0-07-034242-3	Kessler	*ISDN*
0-07-034243-1	Kessler/Train	*Metropolitan Area Networks: Concepts, Standards, and Service*

OTHER RELATED TITLES

0-07-051144-6	Ranade/Sackett	*Introduction to SNA Networking: A Guide for Using VTAM/NCP*
0-07-051143-8	Ranade/Sackett	*Advanced SNA Networking: A Professional's Guide to VTAM/NCP*
0-07-033727-6	Kapoor	*SNA: Architecture, Protocols, and Implementation*
0-07-005553-x	Black	*TCP/IP and Related Protocols*
0-07-005554-8	Black	*Network Management Standards: SNMP, CMOT, and OSI*
0-07-021625-8	Fortier	*Handbook of LAN Technology*

SAA/LU 6.2 Distributed Networks and Applications

John J. Edmunds

McGraw-Hill, Inc.

New York St. Louis San Francisco Auckland Bogotá
Caracas Lisbon London Madrid Mexico Milan
Montreal New Delhi Paris San Juan São Paulo
Singapore Sydney Tokyo Toronto

Library of Congress Cataloging-in-Publication Data

Edmunds, John J.
    SAA/LU 6.2 : distributed networks and applications / John J.
Edmunds.
        p.   cm. — (McGraw-Hill series on computer communications)
    Includes index.
    ISBN 0-07-019022-4
    1: Electronic data processing—Distributed processing.
2. Computer networks.   3. IBM Systems Application Architecture.
QA76.9.D5E36   1992
004'.36—dc20   91-42962
                                                                CIP

1 2 3 4 5 6 7 8 9 0   DOC/DOC   9 8 7 6 5 4 3 2

ISBN   0-07-019022-4

*The sponsoring editor for this book was Jerry Papke, the editing
supervisor was Joseph Bertuna, and the production supervisor was
Donald F. Schmidt.*

Printed and bound by R.R. Donnelley & Sons Company.

To Jarek, Natalia, and Edmund

Contents

Preface

The difficulties involving compatibility and connectivity of mainframes, minicomputers, and personal computers are widespread among computer users. The strategic direction of large cooperations is to interconnect their multivendor environments into a single **Enterprise Information System (EIS)** that appears to programmers and users as a single system. The 1990s are being viewed as the decade of enterprise computing, multivendor interconnections, global networking, open systems, program-to-program communications, and distributed and cooperative processing. Systems Application Architecture (SAA), announced in 1987 by IBM Corporation, is a set of **open architectures** (such as SNA/LU 6.2, OSI, APPC, and CPI-C) that connects mainframes, minicomputers and personal computers as a single Enterprise Information System. SAA is designed to provide the framework for developing common, portable, consistent, and integrated applications across the entire computer enterprise.

The purpose of this book is to provide readers with a comprehensive analysis of the SAA enterprise distributed network based on the SNA logical unit type 6.2 (**LU 6.2**) and the distributed physical unit type 2.1 (**PU 2.1**), the SAA architectures for developing **distributed** and **cooperative processing** applications Advanced Program-to-Program Communications (**APPC**) and Common Programming Interface Communications (**CPI-C**).

THE BOOK 'S ORIGIN

This book has grown out of the author's experiences in designing distributed networks and cooperative processing applications for major corporations and the author's instruction and course development background. The book is based on a 5-day seminar titled *"SAA/LU 6.2 Distributed Networks and Applications"* given by Galaxy Consultants, located in Los Gatos California, a company founded by the author, and well known in the computer industry as education specialists in IBM distributed cooperative transaction processing areas since 1988. These seminars have been developed and taught by the author and have been attended and reviewed by networking and programming professionals from such companies as IBM, Amdahl, Unisys, Hewlett-Packard, Tandem Computers, DEC, Apple Computer, XEROX, NEC, NSA, DCA, Novell, EICON, AT&T, US Sprint, MCI, Pacific Bell, TRW, Citicorp, World Bank, Bank of America, US Customs, Liberty Mutual, Boeing, McDonnel Douglas, PG&E, Chevron, and American Express, just to mention a few. The seminar has consistently received outstanding reviews. The author hopes that the book will be as successful as the seminar and that it will help programming and networking professionals in designing and supporting SAA/LU 6.2 distributed networks and APPC cooperative processing applications applications. For more information on Galaxy Consultants seminars please call (408) 354-2997 or fax (408) 354-2365.

WHO THIS BOOK IS FOR

This book is intended for distributed and cooperative processing application designers, programmers, analysts, and APPC and CPI-C implementors, as well as networking and technical staff, communications specialists, network planners, network designers, system programmers, and anybody who is involved with open system architectures and distributed standards.   A thorough understanding of the SNA logical unit 6.2, APPC, and CPI-C is crucial to programming and networking professionals who will be involved in planning, configuring, or maintaining a company-wide computer enterprise or developing distributed and cooperative processing applications. Developers of APPC/MVS, CICS, OS/2 EE, and AS/400 cooperative processing applications will find that the book applies directly to their specific environments. This book was written and structured in such a way that it can be used as a self-study teaching guide. It can also be used as an excellent source material for a seminar on distributed cooperative processing applications and the SAA distributed network.

PREREQUISITE

The self-study teaching guide approach taken in writing this book assumes that the readers have no prior data communications or cooperative or distributed processing experience. Part 1 of this book introduces the reader to basic SAA, SNA, LU 6.2, APPC, and CPI-C concepts necessary to understand the advanced topics of distributed and cooperative processing application design and implementa-tions, described in subsequent parts. Therefore, readers with any data-processing experience (e.g., CICS, APPC/MVS, OS/2 EE, or OS/400 application and system programmers and networking staff) should be able to understand the concepts of this book after reading Part 1. It was the author's goal in writing this book to provide a comprehensive examination of IBM distributed and cooperative processing concepts and advanced topics in such a way that they can be understood by a wide range of readers with any level of data-processing experience. Thus, readers with a good knowledge of SNA, LU 6.2, APPC, and CPI-C concepts may skip the initial five chapters of the book and start with Part 2.

HARDWARE AND SOFTWARE ENVIRONMENTS

The material covered in this book applies to a variety of hardware platforms (S/390, S/370, AS/400, PS/2, and personal computers and compatible vendors), as well as a variety of software environments, including MVS/ESA, VM/ESA, VSE/ESA, OS/400, OS/2 EE, DOS, and other vendor LU 6.2 emulation packages. The book also covers specific LU 6.2 implementations such as CICS, IMS, DB2, APPC/MVS, CMS, VTAM, OS/2 EE APPC and APPN, OS/400 APPC and APPN, APPC/PC DOS, and other vendor logical unit type 6.2 implementations.

STYLE USED

The book contains a number of figures, diagrams, design flows, and examples that should help the reader in understanding the theory covered in the book. The appendixes contain a summary of configuration, performance, and programming tips discussed in the book, as well as programming design examples and network message flows that should be very helpful while reading the book and as a reference afterward. As an aid to the reader, bold text is used to emphasize important terms, definitions, and conclusions. The book was written as a self-study teaching guide and should be easy to read and understood.

WHAT IS COVERED IN THIS BOOK

Part 1 of the book consists of five chapters and provides the necessary foundation on distributed networks and cooperative processing. Chapter 1 evaluates the major open architectures for enterprise computing in the 1990s: Systems Application Architecture (SAA), Open Systems Interconnection (OSI), and Transmission Control Protocol/Internet Protocol (TCP/IP). Chapter 1 concludes with a comparison of SNA/LU 6.2, OSI, TCP/IP, X.25, and NETBIOS. Chapters 2 through 5 provide an introduction to SNA distributed networks, the logical unit type 6.2, the physical unit type 2.1, Advanced Program-to-Program Communications (APPC), Common Programming Interface Communications (CPI-C), Systems Application Architecture (SAA), and distributed network management issues. Part 2 of this book concentrates on distributed and cooperative processing application design issues using the Advanced Program-to-Program Communications (APPC) and the SAA Common Programming Interface Communications (CPI-C) distributed architectures. Chapter 6 evaluates and compares the APPC and CPI-C architectures. Chapters 7 and 8 cover in depth the APPC and CPI-C architectures and the design issues of distributed and cooperative processing applications. Part 3 of this book covers configuration and performance issues of SAA distributed networks and discusses various LU 6.2 implementations (CICS, IMS, DB2, APPC/MVS, CMS, VTAM, OS/2 EE APPC and APPN, OS/400 APPC and APPN, APPC/PC DOS, and other vendor logical unit type 6.2 implementations). In addition, the appendixes contain configuration, performance, LU 6.2 network message flows, and programming tips, as well as programming design examples.

ACKNOWLEDGMENTS

I would like to express my special thanks to Stella Bryan for making very useful suggestions and clarifications and particularly for the effort she has put into editing the book. My sincere thanks goes to the many networking and programming professionals that attended Galaxy Consultants LU 6.2 seminars, read and corrected various chapters of my manuscript, and gave me invaluable suggestions and tips on the book's content. I would also like to thank Jay Ranade for encouraging me to write this book in the first place. Special thanks go to my parents, in Poland, Natalia and Edmund Chmielnicki for helping me to achieve my professional goals and for moral support and love. Finally, very special thanks to my son Jarek Edmunds Chmielnicki, who has helped me with many diagrams and drawings in the book and who was my best friend during an incredibly difficult time for me of trying to be a good father, writing the book, giving the seminars and managing Galaxy Consultants.

John Edmunds
(Zbigniew Chmielnicki)

SAA/LU 6.2
Distributed
Networks and
Applications

Introduction and Concepts

1

Networking in the 1990s

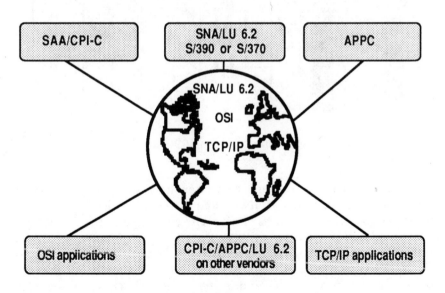

Figure 1.1 Global enterprise networking in the 1990s.

The 1990s will bring unprecedented competition in global markets (see Fig. 1.1). Businesses must adopt a new computing strategy that will allow them to adapt rapidly to the changing global

3

marketplace. This strategy must connect the businesses to the global network in which any information can be shared by the users and decision maker.

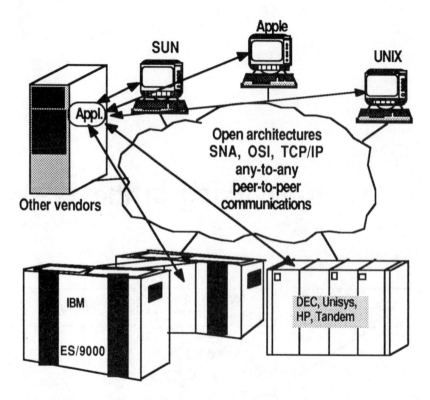

Figure 1.2 End-user requirements of the 1990s.

   The difficulties in current computer networks in the area of compatibility and connectivity of mainframes, minicomputers and personal computers are facts of life. The challenge in the 1990s is to accommodate the existing variety of operating environments and to integrate them into a single **Enterprise Information System (EIS)** that looks to users like a single system. The 1990s are being referred to as the years of multivendor interconnections, open systems enterprise computing, global networking, program-to-program communications, and distributed and cooperative processing. Computer manufactures such as IBM, Digital Equipment, AT&T, Hewlett-Packard, and many others are introducing new networking architectures that eliminate the current differences among the dissimilar operating environments. These architectures will be used by application programs residing on different operating systems via predefined common Application Programming Interfaces (APIs). This interface is independent of the underlying operating environment. The networking architectures of the 1990s must therefore meet the following requirements (see Fig. 1.2):

- **Portability** — businesses should be able to move employees, data, and applications anywhere within the enterprise without any modifications or a need to retrain personnel.

- **Consistency** — users and programmers must be able to perform similar functions on all systems using common techniques.

- **Distribution** — the capability to develop applications that can be used on or distributed among systems residing at different geographic locations.

The ability of a network user or application program to access data and other applications residing anywhere within the network is the major end-user requirement of the 1990s. Therefore, common communications protocols must be adopted that will allow the exchange of information between mainframes, minicomputers, and PCs. The three methodologies currently thought of as contenders for becoming internetworking standards in the 1990s are **Transmission Control Protocol/Internet Protocol (TCP/IP), Open Systems InterconnectionOSI), and Systems Application Architecture/Systems Network Architecture (SAA/SNA).**

1.1 MULTIVENDOR INTERNETWORKING STANDARDS FOR THE 1990s

1.1.1 Transmission Control Protocol/Internet Protocol

With development work having begun in 1972 and first implemented in 1976, TCP/IP, which was developed by the U.S. Department of Defense, was put into heavy production use in 1983. It is the product of the research and academic computer science world and is currently used in a wide range of academic, government, and industrial settings. **Transmission Control Protocol/Internet Protocol (TCP/IP)** is used by over 100 major vendors and is dominant in the UNIX community. It is recognized today as one of the de facto networking standards. The major obstacle that TCP/IP faces in becoming a dominant global networking methodology for the 1990s, is its lack of services at the higher levels. TCP/IP does not define any layers above the **transport layer** (see Fig. 1.7). Therefore, application programs must define all subordinate services, rather than have common services, for managing multiple data streams, performing data transformations, and defining transaction exchanges. The fact that the International Standards Organization (ISO) has chosen to define an altogether new methodology for the OSI transport layer would seem to be cause for its ultimate demise as a dominant networking standard. However, the commercial acceptance of TCP/IP among the UNIX community assures that TCP/IP is going to be one of the communications standards for enterprise computing in the 1990s. IBM has recognized the importance of TCP/IP by implementing it on their AIX computers, PCs (DOS and OS/2), AS/400 and mainframes. TCP/IP is used in such products as:

* X-WINDOW Client/Server

* Network File System (NFS) Client/Server

* File Transfer Protocol (FTP) Client/Server

* Simple Mail Transfer Protocol (SMTP) Client/Server

* Remote Logon Client/Server

TCP/IP is here today and will certainly be one of the widely used networking standards in the 1990s along with OSI/RM and SNA/LU 6.2 distributed architectures.

1.1.2 Open Systems Interconnection

The Open Systems Interconnection Reference Model (OSI/RM) was developed by the International Standards Organization (ISO) in 1976, and the initial protocol specifications were published in the early 1980s. The OSI Reference Model defines a networking platform for a multivendor environment. The OSI architecture (see Fig. 1.3) consists of the full seven layers which define connectivity between two open OSI systems. Even though there are currently several products and services available that take advantage of the full seven layers, such as X.400 electronic messaging, X.500 directory services and File Transfer Access Management (FTAM), the final specifications for the top layer services are not expected to be completed until the mid-1990s. The difficulties that lie ahead within the creation of these services are attributed to the divergence of the members' desires to have their own developments incorporated into the final specifications. Early in 1990, IBM offered greater than expected support for the OSI model by introducing products in the OSI area. This was an important announcement because any wide area networking or enterprise computing connectivity methodology must have a direct connection into the world of IBM mainframe computers, which consist of 80 percent of the mainframes in the market. IBM's participation in the International Standards Organization (ISO) and their 1990 announcement to supply IBM-OSI products, will certainly help the OSI standard to become more important in the years to come.

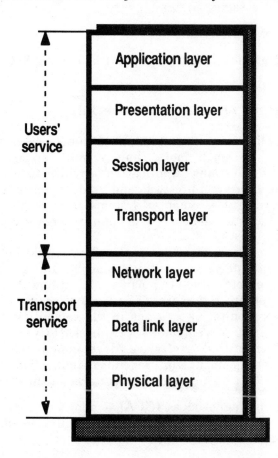

Figure 1.3 Open System Interconnect Reference Model (OSI/RM).

OSI will very likely become a successful multivendor connectivity methodology once ISO provides definitions in several key areas, such as application program standards, and common user access standards. Hopefully these standards will come soon and be innovative because they will probably have a lengthy trial and test period to go through before they gain wide user acceptance. IBM's commitment to Open Systems Interconnection (OSI) is shown in the wide range of products unveiled in the recent year, such as:

- VTAM Version 3 OSI Remote Programming Interface

- OSI/Communications Subsystem

- OSI/CS on AS/400 and OS/2 (IBM direction)

- AIX OSI Messaging System

- X400, X500, FTAM, ACSE

- Presentation, session, and transport layers and X.25

1.1.3 Systems Application Architecture

Systems Application Architecture (SAA), announced in 1987 by IBM Corporation, is much more than a multivendor connectivity methodology. Systems Application Architecture (SAA) is a collection of interfaces, protocols and products (open architectures) that uses mainframe computer systems as repository monitors of global data bases for the sharing of enterprise resources.

SAA is designed to provide the framework for developing consistent and integrated applications across future offerings of the major IBM computing environments. Mainframe Repositories are bringing corporate strategies, definitions of computing enterprise and network monitoring systems to the computing environment. The Automated Development Cycle (AD/Cycle) is bringing rigorous "structured" software development tools for SAA application development via predefined Application Programming Interfaces (APIs). SAA defines architectures in three major areas:

1. **Common User Access (CUA)** — allows consistency in screen layout, keyboard layout, menu presentation, and selection techniques.

2. **Common Programming Interface (CPI)** — allows the design of portable and distributed applications that can easily be integrated into multiple SAA environments.

3. **Common Communication Support (CCS)** — allows connectivity of open SAA systems and programs.

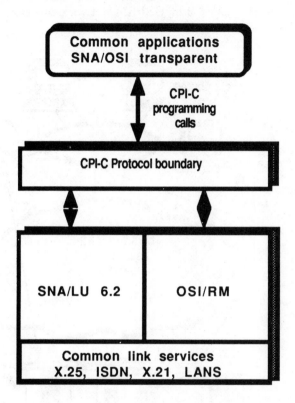

Figure 1.4 SAA application: SNA and OSI transparency.

SAA architecture provides users with many benefits:

• Applications complying with SAA architecture will need little or no redevelopment when ported to other SAA operating systems.

• The end users will require no retraining since the applications will have the same appearance and behave the same in all current and future SAA environments.

• Applications and data can be ported or distributed to run across mainframes, minicomputers, and personal computers.

SAA architecture encompasses both the OSI/RM and the SNA/LU 6.2/PU 2.1 architectures (see Fig. 1.4). The underlying network protocols will be transparent to SAA applications. Applications will access an SAA network via Common Programming Interface-Communications (CPI-C) protocol. The CPI-C call will be translated into SNA/LU 6.2 or OSI/RM network messages and sent to a remote SNA or OSI application partner.

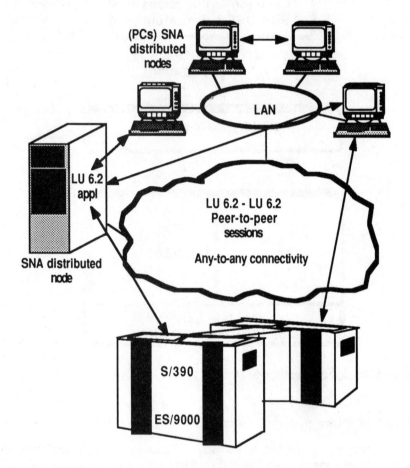

Figure 1.5 SNA/LU 6.2 peer-to-peer communications.

1.1.4 Logical Unit 6.2

The chosen IBM connectivity methodology is Systems Network Architecture (SNA), which has been used in production environments for 16 years. IBM has enhanced this proven methodology to include distributed processing through **logical unit 6.2 (LU 6.2)** and **Advanced Program-To-Program Communications (APPC)**. Figure 1.5 shows an LU 6.2 application, residing on an

SNA distributed node, communicating concurrently with many applications residing on mainframes or any other distributed node in the network. A major advantage of LU 6.2 is that it is the first IBM protocol that recognizes an intelligent entity on both sides of a connection, whether it is a mainframe, a minicomputer, or a personal computer. This recognition of intelligence on both sides of a connection will have a major impact on internetworking in the 1990s. Logical unit LU 6.2 defines the architecture for distributed transaction processing. A distributed transaction (a unit of work) can be executed cooperatively on multiple systems, in the same or different geographic locations. In this environment the user may not even know where the transaction is being processed. The SAA system will automatically contact services on other systems in the network to perform the distributed transaction. The SNA logical unit LU 6.2 does not impinge on the current world of SNA users and represents a method for the corporate world to gradually shift from the old IBM hierarchical networks into SNA distributed networks. Even though the IBM connectivity methodology still revolves around a 16-year-old technology based on SNA architecture, the introduction of logical unit LU 6.2 makes SNA a modern distributed architecture, and as such is just as modern as the Open Systems Interconnection (OSI) Reference Model. IBM plans major product changes years in advance.

1.1.5 APPC and SAA/CPI-C

Advanced Program-to-Program Communications (APPC) is an open architecture designed for writing distributed applications. It is destined for implementation on a very wide range of IBM and other vendor mainframes, minicomputers, and personal computers. It provides a single solution for corporate distributed processing. APPC defines a set of programming calls that allow development of distributed applications. The verbs can be implemented via product specific **Application Programming Interfaces (APIs)**, e.g., CICS API, OS/2 API, AS/400 API (see Fig. 1.6). Generally, the APPC applications are not portable, since APIs differ between various operating systems. Within the SAA environment application programs should be portable across the entire SAA computer enterprise. For this reason IBM announced **SAA/CPI-C Common Programming Interface Communications**. Figure 1.6 shows SAA/CPI-C and APPC applications communicating in peer-to-peer fashion via the SNA/LU 6.2 distributed network. In addition to peer-to-peer communication, SAA/CPI-C provides an interface for the development of portable and distributed applications across different SAA platforms. Therefore it is clear that SNA with a logical unit (LU 6.2), APPC, and CPI-C are the choice for interconnection into the new world of IBM SAA mainframes and SAA enterprise computing. They are also rapidly becoming multivendor internetworking standards replacing the old Remote Job Entry (RJE) and 3270 emulation protocols. The IBM SNA/LU 6.2 and APPC standards have already been adopted by most major software and hardware vendors such as Novell, 3Com Corporation, Network Software Associates, DEC, Apple Computers, Tandem Computers, Unisys, AT&T, HP, and many others.

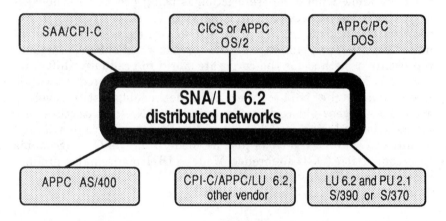

Figure 1.6 SAA/CPI-C and APPC interfaces.

1.1.6 SNA/LU 6.2, OSI, TCP/IP, X.25, and NETBIOS

The relationship and the major differences between SNA/LU 6.2, OSI, TCP/IP, X.25 and Network Basic Input/Output System (NETBIOS) are illustrated in Fig. 1.7. SNA/LU 6.2, OSI, and TCP/IP were discussed in Sec. 1.1 of this book. **OSI** is a full seven-layer open architecture to interconnect dissimilar systems. OSI defines peer-to-peer relationships between equivalent layers. The layers communicate with each other indirectly by inserting headers at the beginning of the information passed from the layer above. These headers are passed down to the physical layer and transmitted to the remote system. The headers are stripped by the corresponding layer in the remote system and then passed to the higher layers. The information is transmitted to the other system via the physical layer. **SNA/LU 6.2** uses similar peer-to-peer protocols to communicate between SNA distributed nodes.

Functionally both OSI and SNA/LU 6.2 are equivalent. The major difference is that in SNA there are fewer headers and that these headers are shared by various SNA layers rather than having a separate header for each layer. Since the headers are different, and as illustrated in Fig. 1.7, there is no one-to-one relationship between SNA and OSI layers, the OSI nodes cannot directly communicate with SNA nodes. SNA/LU 6.2 and OSI are the chosen architecture for the IBM Enterprise Information System (EIS). The SNA/LU 6.2 is already a strongly established standard in the SAA enterprise (e.g., APPC, CPI-C, or the SQL relational databases). IBM also recently showed a strong commitment to the OSI standard. IBM's strategic direction is to provide products that will assure:

- Full OSI and SNA/LU 6.2 integration.

- OSI Local Area Network (LAN) and Wide Area Network (WAN) support.

IBM's announcement of their intention to support OSI Communications Subsystem for MVS and VM (OSI layers 3 to 6 and ACSE), OSI File Server (FTAM) for MVS and VM, X.400 and X.500, OSI Communications Subsystem for OS/2 EE, OSI File Services/2, OS/400 OSI Communications Subsystem and File Server/400 are examples of their commitment to OSI. This provides customers in the SAA enterprise customers with the option to communicate over OSI or SNA/LU 6.2 protocols. IBM will also provide SNA/OSI integration products that will allow for OSI applications to communicate with LU 6.2 applications. The **Transmission Control Protocol/Internet Protocol (TCP/IP)** also has a layered structure which is shown in Fig. 1.7 TCI/IP does not provide the upper three layers. Therefore, the TCP/IP applications themselves have to implement some of the functions equivalent to the top three layers of OSI. Some of the commonly accepted TCP/IP applications are:

- X-WINDOW Client/Server

- Network File System (NFS) Client/Server

- File Transfer Protocol (FTP) Client/Server

- Simple Mail Transfer Protocol (SMTP) Client/Server

- Remote Logon Client/Server (Telnet)

The network interface (the bottom three layers) are not specified by the TCP/IP protocol. TCP/IP can be used, for example, on an Ethernet network. TCP/IP is an established and widespread standard used throughout the UNIX community and as such is a vital part of the IBM AIX/UNIX enterprise. As discussed earlier, TCP/IP is also available on SAA nodes as one of the communication protocols that allows the integration of the SAA and UNIX enterprises.

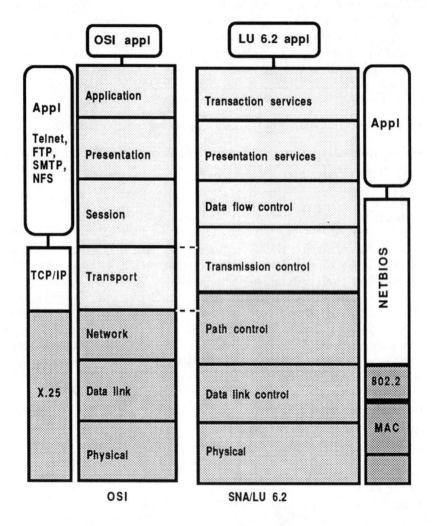

Figure 1.7 SNA/LU 6.2,OSI, TCP/IP, X.25, and NETBIOS.

X.25 Interface is an international standard that complies with the bottom three layers of the OSI/RM. The CCITT Recommended X.25 defines the interface between the Data Terminal Equipment (DTE) and the Data Circuit-Terminating Equipment (DCE) at the physical layer (X.21), the Data Link Control Layer (LAPB) and the network layer (X.25 packets). X.25 has been a widely accepted standard for public computer data networks in most countries, including The United States (SPRINTNET, TYMNET, GTE, etc.), Canada (DATAPAC), France (TRANSPAC), The United Kingdom (PSS), Australia (AUSTPAC), Germany (DATEX-P), and Japan (NTT, KDD). The major strength of X.25 is that it allows sharing of network resources by many users, thereby reducing the overall communication cost. X.25 works similarly to a multiplexer. It allows many users (applications or terminals) to multiplex data over the same communication facilities. The local user, for example, may have only one link connection to its local X.25 provider and can communicate concurrently with multiple users connected to the X.25 network at different geographic locations. This is quite different than the switched telephone connections that were designed for human conversations and allow only two users to communicate at any given time over one telephone line.

The **Network Basic Input/Output System (NETBIOS)** is an IBM local area network protocol for the requestor/server environments on IBM Token Ring networks. It provides a full-duplex programming level interface for the development of LAN applications. NETBIOS is a lower-level interface with fewer functions than the SNA logical unit 6.2. It is well suited for LAN environment rather then wide area network environment. The SNA/LU 6.2 protocol should be used on LANs when the individual workstation needs direct communications with resources residing in the SAA enterprise (e.g., the enterprise-wide distributed databases, distributed office vision, distributed file access.) The NETBIOS interface can still be used for the requestor/server environment, where the server provides LU 6.2 gateway to the resources residing in the SAA wide area network.

1.2 SUMMARY

The addition of the distributed logical unit type 6.2 (LU 6.2), the Advanced Program-to-Program Communications (APPC), and Common Programming Interface Communications (CPI-C) to SNA has made this proven connectivity methodology an advanced distributed processing standard that will tie together the world of mainframes, minicomputers, workstations, and personal computers into a single Enterprise Information System (EIS). Systems Application Architecture (SAA) is the chosen architecture and the strategic direction for IBM's Enterprise Information System.   The SNA logical unit type 6.2 is the dominant communications protocol in the SAA enterprise. Therefore, the new distributed SNA, based on LU 6.2, APPC, and CPI-C, will play a large part in the information age of enterprise computing in the 1990s and is extremely well positioned for the twenty-first century.

2

SNA Concepts

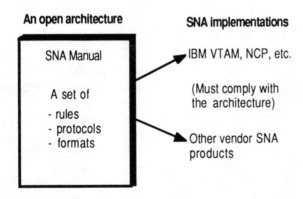

Figure 2.1 SNA architecture and implementations.

2.1 SNA ARCHITECTURE

Introduced in 1974, System Network Architecture (SNA) is an architecture (a set of rules, protocols, and formats) developed and published by IBM for communication between a diverse group of IBM networking products (see Fig. 2.1). The important word is "architecture", which is an open set of specifications that must be followed by IBM and other manufacturers products when communicating with one another using SNA networks. There is a difference between the IBM SNA architecture and an SNA implementation. The architecture is the blueprint (specifications) for the product, and the implementation is architecture and an SNA implementation. The architecture is the blueprint (specifications) for the product, and the implementation is the product itself. Virtual Telecommunications Access Method (VTAM), a product running on an IBM mainframe, or Network Control Program (NCP), a product running on an IBM communication controller, are examples of implementations that comply with the SNA architecture. Also, an important fact is that SNA is an open architecture, which means that other vendors can buy the SNA specifications manuals and implement their own SNA products. SNA has been IBM's strategic networking architecture since its announcement in 1974. Its evolution since then has created a widely accepted connectivity standard of compatible communication protocols. SNA is now a well-established de facto networking standard used by most of the large corporations in the world. IBM is committed to SNA as the strategic architecture for its current and future networking products.

2.2 SNA NETWORK

The purpose of an SNA network is to enable the error-free transmission of data between end-users (application programs and SNA devices, terminals, ect). The end-users are defined as the ultimate sources and destinations of information that flow through an SNA network. The end-users reside outside the SNA network, and they interact with the network to exchange data between each other. In Fig. 2.2 a terminal operator (an SNA end-user) interacts with the network to exchange data with a CICS transaction program (another SNA end-user). The network makes sure that the information passed from the terminal is transferred with no errors to the CICS transaction program. The Virtual Telecommunications Access Method (VTAM) provides protocols for controlling and sharing network resources. The person at a terminal gains access to a network by entering a logon command [e.g., LOGON APPLID (CICS)], which is transferred to VTAM. VTAM will determine if the CICS application is available for access and whether the terminal operator is configured to enable access to the CICS network resource. Only after a successful logon will the operator be able to issue a CICS transaction request (e.g., obtain a customer's account balance) which is routed by the network to CICS. CICS processes the request and generates a reply that is transferred by the network back to the terminal operator.

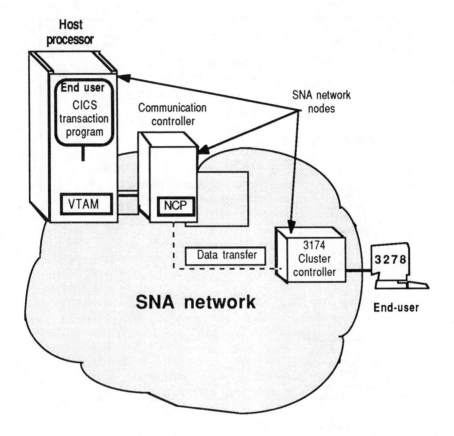

Figure 2.2 SNA network.

2.3 SNA NETWORK COMPONENTS

A network consists of many different hardware and software components. An SNA Network Node (see Fig. 2.2) is a physical package consisting of a hardware component and its associated software component containing a subset of SNA architecture. Each SNA node needs to understand only the small subset of SNA architecture required to perform its specific functions (e.g., a communications controller needs to understand the SNA routing methodology, but it does not need to understand how to manage a network or SNA end-users). SNA defines three types of nodes: host subarea nodes, communications controller subarea nodes, and peripheral nodes (see Fig. 2.3).

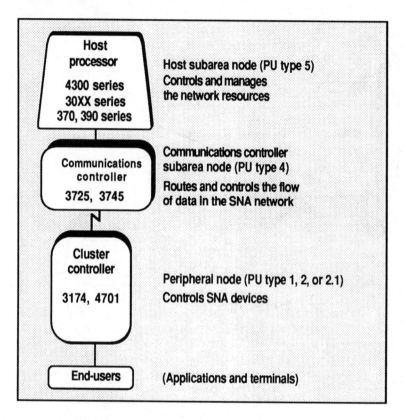

Figure 2.3 SNA network components.

2.3.1 Physical Units

The term **physical unit** (**PU**) is used in SNA to describe a combination of hardware, firmware, and software that manages the SNA node resources. The physical unit is not, as the name may suggest, the physical hardware, but, in actual fact, it is the node's manager responsible for managing the node resources. These tasks include activating and deactivating lines, managing routing, sending management messages to the host in case of a node resource failure, and making sure the node's internal buffers are not overloaded. Terminals and printers do not fall into a PU category and are classified as SNA end-users.

The terms **Host Subarea Node** (node type 5) or **PU type 5** are used within SNA to describe a general-purpose processor (e.g., 43X1, 303X, 308X, 309X, or 370 series) which contains a Telecommunications Access Method (e.g., ACF/VTAM). VTAM implements the SNA System Services Control Point (SSCP) that controls and manages a preconfigured portion of a network. SSCP manages, for example, the "LOGON APPLID (CICS) command" to determine which SNA terminal can have access to CICS transactions. SSCP will also know which SNA nodes in the network are up and running and which nodes need to be activated, and so on.

The terms **communication controller subarea node** (node type 4) and **PU type 4** are used within SNA to describe a front-end processor that contains the Network Control Program (e.g., ACF/NCP), which provides the SNA functions for controlling communication lines and routing and manages the flow of data in the network.

The term **peripheral node** is used within SNA to describe all other SNA nodes (cluster controllers and distributed nodes) that control SNA end-users such as terminals or automatic teller machines (ATMs). The 3174, 3274, 3276, and 4701 ATMs are examples of peripheral nodes. There are two types of SNA peripheral nodes: the **physical unit type 1** (PU 1) cluster controller, which is outdated; and the **physical unit type 2** (PU 2), which is a cluster controller (e.g., 3174, 3274, 4701) that controls SNA end-users and can communicate only with end-users (application programs) residing on mainframes (PU type 5 nodes).

IBM's SNA was originally designed as a terminal-to-host communications network (called a **hierarchical network**) in which the terminals were slaves controlled by masters residing in the host. At that time, all processing power and intelligence did reside on the host and this approach made sense. The 1980s brought minicomputers and personal computers (PCs) to the market which have computing power and intelligence nearly equal to that of mainframes. The SNA hierarchical networks imposed major limitations to end-users that wanted to distribute data or processing tasks and take advantage of the personal computer's intelligence. Treating a powerful PC as a dummy terminal, which can communicate only with applications residing on the mainframe and cannot communicate with other PCs or minicomputers in a network, was a major limitation of IBM's SNA architecture. To overcome the limitations IBM introduced a new physical unit, type 2.1 (PU 2.1), which allows "any-to-any" connectivity, PC to mainframes, minicomputers, and other PCs without host involvement. Networks that allow "any-to-any" connectivity are called **distributed networks**. The physical unit 2.1 node was also chosen by IBM as the SNA node for Systems Application Architecture (SAA), which is IBM's chosen architecture for distributed networks in the 1990s. We will discuss SAA and the SNA distributed networking strategies for the 1990s later in the book.

2.3.2 Logical Units

A **logical unit** (LU) is defined within SNA as a port (an end-user's interface) by way of which the end-user obtains access to an SNA network (see Fig. 2.4).

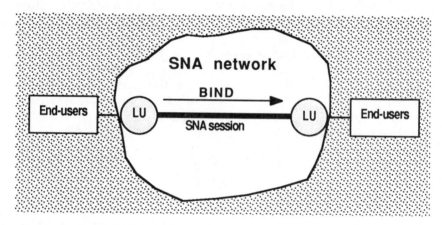

Figure 2.4 SNA logical units.

A logical connection between the logical units is called an SNA **session**. The two LUs (the origin LU and the destination LU) exchange information using the session. An SNA session is established when one LU sends another LU an SNA request, known as a **BIND**, which specifies the rules, upon which both partners agree (e.g., maximum message size exchanged between LUs, or who is responsible for error recovery), for the duration of the session. The BIND sender and receiver are known respectively as the **primary logical unit (PLU)** and the **secondary logical unit (SLU)**. In the original SNA hierarchical network the PLU always resides on the host and the SLU resides on peripheral nodes. The PLU, residing on the host, is considered to be the intelligent entity responsible for error recovery and for establishment of the session rules. The secondary logical units (SLUs), residing on peripheral nodes, are required to have only enough intelligence to control the dummy terminals or printers.

An SNA end-user (e.g., terminal operator) interacts directly with its LU (the end-user manager). For example, when a terminal operator enters a customer's account number to retrieve an account balance from a CICS database, the account number is read by the local LU (which controls the physical port to which the terminal is connected). The local LU uses the SNA session to pass the request to the remote LU (which controls the CICS transaction program). The remote LU receives the information (the customer's account number) and passes it to the CICS transaction program. The CICS transaction program retrieves the account balance and passes it to its LU which in turn uses the SNA session to transfer the answer back to the local LU. The local LU receives the account balance and passes it to the terminal operator.

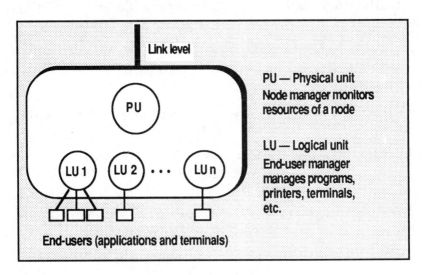

Figure 2.5 An SNA node.

Logical Units (LUs) reside within SNA nodes (see Fig. 2.5). An SNA node contains one physical unit (PU — the node manager) and many logical units (the end-user managers). Most cluster controllers (PU 2 nodes — 3274, 3276, RJE) in an SNA hierarchical network implement one logical unit per SNA end-user (terminal, printer, card reader). This end-user has an exclusive access to the LU and to the session with the remote LU. The SNA LU6.2

architecture does not limit an LU to one end-user but allows many end-users for each logical unit. The end-users residing on SNA distributed nodes (such as PU 2.1 nodes) can share the same logical unit (LU 6.2) and the same session to the remote LU.

To differentiate between the managers of various types of SNA nodes, SNA defines different types of physical units (host — PU 5, communications controller — PU 4, and peripheral node — types 1, 2, and 2.1). SNA also defines 8 different logical unit types. A logical unit that manages an IBM 3278 terminal must understand the 3270 commands and the interaction with that terminal. This LU also exchanges data between the terminal and the host application in both directions (sending the screen data and receiving the answers). A logical unit that manages a 3270 printer must understand how to control the printer. This LU accepts the information sent by the host application and it never has to send any information (other than error status) back to the LU residing in the host. Obviously the LU that manages the printer differs significantly from the LU that manages the 3278 terminal. To differentiate between different classes of devices, the SNA architecture defines different LU types that identify the particular set of SNA functions required to support a particular SNA end-user communication.

LU type 0   —   Provides generalized program-to-program capabilities (e.g., 36XX, 47XX ATMs).

LU type 1   —   Used for Remote Job Entry (RJE) workstation operating in a batch environment (e.g., 377X RJE stations).

LU type 2   —   Used for interactive 327X terminals attached to a 327X or 3174 cluster controller.

LU type 3   —   Used for a printer attached to a 327X or 3174 cluster controller.

LU type 4   —   Used for program to terminal or terminal to terminal data processing and word processing.

LU type 6.2   —   Used for program to program (host to host:
6.1   CICS-CICS and 6.1 IMS- MS, CICS-IMS) data processing.

LU type 6.2   —   Used for program to program "any-to-any" communications in an IBM distributed network (any SNA distributed PU 2.1 node and PU type 5 node).

LU type 7 — Used for programs to communicate with 5250 Display Stations (S/36, AS/400).

The LU 6.0 and 6.1 are for host to host communications only. All the other logical units residing in SNA peripheral nodes (LU 0, 1, 2, 3, 4 and 7) are limited to communications with applications residing on an IBM host. Most of today's PCs emulate LU type 2 terminals (3270 emulation). This means that PCs cannot communicate with each other and must act as dummy 327X terminals instead of as intelligent entities when a part of an SNA network. A logical unit type 0 (program-to-program), frequently used in ATMs, does not act as a dummy terminal, but is limited to host communications only and does not define any rules for how the two programs will communicate with each other (how to contact each other, how to notify each other about application errors, how to start and end transactions, etc.). The LU 0 program-to-program communication is user-defined, which means that different design groups develop applications using totally different rules and whose programs, therefore, may never communicate with programs or services designed by other design groups.

All these limitations are overcome through the use of the most recent SNA logical unit, type LU 6.2, which is used in IBM SNA distributed networks and is a primary focus of discussions within this book.

2.3.3 System Services Control Point

The term **System Services Control Point (SSCP),** implemented in VTAM (see Fig. 2.6), is used within SNA to describe the software running in the host that performs the following functions:

1. Manages network resources (logical units, physical units, and lines)

2. Allows an operator to display the status of network resources, change the states of resources (activate or deactivate lines, LUs, and PUs) and helps an operator in error recovery

3. Knows the details of network configuration

4. Collects network statistics and SNA alerts (error conditions)

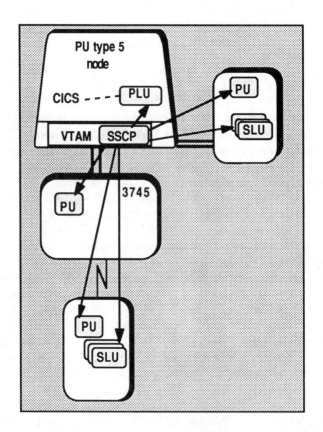

Figure 2.6 System Services Control Point (SSCP).

The SNA network is not limited to one host node. In an SNA network consisting of more than one SNA host the SSCP manages only a preconfigured portion of the network (see Fig. 2.7). At VTAM/NCP system generation a system programmer will decide which SNA communication controllers and peripheral nodes should be managed by each SSCP. A portion of an SNA network managed by one SSCP is called a **domain**. A single host SNA network is called a **single-domain network**, whereas a network containing more than one host is called a **multidomain network**. SSCP1 (see Fig. 2.7) manages all the network resources (PUs, LUs, and host applications) residing in domain 1. An SNA end-user (e.g., 3278 terminal operator managed by LU1 in a 3274 cluster controller) must issue a LOGON command to get access to any of the network resources. The initial LOGON command is always sent to the SSCP in the domain in which the end-user resides. For

example, a LOGON APPLID:CICS1 command would be sent to
SSCP1 and the LU1 to CICS1 session would be established.

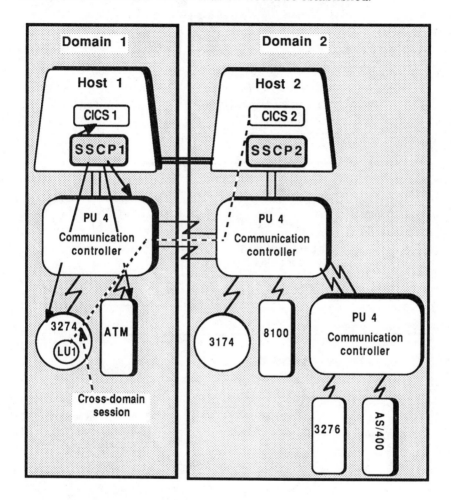

Figure 2.7 Multidomain SNA network.

A LOGON APPLID (CICS2) command would also be sent to
SSCP1. SSCP1 would determine that CICS2 is a cross-domain
resource and would notify SSCP2 of the request. SSCP2 would notify
CICS2 that a resource (LU1) from domain 1 wants to establish a
connection with CICS2. CICS2 establishes the cross-domain session
by sending an SNA BIND request directly to LU1. Once the CICS2-
LU1 session is established information flows directly between
CICS2 and the terminal operator.

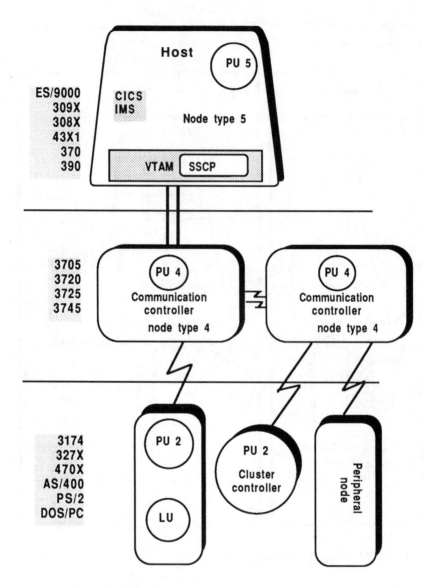

Figure 2.8 IBM terminologies.

2.4 IBM NAMING CONVENTIONS

It is easy to get lost in the different terminologies and abbreviations used by IBM hardware, software, and network personnel. The SNA network actually consists, in fact, of just three major components (see Fig. 2.8):

1. IBM host (mainframe)

   Hardware personnel terminologies:

   309X, 308X, 43X1, 370

   SNA network personnel terminologies:

   node type 5, physical unit type 5, PU type 5, PU 5, host subarea node

   Software personnel refers to host operating systems or host applications:

   VM (virtual machine), MVS (multiple virtual storage) CICS (customer information control system), IMS (information management system), CMS (conversational monitor system)

2. Communication controller

   Hardware personnel:

   3705, 3720, 3725, 3745

   SNA network personnel:

   Node type 4, physical unit type 4, PU type 4, PU 4, communication controller subarea node

   Software personnel:

   NCP (Network Control Program)

3. Peripheral node

   Hardware personnel:

   3174, 3274, 3276, 8100, ATMs, S/36, S/38, AS/400, PS/2, and DOS PC with SNA emulation software (e.g., 3270 emulation, APPC/LU 6.2 emulation)

   SNA network personnel:

   Node Type 1, 2, or 2.1; physical unit type 1, 2, or 2.1; PU type 1, 2, or 2.1; PU 1, 2, or 2.1; SNA peripheral node; cluster controller; distributed processor

Software personnel:

  Reference is to an operating system of different peripheral
  nodes or an SNA emulation software running in personal
  computers or minicomputers (e.g., 3270 emulation, APPC,
  CPI-C, or LU 6.2 emulation).

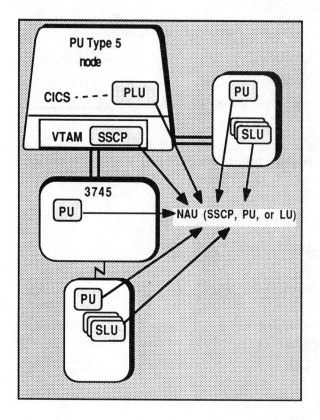

Figure 2.9 SNA network addressable units (NAUs).

2.5 SNA NETWORK ADDRESSABLE UNITS

The System Services Control Point(SSCP), physical unit (PU), and
logical unit (LU) communicate with each other to exchange user
information and network management messages. The messages
flowing in the network carry a unique address of a destination LU,
PU or SSCP. Within SNA these three entities are called **network
addressable units (NAUs)** (see Fig. 2.9). An SNA network consists,

logically, of network addressable units (SSCPs, PUs, and LUs). The end-users do not have to know the unique addresses of NAUs. The end-users specify names (CICS, IMS, CMS, branch 55, etc.) which are mapped by the SSCP to unique network addresses. The communication controllers (PU 4s) are responsible for routing messages throughout an SNA network and must understand the destination address carried in a header preceding each message.

2.6 ADDRESSING IN SNA NETWORK

The routing tables in the communication controllers would have to be very large to store the addresses of all network addressable units (NAUs) in an SNA network. To simplify the SNA routing, a system programmer divides the network into subareas during system definition. A **subarea** (see Fig. 2.10) is defined as a subarea node (PU 5 — host node or PU 4 — communication controller node) and its attached peripheral nodes. The unique number that the system programmer assigns to each subarea becomes the subarea address. Each message flowing in an SNA network carries a network address consisting of a subarea address (identifying the destination subarea node) and an element address (identifying a particular resource within the subarea). For example (see Fig. 2.10), the multidomain network discussed earlier consists of five subareas with unique subarea addresses assigned during system generation (subarea 3, subarea 4, subarea 6, subarea 12, subarea 18). The subarea address for all resources residing in subarea no. 3 is 3; and subarea no. 18 is 18. The messages flowing between CICS2 and LU1 on the cross-domain session will carry a destination subarea address 3 (for messages flowing from CICS2 to LU1) and subarea address 18 (for messages flowing from LU1 to CICS2). Notice that once the message arrives at the destination subarea node 3 (the communication controller), the subarea address is resolved and it is not carried on the remaining portion of the path to LU1. Therefore, the routing headers between subarea nodes are longer (26 bytes) than the routing headers flowing between subarea nodes and peripheral nodes, which are only 6 bytes long. The resources residing in peripheral nodes carry shorter addresses called **local addresses**. Local addresses are unique to their own peripheral node. The boundary function (BF) residing in the communication controller decodes the network addresses and changes them to local addresses. For example, in Fig. 2.10 the local address of LU1 can be configured to be equal to 2 (local LU address) and the 3274 peripheral node PU address equal in hexadecimal code to X'C1'.

One of the logical units in the ATM connected to the same communications controller can also have an address equal to 2 and the ATM PU address equal to X'C1'. Since the ATM and the 3274 cluster controller are connected to the communication controller via different lines the network addresses identifying the two logical units are different. When a message is received from LU1, the BF maps the address (line address, PU address, LU address) to a unique network address (subarea address, element address).

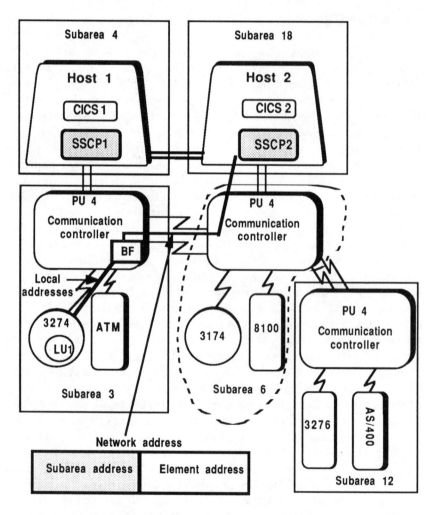

Figure 2.10 Addressing in SNA.

Let us move the ATM peripheral node to the same line as the 3274 cluster controller (such line configuration is called **multipoint configuration** — more than one PU on the same line). Now the combination (line1, PU address X'C1', LU address 2) would be the same for both network resources (LU1 and LUA). This would be illegal within SNA since every resource in an SNA network must be represented by a unique network address. The system programmer would have to redefine one of the two PUs to make the two network addresses unique.

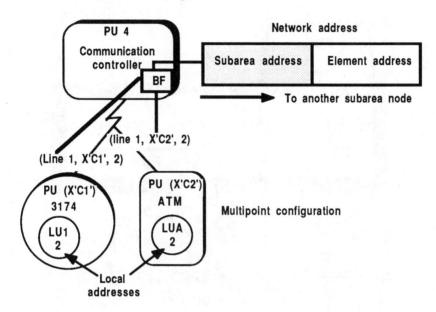

Figure 2.11 Local addresses.

A solution to this problem is shown in Fig. 2.11. By changing the ATM PU address to X'C2' the two resources can be mapped by BF to two unique network addresses. Local addresses are not the same as the corresponding element addresses. The element addresses are indexes to an internal table kept by BF in which lines, PU addresses and local LU addresses are stored for all peripheral nodes attached to this subarea node. The dividing of an SNA network into subareas simplifies significantly the routing in the network. The routing tables of an intermediate communication controller need to contain only information on how to get to a destination subarea and do not have to worry about the element addresses at all. Once the message is received by the destination subarea node, the boundary function (BF) residing in this node maps the element address (line address, PU address, LU address) to

the local address of a destination resource residing in a peripheral
node. Notice that the peripheral nodes do not have to know the
network addresses, but only the local addresses and the SNA **unique
network names** of remote resources. Network names shield the
SNA end-users (programmers, terminal operators) from
complicated network addresses. The System Services Control Point
(SSCP) keeps directories that relate network names to network
addresses.

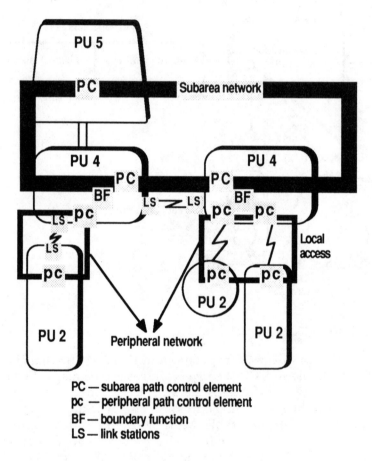

PC — subarea path control element
pc — peripheral path control element
BF — boundary function
LS — link stations

Figure 2.12 Path control network.

2.7 PATH CONTROL NETWORK

The routing network responsible for routing messages between
network addressable units (NAUs) is called, within SNA, **path**

control network (see Fig. 2.12). It consists of subarea node control elements (PCs), peripheral path control elements (pcs), and data link control elements called **link stations** (LS). The data link control elements are responsible for error-free transmission of data from an SNA node to an adjacent node. Link stations only have the knowledge of the adjacent nodes and are not aware of other nodes in the network.

Peripheral path control elements (pcs) route the data between peripheral nodes to adjacent subarea nodes using local addresses and have no knowledge of SNA network addresses. Subarea path control elements (PCs) route data between subarea nodes using network addresses (subarea address, element address). Each subarea node contains one subarea path control element (PC) per subarea node and one peripheral path control element (pc) per adjacent peripheral node. Each peripheral node contains one (pc) per link station (LS). The boundary function (BF) changes the local addresses to network addresses.

2.8 SNA ROUTING

Routing is a mechanism of transporting messages throughout an SNA network from the origin address to the destination address. SNA hierarchical networks use an end-to-end static session routing mechanism. An end-to-end routing mechanism supports multiple routes between nodes if there are multiple physical paths between the nodes.

2.8.1 Explicit and Virtual Routes

The physical route between two subarea nodes (e.g., subarea node SA1 and subarea node SA3; — see Fig. 2.13) is called an **explicit route** or a physical route (e.g., ER0 — explicit route number 0). An explicit route defines an ordered set of nodes and transmission groups (TGs) from one subarea to another. A **transmission group** is a group of one or more links connecting two adjacent subarea nodes and is viewed as as one logical link by the path control layer. Message traffic for a specific SNA session is queued for transmission over any available link within the same transmission group. The receiving end of a TG must reorder any out-of-order messages received on different links belonging to the same transmission group. Transmission groups are assigned statically via VTAM/NCP at system generation.

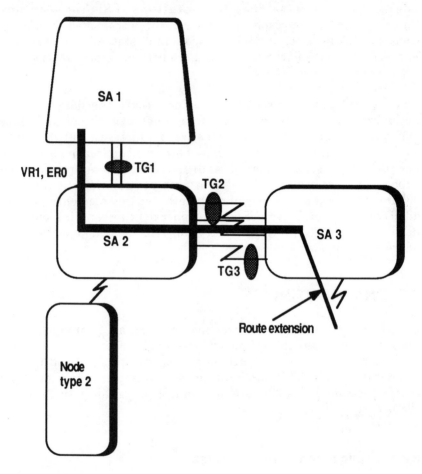

Figure 2.13 Static end-to-end routing.

A logical connection between two subarea nodes is defined as an SNA **virtual route**. A virtual or logical route is used to manage an origin-to-destination subarea routing without being concerned with the explicit (physical) route between the nodes. Each virtual route consists of two parameters: a virtual route number (up to eight) and a **transmission priority** level (up to three — low, medium, and high). A virtual route number (e.g., VR1; — see Fig. 2.13) is mapped at session activation to an explicit route number (e.g., ER0 — the physical path) with a transmission priority (low, medium, high) allowing up to 24 virtual routes. Multiple virtual routes can be mapped to the same explicit route. This SNA routing mechanism was designed to satisfy such service requirements as network load distribution, selection of different priorities (e.g., low for batch and high for interactive) of messages flowing over the same physical paths and to improve network performance by allowing parallel links between nodes. An SNA end-user (e.g., an application program) specifies at session initiation a **class of service** (COS), which is an ordered list of possible virtual routes for the session. The session is then assigned to the first available virtual route in the list.

Networks will continue to become larger in the 1990s because of decreased cost and increased usage of distributed processing. SNA networks with the SNA logical unit 6.2 and the physical unit PU 2.1 are able to function as wide area distributed networks spanning the globe. This network growth will imply the need for dynamic routing and network configurations. A major issue involving dynamic routing is the need to change routing definition more easily than it is accomplished in static tables. Dynamic routing insures continuous network operation by rerouting messages over alternate routes in case of a network failure. We will discuss routing methodologies in SNA/LU 6.2 distributed networks in later chapters.

2.9 SNA SESSIONS

We discussed the LU-LU sessions earlier and defined a session as a logical connection between two logical units (LUs). The LU-LU sessions are used for transferring end-user data. Before an end-user can get access to an SNA network, an SNA session must be established between the local and remote logical units. In an SNA network, all network resources (links, physical units, and logical units), must be activated before an LU-LU session can be established. An operator activates the SNA network resources by issuing network activation commands (e.g., VARY NET, ID= resource name) which are interpreted by the System Services Control Point and sent to the destination network resources as SNA network management messages (e.g., ACTPU — activate physical unit, or ACTLU — activate logical unit). The logical connections between SSCP and PUs, and SSCP and LUs are also called sessions. These sessions are used for SNA network management. Therefore, an SNA session can be defined as a logical connection between two network addressable units (SSCPs, PUs, and LUs; see Fig. 2.14).

2.9.1 Hierarchical SNA Sessions

The following sessions can exist in an SNA hierarchical network:

A. Network management sessions:

  1. An SSCP-PU session is used to manage an SNA node (e.g., a 3174 cluster controller) and its resources. This session is used for activation and monitoring a node and its resources (links, memory, error messages, statistics, traces, etc.).

  2. An SSCP-LU session is used to manage a logical unit (LU) and to help in LU-LU session initiation and termination. A LOGON APPLID(CICS) command typed on a 3278 terminal flows on this session and requests, from SSCP, an LU-LU session between the terminal and CICS.

  3. An SSCP-SSCP session is used to manage cross-domain sessions. For example, the LOGON APPLID (CICS2) command (see Fig. 2.7), requests, from SSCP1, a cross-domain LU-LU session with CICS2. SSCP1 must establish a SSCP1-SSCP2 session in order to notify SSCP2 of the cross-domain request.

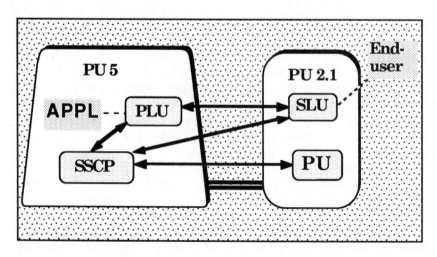

Figure 2.14 SNA sessions.

B.   End-user data transfer session:

1. An LU-LU session is used to exchange data between two SNA end-users (programs, or a program and an SNA device). After a session is initiated with the LOGON APPLID(CICS2) command, the screen information is transmitted between the terminal and CICS2 over an LU-LU session.

There are differences between sessions within SNA hierarchical networks and distributed networks, and we will discuss SNA sessions within IBM physical unit type 2.1 distributed networks in Sec. 3.6.

2.9.2 SNA Network Activation

An operator interacts with the System Services Control Point (SSCP) to activate the resources of the network. Each network addressable unit in an SNA network must be identified by an unique name (e.g., LU1, LU2, LU3, PU1; see Fig. 2.15). The operator first activates the physical units and the logical units in the host nodes, then the links to the adjacent nodes, and then the physical and logical units in the network nodes. Figure 2.15 shows an example of a very simple SNA network. The hierarchy of the network activation within this network is:

1.   Loading and initializing the host hardware, operating system, access methods, and network management programs. Activating all SNA resources in the host node (PU1, LU1, etc.).

2.   Activating the links and all SNA resources in the peripheral node (PU2, LU2, etc.).

The operator command V NET, ACT, ID=PU2 is translated by SSCP to an SNA network management command: Activate physical unit (**ACTPU**) and is transmitted to PU1. Physical unit 1 (PU1) checks that all its local node resources are up and running and it returns an SNA positive response (+RSP) to the SCCP. This sequence of commands establishes an SSCP-PU session that is used for exchanging network management requests and error conditions. Once the SSCP-PU session is established (the node is up and running) SSCP establishes an SSCP-LU session by sending an

SNA network management command: Activate Logical Unit (**ACTLU**) to all remote LUs in the node.

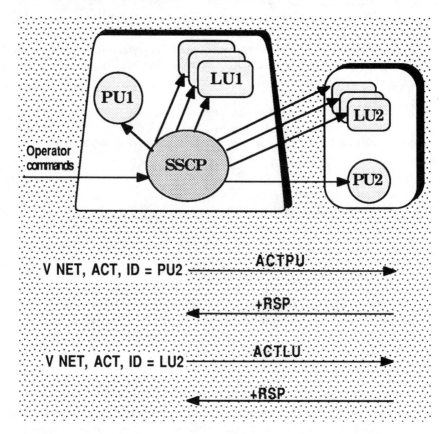

Figure 2.15 SNA session activation.

Large networks may consist of thousands of terminals, LUs, and PUs. Activation and deactivation of these networks would be extremely time-consuming if an operator were required to issue separate commands for each network resource. In large SNA networks, cascaded activation techniques (macros) can be used which allow an operator to enter a single command to activate, display status, or deactivate a group consisting of multiple network resources. Network personnel can set up or change network management command sequences in resource-definition tables. SSCP manages network resources according to the parameters defined in these resource-definition tables.

2.9.3 LU-LU Session Initiation

SNA LU-LU sessions can be activated by one of the two participating logical units, a third logical unit, an operator command, or automatically at system startup. Typically an SNA end-user (e.g., an application program or a person sitting at a terminal) would initiate an LU-LU session. The LU-LU session can only be initiated if all the network resources needed for session initiation have already been activated by an operator via the V NET, ACT, ID=resource name commands described above (all PUs, LUs and applications).

Figure 2.16 shows an example of a typical session activation sequence from a 3278 terminal to a CICS host application. We are assuming that an operator has already loaded, initialized and started all the host resources and the CICS application which is represented by the primary logical unit (PLU).

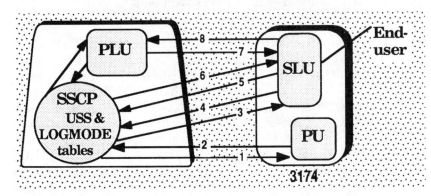

Figure 2.16 SNA network activation.

The following is a sequence of session initiation commands:

1. An operator issues V NET, ACT, ID=PU to SSCP. SSCP sends an Activate physical unit (ACTPU) command to the 3174 cluster controller.

2. The PU (3174's node manager) checks all the 3174 node resources, and if they are up and running, it returns an SNA +RSP to SSCP.

3. An operator issues V NET, ACT, ID=SLU to SSCP. SSCP sends an Activate Logical Unit (ACTLU) command to the 3174 cluster controller.

4.   The LU (3278's terminal manager) returns an SNA +RSP to SSCP. At this point the individual sitting at the 3278 terminal will notice that a "question mark sign" (the terminal is in a local mode, no sessions to a host exist) changes to a "stick man sign" (an SSCP-LU session exists); you can now type the LOGON commands which are going to be sent to the SSCP) (see Fig. 2.17).

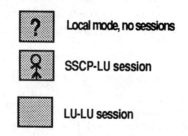

Figure 2.17 3278 terminal — local and session signs.

5. A terminal operator types LOGON APPLID(CICS), which is sent to SSCP on an SSCP-LU session. SSCP uses a LOGMODE table, also called a BIND table (a set of one or more logmode names, each pointing to specific characteristics of a session between logical units) and passes a suggested BIND to the primary logical unit (CICS). CICS agrees on the session with the SLU by sending +RSP to SSCP. Another table that is involved in LU-LU session initiation is called the **unformatted systems services table** (USS). The SCCP calls an unformatted services (USS) routine to convert unformatted (character coded strings) requests, such as LOGON requests, into formatted requests (bit code fields).

6.   SSCP sends a +RSP response to the SLU (controlling the 3278 terminal) to notify the SLU of an incoming BIND from CICS.

7.   CICS modifies the suggested session parameters received from SSCP and sends the BIND command to the SLU establishing an LU to LU session. A terminal operator will notice that the SSCP-LU sign changes to the LU-LU session sign on the 3278 terminal (see Fig. 2.17).

8.   SLU accepts the session rules carried in the BIND request by returning a positive response (+RSP) to CICS.

At this point there are two sessions between the host and the SLU. The SSCP-SLU session for network management and the CICS(PLU)-SLU session for exchanging user data. A terminal operator can switch between the two sessions by pressing the Sys Request key on a 3278 terminal.

In the example above we described the session initiation sequence of a simple single-domain SNA network. The cross-domain LU-LU session initiation involves an additional session between two different SSCPs. Because the two logical units are controlled by separate SSCPs, an SSCP-SSCP session is required to exchange information about each of the logical units as well as to help with the session initiation process.

2.10 SUMMARY

In this chapter we learned the basic SNA architecture concepts and terminologies. The reader is advised to study these concepts and terminologies because they form a basis for many of the chapters ahead.

SNA is an architecture developed and published by IBM for communication between a diverse group of IBM networking products. SNA enables error-free transmission of data between end-users (application programs, terminals, and printers). SNA network nodes consist of host subarea nodes (PU 5s), communication controller subarea nodes (PU 4s) and peripheral nodes (PU 1s, 2s, or 2.1s). A physical unit (PU — a node manager) is a combination of hardware, firmware, and software that manages the SNA node resources. A logical unit (LU — an SNA end-user manager) is a port via which end-users gain access to an SNA network. SNA has eight different logical unit types. LU 6.2 is the newest of the SNA logical units and is used for program-to-program, "any-to-any" communications. System Services Control Point (SSCP) (implemented in VTAM) manages the network resources, knows the details of network configuration, collects network statistics and alerts, and allows an operator to display status and change states and helps an operator in error recovery. The messages flowing in the network carry the unique address of a destination LU, PU, or SSCP [called network addressable units (NAUs)]. The routing network responsible for routing messages between NAUs is called the path control network.

3

SNA Distributed Network Concepts

3.1 SNA GROWTH TRENDS

System Network Architecture (SNA), IBM's hierarchical networking architecture, announced by IBM in 1974, has the hierarchical structure of a tree- the root, a PU 5 and the lower levels of the tree, PU 4s and PU 2s (see Fig. 3.1). The root of the tree is the Mainframe computer (PU 5) that controls and manages all the network resources. Other SNA nodes, such as communication controllers and peripheral nodes (PU 2s), are at the lower-level of the tree and are totally controlled by the System Services Control Point (SSCP) residing in the host. You may think of the relationship between the host (the root of the tree) and other SNA nodes (the lower level nodes of the tree) as a master-slave arrangement. In such networks only one of the conversing entities has an intelligence (the host application such as CICS, IMS, and CMS) and the other side is considered to be a dummy device capable of communicating only with an intelligent entity residing in the host. The peripheral nodes (PU 2s) cannot communicate directly (initiate an SNA session, send BIND command) with other peripheral nodes in an SNA network. SNA was originally designed as a terminal-to-host communications system which assumes no intelligence or computing power at the device end. The hierarchical approach shown in Fig. 3.1 is suitable for this purpose and is valid for such configurations today.

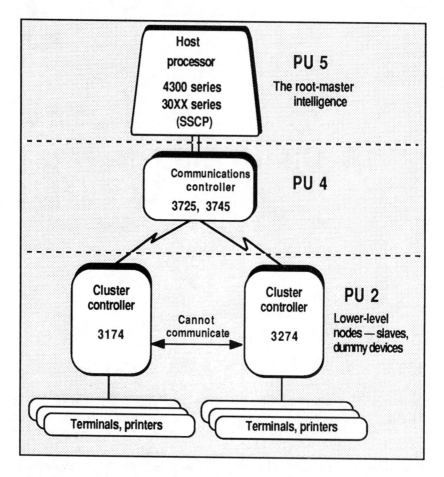

Figure 3.1 SNA hierarchical tree structure.

The rapid improvements in personal computer technologies, together with declining costs, have drastically changed network requirements. The PCs have brought intelligence into host-controlled (intelligent master and dummy slave) environments at the slave side of the connection. Most PC applications emulate 3270 dummy devices (PU 2s and LU 2s) and have the limitations of slaves (PCs which cannot communicate directly with other PCs) in the hierarchical SNA tree (see Fig. 3.1). The only SNA node capable of initiating sessions (sending SNA BIND commands) was the IBM host. Personal computers and minicomputers have had to emulate the functions of an SNA host in order to start SNA sessions and to communicate directly with other nodes within an SNA wide area network. The complexity and the cost of a PU 5 (host) implementation on PCs forced IBM and third-party vendors to implement a PU 2 (peripheral node) emulation rather than a PU 5 emulation on PCs.

3.1.1 User Requirements

Most of the user requirements in the 1980s were for PCs to have the capability to communicate with host application such as CICS, IMS, or TSO, rather than communicate with other PCs in an SNA network. Therefore, PU 2 emulation products satisfied most the customers business requirements. Now, in the 1990s, the business needs of most companies have changed. Customers would like to take advantage of the investments they have made in their purchases of thousands of personal computers. The combined processing power of these PCs is, in many cases, larger than the processing power of customers large investment in mainframes. There is no reason to spend millions of dollars on bigger mainframes before taking advantage of the currently unused (wasted) processing power of PCs which have already been purchased by these companies. To achieve this we must be able to distribute data, applications and processing from the IBM mainframes to the personal computers and minicomputers connected to SNA wide area networks and allow any-to-any connectivity between SNA nodes. The networks today must recognize intelligence on both sides of a connection, not just the host side, and must allow any-to-any rather than host-to-device communications. That suggests that the SNA device dependent hierarchical network is not well suited for modern, peer-to-peer, distributed communications. These things have caused IBM to enhance the SNA hierarchical architecture with a new distributed architecture that allows SNA users to migrate to new, fully distributed, wide area networks.

3.1.2 Token Ring Local Area Network (LAN)

An IBM response to these limitations was the announcement of Token Ring network, IBM's standard for interconnecting dissimilar distributed systems on a local area network (see Fig.

3.2), and the introduction of the SNA device independent logical unit type 6.2 (LU 6.2) and the SNA distributed physical unit type 2.1 (PU 2.1). Personal computers and minicomputers are capable of communicating directly with each other on a Token Ring network without any host involvement.

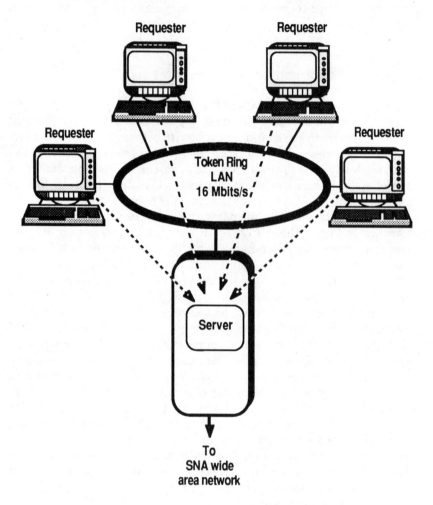

Figure 3.2 Token Ring local area network (LAN).

The requesters (see Fig. 3.2) send requests directly to the server, which processes the data and returns replies to the requesters without any host involvement. If the requests are not for a local resource, the server is capable of passing the requests, via an SNA

network, to a remote host for processing. The reply is then returned
to the server, and the server passes it to the requester. The Token
Ring network is a local area network (LAN) for communications
across short distances (a few miles) and does not address the
limitations of an SNA hierarchical wide area network. For
example, the requesters and the server in Fig. 3.2 cannot
communicate directly with other SNA nodes residing in an SNA
wide area network. The server emulates a PU 2 node and is still
limited to host communications. The Token Ring is an
independent network and it is not an integral part of SNA. The IBM
Token Ring defines only the lower-level communication protocols
below the SNA logical unit protocols. Therefore, the applications
developed on Token Ring do not use SNA but instead use a non-SNA
low-level NETBIOS protocol. The major advantage of the Token
Ring network is that it is much faster (up to 16 Mbits/s) than the
synchronous data link control (SDLC) or the asynchronous
communications and allows host-independent requester-server
processing.

3.1.3 SNA Distributed Wide Area Networks

To address the limitations of the SNA hierarchical wide area
network and to extend the SNA architecture to local area networks it
became necessary to define a new distributed physical unit capable
of any-to-any communications and a new device-independent
logical unit that would recognize intelligence on both sides of a
connection. The logical unit type 6.2 and the physical unit 2.1
enhance SNA wide area networks to fully distributed and peer-to-
peer networks, and allow SNA to be extended to run on Token Ring
and other local area networks.With the introduction of SNA peer-to-
peer logical unit type 6.2 and the distributed physical unit type 2.1,
applications can now be designed on Token Ring using the SNA/LU
6.2 protocols rather than the low-level NETBIOS interfaces. With
these introductions IBM's strategic direction for wide area
networks has changed from the hierarchical SNA approach to an
enterprise computing solution with universal any-to-any
connectivity. Figure 3.3 shows the improvement of an SNA peer-to-
peer network over the tree structured, master-slave connectivity
shown in Fig. 3.1. In the newer distributed network of mainframes,
minicomputers, and personal computers, all nodes are equal (peers)
and an entity residing on any of the network nodes can
communicate directly with other entities residing within the
network. Figure 3.3 shows that in an SNA distributed network all

SNA nodes (PCs, minicomputers, or mainframes) have any-to-any communications capability. Applications residing on any SNA distributed node can communicate directly with any other applications in the SNA wide area network. The announcement of System/390 Enterprise System with MVS/ESA, VM/ESA, and VSE/ESA Enterprise Systems Architecture shows IBM's commitment to provide users with any-to-any connectivity in which theES/9000 mainframe is an SNA PU 2.1 distributed node (see Fig. 3.3) rather than a master PU 5, node which totally controls communications in the hierarchical networks as shown in Fig. 3.1.

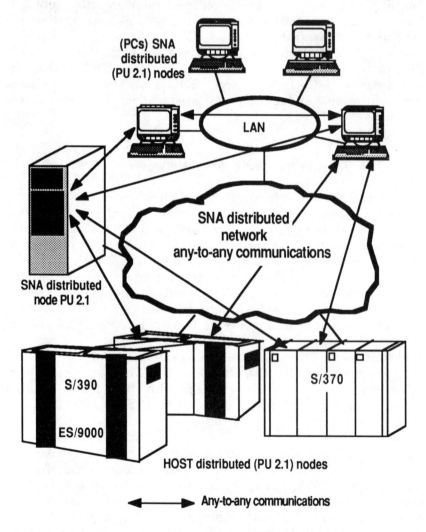

Figure 3.3 IBM SNA distributed network.

3.1.4 Connectivity

The biggest obstacles to distributed networks and distributed processing are the communication links. In moving large amounts of data, communication lines (even at 56 kbits/s) become a performance bottleneck in distributed processing. Token Ring networks at 16 Mbits/s and IBM S/370 (2-Mbytes/s channels) certainly decrease the time needed to move information between distributed nodes. Both Token Ring and the S/370 data channel can be used only locally, however, they do not resolve the problem of moving information fast and efficiently over SNA wide area networks which are generally using leased lines (up to 56 kbits/s). With the introduction of the S/390 (ES9000) Enterprise System, IBM introduced the Enterprise Systems Connection (ESCON), with wideband fiber-optic channels that can transfer data between host systems or between a host and a controller at a rate of 10 Mbytes/s and higher. The communication controllers and I/O devices can be placed on the ESCON channels at a distance of up to 5.6 mi. The introduction of the IBM 3172 model 2 controller, that supports the Fiber Distributed Data Interface (FDDI) 100-Mbits/s international standard, will allow extensions to the ESCON channels for high-speed transmission of data between any computer in the IBM Enterprise Network. The distributed networks and distributed data processing in an SNA network is now more feasible than ever. The enhancements to the SNA architecture (LU 6.2, PU 2.1, Token Ring, ESCON) changes the older SNA hierarchical technology to a brand-new distributed technology. SNA becomes a modern distributed network that will play a very important role in the 1990s along with theOpen Systems Interconnection Reference Model OSI/RM international standard.

3.1.5 Historical SNA Limitations

The major limitations of SNA hierarchical networks are:

1. Intelligent workstations and PCs emulate SNA peripheral nodes (PU 2s). Peripheral nodes (PU 2s) are limited to host communication and cannot communicate directly with other intelligent workstations or minicomputers in the network (see Fig. 3.1). That means, for example, that a file cannot be copied or printed between two personal computers connected to an SNA wide area network.

2. PCs or intelligent workstations emulate dummy SNA devices, mostly a dummy 3270 type terminal (LU 2), and they are not treated as intelligent entities with their own processing power. Programs using 3270 emulations must pretend they are dummy SNA devices and must respond to keyboard events such as Clear key or Enter key. Such programs are not well suited for distributed processing and enterprise distributed networks.

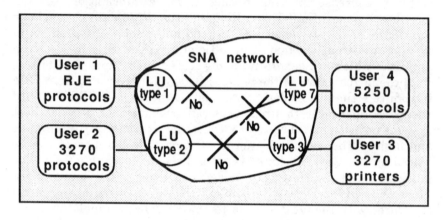

Figure 3.4 SNA incompatible logical units.

3. Different logical unit types use incompatible SNA protocols (see Fig. 3.4). The logical units residing in peripheral nodes were designed to control different SNA devices such as RJE devices (LU type 1), 3270 terminals and printers (LU type 2 and 3), or 5250 terminals (LU type 7). These logical units use specific device-dependent data streams and communications protocols. The LU type 1, controlling RJE devices, is not capable of understanding the data stream or the communication protocols used by other LU types in an SNA network (see Fig. 3.4). Even if all SNA nodes could communicate with one another, the different logical unit types could not understand one another's data streams or protocols and would not allow communications of existing applications that use the different LU types. In a true distributed network any entity (e.g., a logical unit) must understand the network protocols and must be capable of communication with any other entity in the network.

Personal computers (PCs) are capable today of handling presentation services and many other application functions locally without host interaction and control. An intelligent workstation is capable of field editing, screen navigation, dialog with the end-user, printer control, data and application distribution, etc. This reduces line traffic and improves response time. The personal computers and minicomputers connected to an SNA network must be capable of direct communications with other SNA nodes and must be treated as an equal intelligent entity rather than slave dummy devices. Therefore, enhancements to SNA hierarchical architecture would be necessary if SNA were to stay as a leading networking technology of the 1990s.

3.1.6 SNA Architecture Enhancements

The traditional IBM networks had to be changed to overcome the limitations of the SNA hierarchical architecture described above. Users wanted to distribute processing and data among mainframes, minicomputers, and personal computers. Distributed processing was possible under SNA, but it required rather complex programming techniques and nonstandard protocols in order to hide the distributed power of PCs and minicomputers and pretend to be nonintelligent devices to the host. Users also wanted peer-to-peer (not master-slave) relationships among all network entities. That would allow any-to-any (rather than host-to-device only) communications and would recognize intelligence on both sides of a connection of any two SNA nodes (see Fig. 3.3). The addition of thelogical unit type 6.2 (LU 6.2) and the physical unit type 2.1 (PU 2.1) to SNA architecture satisfies the above user requirements. An SNA distributed network can be viewed as a collection of links, distributed nodes (PU 2.1 nodes), and distributed logical units (LU 6.2s) connected via LU-LU peer-to-peer sessions (see Fig. 3.5). A LU 6.2 residing in any of the SNA distributed PU 2.1 nodes can issue an SNA BIND command to establish a peer-to-peer session directly with other nodes in the network. PU 2.1 nodes can be connected by multiple links and contain a variable number of logical units. PU 2.1 is a distributed node capable of direct peer-to-peer, any-to-any communications with other PU 2.1 nodes. LU 6.2 is a device-independent logical unit that recognizes intelligence on both sides of a connection. Therefore, PCs emulating LU 6.2 do not have to pretend to be dummy terminals (screens or keyboards) any more but can be treated as equal intelligent partners when communicating with hosts, minicomputers at other PCs in an SNA distributed network. The extended SNA architecture accommodates smaller distributed systems and extends peer-to-peer connectivity to personal computers (PCs), minicomputers, and other vendor equipment that can emulate the distributed node PU 2.1 and LU 6.2 in an IBM enterprise-wide distributed network.

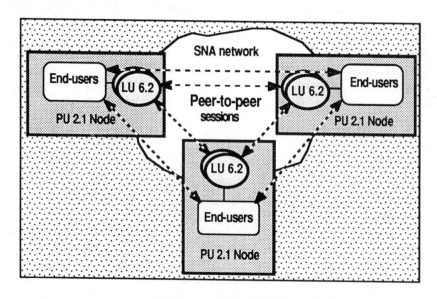

Figure 3.5 The extended SNA/LU 6.2/PU 2.1 architecture.

3.1.7 APPC, CPI-C, LU 6.2, and SAA

IBM's direction toward distributed networks and distributed transaction processing is achieved by bringing products to customers that comply with SAA, SAA/CPI-C, APPC, SNA/LU 6.2, and PU 2.1 architectures.

APPC

Advanced Program-to-Program Communications (APPC) is an open architecture designed for writing distributed applications. It has been designed to provide enhanced SNA support (LU 6.2 and PU 2.1) for distributed processing. Distributed transaction processing means that two or more processors cooperate with each other in the execution of a single unit of work such as a **transaction**. In this sense, APPC defines distributed functions independent of the environments in which they run and assist in providing connectivity (based on LU 6.2 and PU 2.1 architecture) among a wide variety of computer systems and devices.

Recently, the term "APPC" is used differently in IBM SAA literature from the definition described above. The services provided by the logical unit LU 6.2 has been separated from the APPC functions. The APPC is used to describe the function that the LU 6.2 provides to application programs (ALLOCATE, DEALLOCATE, etc., described later in this section) and to control-operator transaction programs (such as CNOS, also described later in this section). Therefore, Advanced Program-to-Program Communications (APPC) describes the functions requested in transaction programs through an application programming interface (API). In the LU 6.2 architecture there is freedom of syntax, which means that the APPC functions can be implemented via product-specific Application Programming Interfaces; (APIs) (e.g., CICS API, OS/2 API, AS/400, API). However, everybody must implement the same LU 6.2 distributed functions.

CPI-C

With the SAA announcement in 1987, one requirement is for SAA applications to be portable between different SAA environments. **SAA/CPI-C Common Programming Interface-Communications** provides a consistent (common syntax) application programming interface for program-to-program communications. SAA/CPI-C provides a common interface for development of portable and distributed applications across different SAA platforms using IBM's SNA logical unit LU 6.2. The APPC programming calls (also called **verbs**) differ from CPI-C communications calls in that CPI-C calls require exact syntax common to all implementations. This would suggest that the APPC implementations should migrate to SAA/CPI-C implementations to comply with the SAA architecture. There are some other differences between SAA/CPI-C calls and APPC verbs that will be discussed in Chap. 6.

Logical Unit Type 6.2

The logical unit type 6.2 is an SNA device independent distributed LU that recognizes intelligence on both sides of a connection and allows peer-to-peer and any-to-any communications. LU 6.2 provides services to both APPC and SAA/CPI-C applications such as:

- Enforcing LU 6.2 session rules and protocols

- Initiating, terminating, and managing sessions and distributed transaction resources

- Processing the APPC or SAA/CPI-C calls

- Building and checking the appropriate SNA headers and network messages

SAA

Systems Application Architecture (SAA) is a collection of interfaces, protocols, and products (open architectures such as SNA/LU 6.2 or SAA/CPI-C) that envisions mainframe computer systems as repositories of global databases for sharing of enterprise resources. SAA is a set of many architectures that not only includes the program-to-program communication standards and the networking standards (such as SNA/LU 6.2 or OSI) but also defines fourth-generation languages, databases, case tools, and common user interface. Using these tools and interfaces SAA will assure:

- Portability — applications can be ported from one system to other SAA systems.

- Consistency — applications are developed using the same techniques (SAA languages, SQL databases, dialog managers for designing a consistent end-user interface, presentation services, etc.).

- Connectivity — communications standards that define communication protocols for the entire computer enterprise.

3.2 SNA DISTRIBUTED NODE TYPE 2.1

The SNA **peripheral nodes** (**PU 2 nodes**) have limited communication capabilities in the traditional SNA hierarchical networks. They are limited to communications with host applications and they are limited to a **single session** between local and remote logical units. In order to provide peer-to-peer rather than terminal-to-host connectivity, IBM enhanced the PU 2.0 node, adding the capability of activation, termination, and management of LU-LU sessions, creating the PU 2.1 node. An **SNA node type 2.1** (**PU 2.1**) is an extension of a PU 2 node that supports peer-to-peer connections of distributed processors (see Fig. 3.6).

The major function of an SNA distributed node type 2.1 is to provide peer-to-peer and any-to-any communications (see Fig. 3.5). Peer-to-peer communications were possible in an SNA network between subarea nodes (CICS-CICS, IMS-CICS, IMS-IMS) using the LU 6.0 or 6.1 protocols. Peer-to-peer communications were also possible on smaller IBM systems (e.g. S/36, S/38, System 34, 8100) using a variety of incompatible product-specific protocols. In an SNA hierarchical network the host (master) is capable of establishing sessions between logical units by only sending an SNA BIND command. The peripheral nodes (PU 2s) may only ask for sessions by sending a LOGON or INITSELF command to the host as described earlier in the book.

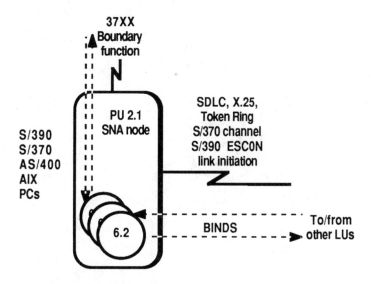

Figure 3.6 SNA distributed node type 2.1.

The physical unit type 2.1 (PU 2.1) node is an extension of the SNA physical unit 2 (PU 2) node with the following added capabilities (see Fig. 3.6):

• Can initiate, terminate and manage links

• Allows any-to-any, point-to-point, and multipoint link connections

• Can initiate, terminate, and manage peer-to-peer host independent sessions (can generate SNA commands such as BIND and UNBIND)

- Supports independent and dependent logical units (LU 6.2s); allows peer-to-peer communications to other distributed nodes and provides support for PU 2 connections to hosts via boundary nodes such as a 3745

- Provides the physical and session level connectivity required for Advanced Program-to-Program Communications (APPC) and SAA/CPI-C cooperative processing which are discussed later in this book

- Can act as an independent distributed node and does not require any connection to the host (SSCP-PU or SSCP-LU sessions)

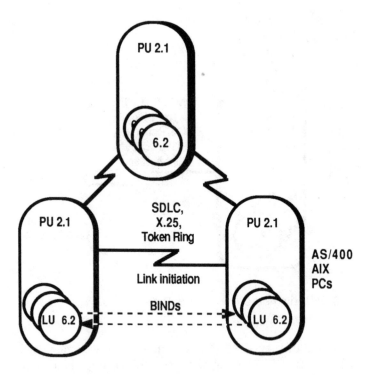

Figure 3.7 Low Entry Networking (LEN) architecture.

3.2.1 Low Entry Networking (LEN)

The network of PU 2.1 nodes is called a **Low Entry Networking (LEN)** architecture for connecting SNA distributed systems (see Fig. 3.7). Figure 3.7 shows the Low Entry Networking (LEN) network consisting of PU 2.1 distributed nodes and LU 6.2s. The LEN architecture defines point-to-point (no routing) PU 2.1-to-PU 2.1 peer-to-peer communications. Notice that there is no master-slave relationship between SNA PU 2.1 nodes and that the logical units (LU 6.2s) are device independent LUs not dummy SNA devices. Two PU 2.1 nodes such as personal computers or AS/400s can be connected directly using a variety of link level protocols such as SDLC, X.25, or the IBM Token Ring. The LEN network can exist as an independent network without any connection to SNA hosts. Most IBM and other vendor computers are capable of emulating the SNA distributed PU 2.1 node. The following is a list of some of the PU 2.1 node implementations.

IBM implementations:

- System/390 Enterprise System ES/9000 with MVS/ESA, VM/ESA, and VSE/ESA

- System/370 with VTAM Version 3 Release 2

- APPC on OS/2 EE

- OS/2 EE Network Services/2

- APPC/PC on DOS PCs

- AS/400, S/3x

- System/88

- AIX (mainframes, RS 6000, and PCs)

There are PU 2.1 emulation products available on most other hardware and software vendor systems, and many third-party PU 2.1 software products run on IBM and other vendor machines; examples include:

- Digital Equipment Corporation (DEC)

- Tandem Computers

- Hewlett-Packard (HP)

- Amdahl Corporation, Unisys

- AT&T

- Apple Computer

- NSA, DCA, Novell, EICON

3.2.2 Advanced Peer-to-Peer Networking (APPN)

Low Entry Networking architecture defines PU 2.1 point to point (no routing) communications. This means that the two PU 2.1 nodes must be connected with each other over a link or a routing network such as X.25, Token Ring, or 37xx subarea network. Advanced Peer-to-Peer Networking (APPN) architecture is a Low Entry Networking (LEN) architecture with two major enhancements:

1. The PU 2.1 node has the ability to perform intermediate network routing.

2. It allows dynamic network configuration.

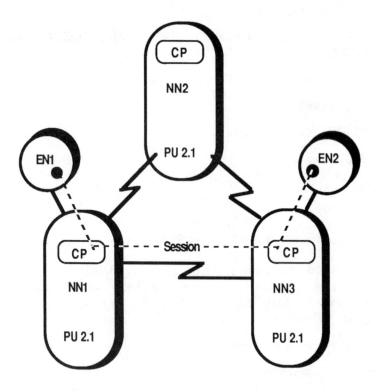

Figure 3.8 APPN networking.

PU 2.1 Network Nodes (NN) and End Nodes (EN)

A PU 2.1 node capable of performing intermediate network routing function is called a **PU 2.1 network node**. A PU 2.1 Low Entry

Networking node is not capable of routing and is called an **PU 2.1 end mode**. In the traditional SNA hierarchical network the routing is done by the path control network (also called **subarea network**) which performs intermediate network routing. The APPN network allows any PU 2.1 node (EN or NN node) to communicate with any other PU 2.1 node attached to theAPPN network. End nodes (PCs or other PU 2.1 nodes) are attached to a network node (such as an AS/400) via SDLC links or a Token Ring network and rely on the network node to provide routing for session requests that involve multiple nodes. Figure 3.8 shows the end node EN1 issuing a request to establish a session with an LU residing in a remote end node EN2. The network node NN1 will perform a distributed directory search to locate the remote LU and selects the **best route** between the two logical units. An LU-LU session can then be established between the local and remote logical units residing respectively in EN1 and EN2. Once the session is established, the intermediate NN nodes simply act as "passthrough" nodes between the two end nodes.

Dynamic Configuration

In the traditional SNA hierarchical approach the VTAM/NCP configuration is static. Each time the hierarchical network resources are added to or deleted from the SNA network, a VTAM system programmer must perform a SYSGEN to update the static NCP tables and routes.

The Advanced Peer-to-Peer Networking (APPN) network supports dynamic configuration. New logical units or entire nodes can be added or deleted dynamically. This information is broadcast to other nodes in the network.

Control Point (CP) is an entity residing in a network node that is responsible for:

• Maintaining and exchanging network topology information with CP residing in other NN nodes

• Conducting Distributed Directory searches in order to dynamically locate the remote logical unit being requested by the local transaction program even if the remote logical unit is not configured at the local network node

• Selecting the best route between the two communicating logical units

3.2.3 PU 2.1 Link Level Connectivity

In an SNA hierarchical network the data link control level commands were totally controlled by the mainframe. Therefore, physical unit type 2 nodes (e.g., 3270 emulation packages) did not have an intelligence required for link activation and management. The SNA physical unit type 2.1 distributed node must be capable of activation, deactivation, and management of links to adjacent nodes. The PU 2.1 node may also support attachment to SNA subarea networks via boundary function nodes such as a 37xx Communication controller (see Fig. 3.6).

The following is a typical physical unit type 2.1 (PU 2.1) node link activation sequence:

- The connect phase — initial establishment of a physical connection between the two PU 2.1 nodes. For example, a dial operation is required on switched facilities.

- Prenegotiation XID phase — initial successful XID exchange. During this phase a null XID may flow and XID collisions may occur.

- Negotiation XID phase — establishes the primary and secondary link station roles and determines link level characteristics.

- Mode-setting phase — initiating the level 2 link level protocol by the primary link station that sends the mode setting command such as (SNRM for the SDLC link level connections or SABM for X.25 network).

PU 2.1 XID-3 Link Negotiation

Once the connect phase has successfully completed, the two PU 2.1 nodes exchange XIDs to establish node link level characteristics (see Fig. 3.9). In the prenegotiation phase a null XID (XID without an I-field) can be used to poll an unknown SNA node type. A PU 2.1 node can be preconfigured as a secondary link station, primary link station, or negotiable link station. The primary and negotiable link stations may send a null XID. The proper response to the null XID is an XID-3. Since the XIDs can be generated asynchronously it is possible for XID collisions to occur. The sending stations detect the collision and retry the XIDs after a random timeout expires. Each time a collision occurs a new random timeout is generated until XIDs are exchanged successfully between the two stations. In the negotiation phase the XID-3s are exchanged to establish the primary and secondary roles and link level characteristics such as modulo and window sizes. X.25 networks use the Asynchronous Balance Mode (ABM) or the Asynchronous Balance Mode Extended (ABME) for the link level protocol.

Primary and Secondary Link Stations

The primary link station (**PLS**) and secondary link station (**SLS**) roles have no meaning for X.25 other than determining which station will send the mode-setting command (SABM) or (SABME). The primary-secondary link station also determines the setting of the Origin Destination Assignor Indicator (ODAI) bit in the transmission header. We will discuss the importance of the (ODAI) bit on LU 6.2 session IDs assignment later in this book. The last phase of the link level activation is the negotiation phase. In this phase the sequence of XID-3 (with predefined Format 3 I-field) is exchanged between the PU 2.1 nodes until the the nodes agree on the link level characteristics (modulo and window sizes, who will send the mode-setting DLC command, etc.).

During network configuration we must assure that any two PU 2.1 nodes that require communication with each other have predefined the appropriate link station roles. If both of the nodes are configured as secondary link stations or primary link stations, the negotiation fails and the link cannot be activated. If one is a negotiable station and the other a primary-secondary station then the negotiable node takes the role of either secondary or primary and the negotiation succeeds. If both PU 2.1 nodes specify negotiable roles (assuming no preconfiguration of one node as a primary link station and the other as a secondary link station), then the node with a greater **node ID** (a configurable parameter) becomes the primary link station. The final exchange carries XID-3s with the appropriate primary-secondary station roles to assure that the two nodes are synchronized with each other. We will discuss the XID-3, in detail, later in the book. Once XID has completed, the primary link station initiates the link by sending the mode-setting command SNRM for SDLC or SABM for X.25. The secondary link station responds to the mode-setting command with an unnumbered acknowledgment UA command. Then the primary link station polls the secondary by sending the RR or RNR command and the link has been established.

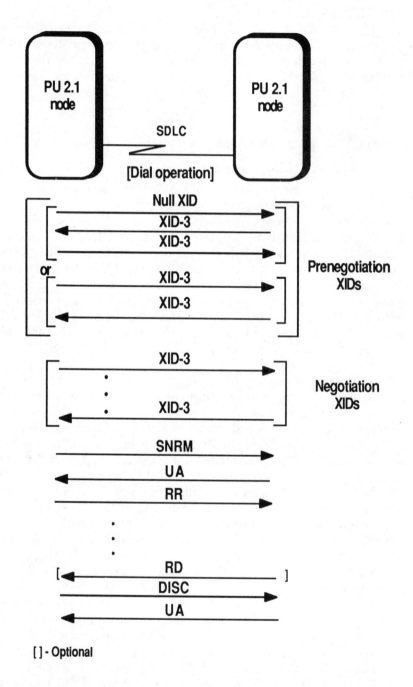

Figure 3.9 PU 2.1 node SDLC role negotiation.

Link Deactivation

Link deactivation can be initiated by either link station. The following is a sequence of link deactivation (see Fig. 3.9).

1. The secondary link station may optionally issue the Request Disconnect (RD) SDLC command to request the primary to deactivate the link connection.

2. The primary link station deactivates the link by sending the SDLC Disconnect (DISC) command.

3. The secondary link station replies with the SDLC unnumbered acknowledgment (UA) command, and both link stations enter disconnect mode.

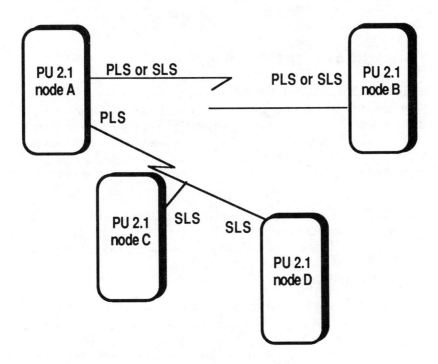

Figure 3.10 Multipoint PU 2.1 link connections.

A PU 2.1 node supports both multiple-link and multipoint link connections to remote nodes. In Fig. 3.10, node A has two link connections, one to node B and the other to nodes C and D. Node A can act as a primary link station (PLS) or a secondary link station

(SLS) when communicating with node B. Node A must act as a primary link station (PLS) when communicating with nodes C or D. Node A can communicate concurrently with nodes B, C, and D. The following restrictions apply to the physical unit type 2.1 multipoint links:

1. Only one primary link station (PLS) is allowed on a multipoint line. All the other nodes on the same link must be configured as secondary link stations.

2. The PLS must know and use the secondary link station address.

3. No negotiable link stations are allowed because the negotiable link stations use the broadcast address when they do not know the address of the secondary link station.

3.3 LOGICAL UNIT TYPE 6.2

A **logical unit** (LU) is defined within SNA as a port (an end-user's interface) via which end-users get access to an SNA network. The end-users of LU 6.2 are applications called **Transaction Programs (TPs)**. The logical unit type 6.2 is an intelligent LU that offers peer-to-peer program-to-program communication between TPs. LU 6.2 is supported by PU 2.1 distributed nodes and PU 5 host nodes. LU 6.2 consists of:

1. The **Application Programming Interface (API)** — the LU's protocol boundary between TPs and the LU itself. The protocol boundary defines a set of primitives (called LU 6.2 **verbs**) for distributed transaction processing. LU 6.2 verbs are discussed later in this section.

2. The SNA logical unit (LU) services — responsible for formatting and encoding messages exchanged on sessions between logical units, understanding the session rules and protocols, and processing a TP's LU6.2 programming calls.

Figure 3.11 shows an SNA network with three logical units. Each LU 6.2 provides an interface between transaction programs (TPs), and the path control network via the LU 6.2 protocol boundary called the Application Programming Interface (API), so that programs need not be aware of the underlying physical network configuration, routing, and addressing.

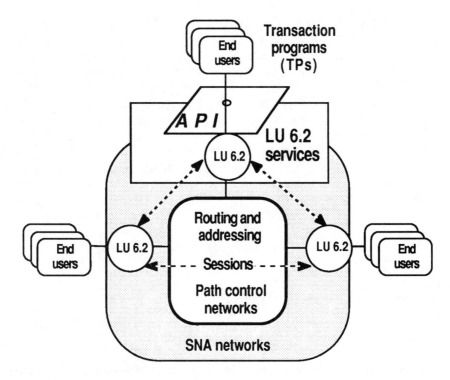

Figure 3.11 SNA logical units.

LU-LU Session

A logical connection between logical units is called an LU-LU
session. The two LUs (the origin LU and the destination LU)
exchange information using the session. An SNA session is
established when one LU sends another LU an SNA request, known
as a **BIND**, which specifies the rules that both partners agree upon
(e.g. maximum message size exchanged between LUs, or who is
responsible for error recovery), for the duration of the session. The
BIND sender and receiver are known respectively as the **primary
logical unit (PLU)** and the **secondary logical unit (SLU)**. In the
traditional SNA hierarchical network the PLU always resided on
the host and the secondary logical unit resided on peripheral nodes.
The PLU, residing on the host, was considered to be the intelligent
entity responsible for error recovery and establishing the session
rules. The secondary logical units (SLUs) residing on peripheral
nodes were required to have only enough intelligence to control the
dummy terminals or printers and they were limited to a single

session. The logical unit type 6.2 does not have the limitations of the hierarchical SNA logical units. Figure 3.11 shows three LUs connected via LU 6.2-LU 6.2 sessions. Notice that each LU may serve many end-users (application programs) concurrently. The LU receives the data from an application program and passes the data to the path control network. The path control network is responsible for building the appropriate routing headers, resolving the network addresses and routing the messages between the network nodes. SNA devices (terminals, printers, etc.) are represented in LU 6.2 by a program controlling the devices. Therefore, the LU 6.2 is an intelligent device independent entity that allows program-to-program and program-to-SNA device communication. Figure 3.11 also shows that the LU 6.2 is not limited to single sessions and can have concurrent multiple or parallel sessions to one or many remote logical units.

Transaction Programs (TPs)

SNA/LU 6.2 architecture defines three types of transaction programs:

1. **Application transaction programs (TPs).** These are end-user applications designed to perform end-user processing.

2. **Service transaction programs (STPs).** SNA LU 6.2 architecture defines service transaction programs (STPs) as programs that provide architected services to other TPs. SNA Distribution Services (SNADS), an architecture allowing for the storing and forwarding of objects (such as documents) between distributed SNA nodes, is an example of a service transaction program.

3. **Control-operator transaction programs.** This is an implementation-specific operator interface to the LU 6.2 architecture. It interacts with the logical unit on behalf of a human operator issuing network commands that control the operational environment of the LU (define, activate, or deactivate LU resources and/or sessions).

Open and Closed Implementations (APIs)

The implementations that expose their LU 6.2 verbs directly to application TPs are called **open implementations (or open APIs).** The implementations that do not expose its LU 6.2 verbs directly to application programs are called **closed implementations (or closed APIs).** All open LU 6.2 implementations must support at least the same LU 6.2 defined function sets (called a **base set**). Closed implementations, such as print processes, resource managers, and other service transaction programs, generally provide product specific functionality and do not have to implement all distributed functions defined in the LU 6.2 base set.

3.3.1 Dependent Logical Units

The PU 2.1 node supports both the SSCP dependent and independent logical units (LUs). The following are the characteristics of a dependent LU6.2 logical unit (see Fig. 3.12):

- It requires assistance from the System Services Control Point (SSCP) to activate an LU-LU session.

- It requires ACTPU and ACTLU commands (SSCP-PU and SSCP-LU network management sessions) prior to LU-LU session establishment.

- It is not able to send an SNA BIND to initiate a session with remote logical units. It always accepts BINDs from the host application such as CICS.

- It may request a session by sending an SNA INITSELF command to the PU 5 host node.

- It is supported from a PU 2.1 node using type 2.0 protocols to a PU 5 node via a boundary function (37xx communication controller).

- It can communicate only with mainframe applications.

- It can act only as a secondary logical unit (SLU) but not the PLU.

- It has the LU-LU session limit equal to 1.

Figure 3.12 illustrates a CICS LU 6.2 transaction program TP A communicating with a PC transaction program TP B. If the user requirements were for a single conversation, then the logical unit residing in the PC may be configured as a dependent LU. Prior to starting the transaction an operator would have to activate the logical and the physical units by issuing VTAM V, NET, ACT, ID = commands. In this case the PC is totally controlled by the host SSCP and the VTAM operator. If such control is required and there is no need for parallel sessions or communications with other LUs in the network, then a dependent logical unit may be the right choice.

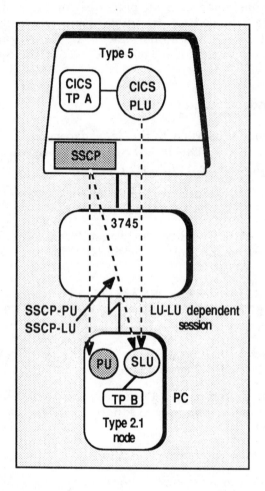

Figure 3.12 LU 6.2 dependent logical units.

3.3.2 Independent Logical Unit

An SSCP **independent LU** (or simply independent LU) is a logical unit capable of initiating sessions by sending SNA BIND commands directly to other LUs residing in the network. The following are the characteristics of an independent LU 6.2 logical unit (see Fig. 3.13):

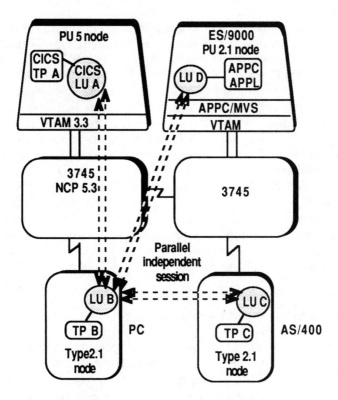

Figure 3.13 LU 6.2 independent logical units.

- It does not require assistance from the SSCP to activate a session.

- It does not require ACTPU or ACTLU commands.

- It is able to send an SNA BIND command directly to other LUs to initiate a session.

- It is supported from a PU 2.1 node to any other PU 2.1 node (not just mainframes) attached directly or via 37xx subarea networks residing within the network.

- It can act as a secondary logical unit (SLU) or a primary logical unit (PLU).

- It supports multiple sessions to remote logical units. Multiple sessions to the same partner LU are called **parallel sessions**.

- It requires only an SNA BIND command for session initiation and only an UNBIND command for session termination.

Figure 3.13 shows a PC transaction program TP B that can concurrently communicate via one independent logical unit LU B with a CICS transaction TP A residing in the PU 5 host node, an APPC/MVS application TP D residing in an ES/9000 PU 2.1 node, and a transaction program TP C residing in an AS/400 attached to the subarea network. Notice that LU B has multiple sessions (six) to the remote LUs, two parallel sessions to each of the LUs (LU A, LU C, and LU D). LU B acts as a PLU for the sessions it initiates by sending an SNA BIND command and as a secondary logical unit (SLU) for the sessions initiated by the other network LUs. What the user gains with a PU 2.1 node and an independent logical unit is the ability to have more than one active session and conversation at the same instance in time with one or many remote transaction programs. With the capability of multiple and parallel sessions, TP B can have multiple requests (transactions) active with remote TPs residing anywhere in the network.

3.3.3 Sessions and Conversations

An SNA **session** is a long-lived logical connection between LUs. When an application program wishes to communicate with another program it asks the LU for the right to exclusively use the session for the duration of a distributed transaction. When the transaction is completed the session is released and is available to other applications. Many transaction programs may use the same session serially (one transaction at a time). The logical connection between a pair of transaction programs (TPs) is called a **conversation**. LU 6.2 conversations are typically short-lived connections corresponding to a single end-user transaction. Sessions connect logical units and conversations connect the transaction programs into pairs for distributed transaction processing. The two transaction programs (TPs) use conversations and cooperate with each other to execute a distributed transaction. The session can be reused serially by many conversations and applications without the interruption of the LU-LU connection.

There are two types of conversations:

1. **Mapped conversations** — intended for application programs written in a high-level language and allowing the exchange of data in any format agreed upon by the two application programmers. Mapped conversations hide, from the programmer, the details of the underlying LU 6.2 data stream.

2. **Basic conversations** — which require that TPs exchange records in a predefined LU 6.2 format that contains a 2-byte record length prefix. Programmers may block many logical records into one "send buffer" and they may request from the LU to receive one or more logical records on one receive call. Basic conversations are typically intended for SNA defined service transaction programs which provide architected services to end-user application programs. An example of a service transaction program is the change number of sessions (CNOS) program that regulates the number of parallel sessions between two logical units.

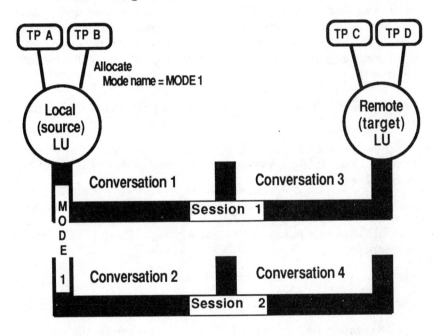

Figure 3.14 Sessions and conversations.

A conversation is allocated to an LU-LU session, but the transaction programs (TPs) do not refer to a specific session but to a group of sessions identified by one of the ALLOCATE parameters called **mode name** (e.g., ALLOCATE Mode name = MODE 1; see Fig 3.14). A conversation is then assigned to the first available session identified by the specified mode name. Conversations may share the same session serially (only one conversation at a time per session). Conversations are usually short-lived logical connections whereas sessions are long-lived logical connections that can be reused in a serial manner by many conversations and different transaction programs. Figure 3.14 shows two logical units, the local LU (also called the **source** LU) and the remote LU (also called the **target LU**), communicating via two parallel sessions (Session 1 and Session 2). The two sessions are identified by one mode name, MODE 1. Transaction programs (TPs) may issue ALLOCATE verbs, supplying the Mode name = MODE 1 as a parameter, to get access to any free (not currently assigned to another conversation) session identified by this mode name. TP B may, for example, establish two concurrent conversations (conversation 1 and conversation 2) over two distinct parallel sessions to TP C and TP D. There can be a maximum of two concurrent conversations active over the two distinct parallel sessions between the local and remote logical units. If both of the sessions are currently in use, then the remaining ALLOCATE verbs (conversation initiation requests) would simply be queued by the logical unit until one of the sessions is released.

The following is a list of LU 6.2 session and conversation characteristics:

- An independent LU may have multiple sessions to one or many partner LUs. Multiple sessions to the same partner LU are called **parallel sessions**.

- An LU may run many TPs successively, concurrently, or both.

- The BIND sender becomes the primary logical unit (PLU) for the session.

- Sessions can be shared by many TPs.

- Successive conversations may share the same sessions serially.

- A conversation has an exclusive use of a session for the duration of the conversation.

- Multiple conversations between different pairs of TPs can be active concurrently using distinct sessions.

- A conversation is initiated by issuing the LU 6.2 ALLOCATE verb.

3.4 DISTRIBUTED NETWORK COMPONENTS

An SNA/LU 6.2 network physically consists of SNA distributed nodes interconnected via links. Distributed nodes are capable of any-to-any connectivity. An SNA node is a physical package that contains a subset of SNA layered architecture. Type 2.1 distributed nodes may connect to other PU 2.1 nodes directly or via a subarea routing network. The transmission media used for link connections can be leased or switched telephone lines, T1 or T3 digital links, microwave, coaxial cable, or fiber-optic links.

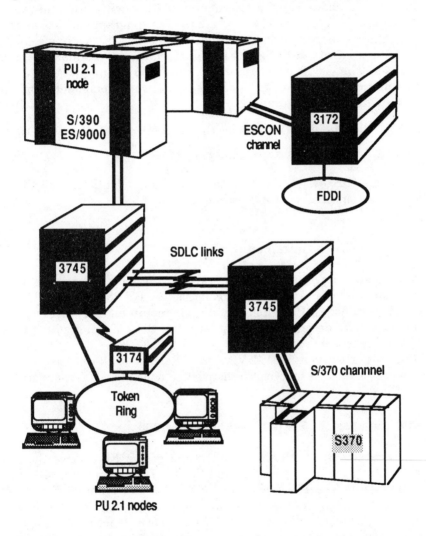

Figure 3.15 Network components.

Figure 3.15 shows an Enterprise System/390 (ES/9000 series) distributed node connected to a 3172 interconnect controller and a 3745 communication controller via ESCON fiber-optic channels.

The 3745 communication controller is connected via multiple SDLC links to another 3745 controller which is connected via an S/370 channel to a S/370 host. The 3745 is also connected to a 3174 establishment controller via a single SDLC link and to a Token Ring local area network via a Token Ring interface card (TIC card). The personal computers on the Token Ring are also PU 2.1 distributed nodes capable of communicating with other network resources via 3745 or 3174 controllers. The diagram also shows the 3172 interconnect controller connected to other resources via Fiber Distributed Data Interface (FDDI) international standard at 100 Mbits/s. The S/370 host connects via S/370 channel to the 3745 communication controller. The major network components of an IBM distributed network are:

- SNA distributed PU 2.1 nodes (hosts, minicomputers, and PCs)

- SNA controllers (3745, 3174, or 3172)

- Links (ESCON, S/370 data channels, SDLC links, FDDI connections, Token Ring, Ethernet, etc.)

3.4.1 PU 2.1 Mainframes

IBM hosts (processors that contain a telecommunication access method such as ACF/VTAM) can act as PU type 5 or PU 2.1 distributed nodes. PU 5 nodes and their role in an SNA hierarchical network were described in Chap. 2. In an SNA distributed network PU 5 nodes can communicate with PU 2.1 nodes using type 2.0 protocols. However, VTAM Version 3 Release 3 allows hosts, such as a S/370, to act as a type 2.1 distributed node in an SNA network.

IBM Enterprise System Architecture/390

The System/390, with the broad range of the Enterprise System ES/9000, is the most powerful and flexible mainframe that IBM has ever offered. The ES/9000 is an SNA PU 2.1 distributed node that supports peer-to-peer communications (no master-slave relationship) with other nodes in the network. It focuses heavily on enterprise wide computing and distributed transaction processing. The ES/9000 replaces the S/370 data channel (2 Mbytes/s) with the fiber-optic ESCON channel that can be connected with peripherals and other mainframes at a higher speed (10 Mbytes/s) and greater distance (5.7 miles) than previously possible. The Virtual

Telecommunications Access Method (VTAM) with the MVS/ESA, VM/ESA, and VSE/ESA operating systems enhance the IBM host to support any-to-any connections at fiber-optic (ESCON) channel speeds. The older S/370 IBM mainframes have also been enhanced with VTAM Version 3 Release 3 that allows hosts to act as type 2.1 distributed nodes. The introduction of CICS/ESA and IMS/ESA and their support for SAA Common Program Interface Communications (CPI-CI) as well as the introduction of the APPC/MVS services show IBM's commitment to distributed transaction processing based on PU 2.1 and LU 6.2 architectures. The IBM host has changed from the hierarchical PU 5 master node to a true distributed node that treats other hosts, minicomputers, and personal computers as equal peer nodes rather than as slaves. Figure 3.15 shows the S/390 and S/370 mainframes as SNA PU 2.1 distributed nodes that recognize equal intelligence with other network PU 2.1 nodes such as PCs. The PCs are treated as peers in a PU 2.1 distributed network. For example, the PCs can initiate sessions with any or both hosts by sending the SNA BIND command without asking permission from either of the hosts. The following is a list of major IBM host and distributed processors with PU 2.1 and LU 6.2 capabilities:

- System/390 — the Enterprise System ES/9000 family of powerful processors with MVS/ESA, VM/ESA, and VSE/ESA operating systems and the Virtual Telecommunications Access Method (VTAM).

- System/370 , 30xx — older IBM host processors. The 3080 and 3090 are the latest representatives of the S/370 series of processors. The S/370 also supports the MVS, VS, and VSE operating systems and the Virtual Telecommunications Access Method (VTAM).

- System/88 — a midrange, fault-tolerant system. It supports SNA PU 2.1 and LU 6.2 architectures.

- AS/400 — the Application System/400 with OS/400 operating system is the SAA family of midrange computers smaller than the ES/9000 or the S/370 processors. AS/400 supports PU 2.1 and LU 6.2 architecture and can act as an intermediate routing node in an Advanced Peer-to-Peer Networking (APPN) PU 2.1 distributed network.

- IBM RISC System/6000 — the very powerful desktop family of IBM processors that run the AIX (UNIX) operating system. The AIX RS/6000 can emulate a PU 2.1 and LU 6.2 SNA distributed node and is capable of running SAA applications.

3.4.2 Controllers

The main purpose of controllers within an SNA network is to:

1. Provide the network routing capabilities and the data flow control between SNA nodes.

2. Act as gateways and multiplexers between devices, local area networks, and hosts.

Communication Controllers (3745)

The 3745 family of communication controllers are the routing nodes in an SNA network. They provide the network routing (subarea network) to SNA nodes and other controllers and assume responsibility for controlling the flow of network messages between different network nodes and devices. The 3745 runs NCP software that controls the routing and flows of the SNA path control network. Communication controllers are capable of receiving data from different network nodes and devices that use different transmission medium, speeds, and link level protocols (e.g., Token Ring, X.25 or SDLC) and convert them into network protocols for transmission to other network nodes. Figure 3.15 shows two 3745 communication controllers that route the data between the PCs on a Token Ring Network and hosts attached via channels. The 3745 performs the function of a gateway between nodes on a Token Ring network and other network nodes.

3174 Establishment Controller

The 3174 models 12L and 22L controllers support directly attached SNA devices (coaxial cable connections) as well as SNA nodes connected via Token Ring interfaces or the ESCON fiber-optic channel. Figure 3.15 shows a 3174 establishment controller acting as a gateway between Token Ring nodes and the subarea network. PCs can communicate via the 3174 gateway with other network resources.

3172 Interconnect Controller

The 3172 interconnect family of controllers is IBM's first product to support the Fiber Distributed Data Interface (FDDI) international standard. FDDI allows data to be transmitted at a rate of up to 100 Mbits/s. For example, the 3172 controller can be used to interconnect two ES/9000 hosts and extend the ESCON 10 Mbytes/s (80 Mbits/s) fiber-optic channel connections to unlimited distances. This means that distributed transaction processing can now be performed at wideband high speed which will improve performance significantly and will give an illusion that distributed transactions are executed on a local system. The 3172 Interconnect controller also supports such protocols as Token Ring, Ethernet, PC LAN, and IEEE802.4 MAP local area networks. The 3172 can be used with SNA, OSI, and TCP/IP networks.

Links and Routing Networks

The SNA nodes (host nodes, distributed nodes, and controllers) are interconnected together via links. **Links** can be defined as physical connections between SNA nodes. The following is a list of link connections typically used in an SNA distributed network.

* ESCON (Enterprise Systems Connection) — a wideband, high-speed (10-Mbyte/s) fiber-optic channel used with the ES/9000 family of processors. ESCON connects other hosts, controllers, and I/O devices at 80 Mbits/s to the ES/9000 family of processors. ESCON allows any-to-any communications and allows the placement of computer devices of up to 5.6 mi (9 km) away from the central processor.

* S/370 — System/370 data channels (2 Mbytes/s or 16 Mbits/s) which connect local controllers and devices to a 370 host processor.

* SDLC (Synchronous Data Link Control) — describes the most commonly used serial transmission interconnecting SNA wide area network nodes such as 3745 nodes. SDLC typically runs on switched or leased telephone lines at speeds of up to 56 Kbits/s. The SNA path control network uses SDLC links to interconnect the 3745 subarea nodes over multiple SDLC links called **transmission groups** (see Fig. 3.14).

* Token Ring — an IBM local area network (LAN). It can operate at a speed of up to 16 Mbits/s. PCs emulating PU 2.1 SNA nodes and with LU 6.2 can communicate directly with each other using LU-LU peer-to-peer communications over the Token Ring network.

• X.25 (CCITT) — International Telegraph and Telephone Consultative Committee standard for packet switching networks. X.25 was designed to share network routing resources among many users. Typically X.25 networks operate on leased or switched connections at a speed of up to 56 Kbits/s.

PU 2.1 emulation products may communicate with each other over many other types of routing networks, link connections, and different transmission medium such as Ethernet local area networks, the Fiber Distributed Data Interface (FDDI), and even the old Binary Synchronous (BSC) protocols.

3.4.3 Gateways

The purpose of a gateway is to interconnect end-users residing in separate networks. Gateway nodes receive data from end-users residing in one network such as Token Ring and route the message to nodes residing in other networks. Figure 3.15 shows an example of a 3174 cluster controller acting as a gateway node. The personal computers residing on a Token Ring network may route all their messages to 3174 gateway. The 3174 gateway node translates the token messages into SNA SDLC frames and passes the data to the 3745 communication controller for transmission to the S/390 or the S/370 host processors. We may also think of a 3745 as a gateway node. The PCs on the Token Ring network can communicate directly via a 3745 controller with other network resources, rather than going over the 3174 cluster controller. The 3174 would be used only if the 3745 controller could not be directly attached to the Token Ring Network. The IBM Personal System/2 with the OS/2 EE operating system and the SNA gateway software can also be used to perform the gateway function. Figure 3.16 shows a typical LAN configuration used for accessing hosts via an **OS/2 EE SNA gateway**. The APPC and SAA/CPI-C LU 6.2 transaction programs residing on a Token Ring or an Ethernet LAN can send data to the SNA OS/2 EE gateway, which routes the data to the SNA hosts. With the ability of OS/2 EE to emulate a network node in an APPN distributed network, the SNA gateway will be able to route data between any two SNA distributed nodes.

Another example of a gateway that can run on **OS/2 EE is CICS 2.1**. CICS can be configured to act as an LU 6.2/PU 2.1 routing server. The personal computers on the Token Ring network can pass data to the CICS gateway, which can perform transactions locally or ship them to CICS residing on the host.

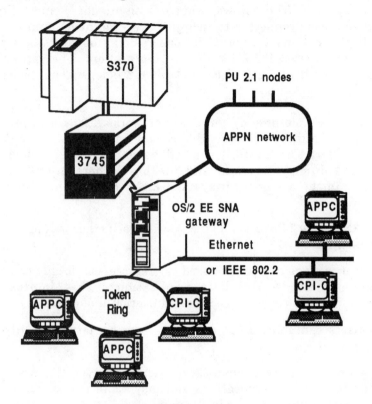

Figure 3.16 OS/2 EE SNA gateway.

The **AS/400** midrange system is also an example of a gateway. The AS/400 can act as an APPN PU 2.1 network node as described earlier in this section. It can accept data from PCs attached directly or via a Token Ring network and route it to hosts or other PU 2.1 nodes attached to the APPN.

The LU 6.2 gateways can be divided into two categories:

1. Gateways that can emulate only a **PU 2.0 node**. This type of gateway is limited to host communications because only type 6.2 dependent logical units are supported. This means that parallel sessions are not supported and that the LUs can communicate only over single sessions with applications residing on type 5 host nodes.

2. Gateways that can emulate a **physical unit type 2.1 node** . This type of gateway has all the capabilities of an SNA distributed gateway node. The gateway supports any-to-any connectivity and end-users connected to such gateways can have parallel or multiple sessions with applications residing on hosts or any other distributed PU 2.1 nodes in the network. The gateway supports both PU 2.1 nodes and LU 6.2 independent logical units.

Formerly, multiple dummy terminals or workstations emulating terminals were attached directly to a cluster controller, such as the 3274 controller. The controller acted as a passthrough device between the dummy terminal and the host. There are several advantages to the use of gateways and LANs rather than dummy controllers.

• The LANs allow TPs to communicate with each other in a peer-to-peer manner.

• Most transactions can be processed or preprocessed locally before shipping them to the host applications. This improves performance and saves on the communication line costs.

• LAN users can share LAN resources such as databases, files, and printers.

• The gateways that can emulate physical unit type 2.1 are not limited to host communications and may route transactions to any distributed PU 2.1 node in the network.

• The gateways allow a mapping of multiple downstream resources (such as LUs, PUs, sessions) to a smaller pool of gateway resources as seen by the hosts and the network. For example, 100 PCs which normally would be represented to the host as 100 logical units and 100 sessions, may be mapped into one gateway PU and the required LUs to satisfy the end-user performance requirements. This reduces, significantly, the number of resources that must be configured and managed on the mainframe.

3.4.4 LU 6.2 Network Resources

The main resource of the SNA/LU 6.2 network is a distributed physical unit type 2.1 node. The main resources of a PU 2.1 node are (see Fig. 3.17):

- **Physical Unit (PU)** — the SNA node manager that manages the resources of the node (buffers, links, LUs, etc.).

- **Control Point (CP)** — the portion of the PU that manages initiation, termination, and management of links (XID-3s) and sessions (BIND, UNBIND).

- **Logical Units (LUs)** — the end-user manager that manages TPs and conversations. They act as a port between transaction programs (TPs) and the routing network. Each PU 2.1 node defines the local logical units and the list of remote logical units. The logical units are referred to by their network names (or alias names), **Local (or Source) LU** and the **Remote (or Target or Partner) LU**.

- **Links** — physical link connections to other nodes in the network.

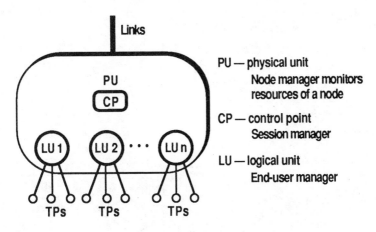

Figure 3.17 Node's resources.

The SNA/LU 6.2 network can be viewed logically as a collection of distributed nodes, logical units, and **transaction programs (TPs)**. The nodes are interconnected together via physical links, the LUs via logical connections called **sessions** and the TPs via logical connections called **conversations**. A logical unit (LU) acts as a port via which TPs get access to the routing network. The LUs residing in a node can establish single or multiple sessions with other LUs residing in any of the distributed nodes. The sessions provide peer-to-peer logical connections and are serving as vehicles that carry the conversation data between any two TPs in the network. Figure 3.18 shows a logical view of a LU 6.2 distributed network. The PU

2.1 nodes A, B, and C are connected via physical links. The LU A is connected with LU B over four parallel sessions and with LU C over a single session connection. The sessions with the same network properties (priority, session rules, message sizes, pacing window sizes, etc.) are grouped together into network resources called modes. The application programmers choose different network properties at allocation time by specifying the appropriate **mode name**. For example, the application program A1 may issue the LU 6.2 ALLOCATE verb and supply MODE 2 as a parameter to choose one of the two parallel sessions identified by MODE 2 to establish a conversation with the application program B1 (Prog B1) residing in node B (see Fig. 3.18). Transaction programs and operators may use installation-specific names (called **alias names**) to refer to network resources (such as logical units, physical units, or modes) rather than the actual network names or addresses.

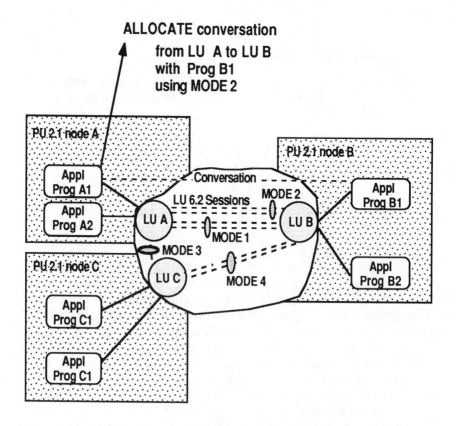

Figure 3.18 Logical view of an LU 6.2 distributed network.

3.4.5 SNA/LU 6.2 Resource Activation

The network resources must be defined and activated for communications to take place between any two distributed nodes. The following is a sequence of steps required for the distributed network shown in Fig. 3.18:

1. An operator (at each of nodes A, B, and C) must load the appropriate physical unit type 2.1 and logical unit type 6.2 emulation software (called **APPC** or **SAA/CPI-C** software in most implementations).

2. A system programmer [at each of nodes A, B, and C must define the network resources (links, PUs, local and remote LUs, number of sessions between local and remote LUs, mode names defining session characteristics and network properties, the local and remote transaction programs, and conversation characteristics)].

3. An operator must activate the links between the communicating nodes. The PU 2.1 link activation was described earlier in this section.

4. Now a session must be activated between communicating logical units. This can be achieved by an operator command (an activate session command issued from an implementation specific operator's subsystem management package) or a programming call. For example, the application transaction program TP A1 may issue an ALLOCATE call (from the local logical unit LU A to the remote logical unit LU B using MODE 2) to establish a conversation with TP B1. If a session is currently available LU A will activate a new session to LU B by sending an SNA BIND command with session parameters pointed by MODE 2 configuration entry. The session will be established if it is not already started or if all the MODE 2 sessions are not currently being used by other conversations and the maximum number of sessions allowed between LU A and LU B does not exceed the preconfigured maximum.

5. Once the session is successfully established, a conversation is established between TP A1 and TP B1.

In the example above we described the steps required to initiate a session and a conversation between the distributed nodes A and B. The same steps are valid for any two PU2.1 distributed nodes in an SNA distributed network.

3.5 LU 6.2 VERBS

Application programmers do not have to be concerned with the SNA/LU 6.2 layers or the underlying network when they are writing their application programs. The logical unit type 6.2 provides system-oriented services and application-oriented services to the application programs. The logical connection between the transaction program (TP) and the logical unit (LU) is called the **TP-LU conversation protocol boundary**. The conversation protocol boundary is referred to as an application programming interface (API) within specific product implementations and consists of a set of LU 6.2 architected verbs. LU 6.2 architecture does not define the syntax of the verbs but defines the set of functions (called **APPC functions**) needed for distributed transaction processing (see Fig. 3.19).

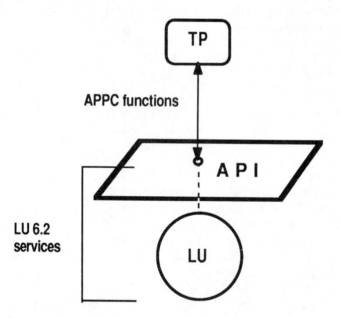

Figure 3.19 LU 6.2 application services and APPC functions.

The LU 6.2 API separates TPs from the logical units. The LU receives programming calls (called verbs) from TPs. The verbs are processed by the LU, which builds the appropriate LU 6.2 data stream and SNA headers and sends the messages across to the remote LU. The LU also enforces the protocols that must be followed between LUs and between the communicating transaction programs.

3.5.1 LU 6.2 Application Services

The following is a list of LU 6.2 application services and the corresponding APPC base-set functions that must be provided by all open API implementations (provide the TP-LU protocol boundary) of the LU 6.2 architecture:

- Allowing users to invoke and terminate transactions.

    APPC ALLOCATE function — the ability to allocate a conversation and attach to a remote transaction program (TP). The ALLOCATE verb invokes the remote program by a special LU 6.2 mechanism called **ATTACH**. The local TP is invoked by an internally generated ATTACH by the local LU to simulate invocation by another transaction program.

    APPC DEALLOCATE function — the ability to end a conversation. The LU notifies the remote LU that the local TP requested an end to the current conversation. The remote LU notifies the remote TP of the transaction termination request and upon agreement by both parties the transaction is ended.

- Confirmation processing.

    CONFIRM — the ability to issue a confirmation request. The remote LU delivers all the data and a confirmation request from the local TP to the remote TP and asks the remote program if all the data has been received and processed successfully. The remote TP acknowledges (replies with CONFIRMED) or rejects (replies with SEND_ERROR) the confirmation request. This information is then passed to the local TP, which can continue processing or recover from the error.

    CONFIRMED — the ability to respond to a confirmation request received form the partner transaction programs.

- Exchanging information.

    SEND_DATA — the ability to send data. This function places the data into the LU send buffer. The local logical unit buffers many SEND_DATA calls into one large network message and transmits its send buffer across only when requested by the TP or when sufficient data has been accumulated. This optimizes the communication facilities between LUs rather than generating a network message for each send. The logical unit also builds the appropriate General Data Stream (GDS) variables for mapped conversation TPs.

RECEIVE_AND_WAIT — the ability to receive data into the program receive buffer. The LU is capable of receiving blocked network messages and deblocking them if requested by the receiving TP. The LU also keeps track of the length of each message received from the partner TP. The logical unit also decodes the GDS variables and passes only the user data to the mapped conversation programs.

• Application program error recovery.

SEND_ERROR — the ability to notify the remote transaction program of application errors. The local and remote logical units will notify the remote TP of an application error and allow the TP that issued the verb to initiate user-defined error recovery.

• Requesting permission to send data.

REQUEST_TO_SEND — the ability to ask for Send state. The LU will send a special expedited message to the remote LU asking the remote TP to allow the local TP to send data.

• Obtaining information from an LU.

GET_ATTRIBUTES — the ability to obtain conversation attributes. This APPC function allows the TP to retrieve information about current conversation and session characteristics.

We will discuss, in detail, all the APPC functions later in the book.

3.5.2 LU 6.2 Operator Services

The SNA logical unit type 6.2 also provides system-oriented services:

• The ability to initialize session parameters and regulate the number of parallel sessions between local and remote logical units

1. Change number of sessions (CNOS) verbs — allow an operator program to control the number of sessions between local and remote logical units.

2. Session control verbs (ACTIVATE, DEACTIVATE) — allow an operator program to activate and deactivate sessions.

3. LU definition verbs (DEFINE, DISPLAY, DELETE) — allow an operator program to define, modify, and control the local LU's operating environment.

The control operator verbs are executed by installation-specific control-operator transaction programs. A human operator interacts with the control-operator transaction program to perform the following functions at the local LU:

* Configure the local logical unit's operating environment

* Activate and deactivate sessions

* Control the number of sessions by issuing the change number of sessions (CNOS) operator verbs

* Manage the configured operating environment

3.6 LU 6.2 SESSION PROTOCOLS

Logical units communicate with each other over a logical connection called a **session**. A session can be initiated by an operator activate session command or by a TP issuing the LU 6.2 ALLOCATE verb (see Fig. 3.20). The operator or the TP can specify a **mode name** to select a particular set of session characteristics (MAXRU maximum message size exchanged between LUs, security requirements, pacing window sizes, etc.). A session is established when an SNA **negotiable BIND** send command is sent from the primary logical unit (PLU) to the secondary logical unit (SLU) and a positive response is returned from the SLU (see Fig. 3.20). The LU 6.2 BIND command can be sent by logical units residing in the PU 5 host nodes or any independent logical unit residing in a distributed PU 2.1 node.

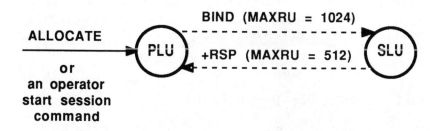

Figure 3.20 Session initiation.

3.6.1 LU 6.2 Session Initiation

Session Establishment — Independent LUs

Independent logical unit LU 6.2 uses the SNA negotiable BIND for LU-LU sessions. The negotiable BIND carries the PLU information which specifies the protocols and rules that both partners have to follow for the duration of the session. The SLU can negotiate the session rules by modifying the received BIND parameters and returning the modified BIND as a part of its SNA positive response to the BIND. The PLU may accept the modified parameters and the session is established successfully or send an UNBIND command and terminate the session. There are LU 6.2 architected negotiation rules on how the parameters can be modified by the SLU. For example, if the PLU requests the maximum message size (MAXRU size) that can be sent from PLU to SLU to be 1024 bytes the acceptable negotiated BIND response may carry a message size smaller than or equal to 1024. Changing the message size to a size greater than 1024 would violate the LU 6.2 defined negotiations rules. The independent LUs are not limited to a single session and can establish multiple or parallel sessions by sending additional BIND commands to the same or other remote LUs.

Session Establishment — Dependent LUs

The dependent logical units can act only as the secondary logical units (SLUs) and are limited to host PU 5 communications. These LUs are limited to a single session at a time and are not capable of sending BIND commands. The System Services Control Point (SSCP), residing in a host, controls session initiation for dependent LUs. The dependent LU can ask for a session initiation by sending an SNA INITSELF command (a bit-oriented logon command) to the SSCP. The SSCP notifies the PLU of the INITSELF request and then the session initiation sequence is the same as for independent LUs (see Fig. 3.20). The PLU sends the negotiable BIND and the session is established.

3.6.2 Send/Receive Protocol

The logical unit type 6.2 uses an SNA half-duplex, flip-flop protocol in which the LUs exchange user data in one direction at a time on a single session. The LU 6.2 half-duplex, flip-flop protocol requires that the two transaction programs follow the send/receive protocol in a single conversation which is assigned to a single session for the duration of the conversation. For example, only one TP at a time can send data in a conversation. The other TP must receive the data until the sender releases Send state by issuing the RECEIVE_AND_WAIT verb. This is similar to a human conversation over the telephone line. Only one person can speak at a time, the other must listen. At any given instance a TP's conversation is in one of the LU 6.2 predefined states (e.g., reset, send, receive, or confirm). The program is allowed to perform only the functions that are allowed in this state. For example, in Receive state the TP must receive data but the receiving TP may break Receive state by aborting the conversation or sending an error (issuing the SEND_ERROR verb). Issuing an error changes the TP from Receive state to Send state and puts the partner TP into Receive state. This gives the TP that issued the SEND_ERROR verb a chance to explain the error. In Send state, the TP is allowed to send data, request confirmation, send error, or deallocate a conversation. When the conversation is deallocated and put into a Reset state, the session used by the conversation is released to another conversation that might already be in the queue for the session from a local or remote LU allocation queue. If a full-duplex exchange between programs is required, two conversations can be started with one always in a Send state and the other in Receive state.

3.6.3 Contention Winner/Loser Sessions

Transaction program TPs exchange data over conversations that correspond to an LU 6.2 bracket, which is discussed later in this section. A single conversation is assigned to a single LU 6.2 session. A conversation has an exclusive use of the session (one conversation at a time per session) for the duration of the conversation and must follow the send/receive mode as described above. It is possible for the local and remote logical units to initiate a conversation by sending the ALLOCATE verbs to each other at the same time (transformed by the LUs to a network message called an ATTACH header). To resolve this contention, an operator must specify a **session contention polarity** for each session. The operator defines the sessions for which the local logical unit is designated to win the allocation race as **conversation winner** (also called a **conwinner** or **first-speaker**) sessions. The sessions for which the local LU is designated to lose the allocation race are called

conversation loser (also called a **conloser** or **bidder**) sessions. The bidder LU must first bid (ask) the first-speaker LU in order to request permission to initiate a conversation. Upon receiving a positive response, the bidder LU may send the allocation request across the session to the first-speaker LU. Notice that it requires three network messages to initiate a conversation on a bidder session and only one network message on a first-speaker session. Also, if there are many allocation requests waiting for the same session, then the bidder is rejected until all conversations are executed on the first-speaker side. Therefore, it is important for an operator to configure the first-speaker sessions for the transaction programs that issue the ALLOCATE verb (request to initiate conversations) and the bidder sessions for the TPs that receive the allocation requests. If the allocation request may come from either side then the operator may tune the **session limits** parameters described in the next paragraph.

3.6.4 Session Limits

Transaction programs (TPs) do not select a particular session. They initiate a conversation by issuing an ALLOCATE verb, supplying, as parameters, the remote TP name, the remote LU name, and the **mode name** that maps to a **session pool** with the same network properties. The operator may preconfigure and regulate the number of sessions in the session pool by specifying the following session limits (configuration entries) at the local logical unit (see Fig. 3.21):

* The **total LU-LU session limit** — the maximum number of active LU-LU sessions. For example, LU A may be configured to have a total LU-LU session limit = 4 for the operator-defined modes — MODE 1 and MODE 2. The **SNASVCMG** mode name is an LU 6.2 architected mode for managing the number of parallel sessions between the local and remote LUs. The two SNASVCMG sessions are not counted into the total number of sessions available to user applications.

* The **(LU, mode) session limit** — the maximum active number of LU-LU sessions with a specific partner LU for a particular (partner LU, mode) pair. For example, LU A may be configured to have the (LUB, MODE 1) session limit = 4. This allows a maximum of four parallel sessions to be active between LU A and LU B and available to application TPs.

- The **automatic activation limit** for a particular (LU, mode) pair — the maximum number of LU-LU sessions that the LU will automatically activate to create the initial session pool. For example, LU A may automatically start one session in the absence of an explicit request from transaction programs or the operator.

- The **local-LU minimum contention winner** for a particular (LU, mode) pair — specifies the minimum number of sessions for which the local LU is allowed to be the contention winner.

- The **partner-LU minimum contention winner** for a particular (LU, mode) pair — specifies the minimum number of sessions for which the partner LU is allowed to be the contention winner.

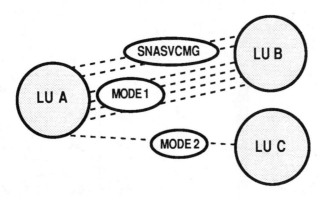

Figure 3.21 Session limits.

Normally these parameters should be planned and agreed upon by the operators that configure the local and the remote nodes. However, this is not a requirement since the local and remote LUs will negotiate the session limits and must comply with architected negotiation rules. Generally the negotiation rules are to be fair and to divide the limits to the closest requested values or a 50/50 rule in a case of a total disagreement. For example, if both LU A and LU B requested four contention winner sessions, the outcome of the LU-LU negotiation would be two winners for each of the LUs. The operator is required to issue the "change number of sessions" (CNOS) verb to regulate the number of sessions and to negotiate the session limits between the local and remote LUs. The SNASVCMG is an architected and dedicated mode name to allow operator commands to be exchanged regardless of the state of sessions between the local and remote logical units.

3.6.5 PU 2.1 LU-LU Session Capabilities

Distributed transaction processing requires an SNA logical unit type that recognizes intelligence on both sides of the communication link and a physical unit type that supports any-to-any connectivity. The physical unit type 2.1 and the logical unit type 6.2 satisfy the above requirements. The PU 2.1 nodes support logical units that can both initiate peer-to-peer sessions and respond to session initiation requests (the SNA LU 6.2 BIND commands) received from other network nodes. The logical unit type 6.2 serves as the port between the end-user (an application program) and the SNA/LU 6.2 distributed network. The logical connection between local and remote LU 6.2s is called an LU 6.2 - LU 6.2 **session**.

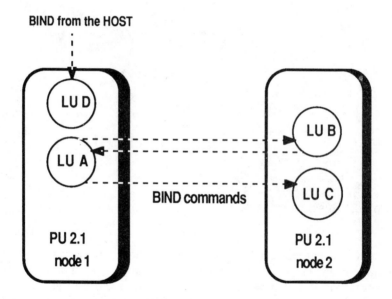

Figure 3.22 PU 2.1 Node session capabilities.

The PU 2.1 node supports the following session capabilities (see Fig. 3.22):

* An LU residing in a PU 2.1 node may initiate a session by sending an SNA BIND command. An LU capable of issuing BIND commands is called an **independent logical unit**. The BIND sender becomes the primary logical unit (PLU) for the LU-LU session and the BIND receiver becomes the secondary logical unit (SLU). When LU A issues two BIND commands to LU B and

LU C residing in node 2, LU A becomes the primary logical unit (PLU) for both the LU A-LU B and the LU A-LU C sessions. If LU A has also received a BIND command from LU B establishing an LU B-LU A session, LU A functions as the secondary logical unit (SLU) for this session and LU B as the primary logical unit (PLU).

• A PU 2.1 can emulate PU 2.0 protocols when receiving BINDs from a host PU 5 node. The PU 2.1 node supports a special type of LU 6.2 called a dependent logical unit. Dependent LUs act as secondary logical units (SLUs) only, and have an LU-LU session limit of 1 managed by an SSCP residing in the mainframe that sent the BIND. LU D is a dependent logical unit that uses PU 2.0 protocols similar to LU 2 when communicating with applications residing in the IBM host. Notice that independent LU and PU 2.1 protocols may be used if the host is configured as a type 2.1 node.

• A PU 2.1 node supports multiple sessions (sessions from one LU to many other LUs in the network). Multiple sessions to the same partner LU are called **parallel sessions**. The independent LU A has two parallel sessions to LU B and multiple sessions to LU B and LU C.

The physical unit type 2.1 node supports both the type 2.0 protocols and type 2.1 protocols. Type 2.0 protocols can only communicate via a subarea node (e.g., 3745 communication controller) to a PU type 5 node. Type 2.1 nodes also known as Low Entry Networking (LEN) nodes support independent logical units that can establish direct peer-to-peer sessions with other type 2.1 nodes in the network. Type 2.1 nodes can also support multiple, parallel and concurrent sessions to remote type 2.1 nodes. PU 2.1 nodes use protocols that reduce system definition requirements. The number of logical units configured in the network can be reduced significantly since we are not limited to single sessions between logical units. Also, the independent logical units do not require preassigned session addresses, and they do not require the SSCP-LU (ACTLU command) or the SSCP-PU (ACTPU command).

3.6.6 Security

The logical unit type 6.2 provides three levels of security:

1. **Session level security** (also called **Partner-LU verification**). This security is checked at session activation time (when an

SNA BIND command is sent). The LUs must have the same **LU-LU password** configured at both local and remote PU 2.1 nodes for successful session establishment. During session activation random data is enciphered using the LU-LU password and exchanged between the LUs. The remote LU enciphers the data received from the local LU and sends it back to the local LU. The local LU compares the received enciphered random data with its own copy of enciphered data, and if a match occurs, the local LU has verified the remote LU. The local LU enciphers random data received from the remote LU and sends it back to the remote LU. The remote LU compares the received enciphered random data with its own copy of enciphered data and if a match occurs, the remote LU has verified the local LU. When both the LUs verify each other's identity the session establishment succeeds.

2. **Conversation level security** (also referred to as **end-user verification**). This is used to check security for each transaction (conversation) at allocation time. Once a session is established, security may be checked for each transaction (conversation). When a transaction program (TP) issues an ALLOCATE verb, it may supply **user ID, password,** and an optional **profile.** The user ID and password are verified by the LU that receives the allocation request. If the user ID and password are incorrect, the LU rejects the allocation request and the conversation is not established. An optional profile may be used to check an authorization list associated with the target TP. The received user ID and profile are additionally checked for access rights to a specific transaction program, and if it fails, the check the conversation is not established. The receiving LU may allow some privileged programs to send ALLOCATEs with a special indicator called **Already Verified Indicator.** The Already Verified Indicator may be sent only by special privileged TPs and must be agreed upon between the local and the remote logical units at BIND time. The allocation requests that carry this indicator bypass the conversation level security. This may be used for an intermediate program (e.g., a security program) that checks system wide security for all transactions and then forwards the transactions to other transaction programs for execution.

3. **Session cryptography.** This type of security uses the Data Encryption Standard (DES) to encipher and decipher all user data exchanged between the logical units for a particular session.

3.7 LU 6.2 MESSAGE UNITS

A message unit (MU) is an SNA defined bit string exchanged between SNA layers and sublayers. The two communicating LUs exchange message units in a predefined LU 6.2 data format called General Data Stream (GDS) variables or logical records (LRs).

3.7.1 Logical Records (LRs)

Logical records are used by basic conversation application programs. The basic conversation programs must build logical records into their application buffer (called a buffer record) before passing the data to the logical unit. A logical record consists of a 2-byte length prefix (LL) followed by the user data. The length field must be equal to at least two since it includes its own length. The logical record is the smallest unit for which the LU detects or reports data truncations. The data portion of the logical records can be in any format agreed upon by the two application programmers and it does not require the 2-byte ID field that is required for TPs on mapped conversations and SNA architected services transaction programs (STPs).

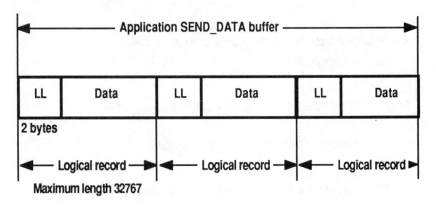

Figure 3.23 Logical records.

A programmer can pack multiple logical records or a portion of a logical record into one application buffer (called a buffer record; see Fig. 3.23). The unit of data that a program sends or receives with a single basic conversation   The LU 6.2 SEND_DATA verb is of arbitrary length determined by the programmer and does not have to consist of complete logical records. The LU 6.2 architecture does not impose any relationship between application buffers and logical records. Therefore, one buffer record may contain one or many complete or or incomplete logical records. The receiving TP may also request, from the remote logical unit, one or many complete or incomplete logical records. The local and remote logical units only check the length field (LL) of each logical record which must be equal to or greater than two before passing the data to the TPs. The ability to block many logical records into an application send buffer and the ability to receive many logical records on one receive call result in a high-level efficiency and performance in the use of basic conversation programs.

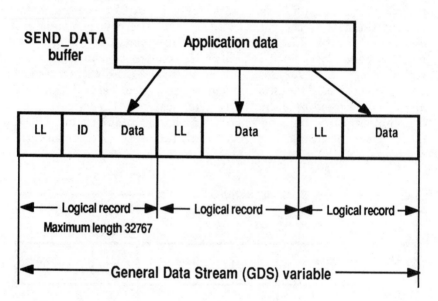

Figure 3.24 General Data Stream (GDS) variable.

3.7.2 General Data Stream (GDS) Variables

Mapped conversations exchange data in an arbitrary record format agreed upon by the two communicating TPs. The logical units transform all mapped conversation data into LU 6.2 data streams called the General Data Stream (GDS) variable (see Fig. 3.24). A GDS variable consists of transaction program data preceded by a 4-byte GDS header (LL field, ID field). The GDS header consists of a 2-byte-length prefix (LL) and a 2-byte ID format identifier describing the type of information contained in the variable (e.g., application data, error data, error log data, null data). The length field must be equal to at least two since it includes its own length. The GDS variable can be of any length, and the application GDS variable corresponds to one mapped MC_SEND DATA verb. Figure 3.24 shows that one GDS variable may consist of multiple logical records. This is true only for an application GDS variable if the application send buffer is larger that a preconfigured maximum logical record length. The SNA service transaction programs (STPs) build their own GDS variables with specific IDs. Notice that the mapped conversation GDS variables are simply changed by the logical units into basic conversation logical records with predefined GDS headers.

3.7.3 BIUs, PIUs, and BLUs

Basic Information Unit (BIU)

The message units exchanged between local and remote logical units are called **Basic Information Units (BIUs)**. The BIU consists of a **request/response header (RH)** and the **request/response unit (RU)** (see Fig. 3.25). The request/response unit (RU) may contain user data or SNA commands. For example, a single RU may carry many basic conversation logical records (LRs) or many mapped conversation GDS variables or an SNA BIND command. The maximum message size that can be exchanged between local and remote LUs is agreed upon at BIND time (MAXRU size). If the user message is longer than the maximum allowed then the LU divides the user conversation message into a sequence of BIUs (called **chain elements**).

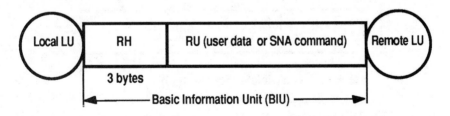

Figure 3-.25 Basic Information Unit (BIU).

The complete TP-TP conversation message is carried as a sequence of chain elements and is called an SNA **chain**. A conversation consists of many data exchanges (chain exchanges) and responses between local and remote LUs. All chains and responses in a particular conversation form an SNA **bracket**. Therefore, a single conversation corresponds to an SNA bracket. A conversation (an SNA bracket) is delineated by special indicators in the request/response (RH) header called the **begin-bracket (BB)** indicator and the **conditional end-of-bracket (CEB)** indicator. Most of the LU 6.2 verbs are not carried across the network as special network messages but they are carried, together with data, as bits in the RH header. For example, the ALLOCATE verb sets the BB bit in the RH, DEALLOCATE sets it in the CEB, and the RECEIVE verb sets the **Change Direction (CD)** indicator bit. The TP data is sent by issuing the SEND_DATA verb and it is carried as logical records or GDS variables in the request/response unit (RU).

Path Information Unit (PIU)

If the BIU is larger than the maximum buffer size allowed for the link connection (maximum frame size) the path control layer divides the BIU into multiple BIU segments (called PIUs). The routing message units exchanged by path control elements of two PU 2.1 nodes are called **Path Information Units (PIUs)**. The PIU consists of a **transmission header** (TH) followed by a BIU (or a portion of a BIU called a **segment**; see Fig. 3.26). Transmission headers (THs) are used to route messages through the network. A **Basic Link Unit (BLU)** size (also referred to as a **frame**) consists of a PIU and a link header (LH) and a link trailer (LT). The Basic Link Units (BLUs) are transmitted across a link connection between two adjacent nodes.

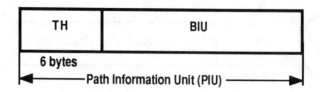

Figure 3.26 Path Information Unit (PIU).

The maximum message size that can be exchanged between two logical units (MAXRU size) and the maximum frame size (e.g., MAXDATA parameter of a 3745) are configurable parameters. Better performance is achieved using large RU and frame sizes. This avoids chaining (MAXRU should be greater than the maximum user message size) and segmentation (MAXRU should not be greater than the maximum frame size). Remember, though, that large frames or large RUs require more memory. If only a small percentage of messages are large, then chaining and segmenting may be appropriate for these messages.

3.8 LU 6.2 ADVANTAGES

The Systems Network Architecture (SNA) with the logical unit type 6.2 and the physical unit type 2.1 is the chosen IBM connectivity methodology for SNA enterprise computing in the 1990s.

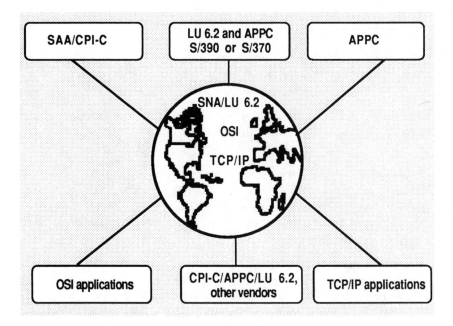

Figure 3.27 SNA/LU 6.2 peer-to-peer communications.

The following is a list of the major LU 6.2 advantages:

- The major advantage of LU 6.2 is that it is a common communication architecture that is independent of any operating system and any vendor computer system. It can be used, effectively, to develop distributed transaction processing in a computer enterprise consisting of multivendor computer systems (see Fig. 3.27).

- The SNA logical unit LU 6.2 has been chosen by IBM to be one of the strategic communication protocols for the SAA distributed networks in the 1990s, and it cannot be ignored by the corporate world.

- LU 6.2 is IBM's first protocol that recognizes an intelligent entity on both sides of a connection, whether it is a mainframe, a minicomputer, or a personal computer. PCs do not have to act as slaves and pretend to be dummy 3278 screens with a keyboard when emulating LU type 2 (3270 emulation).

- SNA/LU 6.2 with the physical unit type 2.1 allows any-to-any (rather than peripheral node to host only) connectivity. LU 6.2 architecture allows direct SNA communications between PCs, minicomputers and any other system platform that supports the SNA logical unit type 6.2. It does not require a host or a 3745 subarea network and may run independently on Token Ring networks, Ethernet, or other local area networks, as well as an X.25 packet switching network and many other networks.

- The LU 6.2 is the best SNA tool for distributed transaction processing and is available on IBM and most other major computer hardware platforms.

- SNA/LU 6.2 provides programmers with architected distributed functions (ALLOCATE, SEND_ERROR,..., DEALLOCATE) for distributed transaction processing. The LU 6.2 verbs make the application development much easier and decrease the time needed to design powerful distributed transaction programs.

- LU 6.2 is capable of multiple or parallel sessions to one or many remote partners residing on the same or different distributed network nodes. This decreases the number of logical units that must be configured and maintained in the network.

- Many transaction programs (TPs) can share the same logical unit and the same session. A conversation (a transaction) has an exclusive use of a session, but successive conversations can reuse the same session.

- The local LU buffers the LU 6.2 verbs and the data to be sent to the remote LU and generates a network message only when the local TP issues a call that requires an answer from the remote TP or when the maximum buffer size is reached. This significantly improves the performance of a network. Verbs and data are blocked together and sent as one network message across to the remote LU that deblocks the information.

SNA Distributed Network Concepts   103

SNA/LU 6.2 was designed to move IBM's 16-year-old SNA technology to a new world of distributed networks and cooperative processing that provides a single solution to the communication requirements of enterprise computing in the 1990s. Logical unit type 6.2 is the chosen IBM strategic communication product for IBM SAA networks but is also becoming a very widely used protocol for interconnecting non-SAA multivendor computer environments within large companies.

4

Distributed and Cooperative Processing Concepts

The terms **cooperative processing** and **distributed processing** are often used interchangeably. IBM defines though the cooperative processing as the relationship between a distributed function residing in a programmable workstation (e.g., the user interface) and a different distributed function residing on a host (e.g., the main program logic). Cooperative processing implies that different functions of an application reside on different machines and cooperate together (work together) to execute a single unit of work (called a transaction). This is different from distributed processing which implies that the same function (e.g., distributed database access) reside in different machines. Distributed transaction processing in SNA distributed networks is based on the logical unit type 6.2 (LU 6.2) architecture. Users have wanted to distribute processing to take advantage of the processing power of PCs, minicomputers, and mainframes.

Distributed and cooperative processing were possible in the traditional hierarchical SNA networks via various nonstandard protocols. These required complex programming in order to hide the intelligence from the host and the processing power of personal computers by emulating a dummy SNA device (such as a 3270 keyboard and the screen). A common standard was required that would make distributed and cooperative processing easier, more efficient, uniform across different systems, and independent of the underlying operating system. The SNA architecture was specifically enhanced with the **logical unit 6.2** and the **physical unit 2.1** to address the needs of distributed and cooperative processing. The **Advanced Program-to-Program-Communication (APPC)** and the SAA **Common Programming Interface Communications (CPI-C)** architectures (common distributed programming standards) were defined to help programmers develop consistent distributed applications across different SAA operating environments. APPC and SAA/CPI-C are based on the LU 6.2 architecture and define common functions (such as transaction initiation and termination, exchanging data, notification of error conditions, confirmation processing, database synchronization processing,) for distributed transaction processing. The LU 6.2 architectures was discussed in Chap. 3. The user is strongly advised to study Chap. 3 thoroughly prior to reading this chapter.

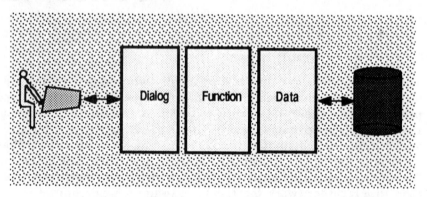

Figure 4.1 Distributed resources.

4.1 LU 6.2 OPERATING ENVIRONMENT

In cooperative processing, different programs perform their own specialized tasks, such as handling the presentation services, screen management, database management, or number crunching. The communicating programs are called transaction programs (TPs). The TPs share distributed resources such as distributed databases, and they can also distribute the user interface (called the **dialog interface**) or the function (the **primary program logic**) in order to process a single transaction. Figure 4.1 shows the three major elements that can be distributed when designing distributed applications. The dialog interface handles the application interaction with the end user (panel navigation, data validation, help and warning messages, scrolling, windowing, etc.). Distributing the dialog interface to a personal computer offloads the host processing and improves network efficiency by exchanging less information over communication links. The local processing of the dialog element provides for more responsive interface to the end user. The distributed function is the primary code of the application that executes the transaction. Distributed applications may be structured to perform some local preprocessing of a transaction on a personal computer before passing the transaction to the host, resulting in more efficient processing as well as more efficient use of network resources. The data itself may also be distributed among PCs, minicomputers, and hosts. Distributed databases are becoming more popular since they may improve performance and data availability. For example, a bank may decide to install local area networks in each branch and to distribute the data to servers residing on PCs or minicomputers connected locally to the LAN. This brings databases closer to the end users improves performance and increases network availability. Most inquiries therefore, (e.g., get account balance, get information about a local customer) may be performed locally. Also, if the host or the network fails, transactions can still be executed for all local customers. The logical unit 6.2 was designed specifically for distributed transaction processing. It provides a common communication interface for program-to-program communications. The major advantages of LU 6.2 are that it is the first logical unit that recognizes intelligence on both sides of the connection and that it fully participates in distributed transaction processing by defining the distributed functions (such as ALLOCATE, SEND ERROR,..., DEALLOCATE) as an integral part of the LU (please review Sec. 3.8, "LU 6.2 Advantages"). Logical units communicate with each other via SNA sessions. Logical unit type 6.2 is capable of multiple sessions to one or many partner LUs. Multiple sessions to the same partner LU are called **parallel sessions**. Transaction programs communicate over conversations. Conversations are short-lived logical connections between transaction programs. A conversation is assigned to a single session, and it does have an exclusive access to the session for the duration of the conversation. A session is a long-lived logical connection between LUs, and it can be reused by many conversations serially (one conversation at a time). The logical unit 6.2 coordinates the communication between transaction programs by enforcing the LU-LU session protocols and managing distributed resources.

Both the SAA/CPI-C and the APPC architectures are based on the logical unit 6.2. The logical unit 6.2 is an SNA device-independent distributed LU that recognizes intelligence on both sides of a connection, and allows peer-to-peer and any-to-any communications. LU 6.2 provides services to both APPC and SAA/CPI-C applications such as:

• Enforcing LU 6.2 session rules and protocols

• Initiating, terminating, and managing sessions and distributed transaction resources

• Processing the APPC or SAA/CPI-C calls

• Building and checking the appropriate SNA headers and network messages

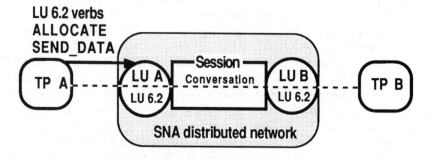

Figure 4.2 Distributed transaction processing environment.

The LU 6.2 manages the data exchange, conversation initiation and termination, security, synchronization levels, contention polarities, and the network message flows. The TPs are concerned only with transaction processing and obeying the LU 6.2 send/receive mode protocols. Figure 4.2 illustrates a typical distributed transaction processing environment. A transaction program TP A communicates directly with the local LU 6.2 (LU A) by issuing SNA/LU 6.2 verbs via an implementation-specific API (e.g., via the APPC OS/2 EE interface — MC_ALLOCATE,

MC_SEND_DATA,..., MC_DEALLOCATE). The local logical unit LU A establishes an LU-LU session to the remote logical unit LU B. TP A residing on an OS/2 workstation establishes a conversation with TP B (for example a CICS host transaction program) by issuing the MC_ALLOCATE verb. The TP A-TP B conversation connects the two TPs and the LU A-LU B session connects the two SNA logical units (the local LU A with the remote LU B). Once the conversation has been established, the two TPs can start exchanging information with one another using the conversation. The remote LU B decodes the messages received from TP A and passes them to the remote TP B (by completing, for example, the EXEC CICS RECEIVE host LU 6.2 verb that has been issued by TP B).

4.1.1 Transaction Programs (TPs)

ALLOCATE

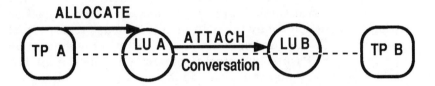

Figure 4.3 An LU 6.2 conversation initiation.

A transaction program (TP) differs from other types of programs by the following characteristics:

• A transaction program is invoked by a special LU 6.2 mechanism called **ATTACH**. In Fig. 4.3 TP A initiates a conversation by issuing the LU 6.2 defined programming call (the **ALLOCATE** verb) which is translated by the LU A to a unique network message (the SNA ATTACH header). The ATTACH header is received by LU B and the remote TP B is invoked. The local transaction program TP A is invoked by an internally generated ATTACH by LU A, to simulate invocation by another transaction program. The LU A simulates the ATTACH in response to an external event such as an operator command or a programming Initialize Conversation call.

• A Transaction Program (TP) uses a conversation to communicate with a remote transaction program. A transaction initiates and uses the conversation by issuing transaction program verbs (described in the *SNA Transaction Programmer's Reference Manual for LU type 6.2*). A single conversation is assigned to a single LU-LU session and it does have an exclusive use of a session. A transaction program may establish many conversations with one or more remote TPs using distinct sessions.

There are three types of transaction programs:

1. **Application transaction programs (TPs).** An application transaction program is designed by an end user to perform specific end-user processing. These programs most commonly use high-level programming languages (FORTRAN, COBOL, C, RPG or PL/I), LU 6.2 mapped conversations, or a specific application interface provided by the SNA service transaction programs (STPs).

2. **Service transaction programs (STPs).** In addition to the end user applications (TPs), the SNA LU 6.2 architecture defines the service transaction programs. The service transaction programs are defined by the SNA architecture as programs that provide LU 6.2 defined services for other transaction programs. STPs are an integral part of the logical unit 6.2. STPs provide users with such services as network management (CNOS), RESYNC, Distributed Data Management (DDM), Document Interchange Architecture (DIA) or the SNA Distribution Services (SNADS). The change number of sessions (CNOS) service transaction program regulates the number of parallel sessions between local and remote logical units. The RESYNC service transaction program resynchronizes resources (e.g., performs a backout on databases) when an error occurs during distributed transaction processing.

3. **Control-operator transaction program.** This is an implementation-specific operator interface to the LU 6.2 architecture. It interacts with the logical unit on behalf of a human operator issuing network management commands. An example of the control-operator program can be an operator console that allows a human operator to define and manage network resources such as logical units, physical units, sessions, or conversations. An operator can, for example, issue a command that regulates the number of sessions between any two logical units in a network. This would cause the control-operator program to communicate with the architected service transaction program (CNOS) residing in the remote LU to negotiate the number of parallel sessions between the two LUs.

4.1.2 APPC and CPI-C Architectures

Advanced Program-to-Program Communications (APPC) is an open architecture designed for writing distributed applications. APPC defines distributed functions independent of the environments in which they run and assists in providing connectivity (based on LU 6.2 and PU 2.1 architecture) among a wide variety of computer systems and devices. The APPC function that the LU 6.2 provides to application programs are also referred to as LU 6.2 verbs (ALLOCATE, DEALLOCATE, SEND_ERROR etc.). The verbs are described in the *IBM Transaction Programmer's Reference Manual for LU type 6.2*. In the LU 6.2 architecture there is freedom of syntax, which means that the APPC functions can be implemented via product-specific **Application Programming Interfaces (APIs)**, e.g., CICS API, OS/2 API, AS/400 API. However, everybody must implement the same LU 6.2 distributed functions. With the SAA announcement in 1987, one of the requirements was for SAA applications to be portable between different SAA environments. The SAA **Common Programming Interface-Communications (CPI-C)** provides a consistent application programming interface for program-to-program communications. This common programming interface allows development of portable and distributed applications across different SAA platforms using IBM's SNA logical unit LU 6.2. The APPC programming calls (ALLOCATE, SEND_DATA, DEALLOCATE) differ from CPI-C communications calls in that CPI-C calls require exact syntax (CMALLC, CMINIT, etc.) common to all implementations. Both the CPI-C and the APPC applications issue the LU 6.2 verbs (APPC applications via an implementation-specific API and SAA applications via the common CPI-C interface) to establish conversations and to exchange data with remote programs. The APPC implementations should migrate to SAA/CPI-C to comply with the SAA architecture. There are some other differences between SAA/APPC and CPI-C standards, which will be discussed in detail in Part 2 of this book.

4.2 LU 6.2 PROTOCOL BOUNDARY

The logical unit 6.2 can also be viewed as layered subsystem (an SNA distributed protocol machine) for program-to-program communications. An SNA state machine is a finite-state machine with a finite number of states, inputs, and outputs, that it can generate. Transaction programs (TPs) must understand the states and the verbs (inputs to the LU 6.2 state machine) that the TPs are allowed to issue in any given state. The logical unit 6.2 enforces the send/receive mode protocol between TPs, which maps to the SNA half-duplex, flip-flop session protocol. A logical unit can be also viewed as a logical port between application programs and the path control network (the routing network).

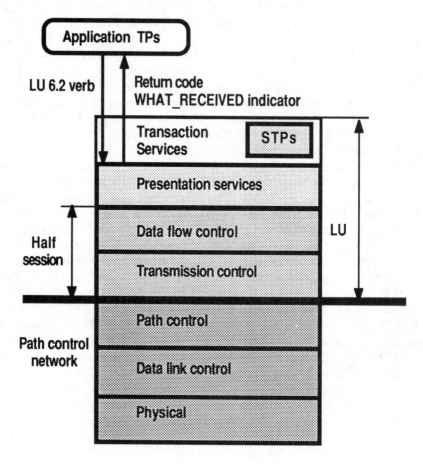

Figure 4.4 LU 6.2 layered subsystem.

Transaction programs (TPs) issue LU 6.2 verbs to the local logical unit (see Fig. 4.4). The local logical unit formats the verbs into unique LU 6.2 network messages Basic Information Units (BIUs) which are passed to the path control layer for transmission over the path control network to the destination logical unit controlling the remote transaction programs. The LU 6.2 consists of the upper four layers of the SNA layered architecture (Fig. 4.4):

1. Transaction services layer — implements the SNA service transaction programs (STPs) such as CNOS, SNADS or DDM.

2. Presentation services layer — defines the protocols for program-to-program communications. It provides the application programming interface directly to the application transaction programs (TPs). It enforces the send/receive mode protocols. This layer is also responsible for handling the incoming allocation requests and loading and initiating of the transaction programs (TPs).

3. Data flow control layer — enforces the session protocols.

4. Transmission control layer — provides end-to-end confirmation by validating the SNA sequence numbers. It also performs pacing of messages exchanged between the local and remote logical units. This is the last layer of the logical unit responsible for direct interaction with the path control network.

The path control network receives the data from the local LU and builds the Path Information Unit (PIU), which is routed to the remote LU. The TP-LU protocol boundary is between the application programs (TPs) and the presentation services layer. The LU 6.2 protocol boundary provides functional definition of verbs, parameters, and state indicators used in distributed transaction processing. It also defines the return codes and WHAT_RECEIVED indicators returned to TPs upon completion of each verb. Programmers use the LU 6.2 verbs to design distributed transaction programs that are independent of the operating environments in which they run. The LU 6.2 protocol boundary uses a pseudo language consisting of verbs (e.g., MC_ALLOCATE, MC_SEND_ ERROR, MC_DEALLOCATE), parameters, and conversation states to describe the architected distributed functions. Each product may implement the LU 6.2 verbs using a syntactically different Application Programming Interface (API), e.g., CICS LU 6.2 API, OS/2 APPC API, DOS APPC/PC API, AS/400 APPC API or ES/9000 APPC/MVS API. All implementations, though, must provide exactly the same LU 6.2 distributed functions. This means that the network messages generated by all implementations for the same distributed functions must be exactly the same. Therefore, different implementations can communicate with each other, and understand each others protocols and network message flows.

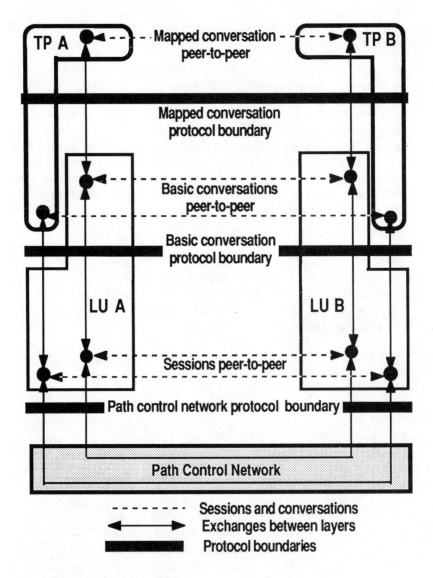

Figure 4.5 Protocol boundaries.

Implementations that define their own operating system dependent APIs must comply with the IBM Advanced Program-to-Program Communications (APPC) architecture. In order to make the applications portable, IBM announced Common Programming Interface-Communications (CPI-C) as a part of Systems Application Architecture (SAA) to enforce exact syntax on the application programming interface. This programming interface is programming interface. This programming interface is independent of the underlying operating system and assures portability across all SAA environments.

The LU 6.2 protocol boundaries can be divided into the following protocols:

- Peer protocols — a protocol boundary between a local LU layer and its peer layer residing in the remote LU. Each of the SNA layers must exchange messages with the corresponding layer at the remote LU. The layers communicate with each other by SNA/LU 6.2 defined headers such as the request header (RH) or the transmission header (TH). See Chap. 2 for more information on the SNA/LU 6.2 network messages and headers.

- Layered protocols — boundaries between layers or sublayers of the node that define the interactions between two layers or sublayers of the same node. For example, an API defines the protocol boundary between a transaction program and an LU (TP-LU protocol boundary) to exchange information between application programs and logical units.

Figure 4.5 shows the mapped and the basic conversation protocol boundaries. Mapped conversations exchange data in any format agreed upon by the two transaction programs TP A and TP B. TP A issues mapped conversation verbs to LU A in order to send data using the conceptual flows on a mapped conversation. The data is passed down the layers to the presentation services layer of LU A. The mapped presentation services component of LU A formats the message received from TP A into an LU 6.2 data stream, called General Data Stream (GDS) variable, and reduces the conceptual mapped conversation to a basic conversation between the mapped presentation services components of LU A and LU B. Notice also that the application transaction program TP A can use basic conversations directly. In this case TP A is responsible for building the LU 6.2 logical records (LRs) by bypassing the mapped services component of the presentation services layer. Therefore, basic conversation programs are more efficient than mapped conversation programs, although they require a programmer's understanding of the LU 6.2 data stream. Figure 4.5 also shows that the conceptual session and the conversation (peer-to-peer) flows are, in actual fact, achieved by passing messages between the adjacent layers and sublayers of the local logical unit (vertical arrows). The actual messages are transmitted across the path control network to the remote logical unit LU B.

4.3 LU 6.2 VERB CATEGORIES

Application programmers do not have to be concerned with the SNA/LU 6.2 layers or the underlying network. The logical connection between the transaction program (TP) and the logical unit (LU) is called the TP-LU conversation **protocol boundary**. The conversation protocol boundary is referred to as an Application Programming Interface (API) in specific product implementations and it consists of a set of LU 6.2 architected verbs. LU 6.2 architecture does not define the syntax of the verbs, but the set of functions needed for distributed transaction processing. The LU 6.2 verbs issued by transaction programs are executed by the presentation services layer of the logical unit. The LU 6.2 verbs are divided into two categories:

1. **Conversation verbs** — used by the service transaction programs (STPs) and application programmers to develop application transaction programs (TPs).

2. **Control-operator verbs** — used by control-operator privileged programs to control the local logical unit. A control-operator program is an implementation-specific program that assists an operator in the LU control and network configuration.

The conversation verbs can be divided into three subcategories:

1. Mapped conversation verbs

2. Basic conversation verbs

3. Operator verbs

4.3.1 Mapped Conversation Verbs

Mapped conversation verbs are intended for use by application transaction programs (TPs) that provide users specific services. The TPs are typically written in a high-level programming language such as COBOL, FORTRAN, or C. The mapped conversation verbs shield application programmers from the LU 6.2 General Data Stream (GDS) variables that must flow between local and remote logical units on mapped conversations. The TP-LU protocol boundary uses a pseudo language consisting of verbs with the prefix MC_ (MC_ALLOCATE, MC_SEND_ERROR, MC_DEALLOCATE, etc.), parameters, and return codes to define the mapped conversation verbs. The following is a short description of LU 6.2 mapped conversation verbs:

- **MC_ALLOCATE** — allocates a mapped conversation. The LU assigns a unique **resource ID** (referred to as **conversation ID**) that must be supplied on every verb following the MC_ALLOCATE verb to uniquely identify this conversation.

- **MC_DEALLOCATE** — ends a mapped conversation. The LU notifies the remote LU that the local TP has requested to terminate the current conversation. The remote LU notifies the remote TP of the transaction termination request and upon agreement by both parties the transaction is ended.

- **MC_CONFIRM** — sends a confirmation request to the partner transaction program. The remote LU delivers all the buffered data and a confirmation request from the local TP to the remote TP and asks the remote program if all the data has been received and processed successfully. The remote TP acknowledges (replies with MC_CONFIRMED) or rejects (replies with MC_SEND_ERROR) the confirmation request. This information is then passed to the local TP which can continue processing or recover from the error.

- **MC_CONFIRMED** — responds to a confirmation request.

- **MC_SEND_DATA** — sends data to the remote TP. The data can be of any arbitrary format agreed upon by the two application programmers. The LU may buffer multiple MC_SEND_DATA verbs into one network message and transmits its send buffer across the conversation only when requested by the TP or when sufficient data has been accumulated (maximum RU size has been reached). This avoids the generation of network messages for each send and optimizes the communication facilities between LUs. The logical unit is responsible for building the appropriate General Data Stream (GDS) variables for mapped conversation TPs.

- **MC_FLUSH** — flushes the local LU's buffers. The LU transmits all the accumulated data to the remote TP.

- **MC_RECEIVE_AND_WAIT** — receives data into the program receive buffer. If there is no partner data the TP is suspended until the data arrives from the partner TP. The LU is responsible for:

  1. Receiving blocked network messages

2. Deblocking the messages before passing the messages to the receiving TP

3. Keeping track of the length of each message received from the partner TP

4. Decoding the General Data Stream (GDS) variable and passing only the user data to the mapped conversation programs

- **MC_RECEIVE_IMMEDIATE** — receives data into the program receive buffer, but does not wait for further information to arrive. The LU checks the receive queue, and if there is nothing to receive it, returns a RC=UNSUCCESSFUL. If there is data to be received, then the MC_RECEIVE_IMMEDIATE verb performs the same function as the MC_RECEIVE_AND_WAIT verb.

- **MC_PREPARE_TO_RECEIVE** — sends the change direction to the remote transaction program. The local LU flushes all data buffered so far and gives Send state to the remote TP. The local TP enters Receive state and may perform local processing before receiving data.

- **MC_SEND_ERROR** — sends an error notification to the remote TP. The local logical unit will notify the remote transaction program of an application error and allow the transaction that issued the MC_SEND_ERROR verb to initiate a user defined error recovery.

- **MC_REQUEST_TO_SEND** — requests a Send state from the remote TP. The LU will send a special expedited message to the remote LU asking the remote TP to allow the local TP to send data.

- **MC_GET_ATTRIBUTES** — retrieves information about current conversation and session characteristics at the local LU side of the conversation.

- **MC_POST_ON_RECEIPT** — requests posting for the specified mapped conversation when information arrives from the remote transaction program on this conversation.

- **MC_TEST** — tests a specific mapped conversation as to whether the conversation has been posted or whether an attention (MC_REQUEST_TO_SEND) has been received from the partner TP.

4.3.2 Basic Conversation Verbs

The Basic Conversation Verbs are intended for use by service transaction programs (STPs) that provide services for other transaction programs (TPs). Basic conversation verbs can also be used directly by application transaction programs (see Fig. 4.5) allowing programmers to bypass the mapped component of the presentation services layer and to develop more efficient applications. The data stream required on basic conversations consists of logical records that can be blocked together by the programmer or the LU into one send message. Each logical record (LR) must be preceded by a 2-byte length field. Other than that, the basic conversation verbs are very similar to the mapped conversation verbs described above. The following is a short description of LU 6.2 basic conversation verbs:

- **ALLOCATE** — allocates a basic conversation. The LU assigns a unique resource ID that must be supplied on every verb following the ALLOCATE verb to uniquely identify this conversation.

- **DEALLOCATE** — ends a basic conversation. The LU notifies the remote LU that the local TP requested to end the current conversation.

- **CONFIRM** — sends a confirmation request to the partner transaction program to synchronize distributed transactions.

- **CONFIRMED** — responds to a confirmation request.

- **SEND_DATA** — sends data in a predefined LU 6.2 format (logical records) to the remote TP. A logical record consists of a 2-byte length prefix (LL) followed by the user data. The data portion of the logical records can be in any format agreed upon by the two application programmers and does not require the ID field that is built by the LU presentation services component for mapped conversations. A programmer can pack multiple logical records or a portion of a logical record into one application buffer (called a **buffer record**). The unit of data that a program sends or receives with a single basic conversation SEND DATA verb is of arbitrary length determined by the programmer and does not have to consist of a complete logical record. The LU 6.2 architecture does not impose any relationship between application buffers and logical records. Therefore, one buffer record may contain one or many complete or incomplete logical records.

- **FLUSH** — transmits all the accumulated LU's data to the remote TP.

- **RECEIVE_AND_WAIT** — receives logical records into the program receive buffer. If there is no partner data the TP is suspended until the data arrives from the partner TP. The receiving TP may request to receive one or many complete or incomplete logical records into its receive buffer. The logical units only check the length field (LL) of each logical record which must be equal to or greater than two when exchanging logical records on basic conversations. A TP's ability to block many logical records into an application send buffer and to receive many logical records on one receive call, may result in improved performance and better network efficiency.

- **RECEIVE_IMMEDIATE** — receives logical records into the program receive buffer, but does not wait for the information to arrive. The LU checks the receive queue, and if there is nothing to receive, it returns a RC=UNSUCCESSFUL. If there is data to be received, then the RECEIVE_IMMEDIATE verb performs the same function as the RECEIVE_AND_WAIT verb.

- **PREPARE_TO_RECEIVE** — sends the change direction to the remote TP, flushes the LU send buffers and changes the conversation From Send state to Receive state.

- **SEND_ERROR** — sends an application error notification to the remote TP. The LU notifies the remote TP of an application error, changes the remote TP to Receive state, and the local TP to Send state and allows the local TP to initiate user defined error recovery.

- **REQUEST_TO_SEND** — requests a Send state from the remote TP. The local LU sends a special expedited message to the remote LU asking the remote TP to release a Send state. The send/Receive states are not affected by this verb, and the receiving TP must still receive data until the sending TP releases a Send state by issuing, for example, the PREPARE_TO_RECEIVE verb.

- **GET_ATTRIBUTES** — retrieves information about current basic conversation and session characteristics.

- **POST_ON_RECEIPT** — requests posting for the specified basic conversation when information arrives from the remote TP on this conversation.

- **TEST** — tests a specific basic LU 6.2 conversation as to whether the conversation has been posted or whether an attention (REQUEST_TO_SEND verb) has been received from the partner TP.

The Basic Conversation Verbs are very similar to the mapped conversation verbs. In actual fact, each mapped conversation verb can be mapped into the corresponding basic conversation verbs. The LU presentation services mapped component (PS.MC) changes the mapped conversation verbs received locally from the transaction program into the LU 6.2 predefined logical record formats (the GDS variables) and uses the basic conversation protocol boundary to transmit the GDS variables to the remote LU.

4.3.3 Type Independent Verbs

The type independent verbs are intended for use with both the basic and mapped conversations. For example, the LU provides TPs with syncpoint services (a SYNCPT type-independent verb) to COMMIT or to BACKOUT all protected resources in a distributed transaction such as databases. The following is a short description of the verbs:

- **SYNCPT** — advances all protected resources (such as distributed databases) to the next synchronization point. The logical unit flushes its send buffers for all conversations allocated with a synchronization level of SYNCPT. Applications define an indivisible **Logical Unit of Work (LUW)** as a sequence of related programming statements (database updates, deletes, etc.). The LU is responsible for committing the LUW to the next synchronization point or restoring all protected resources to the last synchronization point .

- **BACKOUT** — restores all protected resources to the last synchronization point, and sends BACKOUT on all conversations allocated with synchronization level of SYNCPT. The resources are restored to the last synchronization point (either the start of the transaction or the last successful SYNCPT verb issued since the beginning of the conversation).

- **GET_TYPE** — returns the current conversation resource type BASIC_CONVERSATION or MAPPED_CONVERSATION.

- **WAIT** — waits for posting to occur on any mapped or basic conversation from a list of conversations for which MC_POST_ON_RECEIPT or POST_RECEIPT verbs were issued.

4.3.4 Control-Operator Verbs

The control-operator verbs are executed by installation-specific control-operator transaction programs. A human operator interacts with the control-operator transaction program to perform the following functions at the local LU:

- Configure the local LU's operating environment

- Activate and deactivate sessions

- Control the number of sessions by issuing CNOS verbs

- Manage the configured operating environment

The control-operator verbs can also be divided into three subcategories:

1. **CHANGE NUMBER OF SESSIONS (CNOS)** verbs — allow an operator program to control the number of sessions between local and remote logical units.

- **INITIALIZE_SESSION_LIMIT** — initializes the (LU, mode) session limits from a zero to a nonzero value for single or parallel sessions. It also establishes contention-winner polarities for parallel sessions.

- **CHANGE_SESSION_LIMIT** — regulates the number of parallel sessions between the local and the remote logical units for a specific mode name. It establishes the session limit, sets the contention polarities (minimum number of conversation winners), and selects the LU that is responsible for activation or deactivation of LU-LU sessions required as a result of the imposed new limits.

- **RESET_SESSION_LIMIT** — resets the (LU, mode) session limits to zero. All sessions with the specified mode name or all mode names are deactivated in an orderly manner (the current conversations are allowed to complete) as a result of this verb.

- **PROCESS_SESSION_LIMIT** — a verb issued by an LU 6.2 defined "CNOS service transaction program" to process and negotiate the session limits, contention-winner polarities, and related CNOS parameters received from the partner LU.

2. **Session control verbs** — to activate and deactivate LU-LU sessions.

- **ACTIVATE_SESSION** — activates a single or a parallel session for a specific mode name.

- **DEACTIVATE_SESSION** — deactivates the specified LU-LU session. The session may be deactivated normally, after the current conversation is deallocated or the session may be aborted regardless of the current conversation allocated to the session.

3. **LU definition verbs** — used to define, modify, or delete the local LU's operating parameters, such as LUs, modes, or transaction programs (TPs).

- **DEFINE_LOCAL_LU** — defines or modifies the parameters of the local LU.

- **DEFINE_REMOTE_LU** — defines or modifies a remote logical unit as seen by the local LU.

- **DEFINE_MODE** — defines or modifies session characteristics for all sessions with the specified mode name.

- **DEFINE_TP** — defines or modifies parameters describing the local transaction program to the local LU.

- **DISPLAY_LOCAL_LU** —displays current values of the parameters that control the operation of the local LU.

- **DISPLAY_REMOTE_LU** — displays current values of the parameters of the remote LU as seen by the local LU.

- **DISPLAY_MODE** — displays current values of session characteristics (session count, pacing sizes, maximum request (MAXRU) sizes, conversation winners, etc.).

- **DISPLAY_TP** —displays current values of parameters of a local transaction program.

- **DELETE** — deletes the local LU 6.2's parameter values as defined by the DEFINE verbs.

4.4 OPEN AND CLOSED API IMPLEMENTATIONS

Open API implementations are the implementations that provide LU 6.2 TP-LU conversation protocol boundaries directly to application transaction programs. This means that application programmers may use the LU 6.2 basic or mapped conversation verbs directly to write distributed applications. All open implementations must implement at least the base set of LU 6.2 functions. The following is a list of some of the open API LU 6.2 implementations:

• APPC/MVS

• APPC/PC on DOS personal computers

• APPC and CPI-C on OS/2 EE

• LU 6.2 on CICS/VS or CICS/ESA

• APPC products on AS/400, S/38, S/36, S/88, or RT

• CPI-C on ES9000

• VM/CPI-C

• LU 6.2 on DB2

• LU 6.2 on IMS

• Most vendors APPC , CPI-C, or LU 6.2 implementations (NSA, Novell, DCA, EICON, etc.)

Closed API implementations do not provide a TP-LU 6.2 API for end-user applications (TPs). Closed APIs are IBM supplied products that perform LU 6.2 services and do not have to implement the base set of LU 6.2 functions but only the specific functions needed to do implementation-specific tasks. For example, printers such as the IBM 3820 page printer may only implement the secondary LU role and limited LU 6.2 functions that satisfy the printer requirements. The following are examples of some IBM closed LU 6.2 implementations:

• SNA Distribution Services (SNADS) products

- Document Interchange Architecture (DIA) products

- IBM 3820 page printer

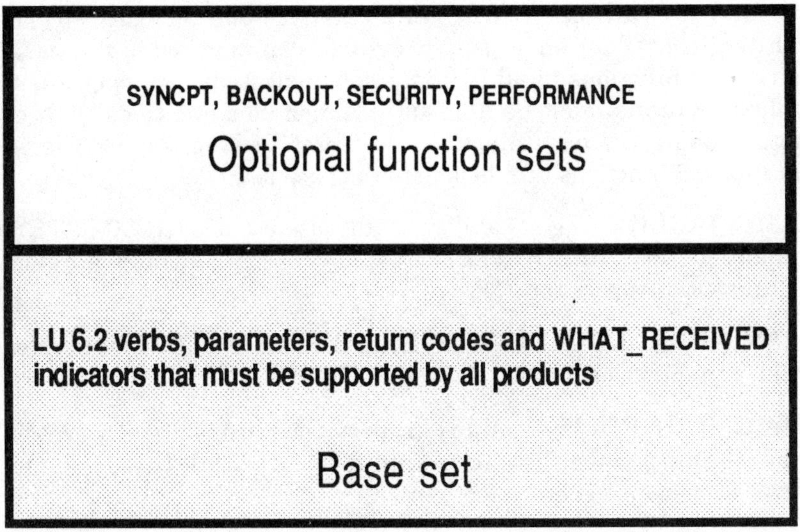

SYNCPT, BACKOUT, SECURITY, PERFORMANCE

Optional function sets

LU 6.2 verbs, parameters, return codes and WHAT_RECEIVED
indicators that must be supported by all products

Base set

Figure 4.6 LU 6.2 functional sets.

4.5 LU 6.2 BASE SET AND OPTION SETS

All implementations complying with the LU 6.2 architecture must
be able to establish conversations with one another. The LU 6.2
architecture defines different functions (grouped into the base set of
functions and the option sets) that allow some flexibility for
different implementations. A **set** is a group of indivisible LU 6.2
functions for products to implement. All functions within a set must
be implemented. The syntax and the manner in which the
APPC/LU 6.2 functions are implemented is left to the
implementors. The variation in the parameters, verbs, and syntax
does not affect the way the different implementations work because
the same LU 6.2 functions must generate the same unique LU 6.2
network messages. The LU 6.2 functions can be grouped into two
function sets (Fig. 4.6):

- A common **base set** of functions

- A number of **option sets** of functions

The Base Function Set

The base set specifies a list of common LU 6.2 verbs, parameters, return codes, and WHAT_RECEIVED indicators that must be provided by all open API implementations of the LU 6.2 architecture. The base set provides common communication distributed functions to all LU 6.2 implementations. All open LU 6.2 implementations must be able to establish conversations with one another using the base function set. The following the SNA logical unit type 6.2 functions that belong to the base set:

- **[MC_]ALLOCATE** — ability to allocate a basic (ALLOCATE) or mapped (MC_ALLOCATE) conversation and attach a remote transaction program (TP)

- **[MC_]DEALLOCATE** — ability to deallocate a conversation (end the conversation)

- **[MC_]CONFIRM** — ability to perform confirmation processing by sending a confirmation request for local to the remote transaction program

- **[MC_]CONFIRMED** — ability to positively respond to a confirmation request

- **[MC_]SEND_DATA** — ability to send data

- [MC_]RECEIVE_AND_WAIT — ability to receive data

- **[MC_]SEND_ERROR** — ability to notify the remote TP of application errors

- **[MC_]REQUEST_TO_SEND** — ability to ask for Send state

- **GET_ATTRIBUTES** — ability to obtain conversation attributes

- **CNOS** verbs (with the exception of CHANGE_SESSION_LIMIT)

The [MC]VERB means both the mapped and the corresponding basic conversation verbs. The GET_ATTRIBUTES verb must be implemented by basic conversation implementations only

The Optional Function Set

LU 6.2 implementations do not have to support option sets. However, if an optional function set is supported, it must include all functions within the set. The following is a list of the principal optional functions:

- **Mapping** — used on mapped conversations. This option allows sending of data that is mapped via user or product-defined maps.

- **FMH** data — used on mapped conversations. This option allows TPs to exchange user defined function management headers (FMHs).

- **PIP** data — allows a local transaction program to allocate a conversation and pass a set of initial parameters to the remote TP.

- **Conversation level security** — allows a local transaction program to supply user_ID, password, and profile at allocation time which can be validated at the remote logical unit for each conversation.

- **Syncpoint** — used with both mapped and basic conversations. It allows a transaction program to COMMIT or BACKOUT protected resources such as distributed databases.

- **Performance options** — allow transaction programs to improve performance. In general the LU controls the session allocation requests and the network message flows. The LU may implement optional functions (such as the immediate parameter on the [MC_]ALLOCATE verb or the [MC_]FLUSH verb or the [MC_]RECEIVE_IMMEDIATE) allowing TPs to request first speaker (allocation winner) sessions, flushing LU 6.2 buffers in order to initiate processing in the partner program or returning to the TP if there is no data available on the receive queue for processing.

Installation-Specific Functions

The logical unit type 6.2 implementations differ because they may implement different LU 6.2 option sets. In addition, some implementation-specific functions not defined by the LU 6.2 architecture may be used by some products. These are always local functions invisible to remote LU implementations. Therefore, the installation-specific functions do not create incompatibility when communicating between different vendor's LU 6.2 products. The following are some examples of installation-specific functions that are used by various vendors:

- TP_STARTED

  A transaction program has requested resources for a new local TP instance. The LU responds by returning a TP_ID uniquely identifying this TP instance. The next verb issued by the local TP is typically an ALLOCATE verb that initiates a conversation for this TP.

- TP_ENDED

  A transaction program has requested to end a TP instance. All resources allocated to this instance are released.

- GET_ALLOCATE (or RECEIVE_ALLOCATE)

  Requests the local LU to dequeue an incoming ALLOCATE and to allocate resources for the new TP and the incoming conversation.

- CREATE_TP

  The local logical unit notifies the TP of incoming allocation requests.

The syntax used to implement the logical unit type 6.2 functions and parameters may also vary for different products. For example, a conversation identification parameter of the LU 6.2 architecture is referred to in different APPC implementations as a conversation IDor a CONV_ID or a resource ID. Therefore applications developed using the implementation-specific APPC/LU 6.2 products are not portable.

4.6 APPC AND CPI-C ADVANTAGES

APPC and SAA/CPI-C are the IBM strategic architectures that define a set of protocols, based on the LU 6.2 architecture, for program-to-program communications, in both IBM's hierarchical (host controlled) networks and distributed networks. They define a set of programming calls used by programs residing on SNA distributed network nodes to carry out an execution of a single transaction. These protocols can be implemented via product-specific APPC Application Programming Interfaces (e.g., CICS API, OS/2 API, APPC/PC, Novell, DCA, ICON or NSA's APPC APIs) or the CPI-C communication calls that require exact syntax (e.g., CMALLC, CMINIT,CMSEND, CMRCV) common to all SAA implementations. Since both APPC and CPI-C are based on LU 6.2, all the advantages described below and the LU 6.2 advantages listed in Chap. 2 (see Sec. 2.3.8 "LU 6.2 Advantages") apply to both APPC and CPI-C distributed standards. Before describing the benefits of APPC and CPI-C, let us look at the problems in designing distributed transaction programs.

4.6.1 Distributed Application Design Problems

Distributed transaction processing between dissimilar systems may be very difficult without a distributed programming standard. Differences in operating systems, communications facilities, hardware, protocols, and the programming interfaces being used on IBM computers, as well as other vendor systems, create barriers in the designing of distributed applications. Without an agreed-upon standard, distributed applications are dependent on the different tools and protocols used in different computer environments as well as on the programming techniques used by programmers designing the applications. Programmers are required to learn completely different skills required for writing distributed applications on different operating systems. Applications are often designed to accept data only from a specific computer, and once designed, they are not capable of receiving data from other computers with different operating systems, data structures, or communication protocols. The application programmers have to learn different communication protocols and programming techniques as used on different machines. Even the common distributed functions used in all distributed applications (such as initiating a transaction or notifying a partner program of an application error) are incompatible between different designs since they have to be designed by individual programmers each time they write a new application. For example, when the PC and the host application designers (see Fig. 4.7) have chosen to exchange application-defined commands [START TRAN.(transaction), SEND_DATA, ERROR, and END TRAN.] to start a transaction, transmit data, notify a partner program of an application error, and end the transaction. Other programmers designing the same applications might have chosen totally different commands to implement the same functions. The lack of standards for writing distributed applications produces incompatible designs totally dependent on the techniques used by individual programmers and the different interfaces provided by different operating systems. Without an established distributed application design standard, the SNA terminal-to-host emulation products have frequently been used to communicate between applications residing on personal computers, minicomputers, and mainframes. The SNA terminal-to-host protocols (LU 2 or 3270 emulation software) were not designed for distributed transaction processing but for a communication between a nonintelligent device (such as 3278 terminal) and the host. These protocols are not suitable for designing distributed transactions. Suppose a PC programmer has to design a very simple function of exchanging data with a host application using the 3270 emulation software (see Fig. 4.7).

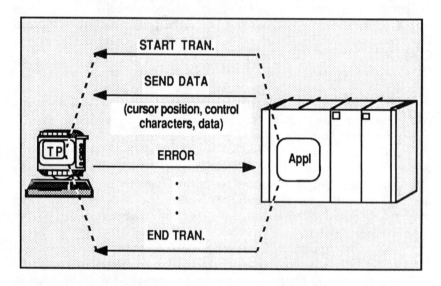

Figure 4.7 LU 6.2 User-defined distributed functions.

The host application builds the 3270 data stream (with special codes for cursor positioning, clearing the screen, displaying protected fields, etc.) appropriate for terminal display. The PC programmer must strip the irrelevant characters to get the requested data. This is time consuming and produces inefficient applications. Also, the additional (not needed) control characters must be sent across communication links using the network resources, such as lines and the network nodes, inefficiently. In addition, the terminal-to-host protocols were designed to communicate with a single host, and they are inappropriate for applications that require simultaneous communications with multiple remote computers to execute a distributed transaction (e.g., updating of distributed relational databases).

4.6.2 APPC and CPI-C Benefits

APPC and CPI Communications are broadly accepted standards for designing distributed applications that address all the above problems. APPC verbs and SAA/CPI-C calls differ only in that CPI-C calls define the application interface in exact syntax that complies with the Systems Application Architecture (SAA). Therefore, the advantages listed below apply equally to both APPC and CPI-C architectures. In addition to APPC advantages, the CPI-C interface provides a consistent and portable interface across all SAA environments (OS/2, AS/400, and mainframes). Therefore, if portability is an important issue, the APPC applications that use implementation-specific APIs should be changed to the SAA common programming interface communications (CPI-C).

The major advantages of designing distributed applications using APPC and CPI-C are listed below.

Any-to-Any Communication

APPC and CPI-C applications are no longer limited to dummy terminal emulation (like 3270 emulation), which can communicate only with applications residing on the host. Notice that the powerful 386 or 486 PCs that emulate dummy 3270 type terminals can not communicate with each other in an SNA network. Applications using the 3270 protocols cannot, for example, copy or print a document from one PC directly to other PCs, minicomputers, or other vendor systems connected to the same SNA network. APPC and CPI-C are based on the SNA logical unit 6.2 which was specifically designed for peer-to-peer communications, and it is the only IBM logical unit that recognizes an intelligent entity on both sides of the connection of any two SNA distributed nodes. LU 6.2 was designed to communicate with single or multiple dissimilar systems and it allows direct communications between PCs, minicomputers and any other system platform that supports the SNA logical unit 6.2 architecture. APPC or CPI-C applications do not have to include any irrelevant control characters (e.g., 3270 data stream) and may send just the desired information across a communication link. This improves performance and uses the network resources efficiently. For example, the file transfer program in Fig. 4.8 may require significantly less data to be transmitted over communication lines in comparison with a 3270 application that would have to send additional control characters with each transmitted record.

Distributed Functions

Most of the functions for developing distributed transaction programs (TPs) are strictly defined and enforced by the LU 6.2 architecture. Application programmers do not have to spend months writing a design document on how to, for example, initiate distributed transactions, send or receive information, notify the remote program of an application error, or terminate a transaction. In the past, hundreds of different design teams would come up with hundreds of different designs to provide the same distributed functions. Therefore, programs designed by one design team could not communicate at all with programs designed by other teams. APPC or CPI-C provide programmers with exactly one design for each distributed function. Figure 4.8 illustrates the use of LU 6.2 distributed functions for a file transfer application design. The transaction initiation code (MC_ALLOCATE) written by one team can communicate with APPC or SAA/CPI-C transaction programs written by other independent teams to accept LU 6.2 transactions. The communicating application programs may reside on any SNA node or other vendor's systems that support the logical unit 6.2 architecture. In actual fact, if the design teams understand the LU 6.2 architecture, a design document for the distributed functions (such as the transaction initiation, termination, error notification, confirmation processing, synchronization processing,) does not have to be written at all. Application programmers need to know the name of the remote transaction program and the name of the remote logical unit (called **remote LU** or **partner LU**), and they need to follow the LU 6.2 protocols.

LU 6.2 Resource Management

The SNA logical unit 6.2 manages the exchange of information between transaction programs (TPs) and informs the local transaction program (the local TP) of actions performed by the remote transaction program (the remote TP). The remote TP might not be active when the allocation request arrives at the remote LU. The remote LU will automatically activate the remote TP when the allocation request arrives. This establishes a conversation between the local and the remote transaction programs. Once the conversation has been established, the LUs manage the data exchange between the local and the remote transaction programs.

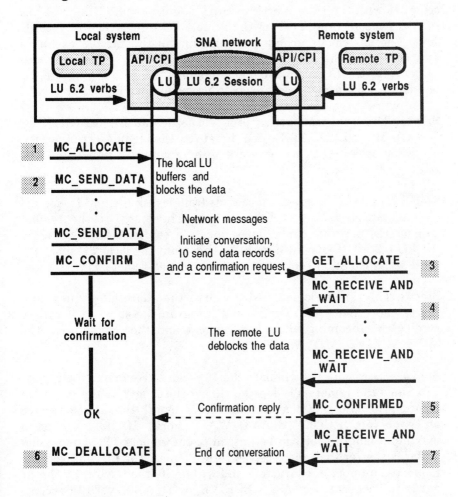

Figure 4.8 APPC file transfer design example.

The remote TP does not have to know how many messages are sent by the local TP, how long the messages are or when the local TP expects a confirmation request from the remote TP. Figure 4.8 illustrates a file transfer program that is required to copy a variable-length record file from a local TP on a DOS PC in the United States, to a remote TP residing on a minicomputer in Poland that supports the SNA logical unit 6.2. We do not have to be concerned at all with the type of the minicomputer or the operating system being used as long as the minicomputer in Poland runs an emulation package (such as APPC/PC on a DOS workstation) that complies with the LU 6.2 architecture. The file sender (the local TP) requires a confirmation from the remote TP after every 10 records sent. The system programmers must install the LU 6.2 packages and configure the required network directories needed on both systems for the LU-LU session establishment. The following are the possible LU 6.2 design steps for both programs (see Fig. 4.8).

Step 1. The local transaction program issues an LU 6.2 (APPC or CPI-C) MC_ALLOCATE verb to start the remote transaction program passing, as parameters, the remote TP name and the remote LU name.

Step 2. The local TP reads 10 records from a disk file and issues LU 6.2 MC_SEND_DATA verbs (one for each record) to the remote transaction program and then requests a confirmation by issuing the LU 6.2 MC_CONFIRM verb. At this point the local TP suspends until a confirmation reply is received from the remote TP.

Step 3. The remote logical unit receives the allocation request and starts the remote TP. The remote program must issue a call to receive the incoming allocation request and then must issue the MC_RECEIVE_AND_WAIT verb.

Step 4. The remote LU will pass the 10 received records to the remote TP. Since the remote TP does not know the length of the incoming records, it has a preset maximum record length that it can receive on each MC_RECEIVE_AND_WAIT verb. If the requested maximum length that can be passed to the remote TP's application buffer is shorter than the received record length, the LU will pass the requested number of characters and will notify the remote TP that it needs to issue another MC_RECEIVE_AND_WAIT verb to receive the remaining portion of data for the same record. Therefore, the number of MC_RECEIVE_AND_WAIT verbs can be greater than 10. After the last record is received the remote LU notifies the remote TP that the local TP requested a confirmation.

Step 5. The remote transaction program must comply with the SNA logical unit type 6.2 architecture and if all data has been received correctly it has to issue the LU 6.2 MC_CONFIRMED verb (confirming the receipt of the 10 correct records). The local logical unit receives the confirmation request and completes the MC_CONFIRM verb with a request code RC=OK (confirmation received). Now steps 2 to 5 can be repeated until the end of file is reached.

Step 6. The local TP issues a MC_DEALLOCATE verb to end the transaction. The local LU (the LU on the local system) notifies the remote LU that the transaction has ended.

Step 7. The remote LU notifies the remote TP that the transaction has ended.

Notice that other than knowing the remote TP name and the remote LU name the two design teams did not have to write or exchange any design documents. Notice also that the same programming codes can now be used to copy/receive files to/from any other computers connected to the SNA/LU 6.2 distributed network. The local TP only has to know the remote TP name and the remote LU name, which could be passed as parameters at the program startup. The remote TP would not have to be changed at all. This example assumes no error during copying of the file. The LU 6.2 distributed error recovery will be discussed in Part 2 of this book.

Network Efficiency

First, let us look at the network efficiency of the most commonly used of the SNA logical units, which is logical unit type 2 (also known as 3270 terminal emulation). The LU 2 is limited to one session at a time and can communicate with only one application residing on a mainframe. The session and the logical unit (LU 2) are used exclusively by one SNA end user (327x terminal or an emulation program). Therefore, the 3270 emulation programs cannot share the same LU at the same time (for the duration of the SNA session), and you are required to configure one LU per 3278 terminal emulation program. In a large SNA network the number of logical units required to support a large number of transactions per second can be significant and may require a lot of memory or large systems. System generation and network management of an SNA network with thousands of different LU names and thousands of sessions is difficult as well. LU 2 was designed for a host application to communicate with an interactive 3278 type terminal not for distributed transactions. Therefore, if you write transaction programs using 3270 emulation, each time a write command is issued a network message flows to the remote partner. LU 2 is not capable of blocking and deblocking application requests for better network utilization. Also, the additional (not needed) control characters (with special codes for cursor positioning, clearing the screen, displaying protected fields, etc., appropriate for terminal display) must be sent across communication link using the network resources, such as lines and the network nodes, inefficiently. Overall, the 3270 emulation is certainly not a protocol for designing distributed applications.

LU 6.2, on the other hand, uses the SNA network resources in a more efficient way than any other SNA logical unit. The applications exchange only the requested data with no additional control characters. Instead of configuring multiple LUs to run multiple transactions at the same time you need to configure only one logical unit 6.2. LU 6.2 can be accessed by many TPs at the same time and allows multiple sessions (sessions with many partners) with many remote LUs. Multiple sessions to the same remote LU are called parallel sessions. Many transaction programs can share the same logical unit and the same session. A conversation (a transaction) has an exclusive use of a session but successive conversations can reuse the same session. If you require many transactions to be executed at the same time using just one LU, you need to start multiple sessions only between the local LU and the remote LUs. The local LU buffers the data to be sent to the remote LU and generates a network message only when the local TP issues a call that requires an answer from the remote TP or when the maximum request unit (MAXRU) size is reached. In our file copy example (see Fig. 4.8) the local LU buffers and blocks the ALLOCATE verb, 10 SEND_DATA verbs and the CONFIRM verb and sends them as one network message across the network to the remote LU. The remote LU deblocks the verbs and passes them, one at a time, to the remote transaction program. The same program written using a 3270 emulation would generate a separate network message for each of the 10 records (at least 10 SDLC frames and acknowledgments). Sending one instead of 10 network messages conserves the transmission bandwidth, improves performance and increases the overall network efficiency.

Other Advantages

• Both APPC and CPI-C are based on the LU 6.2 architecture and they functionally comply with the SAA Common Communication Architecture (CCA). Therefore, APPC programs can communicate with the CPI-C programs. In addition CPI-C complies with the portability requirements of the SAA architecture by providing a common programming interface (syntactically the same) across different SAA platforms (OS/2 EE, AS/400, and mainframes).

- APPC and CPI-C are the best available interfaces for designing distributed applications. LU 6.2 is more efficient than terminal-to-host protocols for applications like file transfer, requester/ server applications on LANs, distributed relational databases, and many other applications.

- Application programs communicate using the LU 6.2 peer-to-peer protocols that are independent of the operating systems and allow direct communications on LANs as well as SNA wide area networks.

- APPC and CPI-C applications may use less expensive personal computers or minicomputers to offload CPU processing from the large mainframes. They allow building less expensive SNA distributed networks that may not include mainframes at all. This is quite important for smaller businesses that may prefer to develop SNA applications on local area networks (LANs), giving them direct control of the network and better response time to the local end users.

- APPC and CPI-C applications provide for distributed error recovery. The terminal-to-host protocols recognized intelligence only on the host side of the connection, so a terminal could not notify a host application of an error condition. Therefore, if any error occurred at the terminal side, the host usually had to abort and restart the SNA session. On the other hand, LU 6.2 recognizes intelligence on both side's of the connection. This allows for the development of more robust and more intelligent applications that are capable of distributed error recovery.

- The APPC and CPI-C applications use a half-duplex, flip-flop protocol which is less error-prone than a full-duplex protocol in which either program may send and receive at the same time. Distributed transactions (e.g., banking transactions) are usually half duplex. If a full-duplex sending and receiving of information is required between different systems, two conversations may be established with one of them always in Send state and the other in Receive state.

- The SNA logical unit type 6.2 provides for transaction level security allowing the secure transfer of sensitive information across the network.

- LU 6.2 hides the details of session establishment, conversation management, and the actual transferring of data to the remote TP. It allows TPs to exchange data in any format agreed upon by the two programmers in a format that is independent of any type of SNA device (such as 3270 or RJE data streams).

5

SAA Enterprise Information System

The difficulties involved within the area of connectivity of dissimilar computers are widely recognized by MIS personnel and directors. In a multivendor environment computers frequently have different operating systems (e.g., OS/2, OS/400, VM, or MVS), different programming interfaces, and different user interfaces. This often causes many inefficiencies and problems with the design of integrated applications. Some of those problems are:

• Applications have to be rewritten for each environment.

• Programmers and users have to be retrained when moved from one environment to another.

• Programs are not easily ported from one environment to another and frequently need extensive modification in order to function on a different system.

• Programmers may have to write several versions of the same application.

• Software purchased or developed today may become obsolete because of lack of compatibility with new system environments.

5.1 USER REQUIREMENTS

User requirements have changed drastically in the 1980s because of the introduction of intelligent programmable workstations. The following are the major requirements for future computing environments:

- **Portability** — businesses should be able to move employees, data and applications anywhere within an enterprise without any modifications or retraining of personnel.

- **Consistency** — users and programmers must be able to perform similar functions on all systems using common techniques.

- **Distribution** — applications that can be used on or distributed among systems residing at different geographic locations must be developed.

5.2 SYSTEMS APPLICATION ARCHITECTURE (SAA) CONCEPTS

As we enter the 1990s many companies, including IBM, are faced with a challenge of integrating their computing environments into a single computing enterprise. The major objective of such an enterprise is to satisfy the user requirements listed above. In March 1987, IBM introduced **Systems Application Architecture (SAA)** which defines an integrated **Enterprise Information System (EIS)** that meets this objective. **SAA is not a product, but a set of open architectures (specifications) to build enterprise-wide products.** The major objective of SAA is that the computer enterprise looks to the user as if it is a single system. This is illustrated in Fig. 5.1. The resources, such as applications or data, are distributed throughout the computer enterprise but the user accesses all the resources as if they were local. Whenever remote access is required, CPI-C or APPC peer-to-peer cooperative processing is used to access the resources as if they were residing on the local system. The SAA enterprise system is composed of the major IBM systems, including mainframes (S/370s and S/390s with MVS/ESA and VM/ESA), midrange computers (AS/400 with OS/400), and programmable workstations (PS/2s with OS/2 EE). Each machine is assigned the distributed functions best suited to its characteristics. The programmable workstation provides the common window (common user interface) to the enterprise. The mainframes and the midrange systems are best suited for multiuser access and sharing resources such as databases. Systems Application Architecture is designed to provide the framework for developing consistent and integrated applications across future generations of major IBM computing environments.

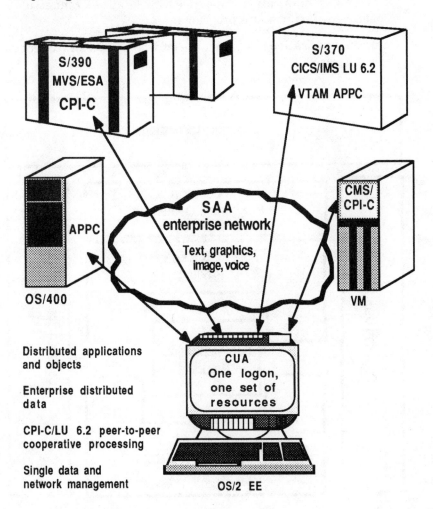

Figure 5.1 SAA single system image.

The IBM SAA architecture consists of four major areas illustrated in Fig. 5.2):

1. Common User Access (CUA) — allows consistency of screen layout, keyboard layout, menu presentation, and selection techniques.

2. Common Programming Interface (CPI) — allows the design of portable and distributed applications that can easily be integrated into multiple SAA environments.

3. Common Communication Support (CCS) — allows connectivity of open SAA systems and programs.

4. Common Applications — provides common services throughout the enterprise.

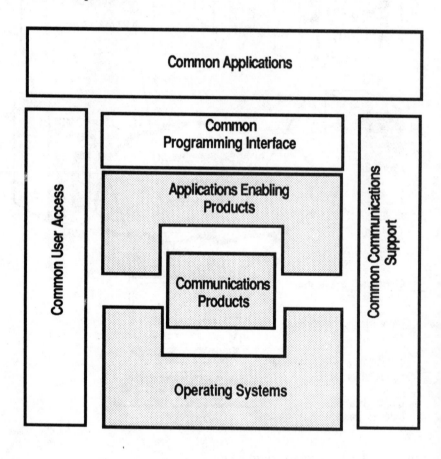

Figure 5.2 SAA Components.

5.2.1 Common User Access (CUA)

Common User Access (CUA) defines the user interface to the SAA enterprise. In the past user interfaces were designed by individual programmers and frequently had significant differences from one application to another. The CUA specifies the design of the user interface as well as the tools for designing the interface. The major objective of CUA is ease of use and consistency across applications. Figure 5.3 illustrates the Personal System/2 with OS/2 operating systems as the chosen programmable workstation for the SAA enterprise system. The information format, the information presentation and the interaction techniques are common across the computer enterprise.

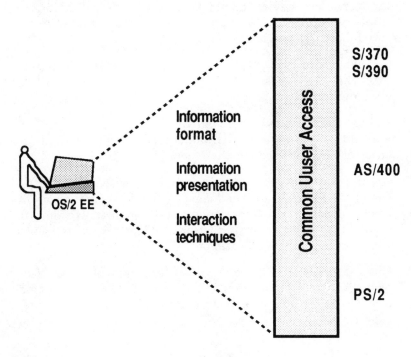

Figure 5.3 SAA Common User Access (CUA).

SAA Common User Access defines two levels of users interfaces:

1. **Entry level**. This user interface is designed for data entry intensive applications that often run on nonprogrammable terminals.

2. **The graphical interface**. This user interface provides a programmer with tools for building menu-driven applications an a programmable workstation using action bars, icons, check boxes, pull-down windows, or pop-up windows. The user can interact with the enterprise via a keyboard or a mouse.

An extension of the graphical interface is a **workplace** which integrates SAA applications into an electronic working environment. The applications appear as objects (represented by icons) in the workplace environment. A mouse interface is used to act on the objects. An example of a workplace environment is the OS/2 Office Vision Family of products, which provide the graphical user interface, as well as various application services for an office environment. An office vision user can, for example, delete a file by dragging the file icon to an icon representing a shredder. Similar workplace environments service will be provided in the future releases of OS/2 CUA. Applications that conform to SAA CUA offer the following benefits:

1. Consistency for users — the appearance of information and the way the users respond to it, is familiar across all SAA environments.

2. Users spend less time learning how to use different applications and their environments. This makes them more efficient and confident in their jobs.

3. Application programmers are provided with software tools, such as the presentation manager or the dialog manager, which assists them with the development of a common user interface. With these tools, many functions can easily be reused and integrated in new applications.

4. Consistency for programmers — programmers can design, write, and change new and existing applications more quickly and easily because the techniques for developing CUAs are common to all programs.

5.2.2 Common Programming Interface (CPI)

Common Programming Interface (CPI) defines languages and services that allow development of SAA applications (see Fig. 5.4). The application programmers uses high-level SAA programming interfaces. This allows the design of portable and distributed applications that can easily be integrated into multiple SAA environments. SAA therefore significantly reduces the impact of operating system variations. It also allows the development of applications without having to be concerned with the specifics of the operating system. Figure 5.4 illustrates the two major components of the CPI interface the languages and the services.

1. Languages

- High-level programming languages (**COBOL** ANS standard X3J11, **C** ANS standard X3.23-1985, **FORTRAN 77, RPG,** and **PL/I**). The high-level languages are sometimes referred to as **third-generation languages.**

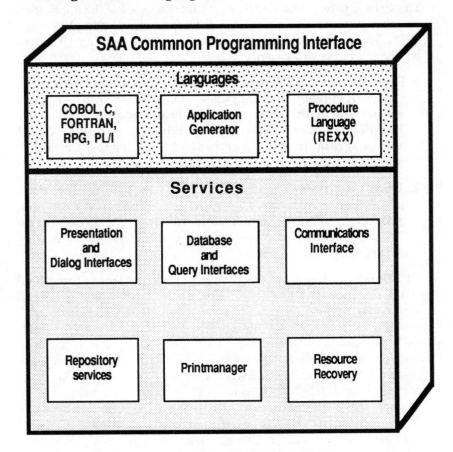

Figure 5.4 SAA Common Programming Interface (CPI).

- The SAA **procedure language** is based on the restructured extended executor language (**REXX**). REXX is a command language common to all SAA systems.

- The SAA **application generator** is based on the IBM Cross System Product (CSP). It is a fourth-generation programming language that significantly increases a programmer's productivity by automatically generating SAA code.

2. Services

* The **Presentation and the Dialog Interfaces** allow the application programmers to design a user interface which complies with CUA. The application development tools for designing CUA can be divided into two categories:

    a. **Procedural** — this allows programmers to define a CUA using the SAA Dialog Tag language. The Dialog Tag language supports both the entry and graphical models. It allows the building of user interfaces which are portable across nonprogrammable terminals and programmable workstations.

    b. **Event-driven** — this allows programmers to develop a graphical event-driven interface. The event driven programming is done via calls to the OS/2 Presentation Manager. This is the recommended model for an SAA user interface.

* **CPI Database Access** is based on the **Structured Query Language (SQL)**. This allows programmers to access (update, delete, modify, or retrieve) a relational database using high-level SQL commands that are consistent across all SAA environments. SQL deals only with the logical access of data so it frees up a programmer from having to write code to the physical database layer. DB/2 under MVS, SQL/DS under VM, OS/400 Database Manager and OS/2 Database Manager are examples of the current IBM SQL databases. At the time of writing this book the OS/2 Database Manager supported only the PC-to-PC requestor/server environment. OS/400 Database Manager provides a relational distributed database residing on AS/400s. The host DB/2 and SQL/DS databases define a relational database which resides on a mainframe. The next challenge facing IBM is to merge these separate databases into one single enterprise-wide relational database.

* The **CPI Query Interface** is based on the Structured Query Language (SQL). It provides a consistent relational database inquiry and report writing services which are common across the SAA enterprise system. By using simple SQL commands a user or a programmer can write reports or query relational

databases interactively (or from within an application program). The queries, procedures, and reports can be separately defined and updated without making any changes to your application program.

- The **CPI-Communications (CPI-C)** provides SAA programmers with a common programming interface for program-to-program communications using SNA logical unit 6.2. Programs communicate with each other by issuing CPI-C calls. CPI-C calls have the same syntax that all SAA implementations must follow (e.g., CMINIT, CMALLC, or CMDEALL). CPI Communications calls are excellent tools for designing cooperative processing applications. Cooperative processing allows the distribution of the processing power, as well as the data, throughout the SAA enterprise. CPI-C interfaces are available on OS/2, APPC/MVS, CMS/VM, and OS/400. Chapter 8 in this book discusses in detail the CPI-C architecture and cooperative processing application design. The SAA direction is to accommodate both the OSI/RM and the CPI-C architectures, as illustrated in Fig. 1.4 in Chap. 1 of this book. Applications can access an SAA network via a Common Programming Interface Communications (CPI-C) protocol. The CPI-C call is translated into SNA/LU 6.2 or OSI/RM network messages and is then sent to a remote SNA or OSI application partner.

- **Repository Services** provides application developers with tools to define, design, develop, and manage the application development life cycle. The Repository Services allows designers and programmers to share data and tools within all phases of the application development cycle (AD/Cycle). The MVS IBM Repository Manager provides common Repository Services for the SAA application development. It provides the single point of control for the application development environment. The SAA Common User Access on the OS/22 EE is used for the Computer-Aided Software Engineering AD/Cycle platform definition.

- **Resource Recovery Interface (RRI)** provides SAA programmers with a two-phase commit capability that allows to **commit** or **backout** of an indivisible logical unit of work across an SAA environments.

- **Printmanager Interface** allows print requests to be routed anywhere within the SAA enterprise. The Printmanager/400 running on IBM AS/400 midrange computers or the SAA Printmanager on MVS and VM, are an example of products that provide the Printmanager Interface.

5.2.3 Common Communication Support (CCS)

Common Communication Support (CCS) provides protocols that allow communication among application, systems, and networks. This allows easy connectivity between computers in an enterprise. Application programmers are isolated from the complexity of the underlying network configuration and protocols. The programmer need only concentrate on application design logic rather than connectivity issues and what communication protocols are being used. CCS supports communication standards as System Network Architecture (SNA) (based on LU 6.2 and PU 2.1) and the Open Systems Interconnection Reference Model (OSI/RM). IBM will provide a common communication interface (CI) to allow programmers the flexibility of using both SAA and non-SAA machines.

Figure 5.5 SAA Common applications.

5.2.4 Common Applications

The applications and products developed by IBM that satisfy the major customer needs and conform to the Systems Application Architecture, are referred to as **Common Applications**. These applications must follow the Common User Access (CUA), Common Programming Interface (CPI) and Common Communication Support (CCS). They will provide SAA users with ready services such as document processing services, document library services, personal services, and distributed data management services. Figure 5.5 illustrates common applications such as **Document Interchange Architecture (DIA), SNA Distribution Services (SNADS), Distributed Data Management (DDM),** and **Office Vision** family. DDM allows SAA applications to access remote files as if they were local resources. When a request for a file is made, the DDM searches the Network Resources Directory and automatically steps up the remote file access. SNADS is an architecture that allows store-and-forward objects (documents, files, etc.) between any two nodes in an SAA enterprise. DIA defines the rules and data structures for exchanging documents within the enterprise.

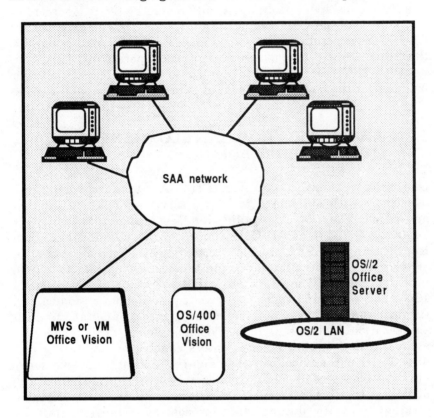

Figure 5.6 SAA Office Vision.

The Office Vision family was introduced in 1989 and was the first significant SAA common application. It demonstrated that a common user interface can be achieved across the major SAA operating systems (OS/2, OS/400, MVS, and VM). Office Vision integrates the office functions across multiple platforms. The Office Vision family consists of Office Vision/2 (a requestor/server LAN environment), OS/400 Office Visions, VM, and MVS Office Vision products. These Office Vision products are not fully integrated yet. In the future IBM will integrate them into a single enterprise-wide Office Vision environment as illustrated in Fig. 5.6. An SAA user will perform office services through the window to the Office enterprise residing on a programmable workstation. The PC users do not have to be aware of where the services are executed because all services appear as if they are performed locally. The SAA enterprise provides the PC's users with a single-system image. The PC requests will be automatically routed by the enterprise to a server residing on OS/2 Office Server, OS/400 Office Server, or the Office Server residing on a mainframe. Figure 5.7 illustrates how the future IBM common applications will operate. To make this possible, IBM introduced the Application Development family of products for the development of SAA enterprise-wide applications.

5.3 SAA APPLICATION DEVELOPMENT ENVIRONMENT (ADE)

One of the most important elements of SAA is to provide application developers with automated tools and services for developing SAA applications. The IBM SAA **Application Development Environment (ADE),** referred to as **AD/Cycle or Computer-Aided Software Engineering (CASE),** provides a comprehensive and integrated set of tools and services for developing, maintaining, and managing SAA applications. The AD/Cycle is IBM's strategic direction for the 1990s and will significantly improve a programmer's productivity. It provides a number of automated tools such as diagramming and specification tools used during design phase, design checkers, analyzers and application generators capable of generating code directly from the specifications. Figure 5.7 illustrates the major building blocks of the AD/Cycle framework. The modeling tools allows the creation of a model SAA enterprise to reflect the company strategy and its unique data processing requirements. The information from a modeling phase is stored in repository and is accessible in the analysis and design phase. The analysis and design tools allow the model to be used as input to design applications that meet the requirements. Once the design document is stored in repository, it can be used as input to produce the application code using either third-generation languages (3GL) such as C, COBOL, or FORTRAN; fourth-generation languages (4GL), such as application generators; or fifth-generation languages (5GL) referred to as **knowledge-base systems** that use artificial intelligence to produce SAA applications.

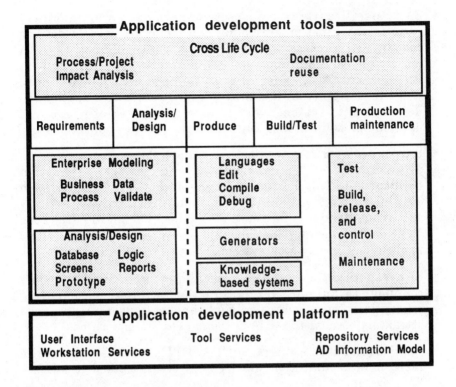

Figure 5.7 SAA AD/Cycle building blocks.

In the final phase the AD/Cycle provides tools for testing and maintaining the applications. Bachman Information Systems, Index Technology Inc., and Knowledge-Ware are three major CASE tool vendors chosen by IBM to supply CASE tools for the SAA Enterprise Information System. AD/Cycle is an open architecture which is an integral part of SAA.

5.4 SAA BENEFITS

The following are major benefits of the SAA architecture:

- SAA allows the design of cooperative processing applications which take advantage of the computing power of personal computers. An example of this would be moving the user interface programming logic to a PC environment.

- SAA significantly increases a programmer's productivity because the same programming skills may be used to develop cooperative processing applications that run on all SAA machines. In addition, the SAA Application Development Environment (ADE), referred to as **Computer-Aided Software Engineering (CASE)**, provides an automated application development system which increases the efficiency of developing, maintaining, and managing large applications.

- SAA provides a common interface that allows programmers to avoid many of the repetitive functions of application development. This is achieved by isolating certain application elements (e.g., user interface, database access) and by specifying standards for those elements. By doing this the code written for one application can easily be reused by other applications on any SAA system.

- SAA significantly increases a user's productivity by providing common techniques for interaction with the computing enterprise. Users who use SAA applications will not need retraining because the CUA is common to all applications.

- Applications that conform to CUA, CPI, and CCS will require little or no modification when ported or distributed to another SAA system.

- Applications will have the same appearance and behave the same way in future SAA environments as they do in the current one.

- Programmers will be able to apply their skills equally in the new environment.

- A customer's investment in future applications will be protected.

- SAA supports distributed relational databases based on SQL. Data can reside on any machine (mainframes, minicomputers, or personal computers) within the enterprise.

- The Common Communication Support (CCS) allows the design of applications that are distributed across an entire SAA enterprise.

A major objective of most companies in the 1990s will be to migrate their hierarchical SNA networks to a distributed computer enterprise. Companies that adopt SAA as their strategic Enterprise Information System will benefit from the tools and various services provides by SAA.

5.5 SAA AND UNIX

UNIX is a widely accepted operating system in government, university, and commercial environments. It runs on a number of computer platforms. In 1986, IBM introduced the AIX/UNIX operating system, which runs on their Personal System/2, RISC System/6000, and mainframe systems. The AIX operating system conforms to the POSIX IEEE standard for open operating systems. It supports X-WINDOW system and AIX windows (based on the OSF/Motif). IBM's strategic direction is to provide tools and protocols that will give a consistent view of applications regardless of whether they are running on the UNIX family of systems or the SAA systems. IBM intends to integrate UNIX enterprise networks with SAA Enterprise Information Systems. A customer will be able to choose between UNIX solutions and SAA solutions. In general the current UNIX customers will follow UNIX standards and the IBM SNA customers will migrate to SAA networks based on SNA/LU 6.2 architecture or OSI/RM. IBM will provide links between SAA and UNIX environments in the following areas:

• Common languages — FORTRAN, C, COBOL.

• Distributed data — ISO and ANSI distributed relational databases SQL standards, the Federal Information Processing Standards (FIPS), and the XPG3 SQL specifications. In addition to sharing databases the NFS architecture will be supported across the SAA and AIX family of systems.

• Presentation services — the AIX X-WINDOW based on OSF/Motif graphical user interface and the Presentation Manager on OS/2 will provide similar user interfaces to AIX and SAA environments.

• Mail exchange — Bridges will be provided to integrate the SAA Office Vision with UNIX Simple Mail Transfer Protocol (SMTP). Also the OSI X.400 protocol will be integrated with the AIX and SAA systems.

• Communication/Connectivity — between SNA/LU 6.2, OSI, TCP/IP, Token Ring (IEEE 802.5), Ethernet, and IEEE 802.3, X.25.

- Network Management — NetView focal point will be compatible with and manage SNA, OSI and TCP/IP networks.

It is IBM's intention to build the enterprise system in which UNIX, SAA, and OSI will be integrated or bridges provided between them.

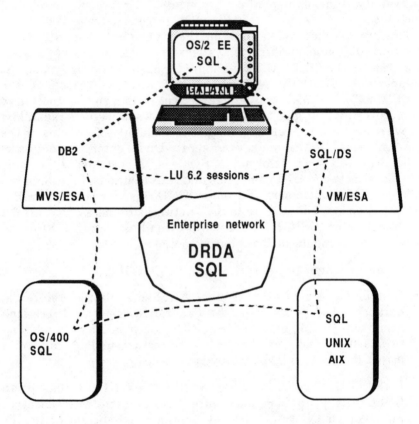

Figure 5.8 Distributed Relational Database Architecture (DRDA).

5.6 DISTRIBUTED RELATIONAL DATABASES

IBM's strategic direction is to provide a distributed relational database across the family of SAA and UNIX systems. The **Distributed Relational Database Architecture (DRDA)** uses the **logical unit 6.2, Distributed Data Management (DDM), SNA Management Services Architecture (MSA), Formatted Data Object Content Architecture (FDOCA),** and **Character Data Representation Architecture (CDRA)** as architectural building blocks for distributed databases operating in SAA and non-SAA environments. DRDA will allow users to share relational data residing anywhere in the SAA or UNIX enterprise (see Fig. 5.8). It uses the industry standard **Structured Query Language (SQL)** to access the database across all IBM platforms. IBM currently provides fully distributed databases on mainframes (DB/2 and SQL/DS), AS/400 (OS/400 Database Manager with SQL 400), and the OS/2 Requestor/Server Manager. On the AIX family of operating systems, IBM provides the ISO, ANSI SQL, the Federal Information Processing Standards (FIPS), and the XPG3 SQL. The SAA and AIX distributed databases will be fully integrated as illustrated in Fig. 5.8. In addition to distributed databases, IBM intends to provide sharing files across AIX and SAA enterprise. The TCP/IP NFS architecture will be supported across SAA and AIX family of systems.

5.7 IBM Network Management

IBM's strategic direction is to provide centralized network management for the enterprise system consisting of the SAA (OSI and LU 6.2) nodes and the UNIX TCP/IP nodes. IBM intends to provide management tools capable of managing multivendor environment. IBM has announced an enterprise-wide structure for system management called **SystemView**. SystemView network management applications are based on the OSI concept of **managers** and **agents**. SystemView will provide a consistent system management environment that focuses on the following areas:

* Integration of system management applications

* Automation of system management tasks

* Enterprise-wide structure (unified and consistent set of management applications)

* Openness (SystemView is based on SAA, OSI and TCP/IP open management standards)

* Multivendor environment

SystemView defines an open and common set of standards for developing system management applications. IBM and third-party vendors will modify and develop new applications that will comply with the SystemView structure. Therefore, system management applications developed by IBM or third-party vendors will have consistent user interface and structure. Therefore, these applications can be easily integrated into a single enterprise-wide system management.

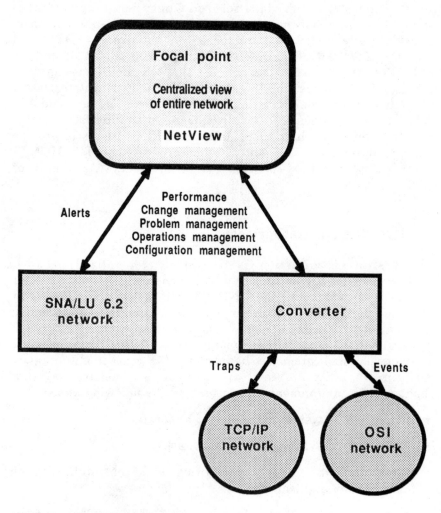

Figure 5.9 IBM network management.

The following is a list of products announced by IBM that will comply with the SystemView structure:

- SAA Asset Manager (SOD)

- SAA Delivery Manager (SOD)

- GraphicsView/2

- Workstation Data Save Facility (VM)

- NetView V2 — NetView Graphics Monitor Facility

- Information/Management (SOD)

- Information/System (SOD)

The centralized view of the networks is achieved by the IBM's **Focal Point (NetView)** as illustrated in Fig. 5.9. The SNA alerts are generated by SNA nodes and forwarded to NetView to be stored in operator log files or to be displayed on the console. The focal point supports such network management functions as performance measurements, change management, problem management, operations management, and configuration management. IBM will also integrate the SNA, OSI and TCP/IP network managements by providing converters capable of changing OSI or TCP/IP network management flows into SNA flows.

Part

2

Distributed and Cooperative Processing

6

APPC and SAA/CPI-C Concepts

Part 2 of this book concentrates on application design issues using the Advanced Program-to-Program Communications (APPC) and the SAA/CPI-C Common Programming Interface-Communications (CPI-C) distributed architectures. The terms **cooperative processing** and **distributed processing** are often used interchangeably. IBM defines though the cooperative processing as the relationship between a distributed function residing in a programmable workstation (e.g., the user interface) and a different distributed function residing on a host (e.g., the main program logic). **Cooperative processing** implies that **different functions** of an application reside on different machines and they cooperate together (work together) to execute a single unit of work (called a **transaction**). This is different from **distributed processing**, which implies that the **same function** (e.g., distributed database access) reside in different machines. IBM has addressed the problem of incompatibilities among various operating systems by defining a set of common communication and programming architectures across a wide range of IBM operating systems (such as OS/2, AS/400, and mainframes). These common architectures are an integral part of the Systems Application Architecture (SAA), which is IBM's strategic direction for enterprise computing in the 1990s.

The SNA logical unit type 6.2 is the SAA common communication protocol that was specifically designed to deal with distributed and cooperative processing environments. Chapters 3 and 4 of this book discussed the basic concepts of LU 6.2 and cooperative processing. The reader is strongly advised to review these chapters. This section compares the APPC and CPI-C architectures and discusses the basic application design issues of distributed transaction programs.

6.1 APPC AND CPI-C INTERFACES

APPC and SAA/CPI-C are IBM's strategic architectures that define a set of protocols, based on the SNA logical unit type 6.2 architecture, for program-to-program communications. The LU 6.2 architecture was introduced in 1982, and its main objective was to define:

• Common functions for designing distributed applications

• The environment for distributed transaction processing

The major differences between APPC and CPI-C standards come from the fact that APPC was introduced in 1984, three years prior to the SAA announcement and it did not impose any syntax rules on application programming interfaces. CPI-C, on the other hand, was introduced in 1988, and it complies with the syntax rules imposed by SAA's common programming interface.

6.1.1 APPC

Advanced Program-to-Program Communications (APPC) has been designed to enhance the SNA network in order to support **distributed** (also called **cooperative**) **processing**. APPC provides application programmers with LU 6.2 defined distributed functions for cooperative processing application design. The distributed **APPC functions** (also referred to as **LU 6.2 verbs**) have a representative syntax (e.g., [MC_]ALLOCATE, [MC_]SEND_DATA,..., [MC_]DEALLOCATE) described in Chaps. 4 and 7 of this book. The representative syntax describes the different distributed functions, and it was not designed to impose any syntax rules on different LU 6.2 implementations. Therefore, the LU 6.2 architecture allows different APPC implementations to implement the most suitable application programming interface (API) for the particular operating system.

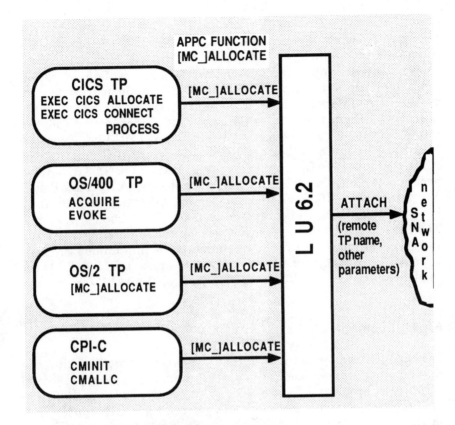

Figure 6.1 CICS, OS/400, OS/2 APIs, and CPI-C.

Figure 6.1 illustrates the different syntaxes used in different environments for the APPC [MC_]ALLOCATE function which allocates a mapped or a basic conversation. The application code written for LU 6.2 CICS, AS/400, and OS/2 transaction programs (TPs) performing the same APPC [MC_]ALLOCATE function differs significantly from one another and from the syntax imposed by the SAA/CPI-C architecture. In the CICS/LU 6.2 environment the allocation process is split into two parts. The EXEC CICS [GDS] ALLOCATE establishes an LU-LU session, if it's not already established, and allocates the session to the local TP. The EXEC CICS [GDS] CONNECT PROCESS completes the allocation process of a mapped or a basic conversation. CICS builds and buffers the SNA ATTACH header which contains the [MC_]ALLOCATE parameters for transmission to the remote LU. Similarly, the allocation process on an AS/400 is split into two parts. The ACQUIRE operation binds the LU 6.2 session, and the EVOKE operation builds the ATTACH header. The Communications Manager of OS/2 EE uses the [MC_]ALLOCATE verb to initiate conversations, which is the same as the APPC architecture representative syntax that describes the conversation initiation function. This shows that different APPC implementations use considerably different syntax rules to perform the same distributed functions. Figure 6.1 also shows that, irrespective of the implementation differences, the [MC_]ALLOCATE function performed by CICS, AS/400, OS/2, or an SAA/CPI-C programmer (CMINIT and CMALLC calls) maps to a unique SNA "ATTACH" header (the same for all LU 6.2 implementations). A remote TP does not detect any difference in the incoming allocation request from CICS, AS/400, OS/2, CPI-C, or other vendor LU 6.2 implementations. The LU 6.2 architecture is independent of the underlying operating systems and maps all the programming verbs into unique SNA/LU 6.2 network messages. These messages are understood by all LU 6.2 implementations (e.g. CICS, AS/400, OS/2, or SAA/CPI-C).

6.1.2 Incompatibilities

Incompatibilities among different types of hardware and the operating systems used on IBM equipment have represented significant problems. Figure 6.1 illustrates the incompatibility of APPC programming interfaces among different IBM environments (OS/2, AS/400, and CICS). The following is a list of some problems encountered by businesses with a diversity of incompatible systems and architectures:

• Applications have to be rewritten for each environment.

• Programmers and end users have to be retrained when moved from one operating environment to another.

• Programmers have to write several versions of the same application.

• The software purchased by customers or developed by the programmers may not run in the future because of a need to migrate to a bigger machine with a different operating system and programming tools.

• Compilers, application generators, and database managers, while similar in function, differ among different operating environments.

6.1.3 SAA Requirements

Many businesses have invested a considerable amount of money in a variety of types of equipment ranging from personal computers, midrange minicomputers, and mainframes. Within the same computer enterprise there exists a need to satisfy the following user requirements:

- Portable resources. Businesses need to move employees, move data and applications, re-use applications and write new applications.

- Consistency for users and programmers. The computer enterprise must provide a consistent user interface which is independent of the hardware and operating systems. The computer enterprise must also provide common programming interfaces allowing the development of consistent and portable applications within the enterprise.

- Distributed applications. Users need to develop applications that can be used on or distributed among systems at different geographic locations within the computer enterprise.

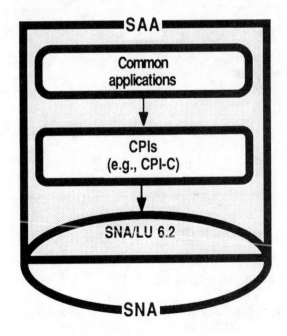

Figure 6.2 Relationships between SAA, SNA, and LU 6.2.

Systems Application Architecture (SAA) was announced in 1987 to address the incompatibility problems among different systems. SAA is a collection of interfaces, protocols, and products designed to provide a consistent environment for programmers and end users across a broad range of IBM systems (OS/2, AS/400, and mainframes). The logical unit type 6.2 architecture was chosen as the common communications architecture for the SAA enterprise. Figure 6.2 shows the relationships between SAA, SNA, and LU 6.2 architectures. SNA is IBM's networking architecture, a set of rules for communication among a diverse group of IBM products. SNA was described in Chap. 2 of this book. SNA supports many logical unit types (e.g., LU 1, LU 2, LU 3, LU 7, or LU 6.2). Only LU 6.2 is an integral part of both the SNA architecture as well as the SAA architecture. SAA defines the networking architecture (e.g., SNA/LU 6.2) as well as the Common User Access (CUA) and Common Programming Interface (CPI) standards. Figure 6.2 shows that CPI-C is an integral part of the SAA CPI standard.

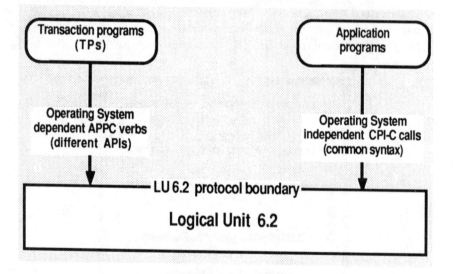

Figure 6.3 APPC and CPI-C interfaces.

6.1.4 CPI Communications (CPI-C)

Even though both CPI-C and APPC are based on the same common communications architecture (LU 6.2), which produces common network messages, the application programming interfaces (APIs) used by different APPC implementations may differ from one environment to another as illustrated in Fig. 6.1. Therefore, the APPC applications are not portable among different operating environments. With the SAA announcement in 1987, one of the most important requirements was for SAA applications to be portable among different SAA environments. The APPC programming verbs needed to be enhanced with an application programming interface that is consistent across the SAA environments. The **Common Programming Interface-Communications (CPI-C)** (also referred to **CPI Communications**) was introduced to provide a consistent application programming interface for program-to-program communications in the SAA environments. Figure 6.3 illustrates the major difference between APPC and SAA/CPI-C programming interfaces. The APPC programming calls differ from CPI-C communication calls in that CPI-C calls require exact syntax common to all implementations (CMINIT, CMALLC, etc.) whereas APPC allows implementation specific syntax. The APPC implementations should migrate to SAA/CPI-C to comply with the SAA architecture. This would assure enterprise-wide portable applications. Portable applications do not have to be re-written for each environment thereby reducing development, maintenance and training costs. Figure 6.1 shows the CPI-C calls for the LU 6.2 [MC_] ALLOCATE function (CMINIT and CMALLC). The application programs on OS/2, AS/400 and CICS need to migrate to CPI-C interfaces to comply with SAA. Then all the applications would issue exactly the same CPI-C calls (CMINIT and CMALLC) and be portable across the different operating environments. The announcements of APPC/MVS on mainframes includes the CPI-C interface. The OS/2 CPI-C and AS/400 CPI-C (or routines that emulate the CPI-C interface) can also be obtained from IBM or third-party vendors. SAA/CPI-C is discussed in detail in Chap. 8.

6.1.5 Functional Relationship

The CPI-C calls have been built on top of the APPC/LU 6.2 verbs. Figure 6.4 illustrates a functional relationship between APPC verbs and CPI-C calls. All the SAA/CPI-C calls can be mapped into corresponding APPC verbs. Then, the local LU maps the APPC verbs into unique SNA/LU 6.2 network messages. The LU 6.2 messages (GDS variables, logical records, or SNA headers) are sent to the remote LU over the LU-LU session. The actual network messages are transmitted via the SNA path control network. The SNA/LU 6.2 network messages were discussed in Sec. 3.7 of this book. For example, the CPI-C CMINIT and CMALLC calls can be mapped into the APPC/LU 6.2 [MC_]ALLOCATE verb. The [MC_]ALLOCATE function is then executed by the local LU, which builds an SNA ATTACH header. This ATTACH header is the unique SNA network message that will be sent to the remote LU to initiate a conversation. The CPI-C CMSEND call can be mapped into the APPC [MC_]SEND_DATA verb, which is changed by the LU into a send GDS variable for mapped conversations or logical records for basic conversations.

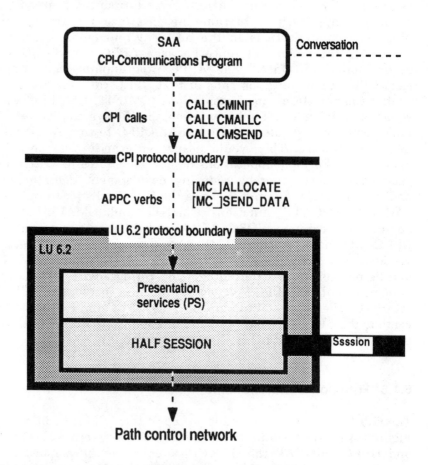

Figure 6.4 Functional relationship of APPC and CPI-C.

Many LU 6.2 implementations may not currently have the SAA/CPI-C interface. It is quite easy, though, to write CPI-C applications on operating systems that currently have only the APPC interface. Application programmers need to develop a set of subroutines, called CMINIT, CMALLC, and CMSEND, that follow the CPI-C syntax rules. Each subroutine may use the current APPC programming interface to execute the CPI-C calls. Then, all other applications may use the written subroutines to perform the LU 6.2 defined distributed functions. The subroutines would provide an interface similar to CPI Communications calls, and they can be later replaced by the SAA/CPI-C programmatic interface. The Common Programming Interface-Communications (CPI-C) uses the following terms and naming conventions:

- A CPI-C **application program** is equivalent to an APPC transaction program (TP).

- SAA/CPI-C programs exchange data using a **conversation**. Both mapped and basic conversations are supported. Read Secs. 4.2 and 4.3 for more information on basic and mapped conversations.

- The communicating CPI-C programs are called **conversation partners**.

- The character set used to name a network resource, such as logical units and transaction programs, is different from the APPC character set. For example, service transaction program (STP) names are not allowed to be used by CPI-C programs. Different implementations may define, installation-specific CPI-C privileged programs, that are capable of communicating with service transaction programs.

The following APPC/LU 6.2 functions are not supported by CPI Communications (CPI-C) architecture:

- **Mapping** — used on APPC mapped conversations. This option allows a programmer to map data via implementation-specific maps prior to sending the data to the remote program.

- **FMH data** — used on APPC mapped conversations. This option allows TPs to exchange user defined function management headers (FMHs).

- **PIP data** — allows a local APPC transaction program to allocate a conversation and to pass a set of initial parameters to the remote TP.

- **Conversation level security** — allows a local TP to supply user_ID, password, and profile at allocation time that can be validated at the remote LU for each conversation.

6.1.6 APPC-to-CPI-C Conversations

The APPC functions that are not supported by the CPI-C architecture belong to the LU 6.2 optional function set. The LU 6.2 base set and the option sets were discussed in Sec. 4.5 of this book. The base set of distributed functions must be implemented by all open APPC implementations. Therefore, programs written using installation-specific APPC interfaces can communicate with programs written using the CPI Communications interface (see Fig. 6.5). The APPC programs that implemented the options listed above would have to be slightly modified. The two programmers would have to agree on the method of implementing the above function. They can be implemented as a part of the user data definition exchanged by issuing the APPC [MC_]SEND_DATA or CPI-C CMSEND verbs. Figure 6.5 shows a CPI-C program B communicating with an APPC transaction program TP A.

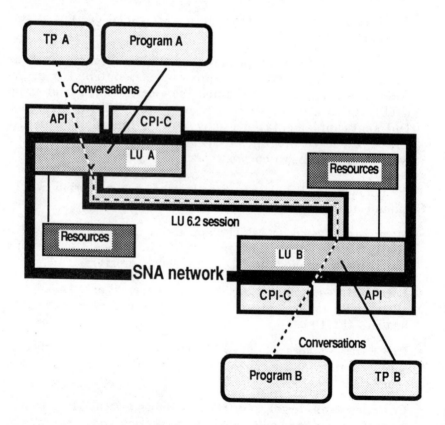

Figure 6.5 APPC-to-CPI-C communication.

The following is a typical exchange that may occur between TP A and program B:

- Program B issues CMINIT and CMALLC calls to initiate a conversation with TP A. The logical connection between a pair of transaction programs (e.g., program B and TP A) is called a conversation. Conversations are typically short-lived connections corresponding to a single end-user transaction.

- LU B establishes a session with LU A, if it was not already established, and it allocates the session to program B. An SNA session is a long-lived logical connection between LUs.

- First, LU B maps the CPI-C CMINIT and CMALLC calls into an SNA/LU 6.2 ATTACH header that carries the name of the remote transaction program to be allocated (the TP A).

- LU A receives the ATTACH header and starts TP A.

- TP A receives the allocation request and accepts the conversation.

- The conversation is assigned to the session, and it has an exclusive use of the session for the duration of the conversation.

- Now program B and TP A use the conversation and cooperate with each other to execute a distributed transaction.

- When the transaction is completed, program B may issue the CPI-C call CMDEAL to deallocate the conversation.

The following is a list of major APPC or CPI-C session and conversation characteristics:

- Sessions connect logical units and conversations connect the transaction programs. LU A is connected with LU B via a logical connection called a session. TP A is connected to program B via a logical connection called a conversation.

- A conversation has an exclusive use of a session for the duration of the conversation.

- A single LU may serve many programs. LU A runs both TP A and program A. Both programs may issue LU 6.2 verbs at the same time. Since there is currently only a single session between LU A and LU B and the session is already assigned to TP A and program B, LU A may buffer all the verbs received from program A until the session is released by the current conversation.

- A session can be shared by many TPs and conversations. Successive conversations may share the same session serially. Once program B or TP A dealloacates the conversation, the session is released to other other programs. For example, program A may establish a conversation with TP B.

- An LU may run many TPs successively, concurrently, or both.

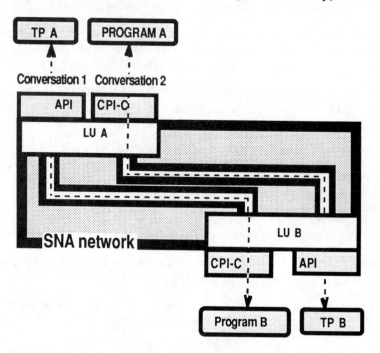

Figure 6.6 Multiple connections.

- The LU 6.2 architecture supports multiple sessions. Multiple sessions to the same LU are called parallel sessions (see Fig. 6.6). The BIND sender becomes the primary logical unit (PLU) for the session and the BIND receiver becomes the secondary logical unit. Figure 6.6 shows parallel sessions between LU A and LU B. Each logical unit might have established one of the sessions. Therefore, LU A may act as PLU for one of the sessions and SLU for the other session.

- Multiple conversations between different pairs of TPs can be active concurrently using distinct sessions. Figure 6.6 illustrates two concurrent conversations. TP A and program B use conversation 1 to exchange data, and at the same time TP B and program A communicate via conversation 2.

6.2 Design Considerations

In cooperative processing, different programs communicate with one another via conversations to execute an indivisible unit of work such as a transaction. A conversation connects an executable local transaction program code (called **TP instance**) with a partner TP instance.

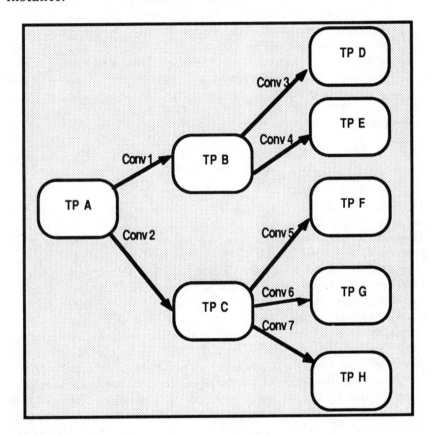

Figure 6.7 Conversations with many TP instances.

6.2.1 TP Instances

A single instance of a program may communicate simultaneously with one or more instances of remote programs. However, both APPC and CPI-C architectures are based on LU 6.2, which defines a conversation as a logical connection between exactly two TP instances (one-to-one relationship only). Figure 6.7 illustrates a transaction program TP A communicating with remote TP instances TP B and TP C over two conversations, Conv 1 and Conv 2. TP B itself may also establish conversations with remote TP instances by issuing the allocation requests to TP D and TP E. This establishes conversations Conv 3 and Conv 4. TP C establishes 3 additional conversations Conv 5, Conv 6, and Conv 7, with TP F, TP G, and TP H, respectively. Each of these conversations is a separate entity with a separate environment and protocol. All the conversations, though, may take a part in the processing of a single distributed transaction. The TPs may share distributed resources such as distributed databases, and they can also distribute the user interface (presentation services) and the function (the primary logic) in order to process the transaction. The transaction programs themselves (TP A, TP B,...,TP H) are responsible for coordinating and managing the individual conversations.

6.2.2 Half-Duplex Design

The LU 6.2 half-duplex, flip-flop protocol requires that the two communicating transaction programs (the local and the remote TPs) follow the send/receive mode protocol. The send/receive mode protocol is enforced by the LU for each conversation. Transaction programs exchange data over a conversation that corresponds to an SNA bracket. A single conversation is assigned to a single session. A conversation has an exclusive use of the session (one bracket is allowed at a time per session) for the duration of the conversation, and it must follow the half-duplex, flip-flop protocol. This means that the local and remote logical units exchange data in one direction at a time on a single session. The program can perform the functions that are allowed only in a particular conversation state. Figure 6.8 illustrates a typical conversation and the rules that must be followed by the source (local) TP and the target (remote) TP. The source TP initiates a conversation by issuing the LU 6.2 [MC_]ALLOCATE (abbreviated to ALLOCATE in Fig 6-8) verb. The TP state changes from the Reset state to the Send state. The source TP is now allowed to send data by issuing the [MC_]SEND_DATA (abbreviated to SEND in Fig. 6.8) verbs. The remote LU receives the allocation request and starts a new instance of the target TP. The target TP enters the Receive state and is allowed to receive information only by issuing the [MC_]RECEIVE_AND_WAIT (abbreviated to RECEIVE in Fig 6.8) verb. The LU 6.2 half-duplex, flip-flop state changes from BETB (between-brackets state) to INB (in bracket-state). Once the session is INB state, no additional brackets can be started until the current bracket (conversation) is over. When the source TP is ready to receive data it issues the [MC_]RECEIVE_AND_WAIT verb and changes the state to the Receive state. The local LU sets the CD (change direction indicator) and sends the accumulated data with the indicator to the remote LU.

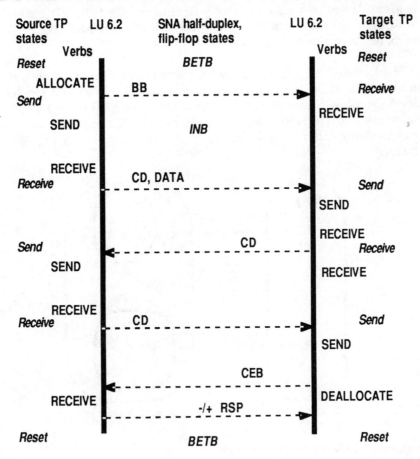

Figure 6.8 Half-duplex design.

The remote LU receives the data with the CD set and changes the target TP state to the Send state. Now, the target TP may send and the source TP must receive. The source and target transaction programs flip-flop the send and receive states by issuing the [MC_]RECEIVE_AND_WAIT verb. Finally, the target TP ends the conversation by issuing the [MC_]DEALLOCATE (abbreviated to DEALLOCATE in Fig. 6.8) verb, which is sent across the session as

CEB (conditional end-of-bracket) indicator. When the LU 6.2 conversation ends successfully, the two TPs again enter the Reset state and the LUs enter the BETB state. The session is now accessible by other conversations. There are some exceptions to the send/receive protocol. The TP that is currently in the Receive state is also allowed to send an error by issuing the [MC_]SEND_ERROR verb, send an attention by issuing the [MC_]REQUEST_TO_SEND verb, or abort the conversation.

The half-duplex, flip-flop protocol should not be confused with the protocols used for the transmission medium. The lines and the link level protocols are independent of the session protocols. The lines, modems and transmission protocols can be full-duplex and they can exchange information for many session partners at the same time.

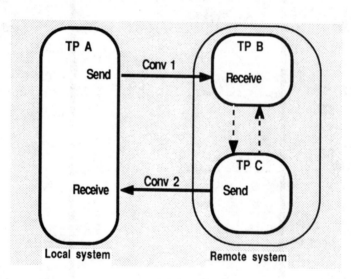

Figure 6.9 Full-duplex data exchange.

6.2.3 Full-Duplex Design

Most distributed transactions require half-duplex application design (e.g., banking transactions such as money deposits, money withdrawals, retrieving information on customers or their banking accounts). The APPC and CPI-C applications use the half-duplex, flip-flop protocol described above, which is less error-prone (only one conversation partner can send at a time) and more secure than the full-duplex protocol in which either program may send and receive at any time. CPI-C or APPC programs are capable of communicating with multiple partners by establishing multiple concurrent conversations. An incoming allocation request starts a new TP instance and a new conversation. Then, the TP instance can initiate additional conversations with other remote partners by issuing the [MC_]ALLOCATE verbs or the CMALLC calls. If a full-duplex operation (sending and receiving of information at the same time) is required between two different systems (e.g., a host and a PC), then two half-duplex conversations may be established.

Figure 6.9 illustrates the full-duplex data exchange between local and remote systems. TP A, residing on a local system, establishes two half-duplex conversations with TP B and TP C, residing on a remote system. Then, TP A uses the unique conversation identifiers (Conv 1 and Conv 2) as parameters that must be present on all CPI-C calls or APPC verbs to distinguish between the two conversations. One of the TP A conversations (e.g., Conv 1) can be put in the Send state and the other in the Receive state. The local and the remote systems may then send and receive data at the same time in a full-duplex mode. The two TP instances (TP B and TP C) residing on the remote system would have to communicate with each other to coordinate the full-duplex operation or to perform error recovery in case of application errors. TP A must be designed in such a way that it is never suspended for a particular conversation (for example, by performing the [MC_]RECEIVE_AND_WAIT function for Conv 1) from which it could not communicate with other partners. TP A should check to see if there is data available for each conversation without waiting for the data to be received. One possible solution would be to use the LU 6.2 defined [MC_] RECEIVE_IMMEDIATE function allowing the checking of the LU's receive buffer for data.

6.2.4 Synchronization Point Services

Error recovery and database consistency are critical to the design of distributed transactions. The LU 6.2 option set defines the highest level of resource synchronization, called called **Synchronization Point Services** (also referred to as **syncpoint**). Syncpoint uses the SNA/LU 6.2 two-phase commit protocol to ensure consistency throughout a distributed transaction. Syncpoint protects and synchronizes changes to protected resources such as distributed databases. The LU 6.2 itself takes the responsibility for ensuring the consistency of all protected resources. The LU will either **COMMIT** (make the changes permanent) or **BACKOUT** (reverse the changes) to protected resources. All conversations allocated with synchronization level set to SYNCPT are considered protected resources.

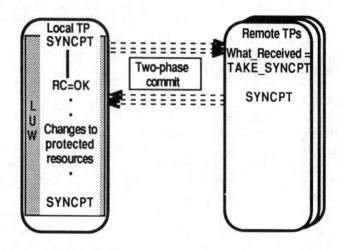

Figure 6.10 Synchronization Point Services.

A transaction program establishes synchronization points in the program logic by performing the SYNCPT or the BACKOUT functions. SYNCPT advances all protected resources to the next synchronization point. BACKOUT restores all protected resources to the previous synchronization point. An indivisible logical unit of Work (LUW) is defined as a collection of autonomous changes to protected resources between two synchronizations (see Fig. 6.10). The LU is responsible for committing the entire LUW to the next synchronization point or for restoring the changes made to the protected resources. All transaction programs participating in the LUW must agree to commit the protected resources. If any of the participating TPs disagrees, the LU 6.2 is responsible for canceling the last LUW and restoring resources to the previous syncpoint. Figure 6.10 illustrates synchronization processing. The local TP issues a SYNCPT verb to the local LU 6.2. The local LU performs an SNA two-phase commit on all conversations allocated with synchronization level set to SYNCPT. The remote TPs receive TAKE_SYNCPT and if there are no errors they also issue a SYNCPT verb to propagate the synchronization on their protected conversations. The SYNCPT verb completes with a return code equal to OK only if all protected resources across all protected conversations were committed without any errors. If a failure occurs during synchronization processing itself, the LU 6.2 defines a resynchronization process which allows the communicating LUs to exchange the status of all protected resources and to recover from the failure. The RESYNC service transaction program is specifically architected to perform the resynchronization processing. Syncpoint is an optional APPC function and is usually implemented in the host environment (e.g., CICS).

6.2.5 Banking Design Example

APPC and CPI-C provide programmers with flexible and powerful LU 6.2 peer-to-peer protocols for designing distributed transactions. Using these protocols application programmers can develop robust and powerful applications that can run on less expensive personal computers. Distributed and cooperative processing can be used effectively for insurance companies, retail businesses, and financial institutions with many small branch offices. The branch offices may be required to keep and preprocess the data locally on their local area networks (LANs). The data can then be used to update corporate host databases and applications. In some cases communications between different branches may be required as well. Transaction programs can be developed on LANs that are capable of establishing conversations with host applications as well as other TPs residing in other branches. As an example, let us look at a network for a typical banking application (such as Current Accounts Balance System). The following are the major network requirements (see Fig. 6.11):

- The network should be available all the time.

- Local-branch customers must be processed locally even if the mainframe is down.

- The data related to local customers should be kept at the branches.

- The branches need to communicate with host applications to access the corporate database.

- The branches need to communicate with one another.

- The response time should be < 1 s for local transactions and < 5 s for interbranch or host transactions.

- Database consistency across the entire computer enterprise is required (the hosts and the LANs).

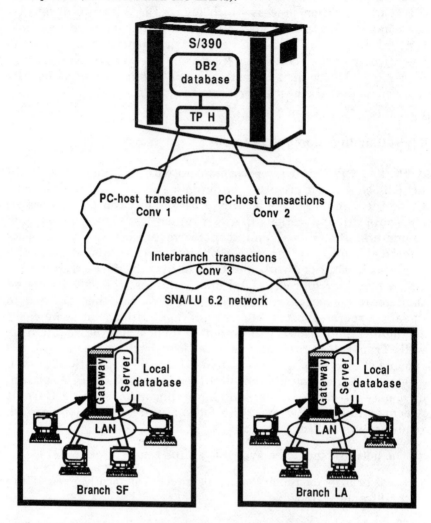

Figure 6.11 Distributed banking application design.

The only SNA protocol capable of host and interbranch communications is the logical unit type 6.2. Therefore, the programming interfaces chosen for such distributed designs must be based on the LU 6.2 architecture. Both CPI-C and APPC are based on the logical unit type 6.2 and are suitable for this design. Figure 6.11 illustrates a suggested network topology. The network will consist of the following components:

1. An IBM S/390 with a DB2 relational database in the New York bank headquarters. The host database is responsible for data integrity, recovery, and reliability.

2. An IBM SNA/LU 6.2 backbone network consisting of front-end processors running NCP.

3. The Local Area Networks (LANs) will be located at the branch offices. Figure 6.11 shows the LANs in the Los Angeles (LA) branch office and in the San Francisco (SF) branch office. Each branch has approximately 10 requester terminals communicating with a local database server via the local network protocols (such as NETBIOS) or via LU 6.2 conversations. The server also can act as an LU 6.2 gateway providing connections to the host applications and interbranch communications. The SNA/LU 6.2 gateways are available from many vendors (e.g., IBM, Novell, NSA, EICON or DCA). For more information on LU 6.2 gateways, read Sec. 3.4.3 of this book.

The network topology with personal computers residing on local area networks, which are connected to mainframes and other branches via SNA/LU 6.2 gateways, is very flexible. It allows programmers to develop distributed applications capable of local processing as well as communications with mainframe applications and applications residing on remote LANs in other branches. Transactions for local customers will be handled by the LAN (client/server) applications that may use LU 6.2 conversations, NETBIOS, or other LANs requester/server protocols. The LAN-based approach allows the processing of most of the local customers' requests by the local LAN database servers, and it has several benefits:

- It offloads the mainframe CPU processing.

- It improves network efficiency. Less information needs to be exchanged over communication links. Presentation services and panel management can be handled locally by the terminal workstations themselves . The data can also be processed locally by the LAN database server and only occasionally exchanged with applications residing on the host.

- It reduces corporate costs by distributing resources, such as databases, and taking advantage of the personal computer's processing power.

- It improves productivity by reducing the reliance on the host and the wide area network and therefore downtime.

- It improves the response time by processing most of the transactions locally (e.g., for all local-branch customers.)

- LAN users may share local resources, such as files, databases, or printers.

- LAN applications may communicate with one another without being affected by host downtime.

The following is a suggested LU 6.2 application design for the Current Account Balance System:

A. A local customer withdraws the money from his or her branch office.

1. The transaction program (called TPPC), residing on the local area network workstation, displays a menu to a teller and waits for a new transaction to be entered. The customer account number and the amount being withdrawn is entered. Let us assume that the LAN workstation communicates with the LAN server using LU 6.2 conversations. TPPC formats the data into its send buffer and establishes a conversation with the LAN server by performing the LU 6.2 MC_ALLOCATE function. Then TPPC sends its request to the server by issuing the MC_SEND_DATA verb and the MC_RECEIVE_AND_WAIT verb. The LAN server receives the request, and since a database update is required, the server establishes a conversation with the application residing on the mainframe (by performing the APPC/LU 6.2 MC_ALLOCATE, the MC_SEND_DATA, and the MC_RECEIVE_AND_WAIT functions) to coordinate account balances between the host and the local server databases. The host application updates the corporate database and returns the response to the LAN server. The LAN server returns the new customer account balance to the TPPC and deallocates the conversation with the host and the TPPC. Notice that for inquiry types of transactions (retrieve an account balance, retrieve information on local customers, generate local reports, etc.), the server may retrieve the data from the local database and it does not have to communicate with the host application at all. In the case of the host or the network being down, the server may update its local database only and log all the transactions locally in the log file. When the network and the host comes up the server must resend the logged transaction to update the corporate database.

B. A remote customer withdraws the money from another branch.

1. The transaction program (called TPPCR) residing on a remote LAN workstation establishes an LU 6.2 interbranch remote conversation with the server residing in the customer's branch office via the LU 6.2 gateways. To establish the conversation the TPPCR performs the   MC_ALLOCATE function. Then TPPCR sends its request on the conversation to the server by issuing   the MC_SEND_DATA verb and the MC_RECEIVE_AND_WAIT verb. The LU 6.2 gateway routes the TPPCR interbranch request throughout the SNA network to the requested branch. The local branch server (residing at the customer's branch office) treats the remote conversations in exactly the same way as if the conversations were started by the local LAN's workstations (e.g., TPPC described above). Then, the local server performs the same functions as described in step A above.

The biggest drawback of this solution is the fact that the application programmers are responsible for the development of distributed transaction programs on PCs and mainframes that must assure **database integrity**. The database integrity is not a trivial issue, particularly if network failure occurs during remote updates. The applications would be required to have quite complicated logic to know when to commit or when to backout the database. It would be much better if we could get products that will assure the database consistency across all the branches and the mainframes rather than relying on the application design itself. IBM has defined a **Distributed Relational Database Architecture (DRDA)** dealing specifically with access and consistency of distributed relational data. DRDA is based on the logical unit type 6.2 (LU 6.2), Distributed Data Management Architecture (DDM), SNA Management Services Architecture (MSA), Formatted Data Object Content Architecture (FDOCA), and Character Data Representation Architecture (CDRA). The IBM strategic directions is to provide products that integrate the OS/2 distributed databases with the AS/400 distributed databases and the DB/2 and SQL/DS distributed host databases. At the time of writing this book, the distributed databases on OS/2, AS/400, and mainframes were not integrated into a single enterprise-wide database. With a single distributed database the design for the banking example described above would assure database consistency throughout the entire enterprise. Instead of writing the actual LU 6.2 calls, the transaction programs would use SQL database calls to access the enterprise-wide distributed data. For example, the remote TPPCR would issue only an SQL "update." The DRDA function receiving the SQL request would determine (using preconfigured network-wide directories) where the data resides and the DRDA server would automatically establish the required LU 6.2 conversations with the remote relational database systems residing on LANs in other branches or on the host. Also, if any failure occurred, the DRDA would automatically rollback or commit the databases to a consistent state throughout the distributed enterprise-wide database.

6.3 Verbs and Message Flows

Advanced Program-to-Program Communications (APPC) and the SAA/CPI-C Common Programming Interface Communications (CPI-C) calls map into the same LU 6.2 distributed functions which generate the same unique network messages. The exact network message flows can be predicted based on the sequence of APPC verbs or CPI-C calls issued by a programmer.

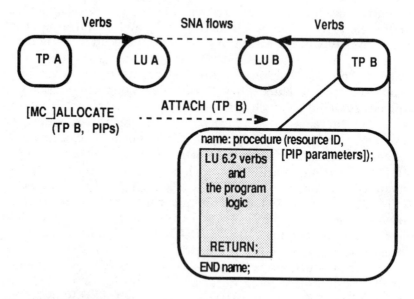

Figure 6.12 Transaction program structure.

6.3.1 Transaction Program Structure

Figure 6.12 illustrates this mapping for the conversation allocation sequence. TP A issues the [MC_]ALLOCATE verb, passing the remote program name TP B and optionally the program initiation parameters (PIPs). The local logical unit LU A builds the appropriate SNA ATTACH header and transmits it to the remote logical unit LU B. Upon receipt of the SNA ATTACH header, LU B creates a new instance of transaction program TP B in an implementation-specific manner. The LU also assigns a unique resource ID (referred to as conversation ID) that must be supplied on every verb following the [MC_]ALLOCATE verb in order to uniquely identify this conversation. Figure 6.12 also shows the general structure of a transaction program containing the following:

name — the transaction program name (e.g., TP B). TP A supplies this name in its allocation request which is also carried in the SNA ATTACH header.

resource ID — when the allocation request is received the LU creates a new conversation and places the unique resource ID (referred to as **conversation ID**) into this variable.

PIP parameters — a variable into which the LU places program initiation parameters. The PIP parameters may be supplied as parameters by the allocating program. TP A supplies PIP parameters on the [MC_]ALLOCATE verb which is transmitted by the LU as a special GDS variable. PIP parameters belong to the optional APPC function set and it is not supported by CPI-C.

6.3.2 Transaction Program Verb Execution

A transaction program issues verbs serially (one at a time) to its local logical unit. The presentation services layer of the local LU is responsible for an interpretation and execution of LU 6.2 verbs. The local LU checks the verb for syntax or any other errors, checks if the verb is allowed to be executed in the current transaction program state, and buffers the verb for later transmission. The TP is suspended until the local LU checks and buffers the verb, and then returns control to the program. Figure 6.13 illustrates an execution of the [MC_]ALLOCATE verb. A local transaction program TP A issues the [MC_]ALLOCATE verb supplying the required parameters and suspends until the verb is processed by the local LU. The local LU executes the verb by checking if the supplied parameters are valid and whether TP A is allowed to issue the verb in the current conversation state. Assuming there are no errors the local LU buffers the [MC_]ALLOCATE verb locally in its send buffer for later transmission to the remote LU and returns control to TP A.

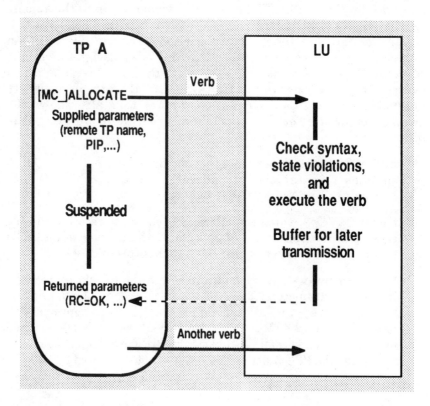

Figure 6.13 LU 6.2 verb execution.

6.3.3 Send/Receive Buffers

The local logical unit buffers all the verbs in its send buffer and it does not send any information across the session. As illustrated in Fig. 6.14, the three TP A verbs (Verb 1, Verb 2, and Verb 3) have been executed by the local logical unit type 6.2 and buffered for later transmission to the partner program. It is important to understand that the RC=OK merely means that the verb was executed and buffered by the local LU. The RC=OK does not imply that the information was delivered to the partner transaction program. The local transaction program (TP A) is responsible for coordinating checkpoints with the remote program. The LU 6.2 architecture defines, specifically for this purpose, the confirmation processing

([MC_]CONFIRM and [MC_]CONFIRMED verbs) and the synchronization processing (SYNCPT and BACKOUT verbs).

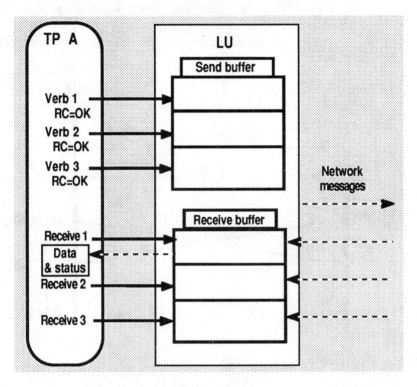

Figure 6.14 LU 6.2 send and receive buffers.

The local LU will transmit the data and control information buffered in its send buffer across the session if one of the following occurs:

1. The local LU accumulates an amount of data equal to an SNA maximum request unit (RU) size (also referred to as MAXRU size) for the session.

2. The transaction program issues a verb that causes the local LU to flush its send buffer. For example, the LU 6.2 [MC_]FLUSH verb flushes the local LU send buffer. The LU transmits all the accumulated data to the remote logical unit. Any LU 6.2 verb issued by the local transaction program that requires a response from the partner program (e.g., [MC_]CONFIRM, [MC_]RECEIVE_AND_WAIT, or SYNCPT) performs an implied MC_FLUSH verb.

Information received from the conversation partner is also buffered by the LU in its receive buffer. The local transaction program TP A may issue the [MC_]RECEIVE_AND_WAIT verb to get the data or the control information (such as change direction, confirmation request or synchronization processing) from the local LU's receive buffer (see Fig. 6.14).

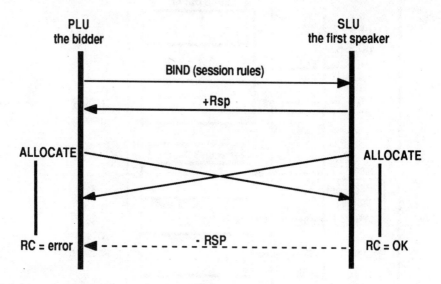

Figure 6.15 Allocation race condition.

6.3.4 Contention Polarities

When a session is established, each of the communicating TPs may start a conversation at the same time, creating an allocation race condition. The operator may define the sessions for which the local LU is designated to win the allocation race as **conversation-winner** (also called a **conwinner** or **first-speaker**) sessions. The sessions for which the local LU is designated to lose the allocation race are called **conversation-loser** (also called a conloser or **bidder**) sessions. Figure 6.15 shows the primary logical unit (PLU) defined as a conversation loser and the secondary logical unit (SLU) to be conversation loser. In the case of an allocation race the first speaker wins the allocation race and gets exclusive use of the session for the duration of the conversation. The bidder side has to wait until the session is released by the conversation winner to get access to the session. An operator may allow parallel sessions between the local and the remote logical units to prevent allocation race conditions.

The operator may then tune the session limits (the number of parallel sessions) and the number of conversation winners at each side of the connection.

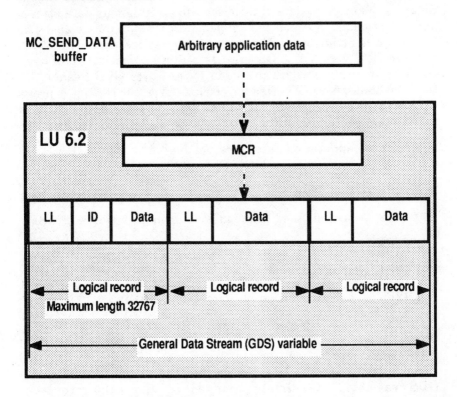

Figure 6.16 Message unit transformation.

6.3.5 Message Unit Transformation

Mapped conversation transaction programs exchange data by issuing the [MC_]SEND_DATA verb. The presentation services of the LU transforms the data into the General Data Stream (GDS) variable format before transmitting it to the remote LUs. Figure 6.16 illustrates the transformation process for mapped conversation data. The application buffer may contain data in an arbitrary record format agreed upon by the two communicating TPs. The application programmer, using mapped conversations, moves the application data (called a **data record**) into the data buffer that corresponds to a data parameter of the [MC_]SEND_DATA verb. The data record is a collection of arbitrary data, variables, and structures defined by the programmer. The LU first transforms the data to a contiguous data string called a **Mapped Conversation Record (MCR)**. The MCR differs from the data record in that it contains the original data transformed to a contiguous data stream and is optionally mapped via implementation specific maps. The logical units transform all mapped conversation data (the MCR) into the GDS variable. A General Data Stream variable consists of transaction program data preceded by a 4-byte GDS header (LL field, ID field). The GDS header consists of a 2-byte length prefix (LL) and a 2-byte ID format identifier describing the type of information contained in the variable such as:

X'12FF' — application data corresponding to one mapped
conversation MC_SEND_DATA verb

X'12F1' — null data

X'12F2' — user-defined function management headers (FMHs)

X'12F3' — map name

X'12F4' — application data

X'12F5' — program initiation parameters (PIPs)

X'12E4' — error log data

The SNA service transaction programs build their own GDS variables with specific IDs. Notice that the mapped conversation GDS variables are simply changed by the LUs into basic conversation logical records with predefined GDS headers. Basic conversations exchange data in logical record (LR) format by bypassing the mapped services component of the LU's presentation services layer. Therefore, the basic conversation programs are more efficient than the mapped conversation programs, although they require a programmer's understanding of the LU 6.2 data stream.

6.3.6 Flow Sequences

It is important to understand the network messages generated as a result of different verb sequences issued by transaction programs. This will allow programmers to design applications that generate less network messages, improve network efficiency and the overall performance. As discussed earlier, the LU buffers and blocks the programming verbs before sending them across the network. The programming verbs before sending them across the network. The verbs are transformed into SNA message units BIUs, PIUs and RUs. Most of the LU 6.2 verbs are carried simply as one or more bits set in the SNA request/response header (RH) or as an SNA function management data (FMH) header (see Fig. 6.17). The [MC_]SEND_DATA verb maps to logical records for basic conversations or a GDS variable for mapped conversations. Figure 6.17 illustrates the mapping of some of the LU 6.2 verbs into BIUs.

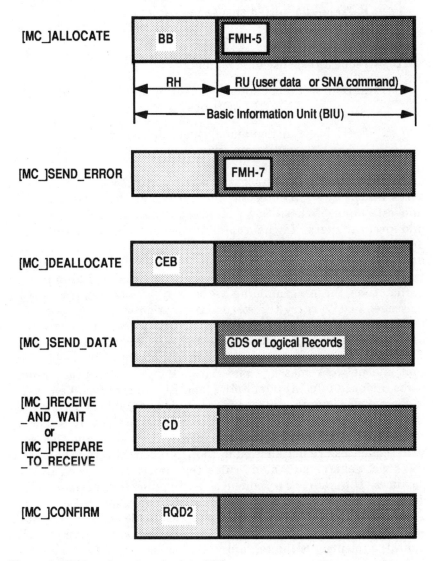

Figure 6.17 Mapping of verbs into BIUs.

SNA notation:

RH — request/response header indicators

   BB — begin-bracket indicator

   CEB — conditional end-of-bracket indicator

   CD — change-direction indicator

   RQD — definite-response indicator

   RQE — exception-response indicator

RU — request/response unit contents

   FMH-5 — function management header type 5, an
   SNA ATTACH header

   FMH-7 — function management header type 7, an
   application error header

The flow of network messages depends on the sequences of LU 6.2
verbs issued by the two communicating transaction programs. An
understanding of these flows is vital to the application designers
and programmers. If the communicating transaction programs
are designed properly, most of verbs are carried with the application
data being sent and they do not generate any additional network
messages. However, if there is no data in the local logical unit send
buffer, then the programming verbs may generate extra network
messages just to carry the status information across the session to
the remote transaction program. Figure 6.17 shows that many verbs
are carried simply as bits in the SNA request/response header.
Therefore, programmers may design applications in such a way
that one network message may carry many LU 6.2 programming
verbs (mapped into RH bits, FMHs, and RU data) across the network
to the partner logical unit. The partner LU is capable of decoding the
RH bits, FMHs, and RU data and can determine the verb sequences
received from the source TP. It is important to understand that some
verb sequences are not allowed in the LU 6.2 architecture because of
the strict send/receive mode rules that must be followed by both
partners. Different verb sequences and application designs will be
discussed in detail in Chap. 7 (for APPC) and Chap. 8 (for CPI-C).
Figures 6.18 to 6.21 show some simple examples of error-free flow
sequences and the resulting SNA chain sequences with the RH
indicator settings, RU data, and FMH headers.

Sequence 1

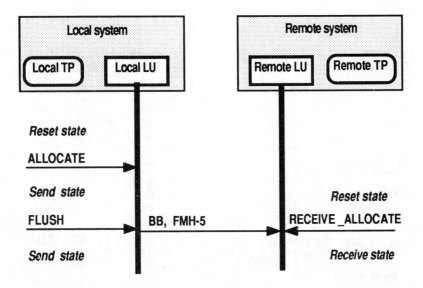

Figure 6.18 Conversation initiation sequence.

Figure 6.18 illustrates a possible sequence for starting conversations. The local TP issues the [MC_]ALLOCATE (abbreviated to ALLOCATE in Fig 6-18) verb. The local LU sets the begin-bracket (BB) indicator and builds the ATTACH header (FMH-5) in its local send buffer. No information is sent across yet. The local TP issues a [MC_]FLUSH verb, which flushes the LU's send buffer. The only information in the LU's send buffer is the [MC_]ALLOCATE verb. The resulting BIU is generated with BB in the RH and FMH-5 in the RU. The remote TP is started by the remote LU on the receipt of the ATTACH header. This design may be appropriate if the application wants to make sure that the remote TP is started successfully before issuing multiple sends. Notice, though, that this design generates an additional network message that carries just the allocation request across the network. Otherwise the ALLOCATE would be buffered locally until the local TP issues a verb that flushes the LU's send buffer or the maximum RU size is reached. Then the allocation request and the buffered data may be combined together into one network message. This approach may be more efficient (it generates less network messages), but in the case of the remote TP being down, a lot of local processing and network messages may be wasted.

Sequence 2

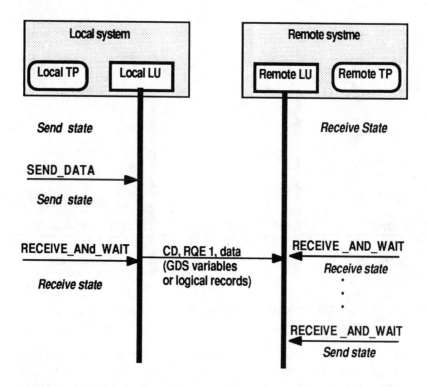

Figure 6.19 Change direction.

Figure 6.19 illustrates a typical data exchange. The local transaction program issues the LU 6.2 [MC_]SEND_DATA verb followed by the [MC_]RECEIVE_AND_WAIT verb. The [MC_] RECEIVE_AND_WAIT verb flushes the local LU's send buffer and gives the Send state to the remote TP. The local LU may buffer many logical records or GDS variables into one RU up to the configurable parameter maximum RU size. Then the LU sets the change direction (CD) and the (RQE) indicators in the request header and flushes all data buffered so far in its send buffer. The resulting SNA network message is generated with CD and RQE indicators in the RH and the buffered data in the RU. The request exception response (RQE) indicator does not require any SNA positive response from the remote LU. The remote transaction program issues the [MC_]RECEIVE_AND_WAIT verbs to receive all the data and finally to receive the Send state. Now the remote TP may start sending data.

Sequence   3

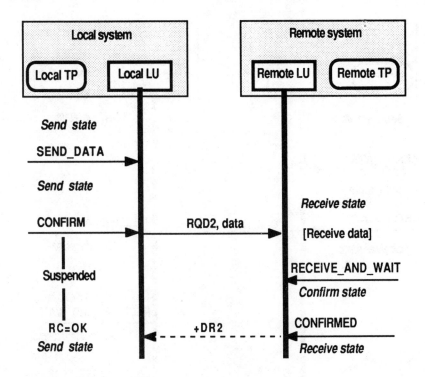

Figure 6.20 Confirmation processing.

Figure 6.20 illustrates how the two communicating TPs can perform checkpointing of all the data exchanged so far on a conversation. The local TP issues [MC_]SEND_DATA verbs which are buffered by the local LU. Then it issues the [MC_]CONFIRM verb to request confirmation of all data sent so far on this conversation. The LU blocks the logical records (for basic conversations) or GDS variables (for mapped conversations) into one RU, sets the definite response 2 (RQD2) indicator, and flushes all data buffered so far in its send buffer to the remote LU. The resulting BIU is generated with the RQD2 indicator in the RH and the buffered data in the RU. The request definite response 2 (RQD2) indicator requires a confirmation reply (an SNA positive response +DR2) from the remote TP. The remote TP issues the [MC_]RECEIVE_AND_WAIT to receive all the data and finally to receive the confirmation request. It replies with the [MC_]CONFIRMED verb, which acknowledges receipt of data without errors and generates an SNA positive response (+DR2).

Sequence 4

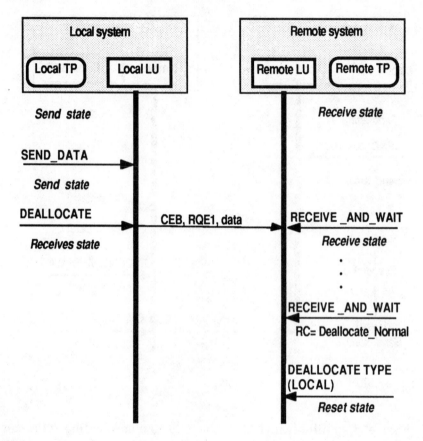

Figure 6.21 Conversation termination sequence.

Figure 6.21 illustrates a possible sequence for ending a conversation without any confirmation or synchronization processing. The local TP issues the [MC_]DEALLOCATE verb. The local LU sets the conditional end-of-bracket (CEB) indicator and flushes all data buffered so far in its send buffer. The resulting BIU is generated with CEB and RQE indicators in the RH and the buffered data in the RU. The request exception response (RQE) indicator does not require any SNA positive response (confirmation) from the remote TP before deallocating. The remote TP receives all the data by issuing [MC_]RECEIVE_AND_WAIT verbs, and it is notified of conversation deallocation (RC=Deallocate_Normal). It then issues DEALLOCATE TYPE

(LOCAL) to deallocate local resources. There are different deallocate types which will be discussed later in this book.

The design in Fig. 6.21 releases the session as soon as a BIU is sent to the remote LU. This allows other TPs to get access to the session to initiate other conversations, but if an error occurs, the data sent with the deallocation request cannot be recovered. This type of deallocate is appropriate for TPs that have already acknowledged all the data and need only to end the conversation.

 The flow sequences shown above are only simple examples of flows. The impact of different application designs on the network message flows and the flows reflecting application error conditions will be discussed in Chap. 7 (for APPC applications) and Chap. 8 (for CPI-C programs).

Chapter

7

Advanced Program-to-Program Communications (APPC)

In the previous chapters, the material presented was intended to provide readers with the concepts of APPC and SAA/CPI-C architectures and the underlying SNA logical unit 6.2. The reader is strongly advised to review these chapters prior to reading this chapter. This chapter covers in detail the Advanced Program-to-Program Communications (APPC) architecture and the issues related to designing distributed applications. It was written for application designers and programmers that design and write transaction programs distributed over many network nodes. The APPC verbs with the prefix [**MC_**] refer to both the mapped and basic conversations. The diagrams in this section do not use the prefix [**MC_**], but they do apply to both mapped and basic conversations unless explicitly specified otherwise.

7.1 APPC ENVIRONMENT

As described earlier, the APPC architecture describes a set of functions (LU 6.2 verbs) that allows program-to-program and peer-to-peer communications directly between any two distributed SNA nodes. The Systems Network Architecture (SNA) consists of physical processors (distributed nodes) interconnected via physical links. Logically the SNA distributed network consists of logical units (LU 6.2s) interconnected via logical connections called sessions. The LU 6.2s act as ports between transaction programs (TPs) and the path control network (see Fig. 7.1).

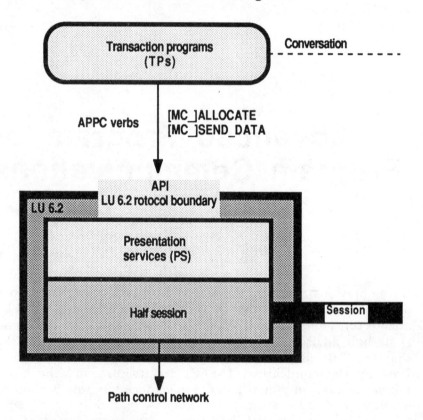

Figure 7.1 APPC environment.

The communicating transaction programs (TPs) exchange messages over a conversation which is assigned to a single session and established between the local and the remote LUs. The TPs share the session to carry many transactions (conversations) in a serial manner. The TPs must follow the send/receive mode protocol established when the conversation is allocated. Basically, one of the TPs is in Send state and may send data, and the other is in Receive state and must receive data. The sending TP may change the send/receive relationship by passing the change direction indicator to the remote TP. The term **APPC** is used to describe the distributed functions (also called verbs) that LU 6.2 provides to application programs via the TP-LU protocol boundary. The TP-LU protocol boundary is between application programs (TPs) and the presentation services layer of LU 6.2 (see Fig. 7.2). It provides functional definition of APPC verbs, parameters, and state indicators used in distributed transaction processing. It also defines the **return codes** and **WHAT_RECEIVED** indicators that are returned to the TPs on completion of each verb. Programmers use the APPC verbs to design distributed transaction programs that are independent of the operating environments in which they run. The LU 6.2 architecture allows a freedom of syntax, which means that the distributed functions (the APPC verbs) can be implemented via product-specific application programming interfaces (APIs). In Fig.7.1 the transaction programs issue APPC verbs such as [MC_]ALLOCATE, [MC_]SEND_DATA,..., [MC_]DEALLOCATE, via a product-specific application programming interface (API) which implements the LU 6.2 protocol boundary. The verbs are executed by the presentation services layer of the LU. The LU formats the verbs into request/response headers (RHs), function management headers(FMHs), and request/response units (RUs) and transmits them across the session to the remote LU.

7.1.1 Configuration Parameters

The network resources must be configured and activated before a transaction program can establish a conversation by issuing the [MC_]ALLOCATE verb. The following is a list of the APPC network resources that must be defined by system programmers:

• Links (SDLC, LANs, or X.25).

• Physical units (PUs) — A PU manages the resources of a distributed node (buffers, links, LUs, etc.).

• Local and remote logical units (LUs) — logical ports via which TPs get access to SNA network.

• Number of sessions between local and remote logical units.

• Mode names defining session characteristics and network properties (cost, priority, performance, routing).

• The local and remote transaction programs (TPs).

Each PU 2.1 node defines the local logical units and the list of remote logical units. The logical units are referred to by their network names, called the **local (source) LU** and the **remote (target or partner) LU.**

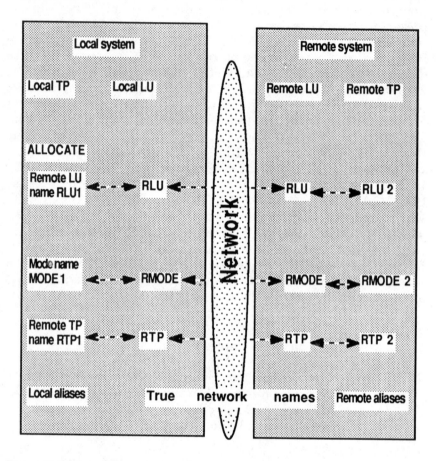

Figure 7.2 Alias names.

Most implementations hide the true network names from the application programmers. Transaction programs and operators may use installation-specific names, called **alias names,** to refer to network resources rather than using the actual network names or addresses. This has some benefits, since the programmers do not have to be concerned with the actual network names and configuration changes. The system programmers may decide to reconfigure the network and change the true network names. The changes will affect only the configuration files at both ends of the connection but the application programs do not have to be changed at all. In Fig. 7.2, the application program issues an ALLOCATE verb supplying alias names rather than the true network names (RLU1 is an alias for the true network name RLU, MODE1 is an alias name for RMODE, and RTP1 is an alias for the true remote TP name RTP). The LU is responsible for mapping the alias name to the true network names before transmitting messages across the network. The alias names are local entities at each SNA node and they are never transmitted across the network. Therefore, the alias names at the remote system may be different than the alias names at the local system (e.g., RLU1 maps to the true network name RLU which maps to an alias name at the remote system RLU2). RLU1 is known only to the TPs on the local system, and RLU2 is known only to the TPs on the remote system. The true network name of RLU must be be defined in configuration files at both the local and remote systems.

The network resources must be activated by an operator command or a programming call. Many APPC implementations, such as APPC/PC on DOS, require the TPs to issue programming verbs in order to define and initialize network resources prior to conversation initiation. The following is a typical sequence of configuration calls that TPs may have to issue prior to the allocation request:

- **DEFINE_PU** — to define or modify the parameters of the physical unit type 2.1.

- **DEFINE_LOCAL_LU** — to define or modify the parameters of the local LU 6.2.

- **DEFINE_REMOTE_LU** — to define or modify the remote LU as seen by the local LU.

- **DEFINE_MODE** — to define or modify LU 6.2 session characteristics for a group of sessions to the remote logical unit with the specified mode name.

- **DEFINE_TP** — to define or modify parameters describing the local transaction program to the local LU.

- **INITIALIZE_SESSION_LIMIT** (or **CHANGE_SESSION_LIMIT**) — initializes or modifies the (LU, mode) session limit from a zero to a nonzero value for a single or parallel session. It also establishes contention winner polarities for parallel sessions.

7.1.2 Verb Parameters

Figure 7.3 shows typical parameters that are supplied by application programmers to refer to different network resources. The local transaction program (LOTP) residing on a local system issues APPC verbs to the local logical unit LU A. LU A currently has configured five sessions to two remote logical units, LU X and LU Y, that may reside on the same or different remote systems. Three of the sessions are identified by the mode name of MODE 2, which specifies a set of characteristics (the same for all the three sessions) that define certain network properties (e.g., cost, security, physical links and routes, performance, priority, or bandwidth). These sessions are connected to LU X and can be used, for example, for interactive types of applications that require an excellent response time. The single session to LU X with the mode name MODE 3 can be assigned to slower links with lower network priority and can be designated for batch jobs. There is also a single session connection identified by MODE 1 to LU Y.

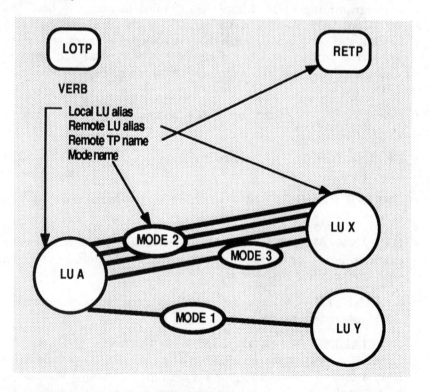

Figure 7.3 Application verb parameters.

7.1.3 Conversation States

The APPC verbs allowed, at any given time in a program, for a particular conversation, depend on the state of the conversation. APPC defines the states and the rules that the programmers must follow when using a conversation. A particular APPC/LU 6.2 implementation enforces the rules by allowing programmers to perform only certain operations in a particular conversation state. A state of a conversation may be changed as a result of an APPC verb issued by the transaction program. The following is a list of APPC states:

- **Reset** — the conversation does not exist, so the TP can allocate the conversation.

- **Send** — the TP can send data, request confirmation, or perform syncpoint processing.

- **Receive** — the TP can receive data from the remote TP.

- **Defer Receive or Defer Deallocate** — the TP can flush the LU's send buffer, request confirmation, or perform syncpoint processing.

- **Confirm, Confirm Send, Confirm Deallocate** — the TP can reply to a confirmation request.

- **Syncpoint, Syncpoint Send, Syncpoint Deallocate** — the TP can reply to a syncpoint request.

- **Deallocate** — the TP may release the local resources.

7.2 CONVERSATION INITIATION

Once the network resources have been defined and activated, the transaction programs may start conversations by issuing the [MC_]ALLOCATE verb.

7.2.1 Initiation States

The APPC verbs that an application programmer is allowed to issue at any given time in a program, for a particular conversation, depend on the state of the conversation. APPC defines the states and the rules that the programmers must follow when using a conversation. A particular APPC/LU 6.2 implementation enforces the rules by allowing programmers to perform only certain operations in a particular conversation state. A state of a conversation may be changed as a result of an APPC verb issued by the transaction program. Figure 7.4 illustrates the state changes for the conversation initiation verb sequence. Initially both of the communicating TPs are in the Reset state. The only operation allowed in this state is to initiate a conversation by using the [MC_]ALLOCATE verb or to accept a conversation by an implementation-specific verb such as GET_ALLOCATE. The [MC_]ALLOCATE verb places the local TP in Send state. An incoming allocation request (the ATTACH header) places the remote TP in Receive state. The local TP is now allowed to send data and the remote TP must receive data. The [MC_].i.RECEIVE_AND_WAIT; verb, issued by the local TP, changes the state from send to receive.

7.2.2 Creating a Transaction Program

Most APPC implementations require an installation-specific call to create a new **TP instance** prior to starting a conversation with a remote application. Typically, the product-specific command (e.g., a TP_STARTED command) requests allocation of resources for a new local transaction program instance. The LU responds by returning an identification number (TP_ID) which uniquely identifies the new TP instance. The next verb issued by the local TP is the [MC_]ALLOCATE verb that initiates a conversation with a remote TP. The GET_ALLOCATE (or RECEIVE_ALLOCATE or CMACCP) verb is used in many implementations to accept an incoming allocation request. The TP_ENDED verb is used to release all the resources associated with this TP instance. An application may start multiple TP instances each identified by a different TP_ID.

7.2.3 [MC_]ALLOCATE Verb

To initiate a conversation, a local transaction program issues the following APPC/LU 6.2 verb:

[MC_].i.ALLOCATE ;
Supplied parameters:
     Remote LU name

Mode name
Remote TP name
Optional parameters:
   Type (Mapped_Conversation, Basic_Conversation)
   Return Control (When_Session_Allocated,
                  Immediate, When_Conwinner_Allocated,
                  When Conversation Group Allocated)
   Conversation_Group_ID
   Sync_Level (None, Confirm, SYNCPT)
   Security
   PIP
Returned parameters:
   RC
   Conv_ID;

Supplied parameters:

Remote LU name — specifies a partner LU name

Mode name — specifies a mode name which defines session characteristics and network properties such as cost, priority, performance, and routing

Remote TP name — specifies the partner transaction program name

Optional parameters:

The **Return_Control** parameter is an indication used when the local LU returns control to the application program. It must be one of the following:

- **When_Session_Allocated** — the local LU returns control to the local TP after successfully allocating a session for use by the conversation. The LU returns control to the program when the session has been successfully established between the local and the remote LUs and it has been allocated to the conversation.

- **Immediate** — only a first speaker (contention winner session) is allocated if such a session is currently available, otherwise an RC=Unsuccessful is returned to the local TP. The LU returns control to the program when the conversation winner is active and it can be successfully allocated to the conversation. The first-speaker session is a session that wins the allocation race

condition.   Normally, which TP initiates a given
transaction is already planned, and therefore the
allocation contention should not occur. The LUs that
initiate conversations should always be configured as
contention winners. The contention loser LU has to bid
(ask) for the right to start a conversation and then, if
allowed by the partner LU, it can initiate the conversation.
This will generate additional network messages.   The
first speaker (contention winner) LU does not have to ask
the partner LU whether it can initiate a conversation but
instead it simply sends the SNA ATTACH header across
the session as shown in Fig. 7.4.

* **When_Conwinner_Allocated** — the local LU returns
  control to the program after successfully allocating a
  contention winner session for use by the conversation.

* **When Conversation Group Allocated** — the local LU
  returns control to TP after successfully allocating a
  session having the specified conversation group ID in the
  Conversation_Group_ID parameter.

The **Conversation_Group_ID** parameter specifies the value of the
conversation group ID which allows multiple TPs share the same
identified session in a serial manner.

The **Sync_Level** parameter specifies the synchronization level
that can be used by the TPs. The two most common options are:

* **N O N E** — no synchronization can be used. This
  conversation cannot issue [MC_]CONFIRM or SYNCPT
  verbs to confirm or synchronize distributed resources.

* **CONFIRM** — confirmation processing can be used on this
  conversation. The [MC_]CONFIRM verb may be used on
  this conversation, but it cannot use the SYNCPT verb.

* **SYNCPT** — both the confirmation and synchronization
  processing may be used on this conversation. Either
  [MC_]CONFIRM, SYNCPT, or BACKOUT verbs are
  allowed on this conversation.

The **Security** parameter specifies the conversation (transaction)
level security that the remote LU utilizes to verify identity and
access rights of an incoming transaction. It consists of user_ID,
password, and a profile.   The remote LU checks the incoming

allocate against user_IDs and passwords allowed to access remote transaction programs and optionally may use the profile to determine the access rights of the local TP. The security parameter can be set to:

- **NONE** — no conversation level security is required for this conversation

- **SAME** — specifies using the user_ID and profile (if present) from the allocation request that started the local TP instance

- **PGM** — the local TP supplies user_ID, password and optional profile that the remote LU uses to verify identity of the end user and check access rights to the remote resources

The **PIP** parameter allows the parameters to be passed from the local TP to the remote TP. A local TP may provide parameters that are passed to the remote TP.

Returned parameters:

CONV_ID (or **conversation ID**) — specifies the conversation identification that uniquely identifies this conversation. The conversation ID must be passed as a supplied parameter in all subsequent verbs for this conversation.

RC (return code) — specifies a return code to be returned on a completion of this verb. An RC=OK indicates that the session was allocated successfully and that the conversation initiation request was buffered by the local LU.

The [MC_]ALLOCATE VERB performs two functions:

1. It establishes an SNA LU 6.2 session between local and remote logical units if a session has not already been started by an operator or another program.

2. It allocates a mapped (issues the MC_ALLOCATE verb) or a basic (issues the ALLOCATE verb) conversation. A conversation is allocated to a single LU-LU session. The transaction programs (TPs) do not refer to a specific session, but to a group of sessions identified by the Mode nameparameter of the LU 6.2 [MC_]ALLOCATE verb (e.g., [MC_]ALLOCATE Mode name=MODE 2). A conversation is then assigned to the first available session identified by the specified mode name.

The parameters of the [MC_]ALLOCATE verb are sent to the partner within an SNA ATTACH header (FMH-5). The local LU does not necessarily send the allocation request to the partner LU when the [MC_]ALLOCATE verb is issued. The LU buffers the transaction initiation request until the requesting program issues a verb that flushes the LU's send buffer.

7.2.4 Initiation Flows

Figure 7.4 shows a typical verb sequence for initiating a mapped conversation, but the same sequence can be used for a basic conversation design. This type of conversation initiation is appropriate for the requester/server model, where the requester allocates a conversation (starts a transaction) and sends a request to the back-end process, called a server. The server receives the request, validates it, and returns information satisfying the request. We assume that the two programs have already issued the verbs required to configure the network resources described earlier and that the local TP has already issued the TP_STARTED verb to start a new TP instance. The following are the design steps appropriate for the client/server design:

Step 1.   The local TP (e.g., a client/requester on a LAN) issues the MC_ALLOCATE verb to start a mapped conversation with the server, called remote TP. The local LU establishes an LU 6.2 session with the remote LU, if the session was not already established. Then it buffers the MC_ALLOCATE verb in its send buffer.

An important thing to remember is that RC=OK on the MC_ALLOCATE verb simply means that:

a.   The verb was syntactically correct.

b.   The local LU builds and buffers the SNA ATTACH header (the FMH-5 containing the MC_ALLOCATE parameters).

c.   The local LU buffers the verb locally and no information is sent to the remote LU.

Step 2.   The client can now send a request to the server by issuing the MC_SEND_DATA verb. The request is changed by the LU into a General Data Stream (GDS) variable and is added to the LU's send buffer.

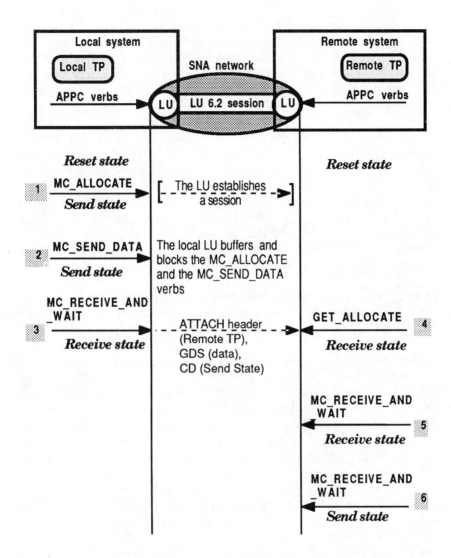

Figure 7.4   Client/server conversation initiation sequence.

Step 3.   The client (local TP) requires an answer from the server. It issues the MC_RECEIVE_AND_WAIT verb that causes the LU to flush its send buffer across the session. The LU sends the allocation request (as an ATTACH header), the GDS variable, containing the request and changed direction together as one network message to the server. The MC_RECEIVE_AND_WAIT verb also changes the client's Send state to Receive state. The client is suspended until the reply is received from the servers.

Step 4.   The remote LU receives the message and starts a new TP instance of the server. The server issues a product specific call (e.g., GET_ALLOCATE or RECEIVE_ALLOCATE or CMACCP) to accept the conversation. The remote LU places the server in the Receive state. The server is not allowed to send until it receives the Send state.

Step 5.   The server issues the MC_RECEIVE_AND_WAIT verb to receive the request. The remote LU moves the request into the server's receive buffer. The state is not changed, therefore the server must issue another MC_RECEIVE_AND_WAIT verb. Some implementations are capable of receiving data and status on the same MC_RECEIVE_AND_WAIT verb. In this case, step 5 could be combined with step 4, and this would increase efficiency because it avoids the processing of additional calls for just the status information (such as receiving Send state).

Step 6.   The remote LU notifies and places the server in Send state. Now the server may format and return the reply by issuing the MC_SEND_DATA verb.

Buffering APPC verbs by the LU and transmitting them as one network message reduces the network message flows, but it may introduce the following problems. If the remote TP is not available, the return code RC=Allocation Failure can be returned on the MC_RECEIVE_AND_WAIT verb. All processing and the network messages sent so far for this conversation are wasted. Since errors do not occur often and the only message processed in the client/server mode is a single request, this design may be appropriate for this model.   In some instances, though, when multiple sends are required before the MC_RECEIVE_AND_WAIT verb is issued or where the remote TP must do a lot of initial processing prior to serving a request, it may be appropriate to send the allocation request immediately.

Flushing [MC_]ALLOCATE

In an application design that requires multiple sends following the conversation initiation request (e.g., file copy), it is not effecient to find out after many records have been sent, that the remote TP was not available in the first place (RC=Allocation Failure). The local TP may want to make sure that the conversation initiation request is sent to the remote TP by issuing the [MC_]FLUSH verb immediately following the [MC_]ALLOCATE verb. The [MC_]FLUSH verb forces the local LU to flush its send buffer. The LU sends the initiation request (an SNA ATTACH header) across the session as a separate network message prior to the first [MC_]SEND_DATA verb. If the remote TP is unavailable the remote LU returns a negative response and the local TP is notified of the allocation failure on one of the initial verbs following the [MC_]ALLOCATE verb. This type of conversation initiation sequence was discussed in Chap. 6 (see Fig. 6.18). In the requester/server model described above it was more efficient to send the ATTACH header and one MC_SEND_DATA verb together as one network message.

Confirming   [MC_]ALLOCATE

Figure 7.5 illustrates an APPC possible sequence of verbs for initiating such conversations:

Step 1.   The local TP issues the [MC_]ALLOCATE verb. The local LU sets the begin bracket (BB) indicator and builds the ATTACH header (FMH-5) in its local send buffer. No information is sent across yet.

Step 2.   The local TP issues a [MC_]CONFIRM verb which flushes the LU's send buffer. The resulting BIU is generated with BB and RQD2 indicators in the RH and FMH-5 in the RU. The RQD2 indicator requires a confirmation reply (an SNA positive response +DR2) from the remote LU. The TP is suspended until the remote TP confirms the allocation request.

Step 3.   The remote TP is started by the remote LU upon receipt of the ATTACH header. The remote TP issues a product-specific call (e.g., GET_ALLOCATE, RECEIVE_ALLOCATE, or CMACCP) to accept the conversation. The remote LU places the remote TP in the Receive state.

Step 4.   The remote TP issues the [MC_]RECEIVE_AND_WAIT to the confirmation request (RQD2).

Step 5.   The remote TP replies with the [MC_]CONFIRMED verb, which acknowledges receipt of the allocation request without errors. The remote LU generates an SNA positive response (+DR2).

Step 6.   The local LU completes the [MC_]CONFIRM verb with a return code OK upon receipt of the +DR2.   The local TP enters the Send state and may start sending data across the session.

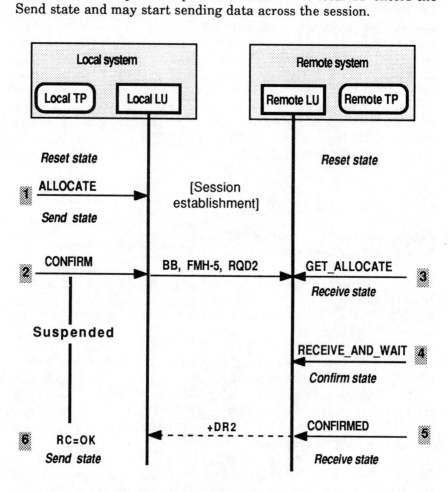

Figure 7.5 Confirmation of [MC_]ALLOCATE.

This design may be appropriate for applications that want to make sure that the remote TP is started successfully before sending any data across the session. The major drawback of this design is that it may significantly slow down the local TP processing.   The [MC_]CONFIRM verb suspends the local TP until the remote TP issues a confirmation reply. Therefore, the remote TP should issue the [MC_]CONFIRMED verb immediately after it is notified of the confirmation request without doing any long local processing. Otherwise the local TP may be suspended for a long time.

7.3 FLUSHING LU 6.2 SEND BUFFER

The logical unit 6.2 is designed to buffer programming verbs for best performance and network utilization. The local LU flushes its send buffer when the maximum request/response unit size (MAXRU size) of information has been accumulated or when an application program issues a call that forces the data to be sent to the partner TP. The [MC_]FLUSH verb can be used to flush the LU's send buffer by sending all buffered information to the partner LU. This may improve performance in instances when the data can be processed by the remote TP while the local TP performs processing (see Fig. 7.6).

7.3.1 [MC_]FLUSH States

The [MC_]FLUSH verb can be issued when the local TP is in Send, Defer Receive, or Defer Deallocate states. Upon successful execution of this verb the TP enters:

Send state — if the verb was also issued in the Send state

Receive state — if the verb was issued in Defer Receive state (immediately following the [MC_]PREPARE_TO_RECEIVE TYPE (SYNC_LEVEL) verb discussed later in this chapter)

Reset state — if the verb was issued in the Defer Deallocate state

7.3.2 [MC_]FLUSH Verb

The [MC]FLUSH verb is used to send the local LU's send buffer. The following is the syntax of this verb:

[MC_]FLUSH
Supplied parameters:
    Conv_ID
Returned parameters:
    RC;

Parameters:

Conv_ID (conversation ID) — the resource ID that uniquely identifies this conversation. This value is returned on the [MC_]ALLOCATE verb for a locally initiated conversation or an incoming allocation request for a remotely initiated conversation.

RC (return code) — specifies a return code to be returned on a completion of this verb.

The [MC_]FLUSH verb can be used immediately following the [MC_]ALLOCATE verb to ensure that the remote TP is started successfully as discussed earlier in this book (see Fig. 6.18). This verb can also be used for optimization of processing between the local and remote TPs. It should be used very carefully, though, since it generally creates additional processing and network messages. However, it may improve performance by allowing the partner TP to receive and process the data while the local TP performs other processing. This is illustrated in Fig. 7.6.

7.3.3 [MC_]FLUSH Flows

This design can be used to improve performance when the data buffered in the local LU's send buffer is needed by the partner TP for immediate processing. For, example a local TP may need to send multiple processing requests to the remote TP. Normally the requests are buffered by the local LU until it issues a [MC_]RECEIVE_AND_WAIT verb in order to receive the answers. At this time the buffered requests would be sent across the session to the remote TP for processing. The remote TP must wait (may be suspended on the [MC_]RECEIVE_AND_WAIT verb) all this time for the requests to be received. The local TP may decide to flush some of the requests earlier. The flushed request could be processed by the remote TP while the local TP performs its local processing or sends additional requests. This minimizes the time that the partner TP has to wait to receive and process the data, which in turn may improve the overall performance. Figure 7.6 illustrates the design steps for the [MC_]FLUSH optimization.

Step 1.   The local TP has already issued [MC_]SEND_DATA verbs to send requests to the remote TP. The requests have been buffered locally by the local LU in its send buffer. The local TP issues the [MC_]FLUSH verb to transmit the requests across the session and to allow the remote TP to start processing the data. The RQE1 indicator does not require an SNA positive response (+RSP) from the remote LU. Therefore, the [MC_]FLUSH verb completes immediately and the local TP is not suspended and can resume its processing immediately.

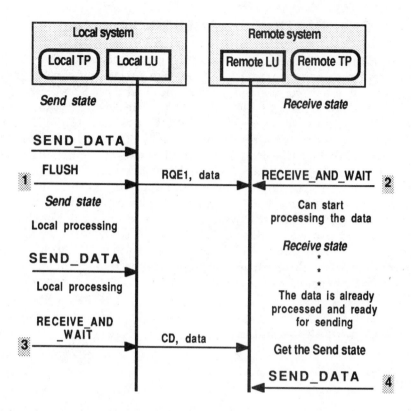

Figure 7.6 [MC_]FLUSH optimization.

Step 2.   The remote TP receives the requests and starts processing. The processed requests can be buffered by the remote TP, and they can be ready for transmission as soon as the Send control is received from the local TP.

Step 3.   The local TP issues the [MC_]RECEIVE_AND_WAIT verb in order to receive the replies from the remote TP. At this time the remaining requests buffered in the LU's send buffer, along with Send state, are transmitted across the session to the remote TP.

Step 4.   The remote TP has already processed most of the requests and has queued the answers ready for transmission. As soon as the remote TP receives the Send control, it may start sending the already processed replies to the local TP. This may significantly improve the overall performance of the two communicating transaction programs.

7.4 CONFIRMATION PROCESSING

Confirmation processing may be used by transaction programs to synchronize their processing. Confirmation processing can be used only on conversations that have been allocated with SYNC_LEVEL (CONFIRM) or SYNC_LEVEL (SYNCPT). The local TP issues the [MC_]CONFIRM verb to send a confirmation request to the remote program and waits for a confirmation reply. The [MC_]CONFIRM verb flushes the LU's send buffer and requests confirmation of receipt of data or completion of some APPC function (e.g., allocation request). It is important to understand that this verb may cause performance degradation if it is misused. The transaction program issuing the [MC_]CONFIRM verb is suspended until the remote TP receives and processes all the data and the confirmation request (see Fig. 7.7). If the partner program requires a lot of local processing before the confirmation reply can be issued, the local TP may be left suspended for a long time.

7.4.1 Confirmation States

Case 1

Normally the [MC_]CONFIRM verb is issued when the local TP is in Send state and the remote TP is in Receive state as shown in Fig. 7.7. The remote TP receives the confirmation request on the [MC_]RECEIVE_AND_WAIT verb and is placed in Confirm state. If there is no errors, the remote TP issues the confirmation reply by issuing the [MC_]CONFIRMED verb. Upon successful completion of the [MC_]CONFIRM verb, (the RC=OK), the local TP remains in the Send state and the remote TP in Receive state. If there is an error, the remote TP replies with [MC_]SEND_ERROR verb and the local TP gets a RC=Program_Error_Purging. In this case the local TP enters Receive state and the remote TP enters Send state.

Case 2

The [MC_]CONFIRM verb can also be issued in the Defer Receive state following the [MC_]PREPARE_TO_RECEIVE verb. In this case the local TP sends a confirmation request with change direction across the session to the remote TP. Upon successful completion of the [MC_]CONFIRM verb, the local TP enters the Receive state and the remote TP enters the Send state.

Case 3

The [MC_]CONFIRM verb can also be issued in Defer Deallocate state following the [MC_]DEALLOCATE verb. In this case the local TP sends a confirmation request with conversation deallocation request across the session to the remote TP. Upon successful completion of the [MC_]CONFIRM verb, both TPs enter the Reset state and the conversation is successfully terminated.

7.4.2 [MC_]CONFIRM and [MC_]CONFIRMED Verbs

[MC_]CONFIRM and [MC_]CONFIRMED verbs are used to synchronize processing between communicating transaction programs. The [MC_]CONFIRM verb is used the most often if the local TP sends data, and requires confirmation that the data was received and processed without errors by the remote TP. Upon successful completion of this verb (RC=OK), the local TP is notified of whether or not the remote TP has received, validated and processed the data. This is illustrated in Fig. 7.7. A transaction program may also issue the [MC_]CONFIRM verb immediately following the [MC_]ALLOCATE verb, to ensure that the remote TP `has been successfully started before sending any data across the conversation. This was illustrated in Fig. 7.5.

The following is the syntax of the [MC_]CONFIRM verb:

[MC_]CONFIRM
Supplied parameters:
    Conv_ID
Returned parameters:
    RC
    Request_To_Send_Received;

Parameters:

.i.Conv_ID; — the resource ID uniquely identifying this conversation. This value is returned on the [MC_]ALLOCATE verb for a locally initiated conversation or an incoming allocation request for a remotely initiated conversation.

RC (return code) — specifies a return code to be returned on a completion of this verb.

Request_To_Send_Received — informs the local transaction program that the remote transaction program issued [MC_]REQUEST_TO_SEND verb, requesting the Send state. The local TP should release the Send state to the Remote TP as soon as possible.

The remote transaction program sends a confirmation reply with the following verb:

[MC_]CONFIRMED
Supplied parameters:
    Conv_ID
Returned parameters:
    RC;

This verb can be issued only as a reply to the received confirmation request from the partner TP. It generates an SNA positive response assuring the partner TP that the information received was processed without any error (see Fig 7.7). The [MC_]CONFIRMED verb enables the local and the remote programs to synchronize their processing.

7.4.3 Confirmation Processing Flows

Sequence 1: [MC_]CONFIRM with   Send State

This design sequence can be used for applications that require confirmation that the partner has received and processed the data that was sent. Upon completion of confirmation processing, the local transaction program needs to remain in Send state in order to continue sending data to the remote TP. A good example would be a file copy program. The copy program needs to check after every "n" records copied, whether the records were received and processed correctly by the receiving program. The copy program may issue an [MC_]CONFIRM verb after every "n" records copied in order to synchronize the processing with the receiving program. Upon successful completion of the confirmation processing, the two programs agree that all records copied so far have been processed without errors. The design steps for this type of confirmation processing are shown in Fig. 7.7.

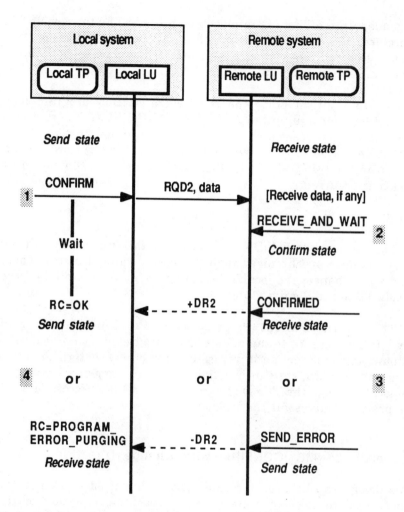

Figure 7.7 Confirmation processing with Send state.

Step 1.   The local TP issues the [MC_]CONFIRM verb. The local LU flushes its send buffer and sends the data and the confirmation request (RQD2) across the session to the remote LU. The SNA request definite response 2 (RQD2) indicator requires a confirmation reply (an SNA positive response +DR2) from the remote TP. The local TP is suspended until it receives the confirmation reply from the remote TP.

Step 2.   The remote TP receives the data and the confirmation request and enters Confirm state. The local transaction program is suspended until all data is received and processed by the remote TP. Therefore, it is very important that the remote TP issues the confirmation reply as soon as possible to resume processing with the local transaction program.

Step 3. In Confirm state the remote transaction program may respond only by issuing the APPC [MC_]CONFIRMED verb. This indicates that it received and processed the information sent by the local transaction program without any errors. The remote TP can also issue the [MC_]SEND_ERROR verb to indicate that an error condition occurred.

Step 4.

a. The return code RC=OK indicates that the two communicating programs have synchronized their processing without errors. There is no state change, the local TP remains in the Send state and the remote TP in the Receive state.

b. The return code RC=Program_Error_Purging indicates that any information sent to the remote TP, since the previous successful acknowledgment may be in error. The remote TP enters the Send state and should a start user-defined error recovery procedure with the local TP (e.g., the TPs may agree to redo all the processing from the previous successful confirmation processing).

Sequence 2: [MC_]CONFIRM with Change Direction

This design can be used for applications that need to change the Send state to Receive state upon successful completion of the confirmation processing. The remote TP receives the Send state and may start sending data to the local TP. For example, a local TP needs to send a request that updates a remote database and requires the remote TP to generate some information that must be sent back to the local TP. After the update is completed, both the local and remote TPs may have to perform some local processing before resuming the exchange of data over the conversation. The update needs to be confirmed to ensure the database consistency. The Remote TP may start sending data immediately following the [MC_]CONFIRMED verb, even if the local TP is still performing other processing. The data is buffered by the local LU and is ready to be passed to the local TP for immediate processing. Figure 7.8 shows the design steps appropriate for such transactions:

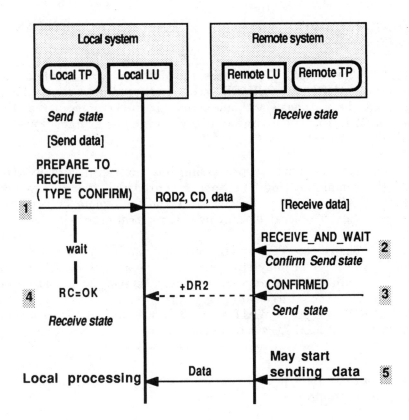

Figure 7.8 [MC_]CONFIRM with change direction.

Step 1. The local transaction program (local TP) issues the [MC_]PREPARE_TO_RECEIVE (TYPE CONFIRM) verb, which combines confirmation processing with change direction. The local LU flushes its send buffer, which contains the buffered database update requests. The resulting network message (BIU) is generated with the RQD2 and CD indicators in the RH and the buffered data in the RU. The request definite response 2 (RQD2) indicator requires a confirmation reply. The change direction indicator gives the Send control to the remote TP upon completion of confirmation processing. Notice that only one network message is needed to pass the data, change direction, and to request the confirmation processing.

Step 2. Once the remote TP receives all the data, it gets the confirmation request with the change direction and enters the Confirm Send state. The Confirm Send indication is received on the

WHAT_RECEIVED parameter of the [MC_]RECEIVE_AND_
WAIT verb.

Step 3. The remote TP updates the database and responds by
issuing the [MC_]CONFIRMED verb to indicate that it received and
updated the database without errors. If an error occurred, the
[MC_]SEND_ERROR verb would be generated as explained earlier
(see Fig. 7.7).

Step 4. The confirmation processing has succeeded with RC=OK
and the communicating TPs have synchronized their processing.
The local TP is placed in Receive state and the remote TP is placed
in Send state. The local TP may now do its local processing.

Step 5. The remote TP may start sending data to the local TP even
though the local TP may still perform some other processing. The
local LU will buffer the incoming data. As soon as the local TP
finishes   its   processing,   it   may   issue   the
[MC_]RECEIVE_AND_WAIT verb and the data may already be
waiting in the local LU's receive buffer.

Sequence 3: [MC_]CONFIRM with Change Direction, an Alternate Design

The design described in sequence 2 can be implemented in another
way. The local transaction program may first perform the
confirmation processing, as shown in Fig. 7.7. Then it can issue the
[MC_]RECEIVE_AND_WAIT or [MC_]PREPARE_TO_RECEIVE
verb to allow the remote TP to start sending data. Figure 7.9
illustrates the additional design steps needed when the
[MC_]CONFIRM verb is followed by the [MC_]RECEIVE_AND_
WAIT verb. The following are the design steps:

Steps 1 to 4. The same as shown in Fig. 7.7. The confirmation
processing completes with RC=OK. The local TP remains in Send
state and the remote TP, in Receive state.

Step 5. The local TP issues the [MC_]RECEIVE_AND_WAIT verb
after it finishes its local processing. At this time the local LU sends
the change direction across the session. Since the previous
confirmation processing flushed and confirmed all the data, an
empty BIU must be sent just to carry the Change Direction (CD) to
the partner TP.

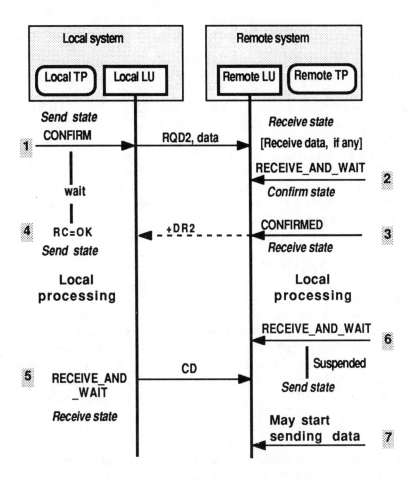

Figure 7.9 [MC_]CONFIRM followed by [MC_]RECEIVE_AND_WAIT.

Step 6.   The remote TP might have finished its local processing
prior to the local TP.   The [MC_]RECEIVE_AND_WAIT verb
suspends the remote TP until the local TP releases the Send state.
This is not very efficient.

Step 7.   Finally the remote TP receives the Send state and may
start processing and sending data to the local TP.

This design is less efficient than the design shown in Fig. 7.8.
One disadvantage of this approach is that the local LU must send an
additional network message just to carry the change direction (CD)
across the session and additional verb processing is required. Also,

the remote TP must wait longer to receive the Send state and cannot start sending data as soon as the confirmation processing completes. This may decrease the overall performance of the communicating programs. Generally application programmers should combine as many APPC functions as they can on one programming call. For example, the [MC_]PREPARE_TO_ RECEIVE (TYPE CONFIRM) verb combines flushing of the LU's send buffer with confirmation processing and also changes the state from Send to Receive. In addition the confirmation processing can be combined with conversation termination and will be discussed later in this chapter. Splitting the APPC functions into many programming calls requires more processing and generates more network messages.

7.5 SYNCPOINT PROCESSING

As described in Sec. 6.2.4 (see Fig. 6.10) the logical unit 6.2 defines the highest level of synchronization processing, called **Synchronization Point Services** (also referred to as **syncpoint**). Syncpoint uses the SNA/LU 6.2 two-phase commit protocol to insure consistency throughout a distributed transaction. A transaction program establishes synchronization points in the program logic by issuing the SYNCPT or the BACKOUT verbs. As an example, consider a typical banking application where a customer needs to transfer money between various accounts that may reside on different systems. The LU 6.2 itself takes the responsibility for updating all the accounts and ensuring the database consistency. The LU will either **COMMIT** (make the changes permanent) or **BACKOUT** (reverse the changes) to protected resources. All conversations, with synchronization level set to SYNCPT, are considered protected resources. A transaction program issues one SYNCPT verb to advance protected resources on all protected conversations to the next synchronization point. In case of a failure, the LU backs out of all the changes to the previous successful synchronization point and notifies all the TPs involved of the failure.

This is significantly different from the confirmation processing, where the communicating application programs are responsible for ensuring the consistency of all protected resources throughout the distributed transaction. The [MC_]CONFIRM and [MC_]CONFIRMED verbs synchronize the processing between the two communicating transaction programs only on a single conversation. The communicating programs are responsible for developing application-specific, synchronization-backout routines and coordinating the updates. If the distributed transaction involves more than one conversation, then the TPs would have to coordinate confirmation processing for each conversation separately. In case of failures, the error recovery across multiple conversations and multiple updates, can be very complicated.

7.5.1 Syncpoint States

Normally the SYNCPT verb is issued when the local TP is in Send state and the remote TP is in Receive state. Upon successful completion of the syncpoint processing, the states for the local TP and the remote TPs do not change. This is illustrated in Fig. 7.11.

When the conversation is allocated with synchronization level SYNCPT and the [MC_]PREPARE_TO_RECEIVE specified TYPE (SYNC_LEVE), then the local TP enters the Defer Receive state. Upon successful completion of the following SYNCPT verb the TP the enters Receive state (see Fig. 7.14).

When the conversation is allocated with the synchronization level SYNCPT and the [MC_]DEALLOCATE verb specified TYPE (SYNC_LEVEL), then the local TP enters the Defer Deallocate state. If the following verb issued is the SYNCPT verb, the conversation is deallocated only upon successful syncpoint processing and the TP enters the Reset state.

7.5.2 SYNCPT and BACKOUT Verbs

The following is the syntax for the SYNCPT verb:

SYNCPT
Returned parameters:
  RC;

Parameters:

  RC (return code) — indicates whether the syncpoint function was successful.

The SYNCPT verb advances all protected resources, such as distributed databases, to the next **synchronization point**. The logical unit flushes its send buffer for all conversations allocated with a synchronization level of SYNCPT. Applications define an indivisible **Logical Unit of Work (LUW)** as a sequence of related programming statements (database updates, deletes, etc.). The LU is responsible for committing the Logical Unit of Work to the next synchronization point or restoring all protected resources to the last synchronization point. The transaction program that initiates the synchronization processing by issuing the SYNCPT verb is called the initiator. In a distributed transaction there can only be one syncpoint initiator. The other programs are called agents or cascaded agents. The agents receive the initial LU 6.2 syncpoint request from the initiator by means of the TAKE_SYNCPT or TAKE_SYNCPT_SEND or TAKE_SYNCPT_DEALLOCATE indication returned on the WHAT_RECEIVED parameter of the [MC_]RECEIVE_AND_WAIT verb. Each program receiving the syncpoint indication may issue a SYNCPT verb to propagate the request to other TPs. These TPs are called **cascaded agents**. A distributed transaction can be viewed as a tree structure with the root of the tree as the initiator and the agents or cascaded agents as nodes of the tree. The branches of the tree represent the conversations participating in the distributed transaction.

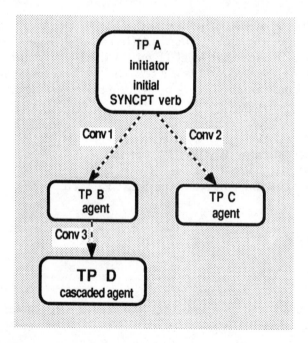

Figure 7.10 Syncpoint initiator and agents.

Figure 7.10 illustrates a distributed transaction that involves four transaction programs communicating via three conversations. TP A (the syncpoint initiator) issues the initial SYNCPT verb. The local LU sends the syncpoint request to its agents over Conv 1 and Conv 2 (both conversations have already been allocated with SYNC_LEVEL(SYCPT)). TP B has already allocated a conversation with TP D with SYNC_LEVEL(SYCPT). Therefore TP D is a cascaded agent participating in the same distributed transaction.

In order to restore all protected resources to the previous synchronization point, a TP issues BACKOUT. The BACKOUT verb restores all protected resources to the last synchronization point, and sends BACKOUT on all conversations allocated with a synchronization level of SYNCPT. Any program participating in the distributed transaction may initiate the backout function at any time if it detects an error condition. The LU notifies all other programs involved in this distributed transaction, by means of a BACKED_OUT return code, and cancels the current LUW.

7.5.3 Syncpoint Flows

Sequence 1: Synchronization Processing

This design can be used for designing distributed transactions that need to update distributed databases to insure data consistency. Figure 7.11 shows typical synchpoint design steps:

Step 1.   The local TP places all protected conversations (e.g., Conv 1 and Conv 2 in Fig. 7.10) in Send state and sends database update requests to all agents (TP B and TP C) by issuing the [MC_]SEND_DATA verbs.

Step 2.   The local TP (the syncpoint initiator) issues the SYNCPT verb which flushes the LU's send buffer for all conversations allocated with SYNC_LEVEL (SYNCPT). The initial syncpoint request is sent to all agents.

Step 3.   The remote TPs (the agents TP B and TP C) receive the data and the TAKE_SYNCPT indication on the WHAT_RECEIVED parameter of the [MC_]RECEIVE_AND_WAIT verb.

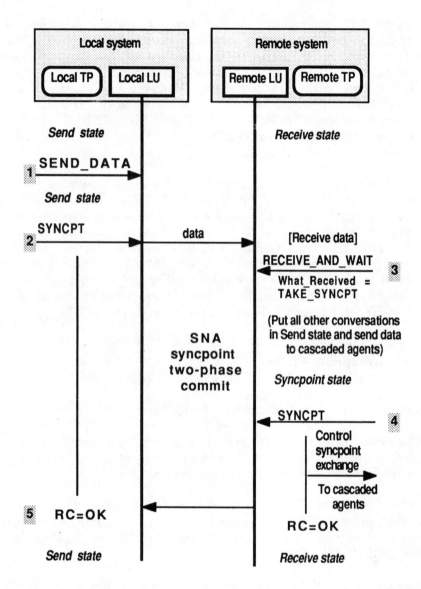

Figure 7.11 Syncpoint processing.

Step 4.   The Remote TPs place all their protected conversations (e.g., Conv 3 in Fig. 7.10) in Send state and sends database update requests to all agents (TP D in Fig. 7.10) by issuing [MC_]SEND_DATA verbs. Then TP B and TP C both issue a SYNCPT verb to complete the synchronization processing. TP B has a protected conversation (Conv 3) to TP D. Therefore, the SYNCPT verb issued by TP B propagates the synchronization processing to TP D.

Step 5. When all participating programs (TP B, TP C, and TP D) respond with a SYNCPT verb and their LUs successfully commit all the protected resources throughout the distributed transaction and coordinate the processing with the local LU, then the SYNCPT verb issued by the initiator (TP A) completes with return code OK. The protected resources are advanced to the next synchronization point and the local TP remains in Send state and the agents in Receive state for Conv 1 and Conv 2. TP B remains in Send state and TP D in Receive state for Conv 3. The TPs may now start a new Logical Unit of Work (LUW).

Sequence 2: Backout Processing

Figure 7.12 illustrates backout processing caused by an error condition. A cascaded agent detects the error and issues the BACKOUT verb. The following are the design steps:

Step 1. The local TP places all protected conversations in Send state and sends database update requests to all agents by issuing [MC_]SEND_DATA verbs. Figure 7.12 shows only one of the agents (e.g., TP B from Fig. 7.10).

Step 2. The local TP issues the SYNCPT verb, which initiates syncpoint processing on all conversations allocated with SYNC_LEVEL (SYNCPT). The TP is suspended until the syncpoint processing completes.

Step 3. The remote TPs (the agents) receive the data and receive the TAKE_SYNCPT indication on the WHAT_RECEIVED parameter of the [MC_]RECEIVE_AND_WAIT verb.

Step 4. The agents place all their protected conversations in Send state, send the required requests to cascaded agents and issue the SYNCPT verb to complete the synchronization processing. The SYNCPT propagates out to the cascaded agents.

Step 5. One of the cascaded agents finds an error condition and replies with BACKED_OUT indication. The remote LU returns control to its TP.

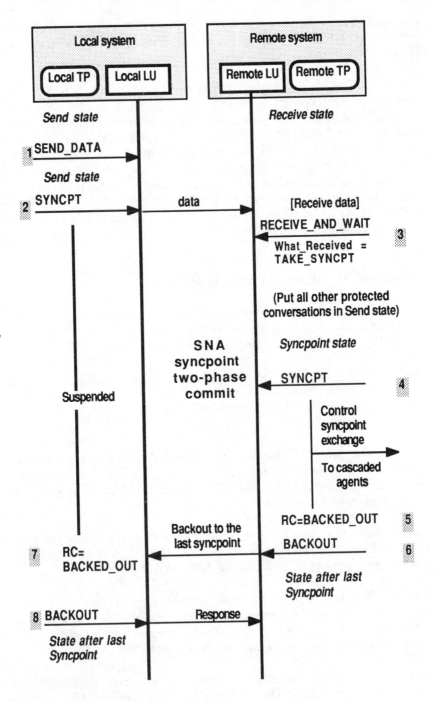

Figure 7.12 BACKOUT processing.

Step 6.   The remote TP issues the BACKOUT verb and restarts its program logic from the last synchronization point. The remote LU restores its protected resources and states to the last synchronization point and propagates the BACKED_OUT indication throughout the distributed transaction to other LUs.

Step 7.   The local LU receives the BACKED_OUT indication and sends back a positive response acknowledging the need for rollback. Then the local LU completes the SYNCPT verb with RC=BACKED_OUT.

Step 8.   The local TP issues the BACKOUT verb, causing the LU to restore all protected local resources to the last synchronization point throughout the distributed transaction. The TP should restart its processing from the last synchronization point.

Synchronization processing should be used very carefully because the local TP is suspended for the duration of syncpoint processing. It also requires logging of the Logical Unit of Work (LUW) throughout the distributed transaction and high usage of system resources. The SNA two-phase commit processing is also time consuming. All of this may cause performance degradation. The synchronization processing is the best tool for ensuring consistency throughout a distributed transaction and therefore should be used when the database consistency is much more important than the response time and system resource usage.

7.6 CHANGING SEND STATE TO RECEIVE STATE

A transaction program may change Send state to Receive state by issuing the [MC_]PREPARE_TO_RECEIVE or the [MC_]RECEIVE_AND_WAIT or the MC_]RECEIVE_IMMEDIATE verbs. The [MC_]RECEIVE_AND_WAIT and the [MC_]RECEIVE_IMMEDIATE verbs will be discussed later in this chapter. The [MC_]PREPARE_TO_RECEIVE verb is very useful for applications that need to perform some local processing before receiving data from the partner TP. Issuing this verb will pass the change direction to the partner program without suspending the local processing. The local TP may perform its local processing while the remote TP may be processing and sending data across the conversation, which is buffered by the local LU. This generally improves the overall performance of the communicating TPs.

7.6.1 [MC]PREPARE_TO_RECEIVE States

The [MC_]PREPARE_TO_RECEIVE verb is issued when the local TP is in Send state and the remote TP is in Receive state, as shown in Fig. 7.13. The remote TP receives the Change Direction (CD) on the [MC_]RECEIVE_AND_WAIT verb and is placed in Send state. The local TP enters Receive state and can immediately resume its processing.

When the conversation is allocated with synchronization level SYNCPT and the [MC_]PREPARE_TO_RECEIVE specifies TYPE (SYNC_LEVEL) then the local TP enters Defer Receive state and the change direction is deferred. Now the local TP issues the SYNCPT, [MC_]CONFIRM, or [MC_]FLUSH verb that flushes the local LU's send buffer and releases Send control to the remote TP. Upon successful completion of the SYNCPT, [MC_]CONFIRM, or [MC_]FLUSH verb, the remote TP gets the Send control and the local TP enters Receive state. Figure 7.14 illustrates synchronization processing with change direction.

7.6.2 [MC]PREPARE_TO_RECEIVE Verb

The following is the syntax of the [MC_]PREPARE_TO_RECEIVE verb:

[MC_]PREPARE_TO_RECEIVE
Supplied parameters:
    Conv_ID
    Type (FLUSH, CONFIRM, SYNC_LEVEL)
Returned parameters:
    RC;

Parameters:

   Conv_ID — the resource ID uniquely identifying this conversation. This value is returned on the [MC_]ALLOCATE verb for a locally initiated conversation or an incoming allocation request for a remotely initiated conversation.

   TYPE

   • **FLUSH** — flushes the local LU's send buffer and places the conversation in Receive state (see Fig. 7.13).

- **CONFIRM** — performs the function of the [MC_]CONFIRM verb which flushes the LU's send buffer and requests the confirmation. This is illustrated in Fig. 7.8.

- **SYNC_LEVEL** — performs the change direction based on the synchronization level for this conversation. If the conversation is allocated with SYNC_LEVEL (NONE), then this is equivalent to TYPE (FLUSH) described above. If the conversation was allocated with SYNC_LEVEL (CONFIRM), then this is equivalent to TYPE (CONFIRM) described above. If the conversation was allocated with SYNC_LEVEL (SYNCPT), then the local TP enters the Defer Receive state and the change direction is deferred until the local TP issues a verb that flushes the LU's send buffer ([MC_]FLUSH, [MC_]CONFIRM or SYNCPT). If [MC_]FLUSH is issued then this is equivalent to [MC_]PREPARE_TO_RECEIVE TYPE (FLUSH). If [MC_]CONFIRM is issued, then this is equivalent to [MC_]PREPARE_TO_RECEIVE TYPE (CONFIRM). If a local TP issues a SYNCPT verb, then upon successful execution of the syncpoint processing, the local TP enters the Receive state and the remote TP enters the Send state (see Fig. 7.14).

RC (return code) — specifies a return code to be returned on a completion of this verb.

7.6.3 [MC]PREPARE_TO_RECEIVE Flows

Sequence 1: [MC_]PREPARE_TO_RECEIVE TYPE (FLUSH)

This design sequence is intended to be used by applications that need to transfer the Send state to the remote TP in preparation to receive data at a later time. The local TP needs to perform some local processing before receiving data from the partner TP and the two TPs do not need to synchronize processing at the time the verb is issued. The [MC_]PREPARE_TO_RECEIVE TYPE (FLUSH) is functionally equivalent to:

- [MC_]PREPARE_TO_RECEIVE TYPE (SYNC_LEVEL) if the conversation was allocated with SYNC_LEVEL (NONE).

- [MC_]PREPARE_TO_RECEIVE TYPE (SYNC_LEVEL) if the conversation was allocated with SYNC_LEVEL (SYNCPT) and the next verb issued was the [MC_]FLUSH verb.

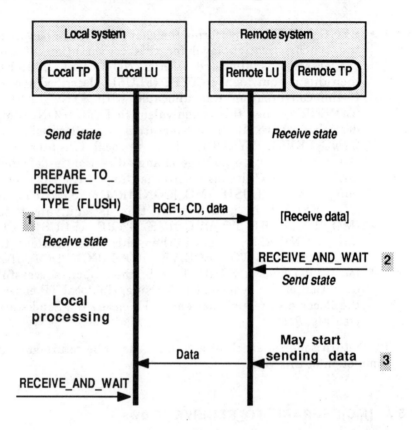

Figure 7.13 [MC_]PREPARE_TO_RECEIVE with no synchronization.

The following are the design steps for passing Send control to the partner TP without any synchronization (see Fig. 7.13).

Step 1.   The local TP issues the [MC_]PREPARE_TO_RECEIVE TYPE (FLUSH) verb. The local LU flushes its send buffer. The resulting BIU is generated with CD and RQE1 indicators in the RH and the data in the RU. The RQE1 indicator does not require a SNA positive response (+RSP) from the remote LU. Therefore the [MC_]PREPARE_TO_RECEIVE TYPE (FLUSH) verb completes immediately. The local TP is not suspended, and it can immediately perform local processing.

Step 2.   The remote TP receives the data and then it receives the Send state on the WHAT_RECEIVED returned parameter of the [MC_]RECEIVE_AND_WAIT verb.

Step 3.   The Remote TP may now start sending data while the local TP performs other processing. Whenever the local TP is ready to receive data, it issues the [MC_]RECEIVE_AND_WAIT verb. The data may already be in the local LU's receive buffer. This may improve the overall performance of the communicating programs.

Sequence 2: MC_]PREPARE_TO_RECEIVE TYPE (SYNC_LEVEL)

This design can be used for applications that need to transfer the Send state to the remote TP upon completion of syncpoint processing. For example, the local TP withdraws money from its local database and updates a remote database.   The databases need to be synchronized to insure consistency throughout the distributed transaction.   Immediately following the synchronization processing, the remote TP will generate a report that should be sent to the local TP. Therefore, the Remote TP needs Send control upon successful completion of the synchronization processing.

Figure 7.14 illustrates the following steps needed for this design:

Step 1.   Assume that the local TP has already allocated the conversation with SYNC_LEVEL (SYNCPT) and the conversation is now in Send state. The last verb issued by the local TP was [MC_]SEND_DATA verb that contains the database update request. The local TP issues the [MC_]PREPARE_TO_RECEIVE TYPE (SYNC_LEVEL) verb and enters Defer Receive state and no information is sent across the session.

Step 2.   The local TP issues the SYNCPT verb, which flushes the LU's send buffer with a change direction and the initial syncpoint request. The local LU performs SNA two-phase commit to synchronize all protected resources (databases) throughout the distributed transaction.

Step 3.   The remote TP receives the data and then it receives the TAKE_SYNCPT_SEND indication on the WHAT_RECEIVED parameter of the [MC_]RECEIVE_AND_WAIT verb.

Step 4.   The Remote TP processes all the protected resources and replies with the SYNCPT verb to complete the synchronization.

Step 5.   Upon successful completion of the synchronization processing, the local TP enters Receive state and the remote TP enters Send state.

Step 6.   Immediately following the synchronization processing the remote TP may start sending data across the session to the local TP.

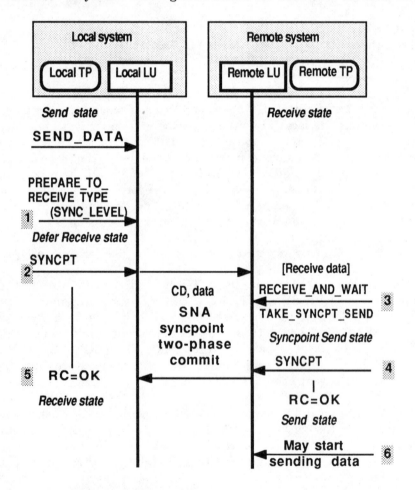

Figure 7.14 [MC_]PREPARE_TO_RECEIVE with syncpointing.

This design could be implemented in another way. The local TP could first perform the synchronization processing (SYNCPT verb) following by the APPC/LU 6.2 [MC_]RECEIVE_AND_WAIT or [MC_]PREPARE_TO_RECEIVE verb to allow the remote TP to start sending data. This design would be less efficient than the design shown in Fig. 7.14. One disadvantage of this approach is that the local LU must send an additional network message just to carry the CD across the session and additional verb processing is required. Also the remote TP must wait longer to get Send control and it cannot start sending data as soon as the confirmation processing completes. This may decrease the overall performance af the communicating programs. Generally application programmers should issue as many functions as they can on one programming call to improve performance. Splitting the APPC functions into many programming calls requires more processing and generates more network messages.

7.7 CONVERSATION DEALLOCATION

A transaction program issues the [MC_]DEALLOCATE verb to end the specified mapped or basic conversation. Upon successful completion of this verb, the LU-LU session assigned to this conversation is released to other conversations. Programmers may choose to deallocate a conversation either unconditionally or conditionally. The unconditional termination ends the conversation immediately as soon as the verb is issued. The conditional termination requires confirmation or synchronization processing before the conversation can be successfully deallocated.

7.7.1 [MC_]DEALLOCATE States

Normally the [MC_]DEALLOCATE verb can only be issued in Send state. Upon successful completion of this verb (RC=OK), the local TP enters the Reset state.

The exception to this rule is when the program discovers an unrecoverable error and wants to abort the conversation. Then the [MC_]DEALLOCATE TYPE (ABEND) can be issued at any time within the conversation. This will abort the transaction and change the conversation state to Reset .

When the conversation is allocated with the synchronization level SYNC_LEVEL (SYNCPT) and the [MC_]DEALLOCATE specified TYPE (SYNC_LEVEL), then the local TP enters Defer Deallocate state and the conversation termination is delayed until the local TP issues the [MC_]FLUSH, [MC_]CONFIRM, or SYNCPT verb. This will flush the local LU's send buffer and confirmation or synchronization processing may also be performed.

When a conversation receives the deallocation request [MC_]DEALLOCATE TYPE (FLUSH) from its partner TP it enters Deallocate state and should issue [MC_]DEALLOCATE TYPE (LOCAL) to complete the deallocation process and enter the Reset state. CPI-C does not require this step and the TP immediately enters the Reset state.

7.7.2   [MC_]DEALLOCATE Verb

The [MC_]DEALLOCATE verb performs the function of the [MC_]FLUSH verb and then deallocates the conversation. The conversation may be deallocated in different ways depending on the TYPE parameter. The following is the syntax for this verb:

[MC_]DEALLOCATE
Supplied parameters:
    Conv_ID
Optional parameters:
    Type (FLUSH, CONFIRM and SYNC_LEVEL, ABEND,
        LOCAL)
Returned parameters:
    RC;

Parameters:

Conv_ID — the resource ID uniquely identifying this conversation.

TYPE

- **FLUSH** — flushes the LU's send buffer and deallocates the conversation normally. APPC deallocates the conversation unconditionally without a need for an acknowledgment from the partner TP. Therefore, the local LU returns control to the local TP as soon as it processes the [MC_]DEALLOCATE verb. The local TP can immediately resume processing on other conversations or initiat new conversations. This type of deallocate is very fast, but it should only be issued if all data sent thus far on this conversation was already checked and acknowledged by the communicating transaction programs. If the data is not confirmed, then it is sent with the deallocation request. Since no confirmation is required from the remote LU the local LU ends the conversation and completes the [MC_]DEALLOCATE verb with RC=OK. As far as the local TP is concerned, the conversation is in Reset state (does not exist). In the meantime the remote TP may still be receiving data and the deallocation request is flushed by the local LU. If any error condition is found, the data cannot be recovered. The [MC_]DEALLOCATE TYPE(FLUSH) was discussed in Sec. 6.3 (see Fig. 6.21).

- **CONFIRM** — APPC performs the function of an [MC_]CONFIRM verb prior to deallocating the conversation. [MC_]DEALLOCATE TYPE (CONFIRM) should be used if the communicating TPs require synchronization of their processing prior to deallocation. The local TP will have to wait for the confirmation reply from the partner TP before the conversation can be deallocated. This type of deallocation is also called a **conditional ending of a transaction**, as it is conditioned on the partner's agreement to end the conversation. If the partner TP does not find any errors in this conversation it sends back a confirmation reply ([MC_]CONFIRMED verb) and the transaction is successfully terminated. If the partner TP finds errors it issues [MC_]SEND_ERROR verb (error notification) and the conversation is not deallocated.

- **SYNC_LEVEL** — performs conversation termination based on the synchronization level for this conversation. If the conversation was allocated with SYNC_LEVEL (NONE), then this is equivalent to TYPE (FLUSH) described above. If the conversation was allocated with SYNC_LEVEL (CONFIRM) then this is equivalent to TYPE (CONFIRM) described above. If the conversation was allocated with SYNC_LEVEL (SYNCPT), then the local TP enters Defer Deallocate state and deallocation is deferred until the program issues the [MC_]FLUSH, [MC_]CONFIRM, or SYNCPT verb. If [MC_]FLUSH is issued, then this is equivalent to [MC_]DEALLOCATE TYPE (FLUSH) described above. If [MC_]CONFIRM is issued, then this is equivalent to [MC_]DEALLOCATE TYPE (CONFIRM) described above. If a local TP issues a

SYNCPT verb, then the TP enters Reset state upon successful execution of syncpoint processing.

• **ABEND** — is intended to be used by a transaction program to unconditionally abort a conversation. This type of deallocate may be used in cases where application error recovery procedures have failed. All TPs that receive an ABEND should restore all the changes performed during this conversation to their initial status. The basic conversations may issue three types of aborts ABEND_PROG, ABEND_SVC, and ABEND_TIMER. The ABEND_SVC and ABEND_TIMER are intended for the LU presentation services mapped component to notify its peer LU services component of an error condition caused by the LU itself or that too much time elapsed without receiving any information from the partner LU.

• **LOCAL** — is intended to be used when the program has received an indication that the conversation has already been deallocated from the session. The TP must then issue [MC_]DEALLOCATE TYPE (LOCAL) to enter Reset state.

RC (return code) — indicates whether the [MC_]DEALLOCATE verb was successful.

7.7.3 Conversation Termination Flows

Sequence 1: [MC_]DEALLOCATE TYPE (CONFIRM)

This design sequence is intended to be used by applications that want to combine the conversation termination with confirmation processing. The partner TP must agree to end the conversation by issuing the [MC_]CONFIRMED verb before the conversation can be deallocated.

The following are the design steps for the [MC_]DEALLOCATE TYPE (CONFIRM) (see Fig. 7.15):

Step 1. The local TP finishes sending data and issues [MC_]DEALLOCATE TYPE (CONFIRM) to deliver and confirm the data and deallocate the conversation. The local LU flushes its send buffer and sends the data along with the confirmation request (RQD2) and the deallocation request (CEB), across the session to the remote LU. The SNA request definite response 2 (RQD2) indicator requires a confirmation reply (an SNA positive response +DR2) from the remote LU before the conversation can be deallocated. Therefore, the local TP is suspended until the confirmation processing is completed. Combining confirmation processing with sending data and deallocation processing is very efficient and saves on network messages (in Fig 7.15 only one network message is generated).

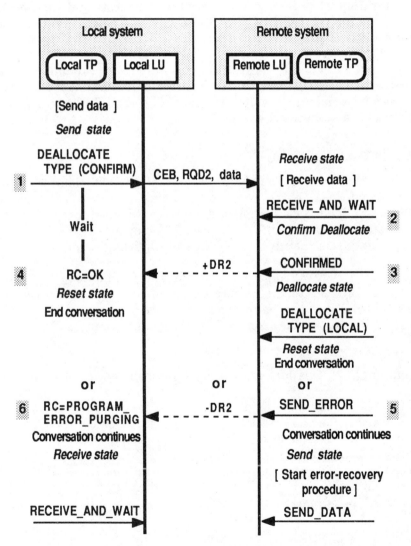

Figure 7.15 Ending a conversation with confirmation processing.

Step 2. The remote TP receives the data, confirmation request, and deallocation request by means of the CONFIRM_ DEALLOCATE indication returned on the WHAT_RECEIVED parameter of the [MC_]RECEIVE_AND_WAIT verb.

Step 3. The remote TP issues the [MC_]CONFIRMED verb to indicate that it received and processed the information sent by the local TP, without errors, and that it agrees to deallocate the conversation. The remote TP enters the Deallocate state and must issue the [MC_]DEALLOCATE TYPE(LOCAL) before entering the Reset state.

Step 4. The RC=OK indicates that the two communicating programs have synchronized their processing without errors and agreed to terminate the conversation. The local TP enters Reset state and the conversation ends.

Or (instead of step 3 and step 4):

Step 5. The remote TP issues [MC_]SEND_ERROR indicating an error condition. The conversation remains allocated. The remote TP enters Send state and should start user-defined error recovery procedure with the local TP (e.g., the TPs may agree to redo all the processing from the previous successful confirmation process).

Step 6. The RC=Program_Error_Purging indicates that any information sent to the remote TP since the previous successful acknowledgment may be in error. The local TP enters the Receive state and waits for the error explanation from the remote TP.

Sequence 2: Deallocation with Synchronization Processing

This design sequence is intended for use in applications that require the synchronization of all protected resources throughout a distributed transaction to a consistent state before deallocating. The [MC_]DEALLOCATE TYPE (SYNC_LEVEL) verb followed by the SYNCPT verb combines the synchronization processing with deallocating the conversation. The following are the design steps for this type of conversation termination (see Fig. 7.16):

Step 1. The local TP finishes sending data and issues [MC_]DEALLOCATE TYPE (SYNC_LEVEL) to defer the deallocation processing.

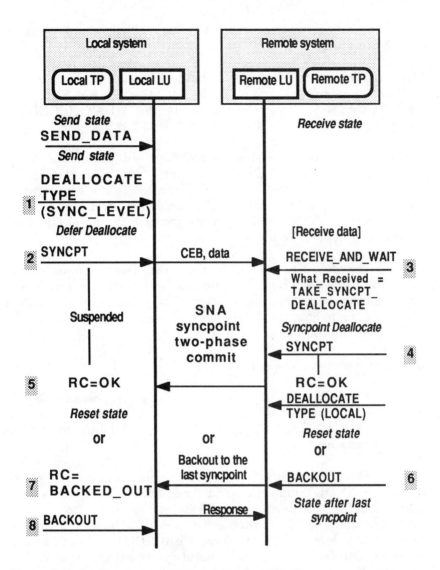

Figure 7.16 Ending a conversation with syncpointing.

Step 2.   The local TP issues the SYNCPT verb to deliver data, synchronize the databases, and deallocate the conversation.   The local LU flushes its send buffer and sends the initial syncpoint request with the deallocation request across the session to the remote LU. The local TP is suspended until the synchronization processing completes.   Combining synchronization processing with sending data and ending the conversation is very efficient and saves on network messages.

Step 3.   The remote TP receives the data, syncpoint request, and deallocation request by means of the TAKE_SYNCPT_ DEALLOCATE indication returned on the WHAT_RECEIVED parameter of the [MC_]RECEIVE_AND_WAIT verb.

Step 4.   The remote TP issues the SYNCPT verb to indicate that it received and processed the information, sent by the local TP, without errors, and that it agrees to deallocate the conversation normally. The TP enters Deallocate state and must issue DEALLOCATE TYPE (LOCAL) before entering the Reset state and ending the conversation.

Step 5.   The RC=OK indicates that the two communicating programs have synchronized their processing without errors and agreed to terminate the conversation. The protected resources are consistent throughout the distributed transaction. The TPs enter the Reset state and the conversation ends.

Or (instead of step 4 and step 5):

Step 6.   The remote TP issues the BACKOUT verb, causing the LU to restore all protected local resources to the last synchronization point and sends a BACKED_OUT indication to all LUs involved in this transaction.

Step 7.   The LU for each TP involved in this transaction, receives the BACKED_OUT indication and sends back a positive response acknowledging the need for restoring its resources to the last synchronization point. It then returns RC=BACKED_OUT to the local TP. The local TP should issue a BACKOUT verb and restart its processing from the last successful synchronization point. The BACKOUT verb causes the LU to restore all protected local resources to the last synchronization point.

TPs that have already acknowledged all the data and only require deallocation processing, should not use conditional deallocation methods described in sequence 1 and sequence 2, but should use the unconditional termination. The conditional deallocation methods require more resource usage and the local TP is suspended until the confirmation or synchronization processing completes. Also, the session is not released immediately (as it is when using the

[MC_]DEALLOCATE TYPE (FLUSH) verb; see Fig. 6.21) for access by other conversations.

7.8 SENDING DATA

This section explains transferring data using the Advanced Program-to-Program Communications (APPC/LU 6.2) architecture. APPC Transaction Programs (TPs), connected via their respective logical units (LUs), issue the mapped MC_SEND_DATA verb or the basic SEND_DATA verb to send data from the local to the remote transaction program. The SNA logical unit 6.2 manages the exchange of data between the communicating TPs. Verbs with the prefix [MC_] mean both the mapped and the corresponding basic conversation verbs. For example, [MC_]SEND_DATA refers to both the mapped conversation verb, [MC_]SEND_DATA, and the basic conversation verb, SEND_DATA.

7.8.1   [MC]SEND_DATA States

The [MC_]SEND_DATA verb can be issued only when the local TP is in Send state as shown in Fig. 7.17. Upon successful completion of this verb the states do not change. The local TP remains in Send state and the remote TP in Receive state. When a successful conversation is established between two TPs, LU 6.2 places the TP that initiated the conversation (local TP) in Send state and places the remote TP in Receive state. The two TPs may now start exchanging data by issuing the APPC mapped or basic conversation verbs. The communicating programs must follow the send/receive mode (half-duplex, flip-flop) protocol as discussed in Secs. 3.6 and 6.2 of this book. Section 6.2 also discusses a possible full-duplex design between systems by using two separate LU 6.2 conversations.

7.8.2   [MC_]SEND_DATA Verb

To send data on a mapped conversation, a transaction program (TP) issues the following APPC/LU 6.2 verb:

[MC_]SEND_DATA
Supplied parameters:
    Conv_ID

           Buffer
           Length
Optional supplied parameters:
    Map_Name
    FMH_DATA
    Encrypt
Returned parameters:
    RC
    Request_To_Send_Received;

Parameters:

Conv_ID — the resource ID uniquely identifying this conversation.

Buffer — used when the mapped conversation [MC_]SEND_DATA verb is issued this parameter contains one complete data record to be sent. The application programmer may move an arbitrary user-defined data record into the buffer. The logical unit formats the data into a single GDS variable as described in Sec. 3.7 of this book.

When the basic conversation SEND_DATA verb is issued, this parameter contains logical records, each preceded by a 2-byte length field (LL) followed by the data. Logical records were discussed in Sec. 3.7 of this book.

Length — specifies the length of the Buffer parameter.

Map_Name — used on mapped conversations. This option allows performing user defined data mapping into a format defined by a user-written exit (or implementation supplied mapping program).

FMH_DATA — used on mapped conversations. This option allows TPs to exchange user-defined function management headers (FMHs). FMH (YES) specifies that the buffer contains data preceded by a user-defined header.

Encrypt — indicates if data encryption is required.

RC (return code) — indicates whether the verb was successful.

Request_To_Send_Received — informs the local TP that the remote TP issued an [MC_]REQUEST_TO_SEND verb requesting Send state. The local TP should release the Send state to the Remote TP as soon as possible.

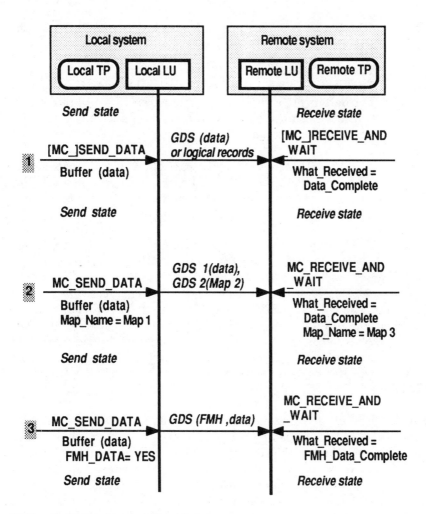

Figure 7.17 Send data processing.

The basic conversation SEND_DATA verb does not contain the optional parameters of Map_Name and FMH_DATA. Also the data buffer must contain logical records as described in Sec. 3.7 of this book. The Request_To_Send_Received parameter, if set to YES, indicates that the partner transaction program asks for permission to send. The sending TP is still in Send state but it should, as soon as possible, release the state to the remote TP by issuing a command such as MC_PREPARE_TO_RECEIVE verb. The LU buffers the data records before sending them to the remote LU until MAXRU size of data has been buffered or the TP issues a call that flushes the

LU's send buffer. It is important to remember that RC=OK on the [MC_]SEND_DATA verb simply means that:

a. The verb was syntactically correct.
b. The local LU added the data to its local send buffer.
c. The data is not sent across to the remote LU until requested by the TP or until a sufficient amount of data has been buffered for transmission.

Figure 7.17 illustrates [MC_]SEND_DATA processing. Normally the local LU buffers the verbs; therefore, the flows in Fig. 7.17 show only conceptual flows that may occur at a later time when the local TP flushes the LU's send buffer.

Step 1. This step can be performed by the mapped MC_SEND_DATA verb or the basic SEND_DATA verb. A programmer moves an arbitrary data record in the case of a mapped conversation, or logical records in case of a basic conversation, to its buffer. The resulting BIU consist of one data GDS variable for the MC_SEND_DATA verb or multiple logical records for the SEND_DATA verb. The remote TP is notified of the received data by means of the data indications returned on the WHAT_RECEIVED parameter of the [MC_]RECEIVE_AND_WAIT verb.

Step 2. The Map_Name option allows a mapped TP to request the data record to be mapped by the user-defined mapping scheme prior to sending the data to the remote LU. The local and remote LUs must maintain the map-name definitions used by the TPs. The TPs specify the map name which is used by the LU to transform the data into a predefined format before sending it to the remote LU. Notice that the local TP specifies the local map name "Map 1." This map name is assigned to a global name of "Map 2" used by the LU. Then the LU assigns "Map 2" to the remote TP's own alias of "Map 3." Therefore, the map name used globally differs from the map name used locally. For example, a programmer may decide to send a COBOL record structure that should be received by the remote program written in C. The local TP moves the COBOL record structure to its buffer and issues the [MC_]SEND_DATA verb using "Map 1." The local LU receives the COBOL structure and "Map1" and calls a user-defined exit routine which is going to map the data to the serialized data to be sent across the session to the remote LU. The user exit returns the serialized data with "Map 2" which describes the serialized data format. The LU sends the data GDS variable containing the serialized data and the GDS variable carrying the map name "Map 2" describing the structure, which is understood by the remote LU. The remote LU maps the received data into the third map name "Map 3," which describes the format of the C data structure. The C data structure and "Map 3" are passed to the remote TP.

Step 3.   The FMH_DATA option is allowed only on mapped conversations. The FMH_DATA option allows mapped TP programmers to build their own headers preceding the data records to be sent to the partner TP. The headers have significance only to the two communicating application programs. For example, the programs may exchange data preceded by the user-defined FMH header of "U," which could be an instruction to update. The LU's only role is to indicate to the receiving TP that the data record contains a user defined header. The receiving TP is responsible for interpreting the headers. The remote TP is notified of the user-defined function management header by means of the FMH_DATA_COMPLETE indication returned on the WHAT_RECEIVED parameter of the [MC_]RECEIVE_AND_WAIT verb.

7.9 MAPPED AND BASIC CONVERSATION DATA FLOWS

Mapped conversation verbs are intended for application transaction programs (end-user applications written in high-level languages). Basic conversations are intended for service transaction programs (STPs) that perform SNA defined services for the end user applications. Basic conversation verbs allow programmers to access an LU at a lower level, bypassing the LU's mapped conversation component. Therefore, the basic conversation verbs are more powerful, and more flexible and allow programmers to develop more efficient applications; however, they are more difficult to use than the mapped conversation verbs. The major difference between mapped and basic conversation verbs is the format of the application data buffer. The basic conversation TPs must build logical records into their application buffer (called a **buffer record**) before passing data to the logical unit. A logical record consists of a 2-byte length prefix (LL) followed by the user data. Mapped conversation programs exchange data in an arbitrary record format agreed upon by the two communicating TPs. The LU first transforms the data to a contiguous data string called a **mapped conversations record (MCR)**. The MCR differs from the data record in that it contains the original data transformed to contiguous data and optionally mapped via implementation specific maps. The logical unit transforms the MCR into LU 6.2 data stream called the **General Data Stream (GDS) variable**. Logical records and the GDS variable were discussed in Sec. 3.7 of this book.

Sequence 1: Mapped Conversation Data Flows

Figure 7.18 shows typical steps performed by the local and remote logical units (LUs) to manage data exchange between two transaction programs (TPs) when using mapped conversations:

Step 1.   The local transaction program (local TP) must be in Send state before it can start sending data to the remote transaction program (remote TP) by issuing the mapped MC_SEND_DATA verb. The application programmer, using mapped conversations, moves the application data (called a data record) into the data buffer that corresponds to a data parameter of the MC_SEND_DATA verb. The data record is a collection of arbitrary data, variables, and structures defined by the programmer. The LU first transforms the data to a contiguous data string and then builds the General Data Stream variable GDS1. GDS1 is buffered in the local LU's send buffer for later transmission.

Step 2.   The local TP issues another MC_SEND_DATA verb containing data 2. The local LU builds and buffers GDS2. The local LU buffers all the data to be transmitted to the remote transaction program until it accumulates a sufficient amount for transmission (e.g., for best network performance the data may be sent when the SNA maximum request/response unit size, also known as MAXRU size, has been reached) or until the local TP issues a verb that forces the LU to flush its buffers. The unique ability of the logical unit 6.2 to block and deblock programming verbs and data, significantly improves network efficiency and performance by reducing the number of network messages transmitted over communication links.

Step 3.   The local TP issues an MC_RECEIVE_AND_WAIT verb or another verb that flushes the LU's send buffer, such as MC_FLUSH or MC_CONFIRM.   The resulting network message (BIU) is generated with the change direction (CD) indicator in the RH and the GDS1 and GDS2 data in the RU.   We are assuming that the MAXRU size is large enough to accommodate both GDS variables.

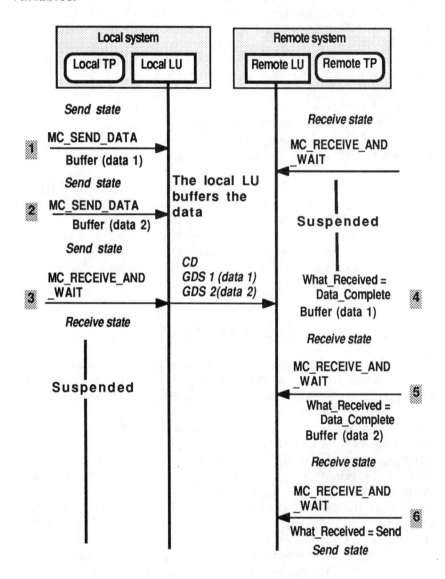

Figure 7.18 Mapped conversation data exchange.

Step 4.   The remote TP receives one complete data record corresponding to the GDS1 even though it issues MC_RECEIVE_ AND_WAIT verb with maximum requested length set to 1920 bytes.

The WHAT_RECEIVED indicator is set to DATA_COMPLETE in order to indicate that a complete data record has been received. If the maximum requested amount of data record the program is to receive were set to 500 bytes, the WHAT_RECEIVED indicator would be set to DATA_INCOMPLETE and another receive call would have to be issued to receive the remaining portion of the first data record. In general this would decrease performance.

Step 5. The remote TP issues another MC_RECEIVE_ AND_WAIT verb with maximum requested length set to 1920 bytes. It receives the second complete data record corresponding to GDS2 (or the MC_SEND_DATA verb issued in step 2).

Step 6. The remote TP must issue another MC_RECEIVE_ AND_WAIT just to receive the Send state. Then it may start sending data. The data will be buffered by the remote LU until the remote program flushes the LU's send buffer. Notice that all this time the local program is suspended and cannot perform any other processing. Compare this design with CPI-C design, discussed in Sec. 8.5 (see Fig. 8.10).

Sequence 2: Basic Conversation Data Flows

Figure 7.19 shows typical steps performed by the local and remote logical units (LUs) to manage data exchange between two transaction programs (TPs) when using basic conversations:

Step 1. The local TP issues a SEND_DATA verb containing two logical records (LL1, data 1, LL2, data 2). The local TP must be in Send state prior to issuing basic SEND_DATA verbs in order to send data to the remote program. The application programmer, using basic conversations, must build logical records into their application buffer (called a buffer record) before passing the data to the logical unit. A logical record consists of a 2-byte length prefix (LL) followed by the user data. The length field must be equal to at least 2 since it includes its own 2-byte length. The logical record is the smallest unit for which the LU detects or reports data truncations. The data portion of the logical record can be in any format as agreed upon by the two application programmers. A programmer can pack multiple logical records or a portion of a logical record into its buffer. The unit of data that a program sends or receives with a single basic conversation SEND DATA verb, is of arbitrary length as determined by the programmer, and does not have to consist of complete logical records. The LU 6.2 architecture does not impose any relationship between application buffers and logical records. Therefore, one buffer record may contain one or multiple complete or incomplete logical records. The ability to block multiple logical records into one application buffer reduces the number of SEND_DATA verbs issued to the local LU and allows programmers to develop more efficient applications.

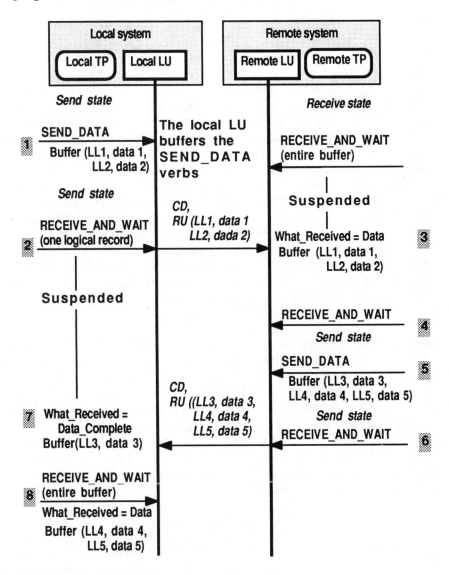

Figure 7.19 Basic conversation data exchange.

Step 2. The local TP issues a RECEIVE_AND_WAIT verb requesting to receive one logical record at a time from the remote TP. The RECEIVE_AND_WAIT verb flushes the local LU's send buffer and passes Send control to the remote transaction program. The resulting network message (BIU) is generated with the change direction (CD) indicator in the RH and the two logical records in the RU.

Step 3. The remote TP has issued the RECEIVE_AND_WAIT verb requesting to receive data independently of the logical record format. The remote TP receives an amount of data equal to or less than the maximum length requested (one of the parameters of the RECEIVE_AND_WAIT verb). Let us assume that the maximum length requested is set to 1920 allowing both logical records (LL1, data 1, LL 2, data 2) to be received on one receive call. The LU passes only the requested length of data from its receive buffer to the application buffer. The remote TP is responsible for interpreting and decoding individual logical records. If the maximum requested length were shorter than 1700 bytes, the remote TP would have to issue more than one call to receive the two logical records. For example, if the maximum requested length were 1600 bytes, then the first RECEIVE_AND_WAIT verb would receive 1600 bytes and the second, the remaining 100 bytes. The remote TP would be responsible for combining the two calls and determining the logical record boundaries. This design would be less efficient and generally decrease the overall performance of the communicating TPs.

Step 4. The remote TP issues another RECEIVE_AND_WAIT verb just to receive the Send state. The APPC architecture defines one WHAT_RECEIVED indicator that separately returns the data indication and status indication. Therefore, most APPC implementations require a separate receive call just to receive the status information. This is not very efficient and would therefore be better to define two indicators, one for data and one for status information (CPI-C defines two indicators). In addition, the Send state and the data indications may be combined into one receive call; then step 4 would not be required.

Step 5. The remote TP issues the basic SEND_DATA verb containing three logical records (LL3, data 3, LL4, data 4, LL5, data 5). The remote LU buffers the logical records until MAXRU size of data has been accumulated or the remote TP issues a verb that flushes the remote LU's send buffer.

Step 6.   The remote TP issues a RECEIVE_AND_WAIT verb to flush the remote LU's send buffer and to release the Send state to the local TP. The remote LU sends the three logical records to the local LU, which queues them on its receive buffer.

Step 7.   The RECEIVE_AND_WAIT issued in step 2 completes with WHAT_RECEIVED=DATA_COMPLETE indicating the a complete logical record was received. This time the local TP requested to receive one logical record at a time. The LU moves only one complete logical record (LL3, data 3) to the applications buffer and waits for another RECEIVE_AND_WAIT verb. We assume that the maximum length requested on the receive call is large enough to accommodate the complete logical record (LL3, data 3). If not, more than one receive calls would be required to receive the logical record which would degrade the performance.

Step 8.   The local TP issues another RECEIVE_AND_WAIT verb requesting to receive data independently of the logical record format. The local TP receives an amount of data equal to or less than the maximum length requested.   Let us assume that the maximum length requested is larger than the combined length for logical record, data 4 and data 5. The LU passes only the requested length of data from its receive buffer to the application buffer. The local TP is responsible for interpreting and decoding individual logical records. Receiving multiple logical records on one receive call is generally more efficient than receiving one logical record at a time.   Application programs usually can pack and unpack logical records much faster than the LU can execute multiple APPC RECEIVE_AND_WAIT calls.

7.10 RECEIVING DATA

This section explains the receiving of data using the APPC architecture. A program issues the mapped MC_RECEIVE_ AND_WAIT verb or the basic RECEIVE_AND_WAIT verb in order to receive data or control information from the remote transaction program.   The received information can be user data, status information (such as state changes), or a request for confirmation or syncpoint processing. In the case of mapped conversations, the received data can be a complete or incomplete data record that corresponds to a single issuance of the [MC]_SEND_DATA verb. In the case of basic conversations, the received data can be one or more complete or incomplete logical records. Successful completion of the

[MC_]RECEIVE_AND_WAIT verb occurs when the local TP receives data or control information from the remote TP. The WHAT_RECEIVED indicator informs the local transaction program of the type of data or control information that has been received.

7.10.1 [MC_]RECEIVE_AND_WAIT States

The [MC_]RECEIVE_AND_WAIT verb can be issued when the local TP is in Send state as shown in Fig. 7.20. In this case the local LU flushes its send buffer with change direction across the session to the remote LU. The [MC_]RECEIVE_AND_WAIT can also be issued in Receive state. Upon successful completion of this verb the program may enter Receive, Confirm, Confirm Send, Confirm Deallocate, Syncpoint, Syncpoint Send, Syncpoint Deallocate, or Deallocate state depending on the return code (RC) and the WHAT_RECEIVED indicator (see Fig. 7.20).

7.10.2 [MC_]RECEIVE_AND_WAIT Verb

To receive data on a mapped or a basic conversation, a transaction program (TP) issues the following APPC/LU 6.2 verb:

[MC_]RECEIVE_AND_WAIT
Supplied parameters:
    Conv_ID
    Fill (Buffer, LL)
Supplied and returned parameters:
    Length
Returned parameters:
    RC
    Request_To_Send_Received
    Buffer
    WHAT_RECEIVED
    Map_Name;

Parameters:

    Conv_ID — the resource ID uniquely identifying this conversation. This value is returned on the [MC_]ALLOCATE verb for a locally initiated conversation or on the incoming allocation request for a remotely initiated conversation.

Fill — used only on basic conversations and specifies whether the program is to receive one or more complete or incomplete logical records using Fill (LL) or data independent of the logical record format using Fill (Buffer).

Length — specifies the maximum length to be received on the [MC_]RECEIVE_AND_WAIT verb. Upon completion of this verb, the Length contains the actual amount of data received by the program.

RC — the return code indicates whether the [MC_]RECEIVE_ AND_WAIT verb was successful.

Request_To_Send_Received — informs the local TP that the remote TP issued an [MC_]REQUEST_TO_SEND verb requesting the Send state. The local TP should release the Send state to the remote TP as soon as possible.

Buffer — specifies the parameter in which the program is to receive data.

WHAT_RECEIVED -- indicates the type of data or control information received (see Fig. 7.20).

Map_Name — used only on mapped conversations. This option allows user-defined data mapping to be specified in a format defined by a user-written exit program (or implementation supplied mapping program). The Map_Name contains the map name identifying the format of received data (e.g., Map 3 in Fig. 7.17).

7.10.3 [MC_]RECEIVE_AND_WAIT Design

The following is the recommended way of processing the [MC_]RECEIVE_AND_WAIT verb (see Fig. 7.20):

STEP A.   The application should first check the return code (RC) for errors. If RC=OK then the program should examine the WHAT_RECEIVED indicator.

IF WHAT_RECEIVED =

DATA_COMPLETE
(a) On mapped conversations a complete data record or the last remaining portion of the data record was received.
(b) On basic conversations a complete logical record or the last

remaining portion of the logical record was received by the program (see Fig. 7.21).

DATA_INCOMPLETE

(a) On mapped conversations, a portion of a data record was received by the transaction program (see Fig. 7.21).

(b) On basic conversations an incomplete logical record was received by the TP. In both cases the TP should issue another [MC_]RECEIVE_AND_WAIT verb to receive the remaining portion of the data.

DATA_TRUNCATED

The program received only a portion of the data record. The LU discarded the remaining portion of the record (only on mapped conversations).

FMH_DATA_COMPLETE, FMH_DATA_INCOMPLETE, FMH_DATA_TRUNCATED

This indicates, in addition to the above, that the data record contains a user-defined function management header (FMH) (only on mapped conversations).

DATA

Data independent of logical record format was received by the TP (Fill (Buffer) on basic conversations only; see Fig. 7.20).

LL_TRUNCATED

The logical record was truncated after the first byte (only on mapped conversations).

THEN

The transaction program should handle the data and issue another [MC_]RECEIVE_AND_WAIT (GO TO STEP A.).

IF WHAT_RECEIVED=SEND

THEN

The TP received change direction (CD) and enters the Send state and may start sending data (GO TO SEND PROCEDURE).

IF WHAT_RECEIVED = CONFIRM

THEN

The partner program issues [MC_]CONFIRM. The TP should reply to the confirmation request with [MC_]CONFIRMED verb or [MC_]SEND_ERROR verb. This was illustrated in Fig. 7.7. [MC_]CONFIRMED acknowledges that the data was received and processed without error. The TP returns to Receive state and should issue another [MC_]RECEIVE_AND_WAIT and then GO TO STEP A. The [MC_]SEND_ERROR verb indicates an error condition. Then the transaction program enters Send state and should perform user-defined ERROR RECOVERY PROCEDURE.

IF WHAT_RECEIVED=CONFIRM_SEND

THEN
The partner program issues [MC_]PREPARE_TO_RECEIVE TYPE(CONFIRM). After issuing [MC_]CONFIRMED the TP enters Send state and may start sending data. Other than that the processing is identical to receiving CONFIRM. This was illustrated in Fig. 7.8.

IF WHAT_RECEIVED=CONFIRM_DEALLOCATE

THEN
The partner transaction program issued [MC_]DEALLOCATE TYPE(CONFIRM).   If there is no error, the transaction program should issue [MC_]CONFIRMED verb and enters the Deallocate state. Then the TP must issue [MC_]DEALLOCATE TYPE(LOCAL) to deallocate the conversation locally.   If there is an error the transaction program should issue [MC_]SEND_ERROR verb and enter the Send state. At this point the conversation should not end until the transaction program has performed the user-defined ERROR-RECOVERY PROCEDURE. This was illustrated in Fig. 7.15.

IF WHAT_RECEIVED=TAKE_SYNCPT

THEN
The transaction program places all its protected resources in Send state and issues a SYNCPT verb to complete the synchronization processing throughout the distributed transaction. After successful completion of the SYNCPT verb, the TP returns to Receive state and should issue another [MC_]RECEIVE_AND_WAIT and then GO TO STEP A. This was illustrated in Fig. 7.11. If there is an error the program should issue the BACKOUT verb to restore all protected resources to the last synchronization point (see Fig. 7.12).

IF WHAT_RECEIVED=TAKE_SYNCPT_SEND

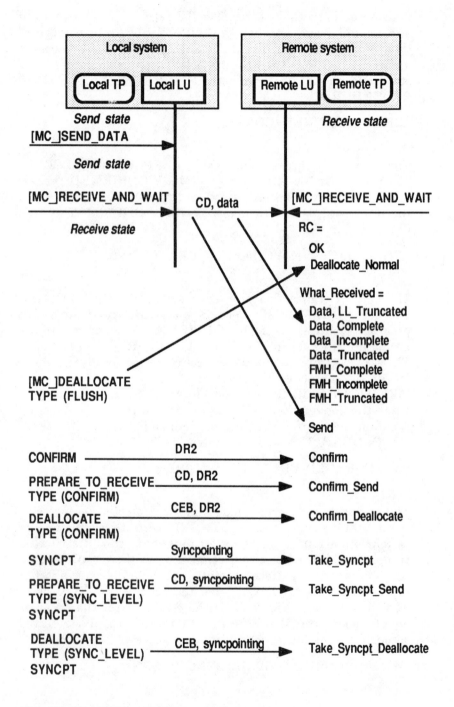

Figure 7.20. WHAT_RECEIVED indicator processing.

THEN
> The partner program issued [MC_]PREPARE_TO_RECEIVE
> TYPE(SYNC_LEVEL) followed by the SYNCPT verb. After
> issuing SYNCPT, the TP enters the Send state and may start
> sending data. Other than that the processing is identical to
> receiving TAKE_SYNCPT. This was illustrated in Fig. 7.14.

IF WHAT_RECEIVED=TAKE_SYNCPT_ DEALLOCATE

THEN
> The partner program issues [MC_]DEALLOCATE
> TYPE(SYNC_LEVEL) followed by the SYNCPT verb. If there
> is no error, the TP should issue SYNCPT verb and enter the
> Deallocate state. Then it must issue [MC_]DEALLOCATE
> TYPE(LOCAL) to deallocate the conversation locally. If there
> is an error the TP should issue the BACKOUT verb to restore all
> protected resources to the last synchronization point. This was
> illustrated in Fig. 7.16.

END of STEP A

ELSE

STEP B.   If RC = DEALLOCATE_NORMAL then the TP should
issue [MC_]DEALLOCATE TYPE (LOCAL) deallocate the
conversation locally. The remote TP issued [MC_]DEALLOCATE
TYPE (FLUSH) and wants to terminate the conversation, or it
may need to handle other error conditions (conversation failures,
session failures, etc.).

7.10.4 Receive Flow Sequences

Sequence 1: Data_Incomplete and Data_Complete Processing

Figure 7.21 illustrates the DATA_COMPLETE and DATA_
INCOMPLETE indications, received on mapped conversations, by
means of the WHAT_RECEIVED indicator of the
MC_RECEIVE_AND_WAIT verb. The verb sequence below can
also be used in designing basic conversation programs when the TP
receives logical records. This is when the FILL (LL) is specified on
the RECEIVE_AND_WAIT verb.

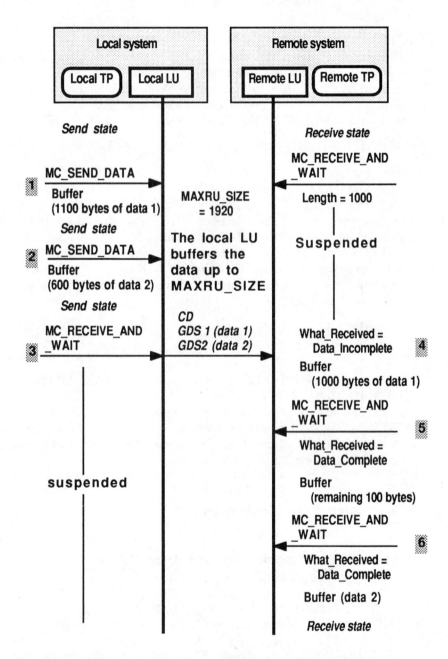

Figure 7.21 DATA_COMPLETE and DATA_INCOMPLETE indications.

Step 1. The local TP issues an [MC]_SEND_DATA verb with a data record of 1100 bytes long. Let us assume that the system managers have configured the maximum request/response unit size (MAXRU size) for the session equal to 1920 bytes. The local LU buffers all data until the MAXRU size is reached or until the local TP issues a verb that forces the LU to flush its buffer.

Step 2. The local TP issues another [MC]_SEND_DATA verb containing data 2 which is 600 bytes long. The local LU builds GDS2 and adds the 600 bytes to its send buffer.

Step 3. The local TP issues an [MC]_RECEIVE_AND_WAIT verb, which flushes the LU's send buffer and releases Send control to the remote TP. The resulting BIU is generated with CD indicator in the request/response header (RH) and the 1708 bytes of data in the RU (GDS1 and GDS2). Each GDS variable contains 4 bytes of header (LL, ID) handled by the two communicating logical units. (The GDS variables were discussed in Sec. 3.7 of this book.

Step 4. The remote LU receives, unblocks, and buffers the two GDS variables in its receive buffer. The TP issues an [MC]_RECEIVE_AND_WAIT verb with a maximum requested length set to 1000 bytes. The remote LU passes the first 1000 bytes of the data record (data 1) to the remote TP and retains the remaining 100 bytes in its receive buffer. The WHAT_RECEIVED indicator is set to DATA_INCOMPLETE to indicate that a portion of a data record was received.

Step 5. The remote TP must issue another MC_RECEIVE_AND_WAIT verb to receive the remaining portion of the first data record. This time the WHAT_RECEIVED indicator is set to DATA_COMPLETE, indicating that the remaining portion of the data record was received. The length parameter contains the actual amount of the data record the program received (in this case 100 bytes). The remote TP must combine the 100 bytes of data with the data received in step 4 in order to get the complete data record corresponding to the [MC]_SEND_DATA verb issued in step 1.

Step 6. Since the RC=OK and the WHAT_RECEIVED indicator is set to DATA_COMPLETE in step 5, no state change occurs (the remote transaction program remains in Receive state). Therefore, the remote TP should issue another [MC]_RECEIVE_AND_WAIT verb. This time all 600 bytes can be moved to the TP's buffer. The WHAT_RECEIVED indicator is set to DATA_COMPLETE, indicating that the remote program received a complete data record (data 2). This data record corresponds to the [MC]_SEND_DATA verb issued in step 2.

Generally transaction programs should allocate a large memory block for incoming data and receive as much data as possible on one [MC_]RECEIVE_AND_WAIT verb. For example, it may be quite efficient to set the requested length to the maximum data length received. Then there would be only one [MC_]RECEIVE_AND_ WAIT verb needed for each corresponding [MC_]SEND_DATA verb. This would require fewer programming verbs to be issued and therefore less processing power. However, a large requested length requires a large memory block to be reserved for the incoming data each time [MC_]RECEIVE_AND_WAIT verb is issued. When many applications are competing for memory resources, the overall system performance may decrease significantly if the memory is not available.

For example, if 99 percent of the messages are shorter than 1000 bytes and only 1 percent of the messages are larger than 5000 bytes, it may be more efficient to set the maximum requested length to 1000 bytes. Although this would require more [MC_]RECEIVE_AND_ WAIT calls to handle the 1 percent of incoming messages, it would use less memory on each receive call. This memory can be used by other TPs and as a result the overall system performance would probably increase. In many cases the remote TP may not know the maximum incoming data length. Therefore, a TP should set the requested length to the maximum possible value that would have a minimal impact on other TPs competing for memory resources.

Sequence 2: Fill (BUFFER) Processing

Basic conversation programmers can write more efficient applications by receiving multiple logical records on one receive call. This reduces the number of RECEIVE_AND_WAIT verbs required and may improve the overall performance of the communicating programs. Figure 7.22 shows typical steps performed by the remote TP while receiving data independent of the logical record format.

Step 1.   The local TP issues a SEND_DATA verb containing two logical records with 1100 bytes in data 1 and 900 bytes in data 2. The 1100 and 900 bytes include the 2-byte (LL) field, therefore the actual data are 1098 and 898 bytes long, respectively. The local TP must be in the Send state before it can start sending data to the remote program. The application programmer, using basic conversations, must build logical records into their application buffer. The data portion of the logical record can be in any format agreed upon by the two application programmers. For more information on logical records, see Sec. 3.7.

Step 2.   The local TP issues a RECEIVE_AND_WAIT FILL (LL) verb requesting to receive one logical record at a time from the remote TP. The RECEIVE_AND_WAIT verb flushes the local LU's send buffer and passes Send control to the remote TP. The resulting network message (BIU) is generated with the change direction (CD) indicator in the RH and the two logical records in the RU.

Step 3.   The remote TP issues a RECEIVE_AND_WAIT FILL (BUFFER) verb requesting to receive data independently of the logical record format. The remote TP may receive an amount of data equal to or less than the length specified on the LENGTH parameter. In Fig. 7.22, the LENGTH=1900 bytes. The remote LU passes the first 1900 bytes (1100 bytes of the logical record containing data 1 and the first 800 bytes of the second logical record containing data 2), and sets the WHAT_RECEIVED indicator to DATA. The program is responsible for interpreting and stripping the 2-byte length (LL) fields.

Step 4.   The remote TP issues another RECEIVE_AND_WAIT verb to receive the remaining portion of data 2. We assume that the maximum requested length is the same for all remote TP receive calls and is set to a LENGTH of 1900 bytes. Upon completion of this verb, the WHAT_RECEIVED indicator is set to DATA indicating that data, independent of the logical record format, was received. When control is returned to the remote TP, the LENGTH is changed to 100 bytes and it shows the actual amount of data that the program received. The TP is responsible for combining the 100 bytes of data with the 798 bytes (after stripping the 2-byte LL field) of data 2 received on the previous call in order to get the complete data contained in the second logical record.

Step 5.   The remote TP issues another RECEIVE_AND_WAIT verb just to receive the Send state. The APPC architecture defines one WHAT_RECEIVED indicator that returns the data indication and the status indication separately.   Therefore, most APPC implementations require a separate receive call just to receive the status information. This is not very efficient and so it would be better to define two indicators, one for data and one for status information (CPI-C defines two indicators). By combining the Send

state and the data indications into one receive call, step 5 would not
be required.

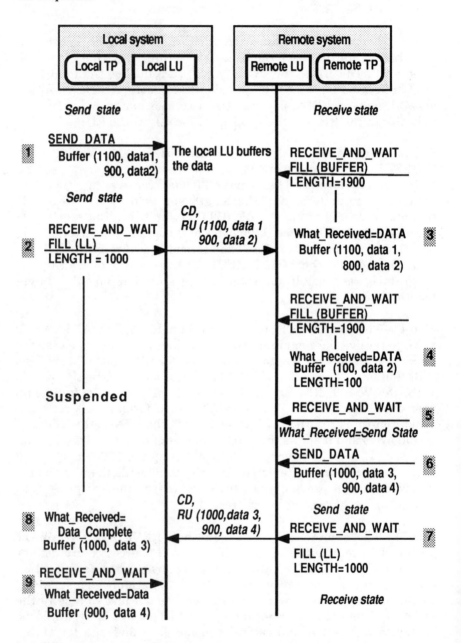

Figure 7.22 FILL (BUFFER) indication.

Step 6. The remote transaction program issues the APPC/LU 6.2 basic SEND_DATA verb containing two logical records (1000 bytes in data 3 and 900 bytes in data 4). The remote logical unit receives and buffers the logical records until maximum request unit (MAXRU) size of data has been accumulated, or the remote TP issues a verb to flush the remote LU's send buffer.

Step 7. The remote TP issues a RECEIVE_AND_WAIT FILL(LL) verb to flush the remote LU's send buffer and releases Send state to the local TP. The remote LU sends the three logical records to the local LU, which then queues them in its receive buffer. Notice that this time the remote TP requested to receive logical records rather than the entire buffer. The FILL(LL) or the FILL(BUFFER) are relevant only at the time the verb is issued and are independent of past use.

Step 8. The RECEIVE_AND_WAIT, issued in step 2, completes with WHAT_RECEIVED=DATA_COMPLETE, indicating that a complete logical record was received. This time the local TP requested to receive one logical record at a time. The LU moves only one complete logical record (1000 bytes of data 3) to the applications buffer and waits for another RECEIVE_AND_WAIT verb. We assume that the maximum length requested on the receive call is set to 1000 bytes.

Step 9. The local transaction program issues another RECEIVE_AND_WAIT verb and receives the second complete logical record. When control is returned to the local TP, the LENGTH is changed, and it now contains the actual amount of data the program received of 900 bytes.

7.11 ERROR RECOVERY

The following is a list of different error types that may occur during distributed processing:

* Local resource failures — failures of non-SNA resources such as databases or disk input/output errors. The local resources are protected by the logical unit when the conversation is allocated with SYNC_LEVEL (SYNCPT). The transaction program may use the LU 6.2 synchronization procedures (SYNCPT or BACKOUT verb) to perform error recovery throughout the distributed transaction. The LU restores all protected resources to their status as of the last synchronization

point. The error recovery of unprotected resources is the responsibility of the transaction program itself.

- Program failures — error conditions that cause abnormal termination of a transaction program. The LU is responsible for deallocating all active conversations for the TP.

- Session failures — unrecoverable session failures due to link failures or invalid LU 6.2 session protocols. They appear to transaction programs as conversation failures. The TPs are responsible for error recovery.

- Conversation failures — failures caused by unrecoverable error conditions on the underlying session. The failure is reported to the program by means of the return code. The transaction program is responsible for establishing a new conversation with another instance of the remote TP and error recovery.

- LU failures — failures as a result of a hardware or software malfunction. These failures are reported to the remote LUs as session failures.

- Application errors — error conditions caused by applications themselves (e.g., program logic errors). TPs are responsible for error recovery.

The LU 6.2 architecture provides confirmation and synchronization protocols that assist transaction programs in error recovery. The confirmation processing was discussed in Sec. 7.4 and the synchronization processing was discussed in Sec. 7.5 of this book. The logical unit type 6.2 also defines [MC_]SEND_ERROR, BACKOUT or [MC_]DEALLOCATE TYPE (ABEND) verbs that were specifically designed to initiate user-defined error-recovery procedures or the LU's backout procedure or terminate the conversation abnormally. The conversation is deallocated abnormally when error recovery failed and it became impossible to continue the conversation because of unrecoverable errors. This Secion concentrates on application errors and error recovery when using [MC_]SEND_ERROR verb. A transaction program issues this verb when it detects errors on a conversation caused by the two communicating programs themselves (e.g., the data received was invalid). The SNA error condition such as conversation or session failures are handled by the logical unit itself. If the LU can not recover from some network failures it notifies the TP of the the unrecoverable error condition on the return code.

7.11.1 [MC_]SEND_ERROR States

The TP that issues an [MC_]SEND_ERROR verb always enters Send state upon successful completion of this verb (RC=OK; see Fig. 7.23). If an [MC_]SEND_ERROR verb is issued in Send state, then no state change occurs. If it is issued in Receive, Confirm or Syncpoint states, then the state is changed to Send state. The remote TP is notified of the application error by means of the return code and it is then placed in Receive state.

7.11.2 [MC_]SEND_ERROR Verb

The following verb is issued to notify the partner transaction program of an application program error detected by the local TP:

[MC_]SEND_ERROR
Supplied parameters:
    Conv_ID
Optional supplied parameters:
    Type
        (PROG, SVC)
    Log_Data
Returned parameters:
    Return_Code
    Request_To_Send_Received;

Parameters:

Conv_ID — the resource ID uniquely identifying this conversation. This value is returned on the [MC_]ALLOCATE verb for a locally initiated conversation or an incoming allocation request for a remotely initiated conversation.

Type (used only on basic conversations) - specifies two levels of an error condition:

• PROG — an application program error.

• SVC — an LU services error. This is an error generated by the mapped conversation manager of the LU itself rather than by the program being served.

Log_Data — contains error information that may be logged throughout the distributed transaction in the local and remote system files.

The Request_To_Send_Received and RC — inform the local TP that the remote TP issued an [MC_]REQUEST_TO_SEND verb requesting the Send state. The local TP should release the Send state to the Remote TP as soon as possible.

RC — specifies the result of the verb execution.

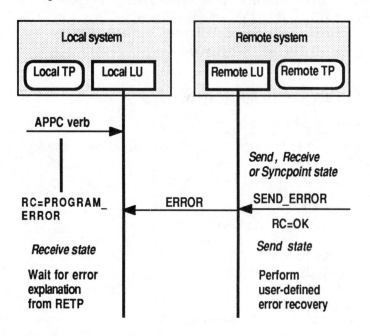

Figure 7.23. [MC_]SEND_ERROR states.

This verb is used by the local TP to inform the partner program of an application error detected by the local TP. For example, the program may issue an [MC_]SEND_ERROR verb to inform the remote TP of an error detected in the received data or to reject a confirmation request or partially truncate a sent logical record.

7.11.3 Error Flows

Sequence 1: [MC_]SEND_ERROR Verb Issued in Send State

This verb sequence shows the error flow when the local TP detects an error during the send operation. The design steps below show data exchange on a basic conversation, but a similar sequence can be applied to mapped conversations as well.

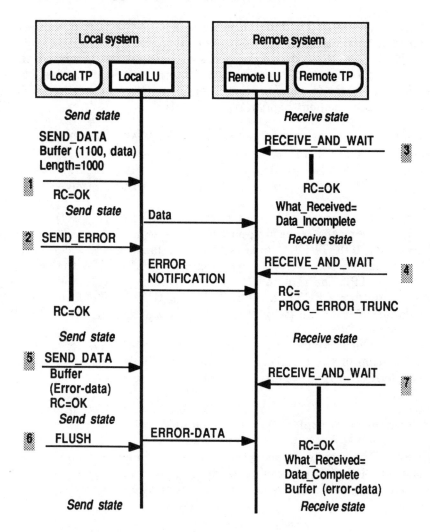

Figure 7.24 [MC_]SEND_ERROR issued in Send state.

Step 1.   The local TP is in the Send state and is sending data to the remote TP by issuing the basic conversation SEND_DATA verb. Notice that the logical records in the buffer show that it is 1100 bytes long. The Length parameter, though, is set to 1000 bytes, showing that the local TP passed only the first 1000 bytes of the logical record to the local LU. The local LU adds the incomplete logical record to its send buffer. If the buffer is full or the MAXRU size is reached, the LU may decide to flush its send buffer to the remote LU.

Step 2.   The local TP finds an error in sending data and wants to abort the current logical record being sent to the remote TP. It issues a SEND_ERROR verb which forces all accumulated data in the LU's send buffer to be sent to the remote logical unit. The local logical unit sends the data and error notification as an SNA function management header type 7 (FMH-7).

Step 3.   The remote TP issues the RECEIVE_AND_WAIT call and receives a portion of the complete logical record. The WHAT_RECEIVED indicator is set to DATA_INCOMPLETE, indicating that only a portion of a logical record was received.

Step 4.   The remote TP issues another RECEIVE_AND_WAIT verb to receive the remaining portion of the logical record. The RC = PROG_ERROR_TRUNC means that the last logical record sent was truncated because of an error condition detected by the sender (the local TP). The remote TP remains in Receive state and should issue another RECEIVE_AND_WAIT verb to receive the error explanation from the local TP.

Step 5.   The local TP issues a SEND_DATA verb that contains an explanation of the error condition and possible information on the user-defined error-recovery procedure.

Step 6.   The FLUSH verb flushes the local LU's buffers in order to deliver the error explanation immediately to the remote TP.

Step 7.   The remote TP receives the error explanation data from the local TP. Further processing is dependent on the error-recovery procedure agreed upon by the two communicating programs.

Sequence 2: [MC_]Send Error Verb Issued in Receive State

This verb sequence shows the error flow when the local TP detects an error during the receive operation. The steps shown in Fig. 7.24 apply to both mapped and basic conversations.

Step 1.   The remote transaction program is in Send state and is sending data to the local TP by issuing APPC mapped or basic conversation [MC_]SEND_DATA verbs.

Step 2. The local TP is in Receive state and receives data by issuing [MC_]RECEIVE_AND_WAIT verbs. The TP finds an error in the received data and wants to notify the remote TP of the error condition.

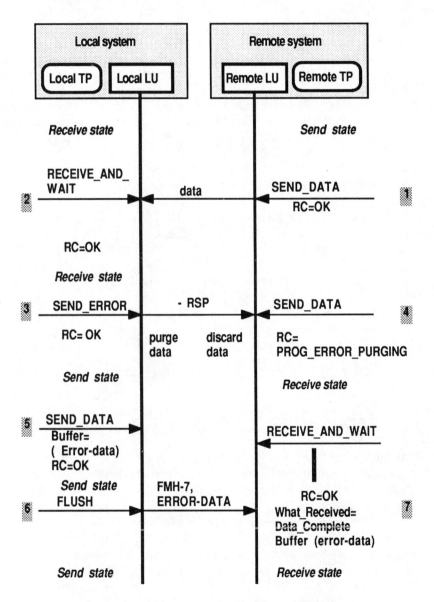

Figure 7.25 [MC_]SEND_ERROR issued in Receive state.

Step 3.   The local TP issues an [MC_]SEND_ERROR verb, which causes an SNA negative response to be sent to the remote LU (see Fig. 7.25). The local LU purges all data it has received from the remote LU that has not been passed to the local TP. The local TP enters the Send state and should start a user-defined error recovery procedure.

Step 4.   The remote LU receives the negative response and discards all the data in its send buffer. The remote TP issues another [MC_]SEND_DATA verb to send additional information to the local TP.   The [MC_]SEND_DATA verb fails with RC=PROGRAM_ ERROR_PURGING, which implies that the local TP has issued an [MC_]SEND_ERROR verb and that some data was purged. The remote TP is placed in Receive state and should issue an [MC_]RECEIVE_AND_WAIT verb to receive the error explanation from the local TP.

Step 5.   The local TP issues a SEND_DATA verb that contains an explanation of the error condition and information on user-defined error-recovery procedure.

Step 6.   The local TP flushes the local LU's buffers, using an instruction such as the [MC]FLUSH verb, and immediately delivers the error explanation to the remote TP.

Step 7.   The remote TP receives the error explanation data from the local TP. Further processing is dependent on the error-recovery procedure agreed upon by the two communicating programs.

7.12 REQUESTING SEND STATE

Transaction programs must follow the send/receive mode protocol established when the conversation is allocated. Basically, one of the TPs is in Send state and may send data, and the other is in Receive state and must receive data.   The sending TP does have control over the conversation and is allowed to perform more APPC functions than the receiving TP. The receiving TP is not allowed to send and normally must receive data until the partner TP releases the Send state. One of the APPC functions that is allowed to be issued in the Receive state is the [MC_]REQUEST_TO_SEND verb, which sends an attention expedited request to the partner TP. The attention request asks the partner TP to release the Send state as soon as possible.

7.12.1 [MC_]REQUEST_TO_SEND States

The TP may issue an [MC_]REQUEST_TO_SEND verb in Receive, Confirm, or Syncpoint state (see Fig. 7.26). The state does not change after the verb is issued, and the program must wait for the partner TP to release the Send state.

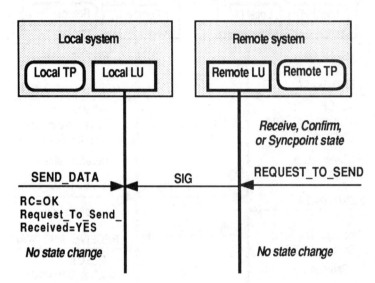

Figure 7.26 [MC_]REQUEST_TO_SEND states.

7.12.2 Requesting Send State Verb Sequence

The verb sequence shown in Fig. 7.27 may be used when the local TP needs to notify the remote TP that the local TP is requesting to enter the Send state on this conversation.

Step 1.   The local TP is in the Send state and is sending data to the remote TP by issuing an [MC_]SEND_DATA verb.

Step 2.   The remote TP issues the [MC_]RECEIVE_AND_WAIT verb in order to receive data from the local TP. The WHAT_RECEIVED indicator is set to DATA_COMPLETE, indicating that a complete data record, for mapped conversations, or logical record, for basic conversations, has been   received. Since RC=OK, the remote TP remains in the Receive state and should issue another [MC_]RECEIVE_AND_WAIT verb. The remote TP knows that it has important information to send to the local TP;

however, the [MC_]SEND_DATA verb is not allowed in the Receive state, therefore the remote TP must first ask the local TP for the Send control.

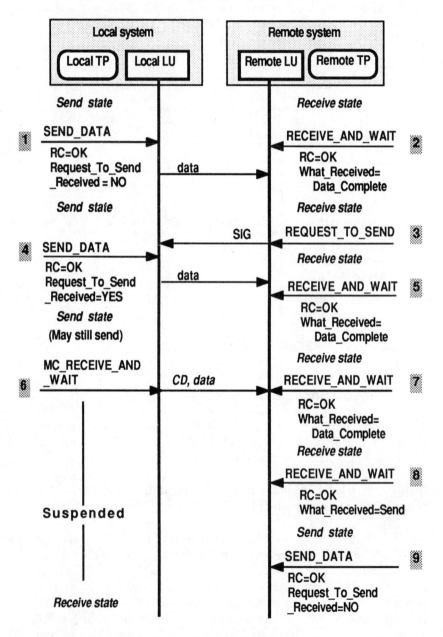

Figure 7.27 Requesting Send state verb sequence.

Step 3.   The local TP issues an [MC_]REQUEST_TO_SEND verb which causes an expedited SNA signal (SIG request) to be sent from the remote LU to the local LU. The SIG request does not change the states of the local and remote transaction programs. The local TP remains in Send state and the remote TP remains in Receive state.

Step 4.   The local LU receives the SIG request and notifies the local TP that the remote TP would like to enter the Send state. This is done by means of the REQUEST_TO_SEND_RECEIVED=YES indicator returned to the local TP on the [MC_]SEND_DATA verb. Notice that the local program stays in the Send state and may finish sending important information to the remote TP. The local transaction program should issue a verb, as soon as possible, to release the Send state to the remote TP.

Step 5.   The remote transaction program issues another [MC_]RECEIVE_AND_WAIT verb and waits for the Send state from the local TP. The WHAT_RECEIVED=DATA_COMPLETE and the RC=OK indicates that another data record was received. Therefore, the remote transaction program must issue another [MC_]RECEIVE_AND_WAIT verb and must still wait for the Send state to be received from the local program.

Step 6.   The local TP issues another [MC_]RECEIVE_AND_WAIT verb and waits for a response from the remote TP.

Step 7.   The remote TP must first receive all the data sent by the local TP before receiving the Send control.

Step 8.   The remote TP finally receives the Send state by means of the WHAT_RECEIVED=SEND indicator received on [MC_] RECEIVE_AND_WAIT verb.

Step 9.   The remote TP may start sending data by issuing an [MC_]SEND_DATA verb.

7.13 SYNCHRONOUS RECEIVING FROM MULTIPLE TPS

A transaction program is capable of communicating simultaneously with multiple remote TPs. APPC defines three functions WAIT, [MC_]POST_ON_RECEIPT, and [MC_]TEST specifically dealing with receiving information from multiple programs. The [MC_]POST_ON_RECEIPT activates posting on a specific conversation. The WAIT and [MC_]TEST functions are intended to be used in conjunction with the previously issued [MC_]POST_ON_RECEIPT verb. Application programs may continue their processing while waiting for information to arrive from one of its partners. When the information is received, the LU posts the specified conversation and returns control to the program by completing previously issued WAIT or [MC_]TEST verbs.

7.13.1 State Changes

The [MC_]POST_ON_RECEIPT, [MC_]TEST (POSTED), or WAIT verbs may only be issued in Receive state. There is no state change upon completion of these verbs (see Fig. 7.28). The [MC_]TEST TEST (REQUEST_TO_SEND_RECEIVED) verb may also be used to test whether a REQUEST_TO_SEND was received from a remote TP. In this case it can be issued in Send, Defer, or Receive state.

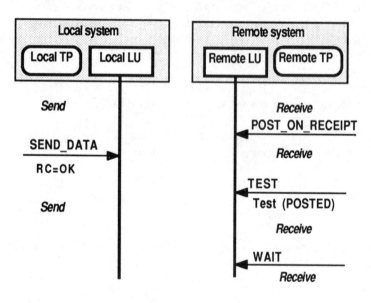

Figure 7.28 POST_ON_RECEIPT, TEST and WAIT states.

7.13.2 [MC_]POST_ON_RECEIPT Verb

A transaction program may communicate with multiple partners over multiple conversations, and it may require that it be informed when information arrives from any of the remote programs. The logical unit is capable of posting a TP when information is received from a partner program. The information can be data, status, or a confirmation or a synchronization request. A local transaction program issues the following APPC verb to activate posting on the specified conversation:

```
[MC_]POST_ON_RECEIPT
Supplied parameters:
    Conv_ID
    Fill
        (BUFFER, LL)
    Length
Returned parameters:
    RC;
```

Parameters:

Conv_ID — contains the resource ID uniquely identifying this conversation. This value is returned on the [MC_]ALLOCATE verb for a locally initiated conversation or on the incoming allocation request for a remotely initiated conversation.

Fill — is used only on basic conversations. It specifies whether the posting is to occur when one complete or incomplete logical record, or data independent of the logical record format, is received by the LU. For the FILL (LL) option, the posting occurs when a complete logical record is received or the amount of data received is equal to the value specified on the LENGTH parameter, or whichever occurs first. For the FILL (BUFFER) option the posting occurs when the amount of data received is equal to the value specified on the LENGTH parameter or when the end of data is reached, whichever occurs first. The end of data is reached when the data is followed by the change direction, confirmation request, syncpoint request, or deallocate verb.

Length — specifies the number of bytes, which, when received, causes the LU to post the conversation.

RC (return) — code indicates whether the verb was executed successfully.

The [MC_]POST_ON_RECEIPT verb should be followed later in the program with a type independent WAIT verb or [MC_]TEST verb in order to find out whether the posting has occurred.

7.13.3 [MC_]POST_ON_RECEIPT, [MC_]TEST, and WAIT Flows

Sequence 1: Testing a Specific Conversation for Incoming Data

This verb sequence flow may be used when the local transaction program needs to communicate with several remote transaction programs over multiple conversations. The local TP needs to be notified by the local LU when information is received on a specific conversation. Figure 7.29 illustrates TP A communicating with three remote programs, TP B, TP C, and TP D. The following are the design steps:

Step 1.   The local TP has already established three conversations, Conv_AB with TP B, Conv_AC with TP C, and Conv_AD with TP D. TP A also has placed all three conversations in the Receive state by, for example, issuing [MC_]PREPARE_TO_RECEIVE TYPE (FLUSH) verb.

Step 2.   TP A issues an [MC_]POST_ON_RECEIPT verb on CONV_AB which causes the LU to post the specified conversation when data, conversation status, request for confirmation or syncpoint is available for the program to receive.

Step 3.   TP A issues an [MC_]POST_ON_RECEIPT verb, on CONV_AC, which causes the LU to post the CONV_AC when information is available for the program to receive.

Step 4.   TP A issues an [MC_]POST_ON_RECEIPT verb, on CONV_AD, which causes the LU to post the CONV_AD when information is available for the program to receive. Now, TP A may continue to perform its processing while waiting for information to be received from one of its partners, TP B, TP C, or TP D.

Step 5.   TP A issues an [MC_]TEST verb to test if any information arrived from TP D. The RC=UNSUCCESSFUL indicates that the conversation has not been posted yet. Posting for this conversation remains active.

Step 6.   The remote TP (TP C) starts sending data to TP A by issuing an [MC_]SEND_DATA verb. The data is buffered by the remote LU managing TP C.

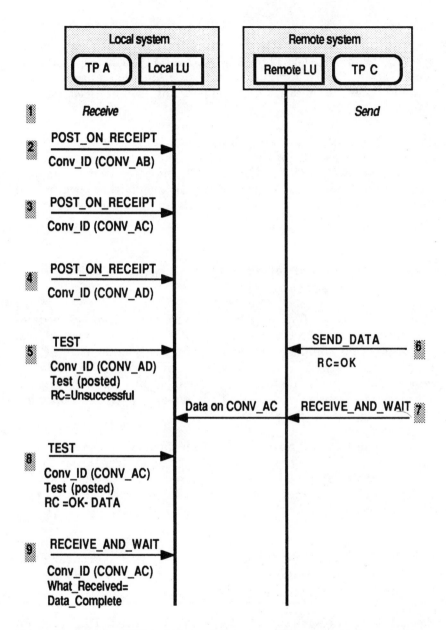

Figure 7.29 [MC_]POST_ON_RECEIPT and [MC_]TEST processing.

Step 7.   TP C issues an [MC_]RECEIVE_AND_WAIT verb, which causes the remote LU to flush its send buffer. The data is sent across the conversation, CONV_AC, to the TP A.

Step 8.   TP A issues an [MC_]TEST verb to test if any information arrived from TP C. The RC=OK-DATA indicates that the conversation (CONV_AC) has been posted and that information is available for TP A to be received. Posting is now reset for this conversation.

Step 9.   TP A should now issue [MC_]RECEIVE_AND_WAIT verb to receive the posted information from the remote program. The WHAT_RECEIVED=DATA_COMPLETE indicates that a complete data record (for mapped conversations) or a complete logical record (for basic conversations) has been received. Now the TP may test other conversations.

Sequence 2: Waiting for Posting to Occur on Multiple Conversations

This verb sequence flow may be used when the local TP needs to communicate with several remote TPs over multiple conversations. The sequence is similar to sequence 1, but this time the local TP (TP A) does not need to check a specific conversation for incoming information. It waits for posting to occur on any basic or mapped conversation from a list of specified conversations. The following are the design steps (see also Fig. 7.30):

Step 1.   The local TP has already established three conversations, Conv_AB with TP B, Conv_AC with TP C, and Conv_AD with TP D . TP A also has placed all three conversations in the Receive state by, for example, issuing [MC_]PREPARE_TO_RECEIVE TYPE (FLUSH) verb.

Step 2.   TP A issues an [MC_]POST_ON_RECEIPT verb on CONV_AB which causes the LU to post the specified conversation when data, conversation status, request for confirmation or syncpoint is available for the program to receive.

Step 3.   TP A issues an [MC_]POST_ON_RECEIPT verb, on CONV_AC, which causes the LU to post the CONV_AC when information is available for the program to receive.

Step 4.   TP A issues an [MC_]POST_ON_RECEIPT verb, on CONV_AD, which causes the LU to post the CONV_AD when information is available for the program to receive. Now, TP A may continue to perform its processing while waiting for information to be received from one of its partners, TP B, TP C, or TP D.

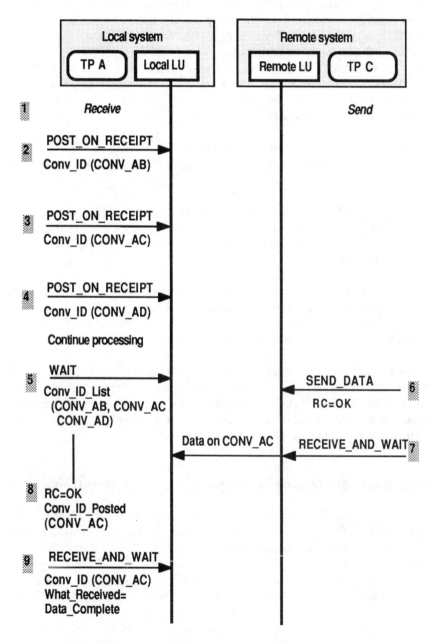

Figure 7.30 [MC_]POST_ON_RECEIPT and WAIT processing.

Step 5.   TP A issues a WAIT verb to test whether information has arrived from any of the remote programs. The local LU suspends TP A until some information arrives on any of the posted conversations specified on the supplied parameter CONV_ID_LIST. WAIT is a type independent verb, which means that it applies to both basic and mapped conversations. The CONV_ID_LIST can specify any combination of basic or mapped conversations. The WAIT verb waits for posting to occur only on conversations for which posting is active, that is, the conversations for which a previous [MC_]POST_ON_RECEIPT verb was issued.

Step 6.   TP C starts sending data to TP A by issuing an APPC [MC_]SEND_ DATA verb. The data is buffered by the remote LU managing TP C.

Step 7.   TP C issues an APPC [MC_]RECEIVE_AND_WAIT verb, which causes the remote logical unit to flush its send buffer. The buffered data is flushed and sent across the conversation, CONV_AC, to TP A.

Step 8.   Information arrives on the conversation from TP C. The WAIT verb completes with RC=OK, and the posted conversation identifier is returned to the program by means of the CONV_ID_POSTED parameter.

Step 9.   TP A should now issue an [MC_]RECEIVE_AND_WAIT verb to receive the posted information from TP C. The WHAT_RECEIVED=DATA_COMPLETE indicates that complete data record (for mapped conversations) or a complete logical record (for basic conversations) has been received.

Sequence 3: Testing a Request_To_Send_Received

The [MC_]TEST verb can also be used to test whether an [MC_]REQUEST_TO_SEND notification has been received from the remote transaction program. In this case the [MC_]TEST verb can be issued in Send, Receive, or Defer state. The design sequence below may be used when the local TP needs to allocate a conversation with multiple remote TPs. Then, the local TP waits for an [MC_]REQUEST_TO_SEND notification to be received on one of the conversations to trigger processing with this TP. The following is the verb sequence showing the local program (TP A) waiting to receive [MC_]REQUEST_TO_SEND notifications from remote programs TP B, TB C, or TP D, (Fig. 7.31 illustrates a possible verb sequence for this design):

Step 1.   The local TP issues the [MC_]ALLOCATE verb. The local LU sets the begin bracket (BB) indicator and builds the ATTACH header (FMH-5) in its local send buffer. No information is sent across yet.

Step 2.   The local TP issues an [MC_]FLUSH verb in order to flush the local LU's send buffer. The allocation request is sent to TP C.

Steps 1 and 2 may now be repeated to allocate conversations with TP B and TP D.

Step 3.   The remote TPs (TP B, TP C, and TP D) are started by the remote LUs upon receipt of the ATTACH headers. Figure 7.31 shows the verb sequence for TP C only. The verb sequences for TP B and TP D would be identical. The remote TP issues a product specific call (e.g., GET_ALLOCATE or RECEIVE_ALLOCATE or CMACCP) to accept the conversation. The remote LU places the remote TP in the Receive state.

Step 4.   The remote TP may now issue the [MC_]REQUEST_TO_ SEND verb, which causes the attention SIG request to be sent to the local LU.

Step 5.   The remote TPs issues an [MC_]RECEIVE_AND_WAIT verb and then waits for data to be received from TP A. The remote LUs suspend the remote TPs until information arrives from TP A.

Step 6.   TP A issues an [MC_]TEST verb to test whether REQUEST_TO_SEND was received from TP B. The RC = UNSUCCESSFUL indicates that REQUEST_TO_SEND has not been received on this conversation.

Step 7.   TP A issues an [MC_]TEST verb to test whether the REQUEST_TO_SEND was received from TP C. The RC=OK indicates that REQUEST_TO_SEND indication has been received on this conversation. The REQUEST_TO_SEND indication informs the local TP that the remote TP issued [MC_]REQUEST_TO_SEND verb requesting the Send state. The local TP should release the Send state to the remote TP as soon as possible. In this design, though, the [MC_]REQUEST_TO_SEND, when received, may trigger distributed processing from the local

TP (TP A) to the remote TP (TP C). Once the processing is finished with TP C, the local TP may test whether [MC_]REQUEST_TO_ SEND was received on other conversations which would trigger processing on these conversations.

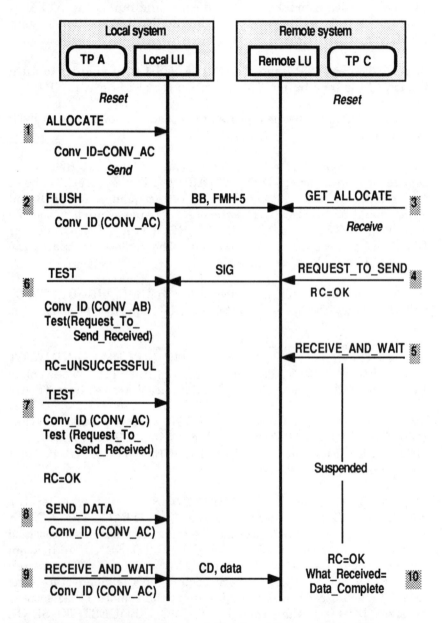

Figure 7.31 Testing [MC_]Request_To_Send from multiple TPs.

Step 8.   The local TP starts processing with TP C and issues an [MC_]SEND_DATA verb. The local LU buffers all the data to be transmitted to the remote transaction program (TP C) until it accumulates a sufficient amount for transmission (e.g., for best network performance the data may be sent when the SNA maximum request/response unit size has been reached) or until the local TP issues a verb that forces the LU to flush its buffers.

Step 9.   The local TP issues and [MC_]RECEIVE_AND_WAIT verb to flush the LU's send buffer and releases the Send control to the remote TP.

Step 10.   The [MC_]RECEIVE_AND_WAIT verb completes with RC=OK. TP C receives and processes the data (e.g., a request from a requester). Then, the remote TP should issue another [MC_]RECEIVE_AND_WAIT verb to receive the Send state, and then it may issue an [MC_]SEND_DATA verb to send a reply to the received request from TP A.

7.14 APPC FLOW DIAGRAMS

In this section we are going to look at several examples of how APPC verbs may be used in designing various types of distributed applications. The examples described in this Sec. apply to both basic and mapped conversations unless specified otherwise. The APPC pseudolanguage (ALLOCATE, ..., DEALLOCATE) is used to describe various APPC functions. The verb parameters in the flows are not complete, and only the significant parameters are shown. A vertical line under a verb indicates that the program is suspended until the LU processes the verb and returns control to the program. The flow diagrams assume that the local and the remote resources have already been configured, started, and initialized. Also, all the initialization calls that may be required by various implementations have already been issued. Many APPC implementations, particularly on DOS PCs, require a programmer to write an application subsystem (management subsystem) that issues implementation-specific verbs to initialize and terminate the local resources. Other implementations may require systems managers to preconfigure and start all the resources and may not require the application subsystem to be written by programmers. In this case the programs are concerned only with starting and ending conversations. Figure 7.32 illustrates typical initialization and termination verbs required by many APPC DOS implementations.

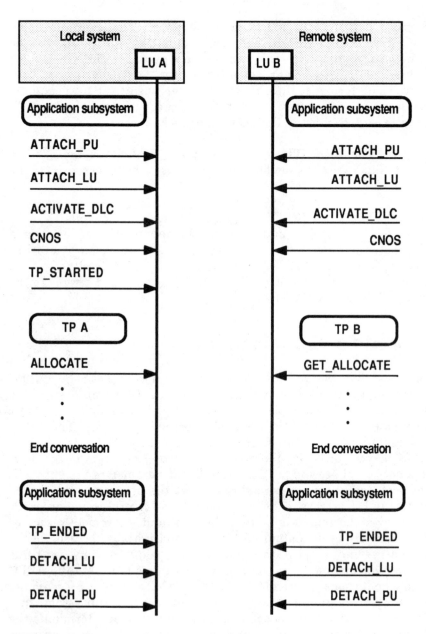

Figure 7.32 Initialization and termination verb sequences.

- ATTACH_PU — identifies the characteristics of the local physical unit to the APPC product.

- ATTACH_LU — identifies characteristics of a local LU and the remote LU.

- ACTIVATE_DLC —activates a Data Link Control Adapter on PCs.

- CNOS — sets the initial number of sessions between the local and the remote LU.

- TP_STARTED — informs APPC that resources need to be allocated for a new TP instance. The remote LU does not have to issue this verb because the resources are automatically allocated when an incoming allocation verb is received.

- DETACH_LU — terminates the local LU. All sessions between local and remote LUs must be terminated prior to this verb. No new sessions can be established from the local LU until another ATTACH_LU verb is issued.

- DETACH_LU — terminates the local PU. No other communication is possible with a detached PU until an application subsystem reissues the ATTACH_PU verb.

- TP_ENDED — ends the TP instance created by the TP_STARTED verb. All conversations for this TP that have not been deallocated are aborted.

The flow diagrams in this section show only the verb sequence performed by the transaction programs (TPs). The calls issued by the application subsystem (or similar calls required by different products) may have to be issued if required by specific implementations.

7.14.1 Sending a Mail Message

This verb sequence flow may be used when the local TP requires to send data in one direction from the local TP to the remote TP. Figure 7.33 illustrates possible design steps for sending a mail message from a local to a remote transaction program. A user sitting at the terminal is asked to enter a mail message. Once the message is entered, the local TP establishes a conversation with the remote TP and sends the message across the conversation to the remote TP, which logs the message in the mail log file. The messages for the log file may then be displayed to the remote users upon request. The following are the design steps:

Step 1.   The local TP (TP A) allocates a conversation with TP B by issuing [MC_]ALLOCATE verb. The supplied parameters, Remote_LU_Name (LU B), Mode name (Mode AB), and the Remote_TP_Name (TP B), direct the local LU to establish an LU 6.2 session with LU B, if the session was not already established. The mode name, Mode AB, defines session characteristics and network properties such as cost, priority, performance and routing. Once the session is established, the MC_ALLOCATE verb is buffered locally. LU A sets the begin-bracket (BB) indicator and builds the ATTACH header (FMH-5) in its local send buffer. No information is sent across yet. The SYNC_LEVEL (NONE) specifies that this conversation cannot issue [MC_]CONFIRM or SYNCPT verbs to confirm or synchronize distributed resources.

Step 2.   The local TP issues an [MC_]SEND_DATA verb to send a mail message to TP B. The application buffer may contain any number of complete or incomplete logical records (for basic conversations) or exactly one data record for mapped conversations. Let us assume that the TP always places and receives exactly one logical record, or a data record at a time, to simplify the flow diagrams. Let us also assume that the data length is shorter than the MAXRU size for the session, therefore no data is sent yet. The local LU (LU A) simply adds the data to its send buffer.

Step 3.   TP A issues [MC_]DEALLOCATE TYPE (FLUSH) verb. LU A sets the conditional end of bracket (CEB) indicator and flushes all data buffered so far in its send buffer to the remote LU. The resulting BIU is generated with BB, CEB, and RQE indicators in the RH and the buffered data in the RU. The request exception response (RQE) indicator does not require any SNA positive response (confirmation) from the remote TP before deallocating. Therefore, TP A deallocates immediately, even before the data is received by TP B. The local LU releases the session at the local side to other conversations. This deallocate type is very fast because the local LU does not have to wait for any acknowledgment from the remote LU before releasing the session for access by other local conversations. Since no confirmation is required from the remote LU, the local LU ends the conversation and completes the [MC_]DEALLOCATE verb with RK=OK. As far as the local TP is concerned, the conversation ended successfully and it is placed in the Reset state. In the meantime the remote TP may still be receiving the data and the deallocation request flushed by the local LU. If any error condition occurs after the local TP deallocates, the transaction cannot be recovered on this conversation.

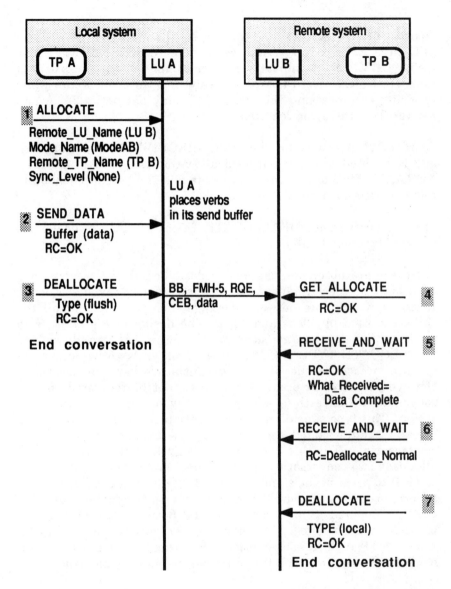

Figure 7.33 Allocate, Send, Deallocate Type (flush) flow.

Step 4.   LU B receives the initiation request and starts TP B. The transaction initiation is done in an implementation-specific manner. Let us assume that TP B receives the incoming allocate by issuing an implementation-defined GET_ALLOCATE verb.

Step 5.   TP B receives and processes the data by issuing an [MC_]RECEIVE_AND_WAIT verb. The WHAT_RECEIVED = DATA_COMPLETE indicates that a complete data record or a complete logical record has been received. If an error occurs while receiving or processing the data, TP B may not notify TP A and recover from the error condition.

Step 6.   TP B issues another [MC_]RECEIVE_AND_WAIT verb and is notified of conversation deallocation (RC=DEALLOCATE_ NORMAL). TP B enters deallocate state and is allowed to deallocate the conversation locally.

Step 7.   TP B issues DEALLOCATE TYPE (LOCAL) to deallocate the conversation locally.

If there are no errors, the design described above is very good from both the performance and network efficiency points of view. Notice that only one network message was generated for all the verbs executed by TP A and TP B. The design in Fig. 7.33 also releases the session as soon as the local LU completes the DEALLOCATE TYPE (FLUSH) verb. This allows other programs to gain access to the session to initiate other conversations. However, if an error occurs the data cannot be recovered on this conversation, since the conversation may not exists on the local system. This type of deallocate is appropriate for programs that have already acknowledged all the data and need only to end the conversation. This design can be significantly improved by allocating two conversations to the remote system: one conversation to TP B to perform the steps shown in Fig. 7.33 and another to TP C for error-recovery purposes. The messages sent from TP A to TP B can be numbered. If an error occurs, TP B may notify TP C of the message in error. Then TP C may send the message in error to TP A on the TP A-TP C conversation. TP A then can then establish a new conversation with TP B and resend the message in error.

7.14.2 PC-to-Host-File Update

This verb sequence flow may be used when the local TP needs to send data in one direction from the local TP to the remote TP, and the data delivery must be confirmed before the conversation is allowed to be deallocated at both ends of the connection. If an error occurs, the local and the remote programs do not deallocate but instead continue the conversation and may start error-recovery procedure. This design can be used when, for example, a PC application sends a data record to update a host file. The PC application needs to be notified whether the update succeeded before the conversation ends. Figure 7.34 illustrates the design steps that can be used by the PC and host applications:

Step 1.   TP A issues the [MC_]ALLOCATE verb requesting a conversation with TP B. The supplied parameter SYNC_LEVEL (CONFIRM) specifies that this conversation may use confirmation processing verbs ([MC_]CONFIRM and [MC_]CONFIRMED verbs are allowed). The local LU buffers the allocation request in its send buffer and returns control to the requester, and nothing is sent across to the remote TP.

Step 2.   TP A issues an [MC_]SEND_DATA verb to send the data to the host application (TP B). The local LU adds the request to its send buffer, and no information is sent to the remote TP.

Step 3.   TP A issues [MC_]DEALLOCATE TYPE (CONFIRM) to deliver, confirm the data, and deallocate the conversation. The local LU flushes its send buffer and sends a single network message to the remote LU. The resulting BIU contains the data, the confirmation request (RQD2), and the deallocation request (CEB). The SNA request definite response 2 (RQD2) indicator requires successful confirmation processing before the conversation can be deallocated. Therefore, the local transaction program is suspended until the confirmation processing is completed. Combining confirmation processing with sending data and deallocation processing is very efficient and minimizes the number of network messages.

Step 4.   LU B receives the initiation request and starts the remote transaction program (TP B). The transaction initiation is done in an implementation-specific manner. Let us assume that TP B receives the incoming allocate by issuing an implementation-defined GET_ALLOCATE verb. Upon completion of this verb TP B eneters Receive state.

Step 5.   TP B receives the data by issuing an [MC_]RECEIVE_AND_WAIT verb. The WHAT_RECEIVED=DATA_COMPLETE indicates that a complete data record or a complete logical record has been received. TP B updates the host file and must issue another [MC_]RECEIVE_AND_ WAIT verb.

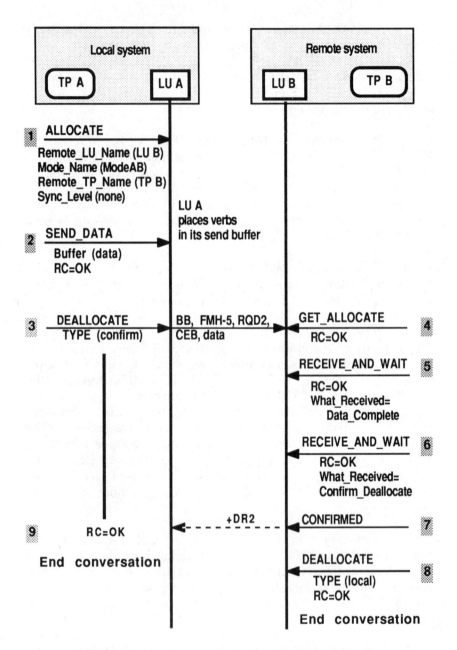

Figure 7.34 Allocate, Send, Deallocate type (Confirm) flow.

Step 6. TP B receives a confirmation request and deallocation request by means of the CONFIRM_ DEALLOCATE indication returned on the WHAT_RECEIVED indicator. Some implementations (and SAA/CPI-C) are capable of receiving status and the data on one receive call. In these implementations, step 6 would not be required. This would be more efficient because it would reduce the number of verbs needed to be processed.

Step 7.   TP B issues the [MC_]CONFIRMED verb to indicate that it received and processed the information sent by the local TP without errors and that it agrees to deallocate the conversation. It then enters the Deallocate state and must issue the [MC_]DEALLOCATE TYPE(LOCAL) before entering the Reset state. Alternatively, TP B may issue an [MC_]SEND_ERROR verb indicating an error condition. The conversation remains allocated. TP B enters Send state and should start user-defined error-recovery procedure. TP A gets RC=Program_Error_Purging and enters the Receive state.

Step 8.   TP B issues DEALLOCATE TYPE (LOCAL) in order to deallocate the conversation and release the session to other conversations.

Step 9.   The RC=OK indicates that TP B has updated the host file without errors and has agreed to terminate the conversation. The local TP enters the Reset state, and the conversation ends.

If there are no errors, the design described above is efficient from both the performance and network usage point of view. Notice that only one network message was generated for all the verbs executed by TP A and TP B. The design in Fig. 7.34 also releases the session as soon as the local LU completes the DEALLOCATE TYPE (FLUSH) verb. This allows other programs to get access to the session and initiate other conversations. However, if an error occurs, the data cannot be recovered on this conversation, since the conversation may have been terminated on the local system. This type of deallocate is appropriate for programs that have already acknowledged all the data and therefore only need to end the conversation. This design can be significantly improved by allocating two conversations to the remote system. One conversation, connected to TPB, would perform the steps shown in Fig. 7.34, and the other conversation, connected to TP C, would be for error recovery purposes. The messages sent from TP A to TP B can be numbered. If an error occurs, TP B may notify TP C of the message in error. Then TP C may send the message in error to TP A on the TP A - TP C conversation. TP A can then establish a new conversation with TP B and resend the message in error.

7.14.3 Requester/Server Design 1

The most common type of conversation is the requester/server model. The local program, also known as the requester, sends a single request to a remote program, also known as the server. The server receives and processes the request and sends back either the data that satisfies the request or a reason why the request was rejected. Once the requester receives the answer, it can then issue another request to the server. Usually the requester/server model is used on local area networks (LANs). However, this model may apply equally well to wide area networks where the server may reside on another LAN network or any other SNA distributed node. Figure 7.35 illustrates possible design steps for the requester/server model. It shows a transaction being entered by a user at a terminal, which is read by the local TP. The local TP then allocates a conversation with the server, sends the transaction request, receives the reply to the request, and displays the answer to the terminal user. The following are the design steps:

Step 1.   TP A (the requester) issues an [MC_]ALLOCATE verb, requesting a conversation with TP B (the server). The supplied parameter, SYNC_LEVEL (NONE), specifies that this conversation cannot issue an [MC_]CONFIRM or SYNCPT verb to confirm or synchronize distributed resources.

Step 2.   The requester issues an [MC_]SEND_DATA verb to send the request to the server. LU A adds the request to its send buffer and no information is sent to the remote TP yet.

Step 3.   The requester issues an [MC_]RECEIVE_AND_WAIT verb and suspends until an answer is received from the server. The [MC_]RECEIVE_AND_WAIT verb flushes the local LU's send buffer and releases the Send state to the remote TP. The resulting network message (BIU) is generated with change direction (CD), begin-bracket (BB), and RQE1 indicators in the RH. The ATTACH header (FMH-5) and data are contained in the RU. The RQE1 indicator does not require a positive response (+RSP) from the remote LU. The change direction (CD) indicator releases the Send state to the server.

Step 4.   LU B receives the conversation initiation request (BB - begin bracket and FMH-5 header) and starts TP B. The remote TP is started in an implementation-specific manner. Let us assume that TP B receives the incoming allocate by issuing an implementation-defined GET_ALLOCATE verb. Once started, the server enters the Receive state, in which it is allowed to receive data.

Step 5. The server receives and processes the data by issuing an [MC_]RECEIVE_AND_WAIT verb. The WHAT_RECEIVED= DATA_COMPLETE indicates that a complete data record or a complete logical record has been received.

Step 6. The server receives the Send state by means of the WHAT_RECEIVED=SEND indicator received on the [MC_] RECEIVE_AND_WAIT verb. Some implementations may receive the data and Send state on one receive call, which is more efficient. Then step 6 would be combined with step 5.

Step 7. The server (TP B) processes the request and issues an [MC_]SEND_DATA verb to send the reply back to the requester. LU B adds the request to its send buffer, and no information is sent yet.

Step 8. The server issues an [MC_]RECEIVE_AND_WAIT verb to flush its send buffer and receive another request from the requester. The [MC_]RECEIVE_AND_WAIT verb flushes the local LU's send buffer and releases the Send state back to the requester. The resulting network message (BIU) is generated with the change direction (CD) and the reply data in the RU.

Step 9. The LU 6.2 [MC_]RECEIVE_AND_WAIT verb issued in step 3 completes with RC=OK. The WHAT_RECEIVED=DATA_ COMPLETE indicates that a complete data record (on a mapped conversation) or a logical record (on a basic conversation) was received from the server.

Step 10. The requester is still in the Receive state and must issue another [MC_]RECEIVE_AND_WAIT verb in order to get the SEND indication and change the state to Send state. Now the requester may display the answer to the terminal user, and if there is no error, it may go to step 2 and send another request to the server. In this case the conversation would not end, and therefore the session would not be released for use by other conversations. This design would be appropriate if the session is not shared by other TPs. The requester could use the session exclusively until it sends all the requests to the server, and then it would need to deallocate the conversation. If there are other TPs competing for the session resources, then the requester should immediately deallocate the conversation (go to step 11) and release the session to other conversations.

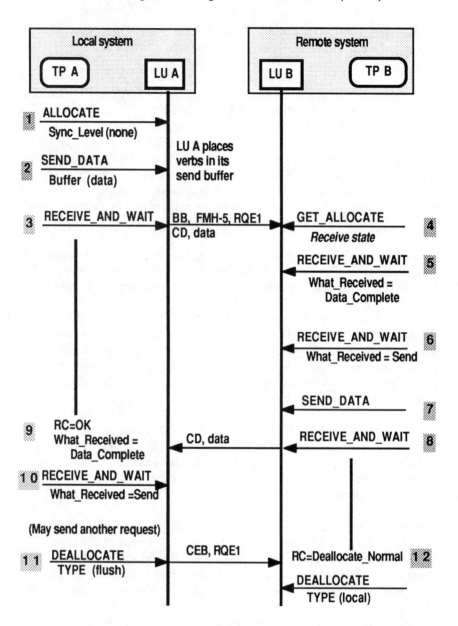

Figure 7.35 Requester/server design 1.

Step 11. The requester issues an [MC_]DEALLOCATE TYPE (FLUSH) verb. LU A sets the conditional end of bracket (CEB) indicator and sends an empty BIU with CEB and RQE1 indicators in the RH. The request exception response (RQE1) indicator does not require any SNA positive response (confirmation) from the remote TP before deallocating. Therefore, the requester deallocates immediately. The local LU releases the session at the local side so it can be accessed by other conversations. Since the requester received and processed the reply to the last request sent, no data can be lost. There is no reason to issue DEALLOCATE TYPE (CONFIRM) and hold the session until confirmation processing completes successfully because all requests have already been processed. In this case the [MC_]DEALLOCATE TYPE(FLUSH) verb is appropriate since the session is released immediately and is then accessible to other conversations.

Step 12. The server issues another [MC_]RECEIVE_AND_WAIT verb and is notified of conversation deallocation request (RC=DEALLOCATE_NORMAL). It then enters the Deallocate state, in which it is allowed to deallocate the conversation locally. Then the server issues DEALLOCATE TYPE (LOCAL), in order to deallocate the conversation locally and release the session to other conversations.

7.14.4 Requester/Server Design 2

Figure 7.36 illustrates another design for the requester/server model. This design is suitable when many requesters need to allocate conversations over the same session. In this case it is important that the local TP does not hold the session for a long time by issuing multiple requests to the server. To avoid this, the server deallocates the conversation as soon as it sends a reply to a single request received from a requester. The following are the design steps (see Fig. 7.36)

Step 1. The requester (TP A) issues an [MC_]ALLOCATE verb, requesting a conversation with TP B (the server). The supplied parameter, SYNC_LEVEL (CONFIRM), specifies that the [MC_]CONFIRM verb is allowed on this conversation to perform confirmation processing.

Step 2. The requester issues an [MC_]SEND_DATA verb to send the request to the server. LU A adds the request to its send buffer. No information is sent to the remote TP yet.

Step 3. TP A issues [MC_]RECEIVE_AND_WAIT verb to receive the reply to the request sent to the server. The [MC_]RECEIVE_

AND_WAIT verb flushes the local LU's send buffer and passes the Send control to the remote TP. The resulting network message (BIU) is generated with change direction (CD), begin-bracket (BB), and RQE1 indicators in the RH. The ATTACH header (FMH-5) and the data are contained in the RU. The RQE1 indicator does not require a positive response (+RSP) from the remote LU. The change direction (CD) indicator releases the Send state to the server.

Step 4.   LU B receives the conversation initiation request (BB - begin bracket and FMH-5 header) and starts TP B. The remote TP is started in an implementation-specific manner. Let us assume that TP B receives the incoming allocate by issuing an implementation-defined GET_ALLOCATE verb. Once started, the server enters the Receive state, in which it is allowed to receive data.

Step 5.   TP B receives and processes the data by issuing the [MC_]RECEIVE_AND_WAIT verb. The WHAT_RECEIVED= DATA_COMPLETE indicating that a complete data record or a complete logical record has been received.

Step 6.   The server receives the Send state by means of the WHAT_RECEIVED=SEND indicator received on [MC_]RECEIVE_ AND_WAIT verb. Some implementations may receive the data and Send state on one receive call which is more efficient. Then step 6 would be combined with step 5.

Step 7.   The server (TP B) processes the request and it issues an [MC_]SEND_DATA verb in order to send the reply back to the requester.   LU B adds the request to its send buffer, and no information is sent yet.

Step 8   The server issues an APPC verb [MC_]DEALLOCATE TYPE (CONFIRM) to deliver the reply and to deallocate the conversation with confirmation processing. The remote logical unit flushes its send buffer and sends a single network message to the remote LU. The resulting BIU contains the data, the confirmation request (RQD2), and the deallocation request (CEB). The SNA request definite response 2 (RQD2) indicator requires successful confirmation processing before the conversation can be deallocated. Therefore, the server is suspended until the confirmation processing is completed.

Step 9.   The [MC_]RECEIVE_AND_WAIT verb issued in step 3 completes with RC=OK. The WHAT_RECEIVED indicator is set to

DATA_COMPLETE, which indicates that a complete data record or a complete logical record has been received.

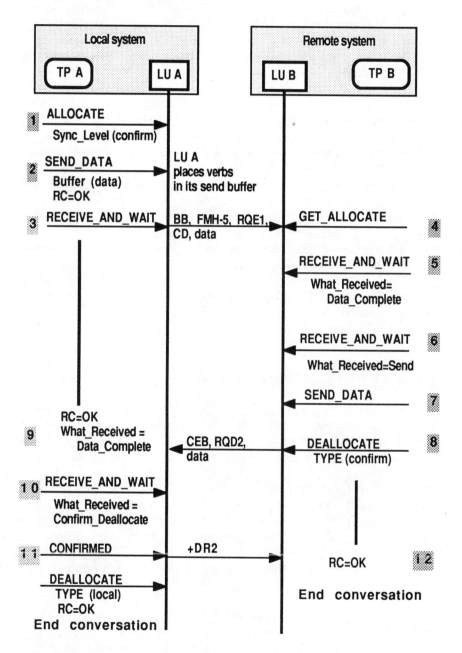

Figure 7.36 Requester/server design 2.

Step 10. The requester receives a confirmation request and deallocation request by means of the CONFIRM_DEALLOCATE indication returned on the WHAT_RECEIVED indicator. Some implementations (and SAA/CPI-C) are capable of receiving status and the data on one receive call. In such implementations step 6 would not be required. This would be more efficient since it would reduce the number of verbs needed to be processed.

Step 11. The requester issues the [MC_]CONFIRMED verb to indicate that it received and processed the reply sent by the server without errors and that it agrees to deallocate the conversation. It then enters the Deallocate state and must issue the [MC_]DEALLOCATE TYPE(LOCAL) before entering the Reset state. Alternatively, TP A may issue an [MC_]SEND_ERROR verb indicating an error condition. The conversation remains allocated. The requester enters the Send state and should start a user-defined error recovery procedure. The server gets RC=Program_Error_Purging, enters the Receive state, and issues an [MC_]RECEIVE_AND_WAIT verb.

Step 12. The RC=OK indicates that the confirmation processing and deallocation completed successfully. The session is released and can be accessed by other conversations.

7.14.5 APPC File Transfer Example

The verb sequence shown in Fig. 7.37 may be used when a file needs to be copied between two systems residing in an SNA/LU 6.2 distributed network. The following are the design steps that can be used by the two transaction programs:

Step 1. The local TP (TP A) issues an APPC [MC_]ALLOCATE verb to start the remote transaction program. The supplied parameter SYNC_LEVEL should be set to CONFIRM to allow confirmation processing to be performed on this conversation. The local LU buffers the allocation request in its send buffer and returns control to the program. Nothing is sent across to the remote TP (TP B).

Step 2. TP A reads "n" records from a disk file and issues an [MC_]SEND_DATA verb (one for each record). The data records are buffered locally by the logical unit, and nothing is sent to the partner yet.

In the case of basic conversations, the "n" records can be moved into the program's buffer and changed into LU 6.2 logical records. Then, only one SEND_DATA verb may be issued to send all the records to TP B. This is more efficient than issuing and processing multiple [MC_]SEND_DATA verbs. The format for blocking and deblocking of logical records on basic conversations is defined by the LU 6.2 architecture. Therefore, any remote transaction program that uses basic conversation verbs will understand the logical record format sent by the local TP. The remote TP may also ask the remote logical unit to "unpack" the received logical records and pass one logical record for each basic RECEIVE_AND_WAIT verb. The SNA/LU 6.2 logical record format was explained in Sec. 3.7 of this book.

In the case of mapped conversations, the local transaction program could also block the records before sending them to the remote TP. Then the local and remote TPs would have to agree on the format and method of blocking and deblocking the data. The data format, and the blocking and deblocking methodology would then be dependent on the design of the local and remote programs. Therefore, the local transaction could not be used to copy a file to another remote mapped conversation TP unless the remote TP was designed specifically to understand the data stream built by the local TP.

Step 3.   TP A issues an [MC_]CONFIRM verb to deliver the "n" records to the remote TP and perform confirmation processing. The local LU flushes its send buffer and sends a single network message (if all the records can be packed into one RU) to the remote LU. The resulting network message (BIU) is generated with the begin bracket (BB) and RQD2 indicators in the RH. The ATTACH header (FMH-5) and the data are contained in the RU. The SNA request definite response 2 (RQD2) indicator requires successful confirmation processing before the local TP can resume its processing. Therefore, the local TP is suspended until the confirmation processing is completed.

Step 4.   The remote logical unit (LU B) receives the conversation initiation request (BB - begin bracket and FMH-5 header) and starts TP B. The remote TP is started in an implementation-specific manner. Let us assume that TP B receives the incoming allocation by issuing an implementation-specific GET_ALLOCATE verb. Once started, the server enters the Receive state and is allowed to receive data.

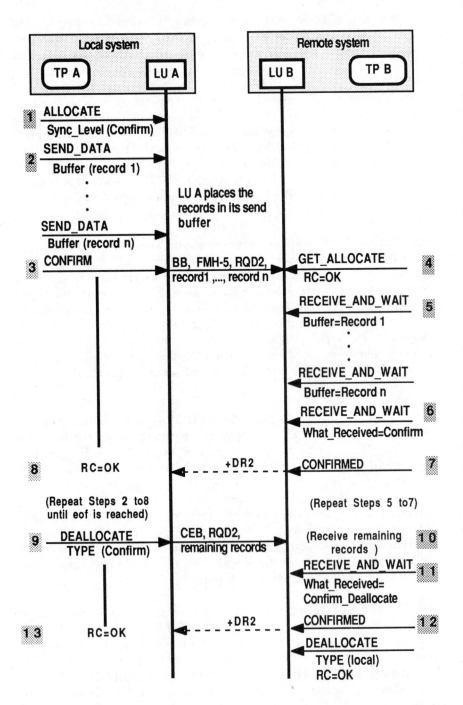

Figure 7.37 File copy example.

Step 5.   TP B receives and processes the data by issuing an
[MC_]RECEIVE_AND_WAIT verb. The WHAT_RECEIVED=
DATA_COMPLETE indicates that a complete data record or a
complete logical record has been received. TP B then continues to
issue [MC_]RECEIVE_AND_WAIT verbs until all the data records
and the confirmation requests are received.

Since TP B does not know the length of the incoming records, it
has a preset maximum record length that it can receive on each
[MC_]RECEIVE_AND_WAIT verb. If the requested maximum
length that is passed to the program's receive buffer is shorter than
the received record length, the LU passes only the requested number
of characters and retains the remaining characters until another
[MC_]RECEIVE_AND_WAIT verb is issued. In this case TP B
would have to issue another [MC_]RECEIVE_AND_WAIT verb to
receive the remaining data for the same record. Therefore, the
number of [MC_]RECEIVE_AND_WAIT verbs can be greater than
the number of corresponding [MC_]SEND_DATA verbs. After the
last record has been received, LU B notifies TP B that TP A has
requested a confirmation reply. In the case of basic conversations
TP B may   receive all the records on one RECEIVE_AND_WAIT
verb by allocating a large enough buffer to accommodate all the
records. TP B itself then would have to deblock the received logical
records. This is generally more efficient than issuing and
processing multiple [MC_]RECEIVE_AND_WAIT verbs.

Step 6.   The confirmation request is received by means of the
WHAT_RECEIVED=CONFIRM indication. TP B should reply to
the confirmation request with an [MC_]CONFIRMED verb or an
[MC_]SEND_ERROR verb.

Step 7.   TP B issues [MC_]CONFIRMED, which acknowledges that
the data was received and processed without errors. Upon successful
completion of this verb TP B returns to the Receive state and should
issue another [MC_]RECEIVE_AND_WAIT verb. Alternatively,
TP B may issue an [MC_]SEND_ERROR verb indicating an error
condition. In this case the TP B would enter the Send state and
should perform user-defined error recovery. Confirmation
processing was discussed in Sec. 7.4 and error recovery, in Sec.
7.11.

Step 8.   LU A receives a positive response (+DR2) from LU B
indicating that TP B confirmed the [MC_]CONFIRM verb issued in
step 3. The control is returned to TP A by completing the

[MC_]CONFIRM verb with RC=OK. TP A and TP B have successfully copied "n" records thus far. TP A may now repeat steps 2 through 8 until the end of file (eof) is reached. TP B would have to repeat steps 5 through 7.

Step 9. TP A issues [MC_]DEALLOCATE TYPE (CONFIRM), to deallocate the conversation and deliver the remaining records to TP B. The deallocation TYPE (CONFIRM) requires successful confirmation processing before the conversation can be deallocated. LU A flushes its send buffer and sends the remaining data, the confirmation request (RQD2), and the deallocation request (CEB) across the session to LU B. [MC_]DEALLOCATE TYPE (CONFIRM) processing was discussed in Sec. 7.7.

Step 10. First, TP B must receive and process all the remaining data by issuing an [MC_]RECEIVE_AND_WAIT verb.

Step 11. LU B notifies TP B of the confirmation and deallocation request by means of the CONFIRM_DEALLOCATE returned on the WHAT_RECEIVED parameter.

Step 12. TP B issues an [MC_]CONFIRMED verb and then [MC_]DEALLOCATE TYPE (LOCAL) to locally deallocate the conversation. If an error occurred, TP B would have to issue an [MC_]SEND_ERROR verb. The conversation would not end, and TP B would have to perform a user-defined error recovery procedure. This was illustrated in Fig. 7.15.

Step 13. The RC=OK indicates that the two communicating programs have copied the file without errors and agreed to terminate the conversation.

The design described above assumes that there are no errors during the copy operation. If an error occurs, the TP that detects an error issues the [MC_]SEND_ERROR verb and always enters the Send state. Then the TP should start a user-defined error-recovery procedure (e.g., the TPs may agree to redo all the processing from the previous successful confirmation processing). The partner TP is notified that an error occurred by means of the RC = Program_Error_Purging. The partner TP then enters the Receive state and should issue an [MC_]RECEIVE_AND_WAIT verb and wait for the error explanation. Error recovery was discussed in Sec. 7.11 .

8

Common Programming Interface Communications SAA/CPI-C

The APPC architecture does not impose any syntax rules on the Application Programming Interfaces (APIs), which may vary from one environment to another. Therefore, the APPC applications are not easily portable in an SAA computer enterprise. **Common Programming Interface-Communications (CPI-C)**, on the other hand, was designed to comply with the SAA architecture. CPI-C ,also referred to as **CPI Communications**, provides a consistent and portable application programming interface that is independent of different implementations. This means that CPI-C programming calls have the same syntax irrespective of whether the programs are running on personal computers, minicomputers, or mainframes. Functionally, though, APPC and CPI-C are very similar. We can think of CPI-C as APPC with defined syntax. CPI-C defines a subset of the APPC/LU 6.2 functions . In actual fact CPI-C calls can be mapped into one or more APPC verbs. This was illustrated in Fig 6.4. Therefore, all the theory and the flow diagrams discussed in Chap. 7, also apply to CPI-C. This Chap. gives a detailed description of the CPI-C architecture and the issues related to designing CPI-C distributed applications.

It was written for application designers and programmers that design and write transaction programs distributed in an SAA computer enterprise. The basic concepts of CPI-C and the major differences between APPC and CPI-C were discussed in Chap. 6 of this book. The reader is strongly advised to review Chaps. 6 and 7 prior to reading this chapter.

8.1 CPI-C ENVIRONMENT

As described earlier, the major differences between APPC and CPI-C standards come from the fact that APPC was introduced in 1984, which was three years prior to the SAA announcement and did not impose any syntax rules on application programming interfaces (APIs). CPI-C, on the other hand, was introduced in 1988 and complies with the syntax rules imposed by the SAA's common programming interface. Similarly to APPC, CPI-C is built on top of the logical unit 6.2. It defines programming calls for program-to-program communications using SNA logical unit 6.2. Programs communicate with each other by issuing CPI-C calls. CPI-C calls have the same syntax that all SAA implementations must use (e.g., CMINIT, CMALLC, CMSEND, or CMDEAL). This syntax is used for both basic and mapped conversations. In this book pseudonyms are used often to refer to actual CPI-C calls rather than the actual syntax. For example, Initialize_Conversation is a pseudonym for the actual CMINIT call, Allocate is a pseudonym for the CMALLC call, Send_Data is a pseudonym for the CMSEND call, and Deallocate is a pseudonym for the CMDEAL call.

When using APPC/LU 6.2 verbs, application programmers have to supply many parameters describing the network environment, such as Remote LU Name, Mode Name, or Remote TP Name. Also the APPC programmer must establish conversation characteristics by specifying, for example, whether the allocation request establishes a mapped or a basic conversation or the maximum synchronization level used on a conversation. This was changed in the CPI Communications (CPI-C) interface by moving most of the parameters into a configuration file and defining initial conversation characteristics. This is illustrated in Fig. 8.1. The CPI-C program issues an Initialize_Conversation call and supplies, as a parameter, sym_dest_name (referred to as symbolic destination name), which points to a configuration file called **side information**. The following information is stored in side information:

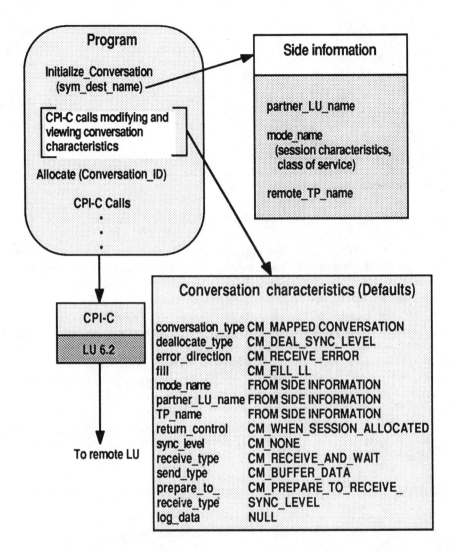

Figure 8.1 CPI-C environment.

- **partner_LU_name** — the name of the partner (remote) logical unit. This name is used by the local LU to establish a session with the remote logical unit and is carried in the SNA BIND command.

- **mode_name** — defining session characteristics and network properties such as cost, priority, performance, or routing.

- **remote_TP_name** — the name of the remote transaction program. This name is carried in the allocation request (ATTACH header) sent by the local LU to the remote LU. CPI-C refers to transaction programs as application programs or simply programs.

A program issues the Initialize_Conversation (CMINIT) call to initialize characteristics prior to allocating the conversation with the remote program. The remote program issues Accept_Conversation (CMACCP) to accept an incoming conversation and initialize characteristics for the remote program. Figure 8.1 illustrates a local CPI-C program issuing an Initialize_Conversation call and supplies as the parameter the symbolic destination name (sym_dest_name), which points to the side information. After issuing the CMINIT call the **conversation characteristics** for the local program are set to values shown in Fig. 8.1. These values are called default values or default conversation characteristics. The program may next issue the Allocate (CMALLC) call, supplying just one parameter conversation_ID, to establish a conversation with a partner transaction program. The conversation automatically assumes all the conversation characteristic set by the default values shown above. The conversation is allocated with a remote program name (remote_TP_name) which is stored in the side information. The underlying session is established to the partner_LU_name with session characteristic, pointed by the mode_name parameter stored in the side information. The conversation characteristic default values may be changed by issuing CPI-C calls prior to the CMALLC call, as shown in Fig. 8.1. The following naming conventions and pseudonyms are used in CPI-C to enhance clarity and readability:

- **CPI-C calls** — begin with the prefix CM (e.g., CMINIT). The pseudonyms describing the calls start with capital letters (e.g., Initialize Conversation).

- **Conversation characteristics** and **variables** — hold the values of characteristics (see Fig. 8.1). For example, the conversation characteristics conversation_type is set to the value CM_MAPPED_CONVERSATION. The values appear in all-capital letters.

- **States** — define CPI-C states and begin with a capital letter (e.g., Initialize, Send, or Receive state).

8.1.1 CPI-C Programming Calls

CPI-C programs exchange messages over a conversation which is assigned to a single session established between the local and the remote LUs. The programs share the session to carry multiple transactions (conversations) in a serial manner.

Figure 8.2 shows program A issuing CPI-C calls to communicate with program B. The calls are executed and buffered by the local LU, changed to appropriate network messages, and sent across the session to the remote logical unit. The remote LU unblocks and decodes the network messages and passes them to program B.

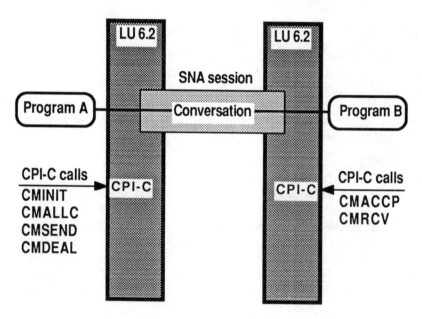

Figgure 8.2 CPI-C calls.

SAA/CPI-C program calls can be divided into two groups:

* **Starter-Set calls.** These calls are used for simple communications that assume the default conversation characteristics shown in Fig. 8.1. The starter-set calls include Initialize_Conversation, Accept_Conversation, Allocate, Send_Data, Receive, and Deallocate calls.

• **Advanced-Function calls**. These calls are used to perform more specialized distributed functions that are not provided by the default set of conversation characteristics shown in Fig. 8.1. For example, advanced-function calls are used, when an LU 6.2 distributed function such as synchronization processing, confirmation processing, or error recovery is required. The default conversation characteristics may be changed or examined by issuing CPI-C advanced-function calls specifically designated for this purpose.

The following is a list of CPI Communications starter-set calls and their major functions:

Conversation Initiation and Termination

• **Initialize_Conversation (CMINIT)** — issued by the local program to initialize resources for the conversation and to set the default conversation characteristics. The local logical unit (LU) assigns a unique **conversation_ID** that must be supplied on every verb following the CMINIT call in order to uniquely identify the local end of a conversation.

• **Allocate (CMALLC)** — allocates a CPI-C mapped or a basic conversation with a partner program. A CMALLC call supplies just one parameter conversation_ID that was returned on the previously issued CPI-C CMINIT call. The conversation automatically assumes all the conversation characteristics set by the default values and the side information as shown in Fig. 8.1. At this time the local LU establishes a session between the local and remote logical units if one does not already exist. The CMINIT and CMALLC calls combined can be mapped into the APPC ALLOCATE verb.

• **Accept_Conversation (CMACCP)** — issued by the remote program to accept an incoming conversation. It also initializes resources for the conversation and sets the default conversation characteristics for the remote program. The LU assigns a unique **conversation_ID** that must be supplied on every verb following the CMACCP call.

• **Deallocate (CMDEAL)** — ends a conversation. The local LU notifies the remote LU that the local program requested to end the current conversation. The remote LU notifies the remote program of the conversation termination request and upon agreement by both parties the conversation is ended.

Exchanging Data

- **Send_Data (CMSEND)** — sends data to the remote TP on a basic or a mapped conversation. The data can be of any arbitrary format agreed upon by the two application programmers. The local logical unit may buffer multiple CMSEND calls into one network message and transmit its send buffer across the conversation when requested by the program or when sufficient data has been accumulated (maximum RU size has been reached). This avoids generating network messages for each send and optimizes the communication facilities between logical units (LUs). The LU is responsible for building the appropriate General Data Stream (GDS) variables for mapped conversations. An application programmer is responsible for building the logical records for basic conversations.

- **Receive_Data (CMRCV)** — receives information into the program receive buffer. This call performs a similar function to the [MC_]RECEIVE_AND_WAIT verb when the receive type is set to the default value CM_RECEIVE_AND_WAIT (see Fig. 8.1). When the receive type is set to CM_RECEIVE_ IMMEDIATE, then this call performs a similar function to the MC_RECEIVE_IMMEDIATE verb.

  The LU is responsible for:

  1. Receiving and buffering network messages

  2. Deblocking the messages before passing them to the receiving program

  3. Keeping track of the length of each message received from the partner program

  4. Decoding the GDS variables and passing only the user data to the mapped conversation programs

  5. Blocking and deblocking logical records

The following is a list of CPI-C advanced-function calls and their major functions:

Synchronization and Control

- **Confirm (CMCFM)** — sends a confirmation request to the partner transaction program. The local program is suspended until a confirmation reply is received from the partner program.

- **Confirmed (CMCFMD)** — sends a confirmation reply to the received confirmation request. This synchronizes processing between local and remote transaction programs on a specific conversation.

- **Flush (CMFLUS)** — flushes the local LU's send buffer.

- **Prepare_To_Receive (CMPTR)** — sends the change direction (CD) indicator to the remote program. The LU flushes all data buffered so far and releases the Send state to the remote program. The local program enters the Receive state and may perform local processing before receiving data.

- **Send_Error (CMSERR)** — sends an error notification to the remote program. The remote program is notified of an application error and is placed in Receive state. The program that issued the CMSERR call enters the Send state and should initiate user-defined error recovery.

- **Request_To_Send (CMRTS)** — requests a send state from the remote program. The local LU will send a special expedited message to the remote LU notifying the remote program that the local program wants to send data.

- **Test_Request_To_Send (CMTRTS)** — tests whether a specific request-to-send notification has been received from the partner program.

Modifying Conversation Characteristics

- **Set_Conversation_Type (CMSCT)** — sets the CPI-C conversation_type conversation characteristic to basic or mapped conversation.

- **Set_Deallocate_Type(CMSDT)** — sets the conversation deallocate_type to FLUSH, CONFIRM, or SYNC_LEVEL.

- **Set_Error_Direction(CMSED)** — sets the error_direction characteristic to SEND_ERROR or RECEIVE_ERROR.

- **Set_Fill(CMSF)** — sets the fill conversation characteristic for a basic conversation to LL or BUFFER.

- **Set_Log_Data(CMSLD)** — sets the log_data conversation characteristic. It is used only on basic conversations. The LU generates a special log GDS variable when a program issues CMSERR call or CMDEAL call with deallocate_type set to CM_DEALLOCATE_ABEND.

- **Set_Mode_Name(CMSMN)** — sets the mode_name characteristic.

- **Set_Partner_LU_Name(CMSPLN)** — sets the partner_LU_name characteristic.

- **Set_Prepare_To_Receive_Type(CMSPTR)** — sets the prepare_to_receive_type conversation characteristic to FLUSH, CONFIRM, or SYNC_LEVEL.

- **Set_Receive_Type(CMSRT)** — sets the receive_type characteristic to RECEIVE_AND_WAIT or RECEIVE_IMMEDIATE.

- **Set_Return_Control(CMSRC)** — sets the return_contol characteristic to WHEN_SESSION_ALLOCATED or IMMEDIATE. This is used to determine when a control should be returned to the program after issuing a CMALLC call.

- **Set_Send_Type(CMSST)** — sets the send_type characteristic. This allows the combination of flushing, confirmation processing or conversation termination when sending data to the remote program.

- **Set_Sync_Level (CMSSL)** — sets the sync_level characteristic to NONE, CONFIRM or SYNC_POINT. This synchronization level, when issuing a CMALL call, will be sent to the remote program at conversation initiation.

- **Set_TP_Name (CMSTPN)** — sets the TP_name conversation characteristic. This is the name of the remote transaction program that is sent with the allocation request to the remote logical unit.

Extracting Conversation Characteristics

- **Extract_Conversation_Type (CMECT)** — allows viewing of the conversation_type characteristic. This can be used, for example, to determine whether the incoming conversation is basic or mapped.

- **Extract_Mode_Name(CMEMN)** — allows viewing of the mode_name characteristic.

- **Extract_Partner_LU_Name(CMEPLN)** — allows viewing of the partner_LU_ name characteristic.

- **Extract_Sync_Level(CMESL)** — allows viewing of the sync_level characteristic.

Synchronization Point Services

The logical unit 6.2 provides programs with synchronization point services. The LU performs the SNA two-phase commit protocol to synchronize changes to protected resources throughout a distributed transaction. All conversations allocated with sync_level set to CM_SYNC_POINT are called **protected conversations**. CPI-C issues a generic **commit** or **backout** call to use the synchronization point services. The commit and backout calls establish a new synchronization point (called syncpoint) or returns to a previous syncpoint.

The following is a short description of the synchronization processing CPI-C calls:

- **commit** — advances all protected resources, such as distributed databases, to the next synchronization point. The local logical unit flushes its send buffer for all LU 6.2 conversations allocated with a synchronization level of CM_SYNC_POINT. Applications define an indivisible **logical unit of work (LUW)** as a sequence of related programming statements (database updates, deletes, etc.). The LU is responsible for committing the logical unit of work to the next synchronization point or restoring the LUW to the last synchronization point.

- **backout** — restores all protected resources to the last synchronization point, and sends backout on all conversations allocated with synchronization level of CM_SYNC_POINT. The resources are restored to the last synchronization point, which would be either the start of the transaction or the last successful commit call issued since the beginning of the conversation.

The transaction programs are notified of synchronization point services by the return_code (e.g., RC=CM_TAKE_BACKOUT indicating an error condition) or status_received parameters (e.g., CM_TAKE_COMMIT).

The APPC/LU 6.2 architecture, discussed earlier, defines the **SYNCPT** and **BACKOUT** verb to perform a distributed function equivalent to the **commit** and **backout** verb described above. For more information on synchronization services, see Sec. 7.4 and 7.5 in this book.

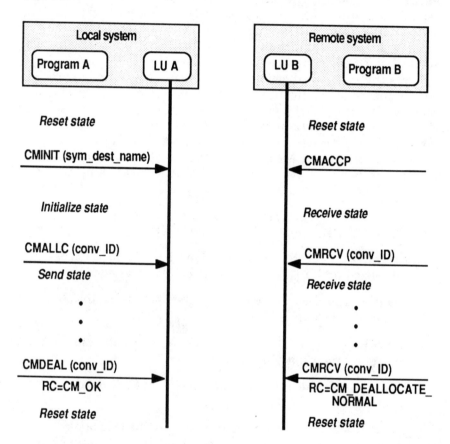

Figure 8.3 CPI-C state transitions.

8.1.2 CPI-C Programming States

The SAA CPI-C calls that are allowed, at any given time in a program and for a particular conversation, depends on the state of the conversation. CPI-C defines the states and the rules that the programmers must follow when using a conversation. Initially the conversation is in the Reset state for both programs (see Fig. 8.3), and then the states change depending on the CPI-C call made by the program and the information received from the remote program. The conversation states at each end of the conversation may be different. The communicating programs must follow the send/receive mode protocol established when the conversation is allocated. Basically, one of the programs is in Send state and may send data and the other is in Receive state and must receive data. The sending program may change the send-receive relationship by passing the change direction indicator to the remote program. The send/receive mode protocol was discussed in Sec. 3.6.2. CPI-C enforces the rules by allowing programmers to perform only certain operations in a particular conversation state. The state of a conversation may be changed as a result of a CPI-C call issued by the transaction program. When a conversation leaves a state, it makes a state transition to another state. For example, when Program A issues a CMALLC call, then a state transition occurs from the Initialize to the Send state. The following is a list of CPI-C states:

- **Reset** — The conversation does not exist. The program is allowed to issue the CMINIT or CMACCP call.

- **Initialize** — The conversation has been successfully initialized and a conversation_ID has been assigned.

- **Send** — The program can send data, request confirmation, or perform syncpoint processing.

- **Send-Pending** — The program has received data and the Send control on the same Receive call.

- **Receive** — The program can receive data from the remote program.

- **Defer Receive or Defer Deallocate** — The program can flush the LU's send buffer, request confirmation, or perform syncpoint processing.

- **Confirm, Confirm Send, Confirm Deallocate** — The program can reply to a confirmation request.

- **Syncpoint, Syncpoint Send, Syncpoint Deallocate** — The program can reply to a syncpoint request.

A programmer is responsible for tracking a conversation's current state. A return_code CM_PROGRAM_STATE_CHECK is returned to the program if an invalid CPI-C call is issued for this state.

8.2 CONVERSATION INITIATION

Once the network resources such as SNA nodes, side information, and conversation characteristics have been defined and activated, the CPI-C transaction programs may initiate conversations. A program can be started by receiving an allocation request from a remote program or by an operator command.

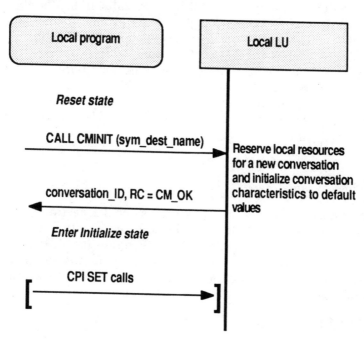

Figure 8.4 Initialize_Conversation (CMINIT) call.

8.2.1 Initialize_Conversation

As described earlier, the CPI-C calls that an application programmer can issue, at any given time in a program and for a particular conversation, depends on the state of the conversation. Initially the local and remote programs are in the Reset state. Fig. 8.4 illustrates the Initialize_Conversation (CMINIT) call. A local program uses the call and the side information to initialize conversation characteristics. Upon successful completion of this call, a conversation_ID is returned to the program. This conversation_ID must be used in all subsequent local program calls using this conversation. The program is not required explicitly to specify parameters, such as partner_LU_name, mode_name or remote_TP_name, in order to start a conversation with a remote program because these parameters are taken from the side information. The remaining conversation characteristics, such as conversation_type, return_control, prepare_to_receive_type, send_type, sync_level, deallocate_type or error_direction, are set to their default values (see Fig. 8.1). If a program wants to change the default values, it may issue CPI-C Set calls immediately after issuing Initialize_Conversation. CPI-C programs are not allowed to modify or examine the security parameters. The default security is set to SECURITY=SAME. The security parameters can be changed via implementation specific calls. For more information on LU 6.2 security, see Sec. 7.2.3 in this book.

The following is the syntax of the Initialize_Conversation call:

CALL CMINIT   (conversation_ID, sym_dest_name,
                   return_code)

Supplied parameters:

sym_dest_name — specifies the symbolic destination name that points to an entry in the side information containing partner_LU_name, mode_name, TP_name (see Fig. 8.1). If sym_dest_name is set to blanks, then the program is responsible for setting the side information prior to issuing the Allocate call.

Returned parameters:

conversation_ID — specifies the conversation identification that uniquely identifies this conversation. The conversation_ ID must be passed as a supplied parameter in all subsequent calls for this conversation.

RC — specifies a return code to be returned on completion of this call.   RC=OK indicates that a new conversation_ID was successfully assigned and that conversation characteristics were initialized to default values.

A program must issue an Initialize_Conversation call each time it wants to establish a new conversation. CPI-C allows a program to communicate with multiple remote programs using concurrent conversations. Multiple conversations can be established by issuing multiple Initialize_Conversation calls, or by issuing the Accept_Conversation call followed by one or multiple Initialize_ Conversation calls. When communicating concurrently with multiple programs it may be advantageous to set the receive_type to CM_RECEIVE_IMMEDIATE. Then the program will not be suspended when a Receive call is issued for a particular conversation even if no data is available from the partner program. The program simply is notified that there is no data for this conversation and it can start processing other conversations. The default receive_type is set to CM_RECEIVE_AND_WAIT. Then a Receive call suspends the program until some information arrives from the remote program. At this point the program cannot perform any other processing.

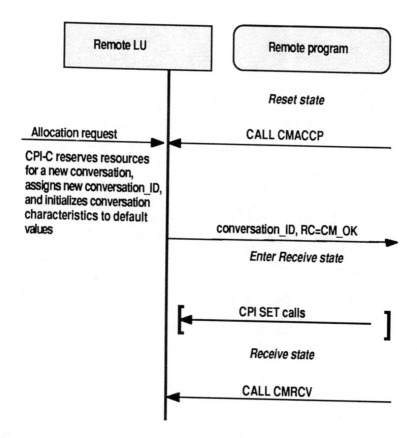

Figure 8.5 Accept_Conversation (CMACCP) call.

8.2.2 Accept_Conversation

A remote program issue Accept_Conversation (CMACCP) in order to accept an incoming conversation and initialize characteristics for the remote program. Figure 8.5 illustrates a remote CPI-C program issuing the Accept_Conversation call to accept an incoming allocation request. The incoming allocation request carries such conversation characteristics as conversation_type and sync_level. The conversation characteristics received in the allocation request cannot be modified by the remote program. The remaining conversation characteristics (deallocate_type, error_direction, prepare_to_ receive_type, or send_type) are set to default values. These characteristics can be changed by issuing CPI-C Set calls following an Accept_Conversation call. Upon successful completion of the call, the conversation enters the Receive state and the program should issue the Receive call and wait for information from the local program. CPI-C allows only one Accept_Conversation call (only one transaction program can be started by the incoming allocation request), but this does not limit the program to just one conversation. Once started, the program may issue multiple Initialize_Conversation calls to start other conversations with multiple partner programs.

8.2.3 Allocate Call

Upon successful completion of the Initialize_Conversation (CMINIT) call, a program enters the Initialize state as shown in Fig. 8.6. The conversation has been successfully initialized and a unique conversation_ID has been assigned. The Initialize_Conversation call initializes the conversation for the local program only and no information is sent to the partner program yet. The conversation_ID returned to the program is also a local entity and identifies the conversation at the local end only. After issuing the CMINIT call, the program may additionally issue Set calls to change the default conversation characteristics and then it should issue the Allocate (CMALLC) call to allocate a conversation with a partner transaction program. At this time the local LU sends a session initiation BIND command to the remote LU in order to establish a session between the local and remote LUs if one does not already exist. The local LU does not necessarily send the allocation request to the partner LU when the Allocate call is issued. The LU buffers the allocation request (an SNA ATTACH header FMH-5) until the local program issues a call that flushes the LU's send buffer. Therefore, successful execution of the Allocate call does not guarantee that the remote program has been contacted or even started. The local LU is not required to flush its send buffer until requested explicitly by the local program or until it accumulates a sufficient amount of information for transmission from one or more subsequent Send_Data calls. The sufficient amount of information for transmission can vary from one session to another depending on the configured maximum request/response unit size (MAXRU size). Upon successful completion of the Allocate call the local program enters the Send state. Now the local program may start sending data by issuing Send_Data calls. When MAXRU size of information is accumulated, the local LU will send the allocation request together with the accumulated data to the remote LU. Optionally, the local program may issue the Flush or Confirm calls immediately following the Allocate call to ensure that the allocation request is sent as soon as possible to the remote program.

The following is the syntax of the Allocate call:

CALL CMALLC   (conversation_ID, return_code)

Supplied parameters:

conversation_ID — specifies the conversation_ID returned on the Initialize_Conversation call

Returned parameters:

RC — specifies the result of the call execution. CM_OK indicates that the conversation was allocated successfully

The CPI-C Allocate call performs two functions:

1. It establishes an SNA LU 6.2 session between local and remote logical units if a session has not already been established.

2. It allocates a mapped or a basic conversation with a partner program (depending on the conversation_type characteristic). The CMALLC call supplies just one parameter conversation_ID that was returned on the previously issued CMINIT call. The partner_LU_name, mode_name and TP_name are taken from the side information, or they can be overwritten by the previously issued CPI-C Set calls.

8.2.4 Initiation Flows

Figure 8.6 shows a typical call sequence for establishing a CPI-C conversation. The following are the steps:

Step 1. The local program (program A) issues the Initialize_ Conversation call to initialize local resources for a new conversation. CPI-C performs the following tasks on the local system:

- It initializes local resources for a new conversation.

- It assigns a conversation_ID (conv_ID 1) that uniquely identifies this conversation.

- It identifies a session partner_LU_name, mode_name, and the partner program TP_name. These parameters are taken from the side information. It establishes a set of conversation characteristics (see Fig. 8.1) for example, the default conversation_type is set to CM_MAPPED_CONVERSATION.

- Upon successful completion of this call the control is returned to the program with RC=OK and the new conversation_ID to identify the local end of this conversation (e.g., Conv_ID 1 in Fig. 8.6). The local end of the conversation enters the Initialize state. Notice that all the processing so far is local and no conversations exists yet on the remote system.

Now, program A may issue CPI-C Set calls to change the side information or conversation characteristics. For example, the program may change conversation_type to basic conversation, or it may set the TP_name to program B if it was not already preset to this value in the side information. CPI-C does not allow the change of conversation level security parameters from a program. The default security is set to SAME, and it can be changed in an implementation-specific manner. The conversation level security parameters were discussed in Sec. 7.2 of this book.

Step 2. Program A issues an Allocate call to start a basic or a mapped conversation with program B. The local LU (LU A) establishes a LU 6.2 session with the remote LU (LU B), if it hasn't already been established. The session characteristics are specified by mode_name, taken from the side information, or set by the Set_Mode_Name call issued prior to the Allocate call. Once the session has been established and the conversation is successfully allocated to the session, then the local LU buffers the Allocate call in its send buffer and returns control to the program. The important fact to remember is that RC=OK on the Allocate call simply means that:

a. The call was syntactically correct.

b. The local LU builds and buffers the SNA ATTACH header (the FMH-5 containing the allocation parameters).

c. The local LU buffers the allocation request locally and no information is sent to the remote LU (some implementations may choose to send the allocation request to the remote program immediately rather than storing it in the LU's local send buffer). The local program enters the Send state.

Step 3.   Program A may start sending data by issuing Send_Data calls. The local LU buffers the Send_Data calls until it accumulates enough data for transmission (from one or more subsequent Send_Data calls). Then the allocation request (the ATTACH header) and the data is sent to the remote LU as one network message. Combining the data with the allocation request reduces the number of network messages and generally improves performance. In some cases, though, when the remote program is not available, a lot of processing can be wasted. The local program is informed of an allocation failure on one of the subsequent calls following the Allocate call. All processing and the network messages sent so far for this conversation are wasted. Therefore in some instances, when, for example multiple sends are required or the program must perform a lot of initial preprocessing prior to sending data across the conversation, it may be more appropriate to send the allocation request as soon as possible rather than buffering it in the LU's send buffer.

Or:

Program A may issue the Flush (CMFLUS) call immediately following the Allocate call. The CPI-C Flush call flushes the LU's send buffer. Notice, though, that in this case an additional network message is generated that carries just the allocation request across the network. This case was discussed in Sec. 6.3 (see Fig. 6.18).

Or:

Program A may issue the Confirm (CMCFM) call immediately following the Allocate call. This time program A will be suspended until confirmation processing completes. Upon successful completion of confirmation processing, the local program is assured that the remote program was contacted and that it replied positively to the confirmation request. The major disadvantage of the confirmation processing is that the local program is suspended and therefore cannot perform any processing until the remote program is started and a confirmation reply is received from the remote program. This case was discussed in Sec. 7.2 (see Fig. 7.5).

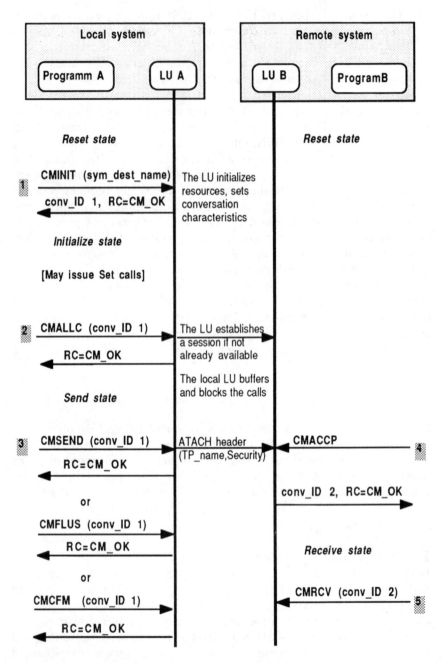

Figure 8.6 Conversation initiation sequence.

Step 4. The remote logical unit receives the allocation request and starts a new instance of program B. Program B issues the Accept_ Conversation (CMACCP) call to accept the incoming allocation request. Upon successful completion of the call the remote logical uni returns control to program B. The RC is set to OK and the conversation_ID is set to conv_ID 2, which uniquely identifies this conversation at the remote end of the conversation. Notice that conv_ID 2 is local to program B only and differs from conv_ID 1, which identifies the same conversation at the local end. Program B is placed in the Receive state and must supply conv_ID 2 in all subsequent calls for this conversation. Also at this time the conversation characteristics are set to default values at the remote end of the conversation.

Step 5. In the Receive state program B is allowed to issue the Receive call and then wait for information to arrive from program A. The received information can be user data or a confirmation request, if program A issued the Confirm call immediately following the Allocate call. The reader should review the APPC [MC_]ALLOCATE verb and initiation flows discussed in Sec. 7.2.4. The functionality of the APPC flows apply to CPI-C as well. The only differences are that the local TP must issue an Initialize_Conversation call prior to issuing an allocation request and the remote TP uses the Accept_Conversation call to explicitly receive an incoming allocation request.

8.3 CONVERSATION TERMINATION

The CPI-C program issues the Deallocate (CMDEAL) call to end a specified mapped or basic conversation. Upon successful completion of this call the LU-LU session assigned to this conversation is released to other conversations. The APPC conversation termination was discussed in detail in Sec. 7.7 in this book. Since APPC and CPI-C are almost functionally equivalent, the reader is strongly advised to review especially Sec. 7.7.3. In this section we will concentrate on the difference between the APPC and CPI-C conversation termination flows.

8.3.1 Deallocate Call

The following is the syntax of the Deallocate call:

    CALL CMDEAL (conversation_ID, return_code)

Supplied parameters:

conversation_ID — specifies the conversation_ID returned on the Initialize_Conversation call or the Accept_Conversation CPI-C call.

Returned parameters:

RC (return code) — specifies the result of the call execution. CM_OK indicates that the conversation was deallocated successfully.

The CPI-C Deallocate call ends a conversation with a partner program. The conversation may be deallocated in different ways depending on the deallocate_type conversation characteristic. The major difference between an APPC and CPI-C conversation termination is the syntax of the CPI-C Deallocate call. CPI-C programs do not explicitly provide a deallocate type parameter (the APPC TYPE parameter FLUSH, CONFIRM, SYNC_LEVEL, ABEND). This parameter is already preset to a conversation characteristic default value (CM_DEALLOCATE_SYNC_LEVEL) after the conversation is successfully established (see Fig. 8.1). Once the conversation is established the deallocate_type conversation characteristic can be overwritten with the CPI-C Set_Deallocate_Type (CMSDT) call.

Normally the CPI Communications Deallocate call can be issued only in the Send state (see Fig. 8.7). The exception to this rule is when the transaction program discovers an unrecoverable error condition and wants to abort the conversation by issuing a Deallocate call with the deallocate_type set to CM_DEALLOCATE_ ABEND. The conversation can be aborted in any state other than the Reset state.

Upon successful completion of the Deallocate call (RC=OK) the local program enters the Reset state. There is no Deallocate state in CPI-C. Therefore, there is no need for the remote program to deallocate the conversation locally after receiving a deallocation request from a partner. When the conversation is allocated with the synchronization level (sync_level) set to CM_SYNC_POINT and the deallocate_type set to CM_DEALLOCATE_SYNC_LEVEL, then the local program enters the Defer-Deallocate state. The program must complete the conversation termination by performing synchronization processing, confirmation processing, or flushing the LU's send buffer.

8.3.2 Conversation Termination Flows

The following are the design steps for terminating a CPI-C conversation (assuming that a conversation has already been allocated, as shown in Fig. 8.6):

Step 1. Prior to deallocating the conversation, the local program may issue a Set_Deallocate_Type (CMSDT) call to overwrite the default deallocate_type conversation characteristic (CM_DEALLOCATE_SYNC_LEVEL), or it can issue the Set_Log_Data (CMSLD) call to set the log_data characteristic. The log_data is used only by basic conversation programs to log error information throughout the distributed transaction when a program ends the conversation with the deallocate_type set to CM_DEALLOCATE_ABEND. In this case the remote program is notified by means of RC=CM_DEALLOCATE_ABEND and the conversation ends unconditionally.

Step 2. The local program issues the Deallocate call. If there are no errors, the local program may choose to deallocate a conversation unconditionally or conditionally. The unconditional termination ends the conversation as soon as the call is issued and does not require any acknowledgment from the partner program. The conditional termination requires confirmation or synchronization processing before the conversation can successfully deallocate.

Step 3. The local LU returns to the program immediately (RC=OK) without a need for any acknowledgment from the partner program. This means that the Deallocate call issued in Step 2, requested unconditional termination of the conversation. This occurs when prior to Step 2 either of the following conditions have been met:

- The deallocate_type was set to CM_DEALLOCATE_FLUSH.

- The deallocate_type was set to CM_DEALLOCATE_SYNC_LEVEL and the conversation was allocated with the sync_level set to CM_NONE. These are the CPI-C default values.

This type of CPI-C deallocate call is equivalent to the APPC DEALLOCATE TYPE(FLUSH) verb and was discussed in detail in Sec. 6.3 (see Fig. 6.21) and Sec. 7.7 in this book. Notice that in this case the local program may end the conversation at the local end before even the remote program was started. This was illustrated in Fig. 7.33. The reader should review Fig. 7.33 keeping in mind the syntax differences between the APPC verbs and the CPI-C calls and also that CPI-C does not need DEALLOCATE TYPE (LOCAL).

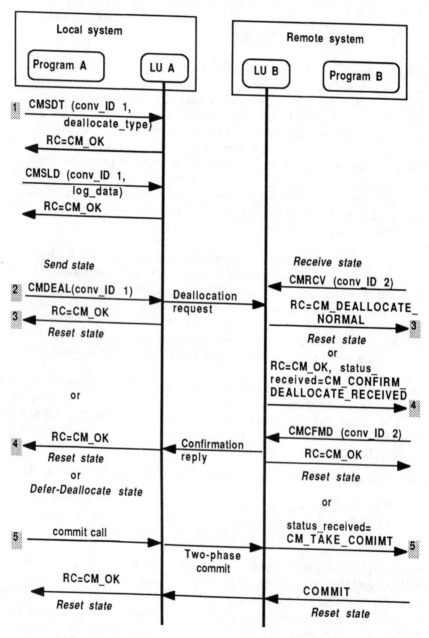

Figure 8.7 Ending CPI-C conversation.

The remote program issues the Receive call, and it gets RC=CM_ALLOCATE_NORMAL. The remote program immediately enters the Reset state (not the Deallocate state like in APPC), and the conversation ends normally. This completes the CPI-C unconditional conversation termination.

Or:

Step 4. The LU returns to the program after successful confirmation processing. This occurs when prior to Step 2 the following conditions are met:

- The deallocate_type was set to CM_DEALLOCATE_ CONFIRM.

- The deallocate_type was set to CM_DEALLOCATE_SYNC_ LEVEL and the conversation was allocated with the sync_level set to CM_CONFIRM.

The local LU flushes its send buffer and sends the data, the confirmation request, and the deallocation request, across the session to the remote LU. The local program is suspended until a confirmation reply is received from the remote program. This type of CPI-C deallocate is equivalent to an APPC DEALLOCATE TYPE(CONFIRM) verb, which was discussed in detail in Sec. 7.7 (see Fig. 7.15).

Or:

Step 5.   The conversation was deallocated with synchronization point processing in Step 2. This occurs when the following conditions are met:

- The deallocate_type is set to CM_DEALLOCATE_SYNC_ LEVEL and the conversation was allocated with the sync_level set to CM_SYNC_POINT and commit is performed immediately following the deallocation request.

The local LU defers the deallocation request (the program enters Defer-Deallocate state) until the synchronization point services commit call is issued. If commit processing succeeds, then the conversation deallocates normally. If the commit fails, then all protected resources are restored to the previous synchronization point. This type of CPI-C deallocate is equivalent to APPC DEALLOCATE TYPE(SYNC_LEVEL) verb and was discussed in detail in Sec. 7.7 (see Fig. 7.16).

8.4 SENDING DATA

This Secion explains the transfer of data using the CPI Communications Send_Data call. A CPI-C program issues the Send_Data (CMSEND) call to send one data record on a mapped conversation, or one or more logical records on a basic conversation to the remote program. The remote transaction program receives the data by issuing the CPI-C Receive (CMRCV) call. The APPC [MC_]SEND_DATA verb and the CPI-C Send_Data call are functionally very similar. The reader should review Sec. 7.8, which discusses in detail the APPC [MC_]SEND_DATA verb. CPI-C performs a function equivalent to the APPC [MC_]SEND_DATA verb and additionally allows the combination of multiple APPC functions into one Send_Data call. A CPI-C program may issue Set_Send_Type (CMSST), Set_Prepare_To_Receive_Type (CMSPTR), and Set_Deallocate_Type (CMSDT) calls prior to sending data to combine multiple LU 6.2 distributed functions following the Send_Data call.

The following functions can be combined together:

- Sending and flushing data buffered in the LU's sending buffer

- Sending and flushing data, and releasing the local program Send state to the remote program

- Sending data and performing confirmation processing

- Sending data, performing confirmation processing, and release the Send state to the remote program

- Sending data and performing LU 6.2 synchronization processing

- Sending data, performing synchronization processing, and release the Sending state to the remote program

- Sending data and deallocating a conversation, and performing LU 6.2 confirmation or synchronization processing

Combining multiple distributed functions is very efficient and improves the overall performance of CPI-C distributed transactions. In this Sec. we will concentrate on the differences bewteen the CPI-C Send Data call and the APPC [MC_]SEND_DATA verb.

8.4.1 Send_Data States

The Send Data call can be issued only when the local program is in Send state or Send-Pending state. Upon successful completion of this call the conversation enters the Send state if the send_type conversation characteristic was set to CM_BUFFER_DATA (default value), CM_SEND_AND_FLUSH, or CM_SEND_AND_CONFIRM. The local program remains in the Send state and the remote program, in the Receive state. When a successful conversation is established between the local and remote logical units, LU 6.2 places the local program that initiated the conversation in Send state and the remote program in Receive state. The two programs may now start exchanging data by issuing the CPI-C Send_Data and Receive calls. The communicating programs must follow the send/receive mode (half-duplex, flip-flop) protocol as discussed in Secs. 3.6.2 and 6.2.2 of this book. Section 6.2 also discusses a possible full-duplex design between systems using two separate LU 6.2 conversations.

The conversation may also enter Receive, Defer-Receive, Reset, or Defer-Deallocate state depending on the setting of the send_type characteristic.

8.4.2 Send_Data Call

The following is the syntax of the CPI Communications Send_Data call:

CALL CMSEND
    (conversation_ID, buffer, send_length,
    request_to_send_received, return_code)

Supplied parameters:

conversation_ID — specifies the conversation_ID returned on the Initialize_Conversation call.

buffer — data buffer containing one data record for mapped conversations or logical records for basic conversations.

send_length — the length of the buffer parameter. For mapped conversations, this is the actual length of the data record to be sent. For basic conversations, send_length specifies the size of the buffer parameter and is not related to the length of a logical record.

Returned parameters:

request_to_send_received — if set to CM_REQ_TO_SEND_
RECEIVED, the local program is informed that the remote
program issued the Request_To_Send (CMRTS) call
requesting the Send state. The local program should release the
the conversation Send state as soon as possible. Notice that
CM_REQ_TO_SEND_RECEIVED asks only for the Send state
and does not have any impact on the conversation state. The
local program is allowed to continue sending data if it has
something very important to finish and then should issue a call
that releases the Send state to the remote program.

RC (return code) — specifies the result of the call execution.

Prior to the Send_Data call a program may issue the
Set_Send_Type (CMSST) call to set the send_type conversation
characteristic. The following are the possible send_type values:

• CM_BUFFER_DATA

The Send_Data call performs the functional equivalent of the
APPC [MC_]SEND_DATA verb (see Sec. 7.8). CPI
Communications does not support the APPC function
management header (FMH) and the MAP_NAME options
discussed earlier in Sec. 7.8.2. The local logical unit buffers
the data until a sufficient amount is accumulated for
transmission.

• CM_SEND_AND_FLUSH

The Send_Data call performs the Send and Flush functions
combined. This may be useful if, for example, the local
program requires a lot of processing between sends. Flushing
the LU's send buffer allows the remote program to start
processing the received data while the local program performs
other processing. When using APPC, a program must issue two
verbs, [MC_]SEND_DATA followed by [MC_]FLUSH, to send
and flush the LU's send buffer. The CPI-C Send call is very
efficient because the logical unit sends the data at the time the
call is issued rather than buffering the data and waiting for
another call to flush the LU's send buffer..

• CM_SEND_AND_CONFIRM

The SAA/CPI-C Send_Data call is functionally equivalent to
the APPC [MC_]SEND_DATA verb followed by confirmation

processing. Combining the two functions into one Send_Data call improves performance in applications that, for example, need to perform confirmation processing for each data record sent to the partner program (e.g., file updates). The CPI-C program needs to issue only one Send_Data programming call to send the data and perform confirmation processing. Upon successful completion of the call the local program is assured that the data was received and confirmed by the partner program.

- CM_SEND_AND_PREP_TO_RECEIVE

  The Send_Data call is functionally equivalent to the APPC [MC_]SEND_DATA verb followed by [MC_]PREPARE_TO_RECEIVE verb. This can improve performance in, for example, interactive requester/server types of applications. Normally an APPC requester issues an [MC_]SEND_DATA verb followed by an [MC_]PREPARE_TO_RECEIVE verb. SAA/CPI-C transaction program needs to issue only one Send_Data call to flush the LU's send buffer and change the direction indicator across the conversation at the time of call issuance. The local program may perform its local processing while the remote program may process the received request. When the local program is ready to issue the Receive call, the reply may already be processed and returned to the local LU. Depending on the prepare_to_receive_type conversation characteristic, this call may also require confirmation or synchronization processing.

- CM_SEND_AND_DEALLOCATE

  The Send_Data call is functionally equivalent to the APPC [MC_]SEND_DATA verb followed by the [MC_]DEALLOCATE verb. The LU's buffer is flushed and is sent to the remote LU together with the deallocation request. Depending on the deallocate_type characteristic, this call may require confirmation or synchronization processing before the conversation can be deallocated.

8.4.3 Send_Data Flows

The flow diagrams for data exchanges on mapped and basic conversations were illustrated in Figs. 7.18 and 7.19. The reader should study Sec. 7.9 keeping in mind the difference between the APPC [MC_]SEND_DATA verb and the CPI-C Send_Data call.

Sequence 1

Let us look at the design steps for a mapped conversation program that needs to perform the following functions:

1. Send a data record to the remote program

2. Perform confirmation processing

3. Perform local processing or process other conversations before receiving data from the remote program

Let us also assume that the program needs to perform these three functions many times. A simple solution could be for the local program to issue a CPI Communications Send_Data call, followed by the Confirm call to perform the first two required functions. Then the program could perform local processing, or it could process other conversations before issuing the Receive call. This design would be very inefficient because of the following:

- The local program would have to issue three calls each time to perform the above functions.

- The remote program would not be allowed to send data back to the local program until the local program had completed its processing and issue a Receive call.

- The Receive call would generate a redundant additional network message to carry the change direction (Send state) across the session to the remote program.

This design can be significantly improved by combining the three functions into one Send_Data call. The following are the design steps to achieve this:

Step 1. The local program (program A) issues the CPI-C Initialize_Conversation call to initialize local resources for a new conversation. The local logical unit allocates local resources for a new conversation and assigns a unique conversation_ID identifying this conversation. Upon successful completion of this call the control is returned to the program with RC=OK and the new conversation_ID set to for example to conv_ID 1. The conversation characteristics are set to default values as shown in Fig. 8.1. The conversation enters the Initialize state.

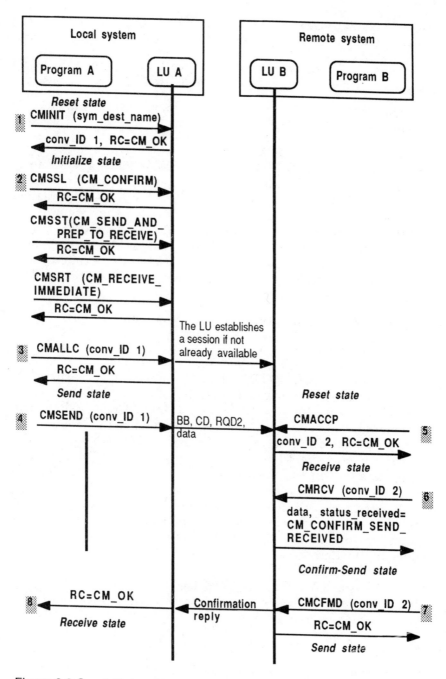

Figure 8.8 Send_Data with confirmation and change direction.

Step 2.   Now, program A may issue CPI-C Set calls to set the conversation characteristics. The following characteristics are set:

- The Set_Sync_Level (CMSSL) call sets the sync_level conversation characteristic to CM_CONFIRM.

- The CMSST call sets the send_type conversation characteristic to CM_SEND_AND_PREP_ TO_RECEIVE.

- The conversation default prepare_to_receive_type is set to CM_PREP_TO_RECEIVE_SYNC_LEVEL. Then the value of the prepare_to_receive_type depends on the sync_level conversation characteristic. Since the sync_level conversation characteristic is set to CM_CONFIRM, the prepare_to_ receive_type is set to CM_PREP_TO_RECEIVE_CONFIRM by default. Therefore, there is no need to issue the Set_Prepare_ To_Receive_Type (CMSPTR) call in order to explicitly set prepare_to_receive_type conversation characteristic to CM_ PREP_TO_RECEIVE_CONFIRM.

- The conversation_type is set to the default value CM_MAPPED_ CONVERSATION.

- The Set_Receive_Type call sets the receive_type to CM_ RECEIVE_IMMEDIATE. When communicating concurrently with multiple programs it may be advantageous to set the receive_type to CM_RECEIVE_IMMEDIATE. Then the program will not be suspended when a Receive call is issued for a particular conversation even if no data is available from the partner program. The program simply is notified that there is no data for this conversation and it can resumet processing.

Step 3.   Program A issues the Allocate call to start a mapped conversation with program B. LU A establishes an LU 6.2 session with the remote LU (LU B). The LU buffers the allocation request and no information is sent to the partner program yet.

Step 4.   Program A issues the Send_Data call to send data to the remote program. The conversation characteristics are currently set to the following values:

- sync_level is set to CM_CONFIRM.

- send_type is set to CM_SEND_AND_PREP_TO_RECEIVE

- prepare_to_receive_type is set to CM_PREP_TO_RECEIVE_ CONFIRM.

Therefore, the Send_Data call actually performs three functions:

1. **Send_Data** — the data is added to the LU's send buffer.

2. **Prepare_To_Receive** — releases the Send state to the remote program.

3. **Confirm** — performs confirmation processing which also flushes the LU's send buffer.

The resulting network message carries the data record in the request/response unit (RU), the change direction (CD) and confirmation request (RQD2) as bits set in the request/response header (RH). Since this is the first call following the Allocate call that flushes the LU's send buffer, the allocation request is also carried with the message partly in the RU (ATTACH header) and in the RH (BB — begin-bracket indicator). Notice that so far program A has generated only one network message which carries multiple programming calls across the conversation to the remote LU.

Step 5.   The remote LU receives the allocation request and starts a new instance of program B. Program B issues the Accept_Conversation (CMACCP) call to accept the incoming allocation request. Upon successful completion of the call the remote LU returns control to program B. The RC is set to OK and the conversation_ID is set to conv_ID 2, which uniquely identifies this conversation.

Step 6.   Program B issues the receive call and receives the data record sent by the local program. The data_received is set to CM_COMPLETE_DATA_RECEIVED, indicating that a complete mapped conversation data record has been received. The status_received indicator is set to CM_CONFIRM_SEND_RECEIVED, indicating that program A requested confirmation processing. Also the SEND portion indicates that after sending a confirmation reply, program B enters Send state and may start sending data to program A.

Step 7.   The remote program issues the Confirmed (CMCFMD) call to send a confirmation reply to program A and then enters Send state.

Step 8.   The Send call issued in Step 4 completes with RC=OK. Now the local program may perform local processing, or it can start processing other conversations. Upon successful completion of the call, the local program enters the Receive state and the remote program enters the Send state. This allows the remote program to start sending data while the local program performs other processing.

Sequence 2

Let us look at the design steps for a typical banking application which transfers money between various accounts that may reside on different systems. The customer wants to transfer $1000,000.00 from his banking account in Los Angeles and deposit the money in his wife's account in Poland. Figure 8.9 illustrates the design steps for the CPI-C program residing on a system in Los Angeles. The program must perform the following tasks:

1. Withdraw $1000,000.00 from the customer's account stored in a database in LA.

2. Contact the bank in Poland and deposit $1000,000.00 in his wife's account.

The program must insure that the money is withdrawn from the database in LA only if it is successfully deposited to the database residing in the bank in Poland. The communicating programs would have to develop application-specific synchronization and backout routines in order to coordinate the changes throughout the distributed transaction. In case of failures the error recovery can be very complicated. To avoid developing complicated backout routines we are going to use in our design the CPI-C commit and backout function that are specifically defined for this purpose. In doing so LU 6.2 takes the responsibility for updating all the accounts and ensuring database consistency. The LU will either **commit** (make the changes permanent) or **backout** (reverse the changes) to protect resources in case of failure. Our example shows just one conversation from a program in LA to the remote program in Poland. In a more complicated distributed system, more than one conversation can be involved in the same distributed transaction. The **commit** function is executed on all protected conversations. All conversations allocated with the synchronization level set to CM_SYNC_POINT are considered protected resources. A transaction program issues one commit call to advance protected resources on all protected conversations to the next synchronization point. In case of a failure the LU backs -out of all the changes to a previous successful synchronization point and notifies all programs involved of the failure. This is significantly different from the confirmation processing where the communicating application programs are responsible for ensuring the consistency of all protected resources throughout the distributed transaction.

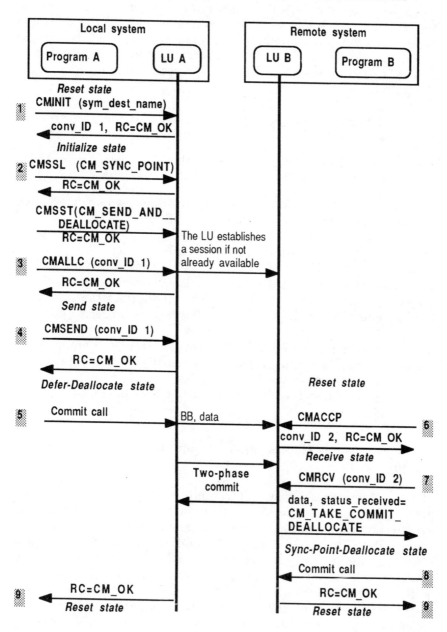

Figure 8.9 Send_Data with Deallocate and synchronization processing.

The following are the design steps:

Step 1.   The local program (program A in Los Angeles) issues the Initialize_Conversation call to initialize local resources for a new conversation. Upon successful completion of this call the control is returned to the program with RC=OK and the new conversation_ID is set to conv_ID 1. The conversation characteristics are set to default values as shown in Fig. 8.1. The conversation then enters the Initialize state.

Step 2.   Program A issues CPI-C Set calls to define conversation characteristics. The following characteristics are set:

- Set_Sync_Level (CMSSL) — sets the sync_level conversation characteristic to CM_SYNC_POINT.

- Set_Send_Type (CMSST) — sets the send_type conversation characteristic to CM_SEND_AND_DEALLOCATE.

Step 3.   Program A issues an Allocate call to start a conversation with program B. The local LU (LU A) establishes an LU 6.2 session with the remote LU (LU B residing on the system in Poland) if the session is not already established. The LU buffers the allocation request, and no information is sent to the partner program yet.

Step 4.   Program A withdraws $1000,000.00 from its database and issues a Send_Data call to deposit the money in the database in Poland. The conversation characteristics are set in such a way in Step 2 that the Send_Data call performs the following tasks:

1. It buffers the data to be sent in the LU's send buffer.

2. It deallocates the conversation and performs syncronization processing.

Step 5.   Program A issues a commit call to advance all the protected resources (the local and remote databases) to the next synchronization point. If the commit call is successful the conversation deallocates normally and programs A and B are assured that the money transfer succeeded and that the distributed database is in a consistent state. If the commit call is not successful or if program B issues a backout call, then the logical units are responsible for backing out the update to the database in Poland and cancelling the withdrawal of the money in LA. The backout procedure occurs throughout the distributed transaction and returns to the state of the last successful synchronization point (in our case the beginning of the conversation).

Step 6.   The remote LU receives the allocation request and starts a new instance of program B. Program B issues the Accept_Conversation (CMACCP) call to accept the incoming allocation request. Upon successful completion of the call the remote LU returns control to program B. The RC is set to OK and the conversation_ID is set to conv_ID 2 as a unique identifier for this conversation.

Step 7.   Program B issues the receive call and receives the $1000,000.00 sent by the local program. The status_received indicator is set to CM_TAKE_COMMIT_DEALLOCATE indicating that program A requested synchronization processing before the conversation can be deallocated successfully.

Step 8.   The remote program does not find any error, and so it issues a commit call to complete the synchronization processing.

Step 9.   The commit call completes with return code RC=OK indicating that the transaction was successful. The two programs enter the Reset state, and the conversation terminates successfully.

8.5 RECEIVING DATA

This section explains receiving data using the CPI-C architecture. A program issues a Receive (CMRCV) call to receive data or control information from the remote transaction program. The received information can be user data, status information (such as state changes), a request for confirmation or synchronization processing. In the case of mapped conversations the received data can be a complete or incomplete data record that corresponds to a single issuance of the Send_Data (CMSEND) call. In the case of basic conversations the received data can be one or more complete or incomplete logical records. The CPI-C Receive call performs a similar function to the APPC [MC_]RECEIVE_AND_WAIT verb when the receive_type conversation characteristic is set to the default value CM_RECEIVE_AND_WAIT. When the receive_type is set to CM_RECEIVE_IMMEDIATE, this call performs a similar function to the APPC MC_RECEIVE_IMMEDIATE verb. The reader is strongly advised to review Sec. 7.10 which discusses receiving data using APPC verbs.

8.5.1 Receive States

The Receive call can be issued when the local program is in the Send state or Send-Pending state. In this case the local LU flushes its send buffer with the change direction across the session to the remote LU. The Receive call can also be issued in Receive state to continue receiving information from the partner program. Upon successful completion of this call the program may enter the Receive, Confirm, Confirm-Send, Confirm-Deallocate, Syncpoint, Syncpoint-Send, or Syncpoint-Deallocate state depending on the return code (RC) and the status_received parameter.

8.5.2 Receive Call

To receive data on a mapped or a basic conversation a program issues the following CPI-C call:

```
CALL CMRCV
    (conversation_ID, buffer,
    requested_length,
    data_received,
    received_length,
    status_received,
    return_code)
```

Supplied parameters:

conversation_ID — the resource ID uniquely identifying this conversation.

requested_length — the maximum amount of data that can be received on one Receive call (0 to 032767 bytes).

Returned parameters:

buffer — specifies the parameter in which the program is to receive a data record on a mapped conversation or logical records on a basic conversation.

data_received — indicates whether data was received.

status_received — indicates the type of control information received.

received-length — specifies the actual length received on this Receive call.

Request_To_Send_Received — informs the local program that the remote program issued the Request_To_Send call requesting the Send state. The local program should release the Send state to the Remote program as soon as possible.

RC (return_code) — specifies the result of the call execution.

If the **receive_type** conversation characteristic is set to **CM_RECEIVE_AND_WAIT,** the Receive call does not complete until data arrives from the partner program. If the information is not available, the program is suspended and cannot perform other processing.

If the **receive_type** conversation characteristic is set to **CM_RECEIVE_IMMEDIATE** , then the program does not wait for the information to arrive. The call completes immediately with RC=CM_UNSUCCESSFUL indicating that there is no information in the local LU's receive buffer. This option is very useful when communicating with multiple partners over multiple concurrent conversations. A programmer may set the receive_type conversation characteristic to CM_RECEIVE_IMMEDIATE in order to periodically check each conversation for data. If no information arrives on a specific conversation, the program is not suspended and may start processing other conversations.

8.5.3 Receive Call Processing

The following is the recommended way of processing the Receive call:

STEP A. Issue the Receive call. The application should first check the return code (RC) for errors.

IF the **RC=OK THEN** the program should examine the data_ received and status_received parameter

ELSE

  BEGIN

   • **IF RC=CM_DEALLOCATE_NORMAL THEN** the conversation ends normally.

   • **IF receive_type=CM_RECEIVE_IMMEDIATE AND RC=CM_ UNSUCCESSFUL** (indicating that there is no information in the local's LU's receive buffer) **THEN** the program should examine the data_received and status_received parameter.

- **IF error or backout condition THEN GO TO USER-DEFINED ERROR RECOVERY PROCEDURE ;**

END;

(RC=OK)

IF data_received=CM_COMPLETE_DATA_RECEIVED THEN

- On a mapped conversation, a complete data record or the last remaining portion of the data record was received.

- On a basic conversation, a complete logical record or the last remaining portion of the logical record was received by the program (possible only on a basic conversation when the fill conversation characteristic is set to CM_FILL_LL).

- The program should handle the data and **GO TO STEP B**;

IF data_received=CM_INCOMPLETE_DATA_RECEIVED THEN

- On mapped conversations, a portion of a data record was received by the transaction program (see Fig. 7.21).

- On basic conversations an incomplete logical record was received by the program (possible only on a basic conversation when the fill conversation characteristic is set to CM_FILL_LL).

- The program should handle the data and **GO TO STEP A;**

IF data_receive=CM_NO_DATA_RECEIVED THEN

- No data is received by the program.

- **GO TO STEP B;**

IF data_received=CM_DATA_RECEIVED THEN

- Data independent of the logical record format was received by the program (possible only on a basic conversation when the fill conversation characteristic is set to CM_FILL_BUFFER).

- The program should handle the data and **GO TO STEP B;**

STEP B. Check the status_received indicator.

IF status_received=CM_NO_STATUS_RECEIVED THEN GO TO STEP A;

IF status_received=CM_SEND_RECEIVED THEN

- The CPI-C transaction program enters the Send state (**IF data_receive=CM_NO_DATA_RECEIVED**) or the Send_ Pending state (if data and the Send state was received on this call). The program may now start sending data (**GO TO Send_Call Procedure**).

IF status_received=CM_CONFIRM_RECEIVED THEN
the program enters the Confirm state. The partner program requested confirmation processing. The program should respond by:

- Issuing the Confirmed call (if there are no errors). Upon completion of Confirm the program enters the Receive state and should **GO TO STEP A**.

- Issuing the Send_Error call (if errors are found), the program enters the Send state and the partner program enters the Receive state. Further processing is dependent on user-defined error recovery. **GO TO USER-DEFINED ERROR RECOVERY PROCEDURE** (e.g., ask the partner to resend all information since the last successful confirmation processing).

  Issuing the Deallocate call with deallocate_type set to CM_DEALLOCATE_ABEND (if an unrecoverable error has occurred). The **conversation ends unconditionally** and the two programs must re-establish a new conversation to perform user-defined error recovery.

IF status_received=CM_CONFIRM_SEND_RECEIVED THEN
The program enters the Confirm-Send state. The partner program requested confirmation processing and released the Send state. The program should respond by:

- Issuing the Confirmed call (if there are no errors). Upon completion of Confirm the program enters the Send state and may now start sending data (**GO TO Send_Call Procedure**).

- Issuing the Send_Error call or the Deallocate call with the deallocate_type set to CM_DEALLOCATE_ABEND (if errors are found as described above).

IF status_received=CM_CONFIRM_DEALLOCATE_RECEIVED THEN

The program enters the Confirm_Deallocate state. The partner program has deallocated the conversation and requested confirmation processing. The program should respond by:

- Issuing the Confirmed call (if there are no errors). Upon completion of Confirm the program enters the Reset state and the conversation ends normally.

- Issuing the Send_Error call (if errors are found). The program then enters the Send state, and the partner program enters the Receive state. The conversation does not end. Further processing is dependent on user-defined error recovery. **GO TO USER-DEFINED ERROR-RECOVERY PROCEDURE.**

- Issuing the Deallocate call with the deallocate_type set to CM_DEALLOCATE_ABEND (if an unrecoverable error has occurred). The **conversation ends unconditionally** and the two programs must reestablish a new conversation to perform user-defined error recovery.

STEP C. Check for the synchronization processing.

IF sync_level is set to CM_SYNC_POINT and

status_received=CM_TAKE_COMMIT THEN

The CPI-C transaction program enters the Syncpoint state. This implies that the partner program requested synchronization processing (has issued a commit call). The program should respond by:

- Issuing a commit call to advance all protected resources, such as distributed databases, throughout the distributed transaction to the next synchronization point (if there are no errors). The logical unit flushes its send buffer for all conversations allocated with a synchronization level of CM_SYNC_POINT. LU 6.2 defines an indivisible **Logical Unit of Work (LUW)** as a sequence of related programming statements (database updates, deletes, etc.). The logical unit is responsible for committing the LUW to the next synchronization point or restoring the LUW to the last synchronization point. Upon successful completion of synchronization processing (RC=OK) the program enters the Receive state and should issue another CPI-C Receive call (**GO TO STEP A.**).

- Issuing a backout call to restore all protected resources to the last synchronization point. The LU sends backouts to all conversations allocated with synchronization level of CM_SYNC_POINT. The resources are restored to the last synchronization point, which is either the start of the transaction or the last successful commit call issued since the beginning of the conversation. All the programs taking part in this synchronization point processing enter the states they were in at completion of the most recent successful synchronization point.

status_received=CM_TAKE_COMMIT_SEND THEN

The program enters the Syncpoint-Send state. The partner program requested synchronization processing and released the Send state (the program has issued a commit call with a Prepare_To_Receive call). The program should respond by:

- Issuing a commit call as described above. Upon successful completion of the synchronization processing (RC=OK) the program enters the Send state and may now start sending data (**GO TO Send_Call Procedure**).

- Issuing a backout call as described above.

status_received=CM_TAKE_COMMIT_DEALLOCATE THEN

The program enters the Syncpoint-Deallocate state. The partner deallocated the conversation with synchronization processing. The program should respond by:

- Issuing a commit call as describe above. Upon successful completion of the synchronization processing (RC=OK) the program enters the Reset state and the conversation ends normally.

- Issuing a backout call as described above. The conversation does not end.

Notice that the major difference between the CPI-C Receive call and the APPC [MC_]RECEIVE_AND_WAIT verb is the fact that the APPC architecture defines one WHAT_RECEIVED indicator that separately returns the data indication and the status indication. Therefore most APPC implementations require a separate [MC_]RCEIEVE_AND_WAIT verb just to receive the status information. This is not very efficient and it is much better to define two indicators, one for the data (CPI-C receive_data) and another for status information (CPI-C status_received). Then the control information and the data may be received on one Receive call which saves CPU processing. Other than that the CPI-C call and the APPC [MC_]RECEIVE_AND_WAIT verb are very similar.

8.5.4 Receive_Data Flows

Let us look at the mapped and basic conversation data flow examples that were illustrated in Fig. 7.18 and 7.19 for the APPC environment. The design flows below show the major differences and advantages of a CPI-C design over an APPC design. The reader should read Sec. 7.9 explaining the major difference between mapped and basic conversation flows and discussing in detail the APPC verb sequences for the two CPI-C examples below.

Sequence 1: Mapped Conversation Data Flows

Figure 8.10 shows typical steps performed by the local and remote CPI-C programs to exchange data on a mapped conversation:

Let us make the following assumption for the local program (program A):

- The conversation is already established with all the default characteristics (see Fig. 8.1) and program A's end of the conversation is in the Send or Send_Pending state. Program A sends multiple data records to program B.

Let us make the following assumption for the remote program (program B).

- The allocation request has already been received. Program B always sends one data record to program A and then does local processing or receives more data from program A. Since program B always replies by sending one data record, it is advantageous to flush the LU B's send buffer and release the Send state at the time of issuing the Send Data call.

- Program B issues the CPI-C Set_Send_Type (CMSST) call to set send_type conversation characteristic to CM_SEND_AND_PREP_TO_RECEIVE. This allows the program to flush the LU B's send buffer and release the Send state when issuing a second data call.

• The default prepare_to_receive_type is CM_PREP_TO_
RECEIVE_SYNC_LEVEL. Then the value of the prepare_to_
receive_type depends on the sync_level conversation
characteristic. Since program A allocated the conversation
with the default sync_level set to CM_NONE, the
prepare_to_receive_type is set CM_PREP_TO_RECEIVE_
FLUSH by default. There is no need then to issue a
Set_Prepare_To_Receive_Type (CMSPTR) call to explicitly set
prepare_to_receive_type characteristic to CM_PREP_TO_
RECEIVE_FLUSH. Now every time program B issues the Send
call, the LU's buffer is flushed with change direction. Program
B enters the Receive state and may perform local processing,
and program A enters the Send_Pending state and may start
sending data.

• The conversation_type is set to the default value CM_
MAPPED_CONVERSATION. This value cannot be changed
by program B for this conversation.

• The receive_type is set to the default value CM_RECEIVE_
AND_ WAIT.

Step 1. The local program (program A) must be in the Send or
Send_Pending state before it can start sending data to the remote
transaction program (program B) by issuing a Send_Data call. The
application programmer, using a mapped conversation, moves the
application data (called a **data record**) into the data buffer that
corresponds to the Buffer parameter of the Send_Data call. The data
record (data 1 in Fig. 8.10) is a collection of arbitrary data,
variables and structures defined by the programmer. LU A first
transforms the data to a contiguous data string and then it builds the
General Data Stream variable GDS1. GDS1 is buffered in the local
LU's send buffer for later transmission. The GDS variable was
discussed in Sec. 3.7 of this book.

Step 2. The local program issues another Send_Data call
containing data 2. The local logical unit buffers all the data to be
transmitted to the remote transaction program until it accumulates
a sufficient amount for transmission (e.g., for best network
performance the data may be sent when the SNA maximum
request/response unit size, also known as MAXRU size, has been
reached) or until program A issues a call that forces the LU to flush
its send buffer. The unique ability of LU 6.2's blocking and
deblocking capabilities with regard to programing calls and data,
significantly improves network efficiency and performance by

reducing the number of network messages transmitted over communication links.

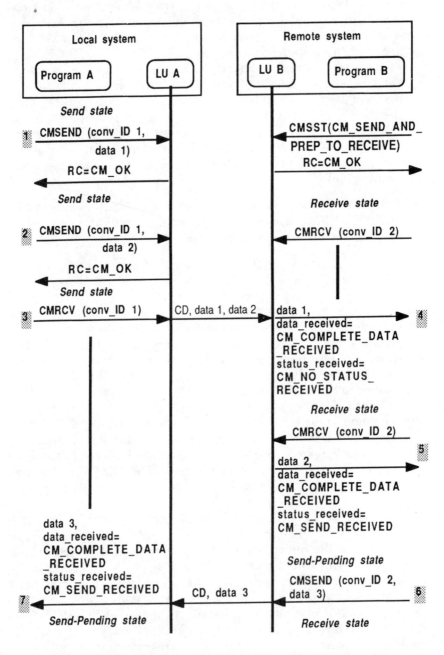

Figure 8.10 CPI-C mapped conversation data exchange.

Step 3.   Program A issues a Receive call. Since the default receive_type is CM_RECEIVE_AND_WAIT, the program is suspended until some information arrives from program B. LU A flushes its send buffer. The resulting network message (BIU) is generated with the change direction indicator in the RH, and the GDS 1 and GDS 2 variables containing data 1 and data 2 in the RU. We are assuming that the MAXRU size is large enough to accommodate both general data stream variables. For example, MAXRU size is equal to 1920, and the two sends are 900 and 800 bytes, respectively.

Step 4.   The remote program (program B) receives one complete data record corresponding to the GDS1 even though it issues the Receive call with the maximum requested_length set to 1920 bytes. The data_received parameter is set to CM_COMPLETE_DATA_ RECEIVED indicating that a complete data record is received. If the maximum requested_length were set to 500 bytes, then the data_received parameter would be set to CM_INCOMPLETE_ DATA_RECEIVED and another receive call would have to be issued to receive the remaining portion of the first data record. This would generally decrease performance.

Step 5.   The remote program issues another Receive call with the maximum requested_length set to 1920 bytes. It receives the second complete data record corresponding to the General Data Stream variable GDS2 (or the Send_Data call issued in Step 2).   The data_received parameter is set to CM_COMPLETE_DATA_ RECEIVED indicating that complete data was received. The status_received parameter is set to CM_SEND_RECEIVED indicating that program B received the Send state on the same Receive call. Compare this to the APPC design illustrated in Fig. 7.18. The APPC program had to issue an additional call to receive the Send state, which is less efficient than one CPI-C Receive call. Program B enters the Send_Pending state and may start sending data.

Step 6.   Program B issues the Send_Data call containing data 3. After the call, program B wants to perform local processing or issue a Receive call to receive data from program A.

Step 7.   The Receive call issued in Step 3 completes with RC=OK. The data_received parameter is set to CM_COMPLETE_DATA_ RECEIVED indicating that a complete data record is received. The status_received parameter is set to CM_SEND_RECEIVED indicating that program A received the Send state on the same

Receive call. Program A enters the Send-Pending state and may start processing or sending data to program B, which may be doing some other processing at this time.

The CPI-C design described above is more efficient than the APPC design illustrated in Fig. 7.18. Fewer CPI-C calls are required to perform the same distributed functions. The CPI-C Receive call is capable of receiving the data and Send state on the same call (see steps 5 and 7 in Fig. 8.10). Also by combining Send with Prepare_To_Receive in Step 6, the data and the Send state are sent to Program A at the time of call issuance. This releases program A from the wait state and allows both programs to resume processing earlier than it would in the corresponding APPC design. An APPC program would have to issue an MC_SEND_DATA verb followed by an MC_PREPARE_TO_RECEIVE verb to perform the distributed functions carried out by the Send_Data call issued in Step 6. The CPI-C design should improve the overall performance of the communicating programs.

Sequence 2: CPI-C Basic Conversation Data Flows

Figure 8.11 shows typical steps performed by CPI-C programs that need to exchange data over a basic conversation. The corresponding APPC verb sequence was illustrated in Fig. 7.19. The reader should compare Fig. 7.19 with Fig. 8.11 to evaluate the differences between APPC and CPI-C designs.

The following are the CPI-C design steps (see Fig. 8.11):

Step 1.   The remote program (program B) issues a Set_Fill (CMSF) call to set the "fill" characteristic to CM_FILL_BUFFER and to receive data, independent of logical record format, on the subsequent Receive calls for this conversation.

Step 2.   The local program (program A) issues the Send_Data call containing two logical records (LL1, data 1, LL2, data 2). The application programmer must build logical records into the application buffer (called a buffer record) before passing the data to the logical unit. A logical record consists of a 2-byte length prefix (LL) followed by the user data. The length field must be equal to at least 2 since it includes its own 2-byte length. A basic conversation logical record format was discussed in Sec. 3.7. A programmer can pack multiple logical records or a portion of a logical record into its buffer. The unit of data that a program sends or receives, with a single Send_Data call, is of arbitrary length determined by the programmer and does not have to consist of complete logical records. The LU 6.2 architecture does not impose any relationship between application buffers and logical records. Therefore, one buffer record may contain one or multiple logical records. The last logical record does not have to be a complete logical record. The ability to block multiple logical records into one application buffer reduces the number of Send_Data calls and allows programmers to develop more efficient applications.

Step 3.   Program A issues a Receive call. Since the default conversation characteristic "fill" is set to CM_FILL_LL, the Receive call is requesting to receive one logical record at a time from program B. The Receive call flushes the local LU's send buffer and passes the Send state to program B. The resulting network message (BIU) is generated with the change direction (CD) indicator in the RH and the two logical records in the RU. We are assuming that the MAXRU size is large enough to accommodate both logical records.

Step 4.   Program B issues the Receive call requesting to receive data independent of the logical record format. Let us assume that the requested_length is set to 1920, which allows both logical records (LL1, data 1, LL2, data 2), to be received on one receive call. Upon successful completion of the call (RC=OK) the data_received parameter is set to CM_DATA_RECEIVED, indicating that data independent of its logical record format has been received. The LU only passes the requested_length of data from its receive buffer to the application buffer. Program B is responsible for interpreting and decoding individual logical records. If the requested_length parameter were shorter than 1700 bytes, program B would have to issue more than one call to receive the two logical records. This would be less efficient and should be avoided. The status_received parameter CM_SEND_RECEIVED indicates that the change direction was received on this call together with data. Program B enters the Send_Pending state and may immediately start sending data to Program A. The APPC program illustrated in Fig. 7.19 had to issue an additional RECEIVE_AND_WAIT verb just to change the Receive state to Send, which is less efficient than the CPI-C design.

Step 5.   Program B issues a Send_Data call containing three logical records (LL3, data 3, LL4, data 4, LL5, data 5). LU B buffers

the logical records until MAXRU size of data has been accumulated
or until program B issues a call that flushes the LU's send buffer.

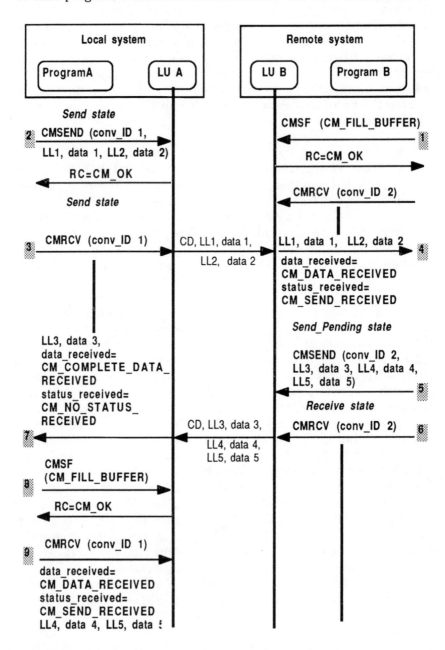

Figure 8.11 CPI-C Basic conversation data exchange.

We are assuming that the send_type conversation characteristic is set to the default value CM_BUFFER_DATA. This means that the LU buffers the data in its send buffer until a sufficient amount of data is accumulated for transmission. Program B could set the send_type characteristic to CM_SEND_AND_PREP_TO_RECEIVE and the prepare_to_receive_type conversation characteristic to CM_PREP_TO_RECEIVE_FLUSH. Then, the data and the change direction would be flushed when the Send_Data call is issued. Upon completion of the Send_Data call program B can enter the Receive state and can perform other processing before issuing the Receive call to receive additional data from program A.

Step 6.   Program B issues the Receive call in order to flush LU B's send buffer if the buffer is not already flushed, and to release the Send state to program A. LU A receives and buffers the three logical records sent by LU B.

Step 7.   The Receive call issued in Step 2 completes with data_received=CM_COMPLETE_DATA_RECEIVED, indicating that a complete logical record was received. The default "fill" characteristic is set to CM_FILL_LL. Therefore, program A requested to receive one logical record at a time. The LU moves only one complete logical record (LL3, data 3) to the application buffer and waits for another Receive call. We assume that the requested_length on the Receive call is large enough to accommodate the complete logical record (LL3, data 3). If not, more than one Receive call would be required to receive the logical record (LL3, data 3) and would therefore degrade the performance.

Step 8.   Program A issues a Set_Fill (CMSF) call to set the "fill" characteristic to CM_FILL_BUFFER and to receive the data independent of the logical record format on subsequent Receive calls for this conversation. Normally, a program sets the "fill" conversation characteristic immediately after the conversation is initialized. This "fill" value is then used on all subsequent Receive calls for this conversation. This example shows that a programmer may change the value of the "fill" characteristic depending on whether the program wants to receive one logical record at a time or it wants to receive data independent of logical record format.

Step 9.   Program A issues another Receive call and requests to receive data independently of the logical record format. It receives an amount of data equal to or less than the requested_length. Let us assume that the requested_length is larger than the combined length of the logical records (LL4, data 4 and LL5, data 5). The LU passes the requested_length of data from its receive buffer to the application buffer. Program A is responsible for interpreting and decoding individual logical records. The receiving of multiple logical records on one receive call is generally more efficient than receiving one logical record at a time. The reason for this is because application programs can usually pack and unpack logical records much faster than they can execute multiple CPI-C Receive calls.

8.6 CPI-C CALLS AND APPC VERBS

Most of the CPI Communications calls are functionally equivalent to the corresponding APPC verbs. Some CPI-C calls, such as Confirm, Confirmed, Flush, or Request_To_Send, are almost functionally identical to the corresponding APPC verbs. Therefore, the reader should review Chap. 7 for the functional description of these calls. While reading Chap. 7, the reader should keep in mind the following differences between CPI Communications (CPI-C) and Advanced Program-to-Program Communications (APPC) verbs:

- The CPI-C does not support the program initial parameters PIP data, MAP_NAME FMH_DATA discussed in Sec. 6.1.

- Conversation Level Security (user_id, password, and profile) cannot be modified or examined by issuing CPI-C calls. The default CPI-C SECURITY=SAME.

- CPI-C programs are capable of receiving data and control information on the same Receive call. When this occurs the program enters the Send-Pending state The Send-Pending state is discussed in Sec. 8.7.

- The CPI Communications Initialize_Conversation (CMINIT) call is used to explicitly initialize conversation characteristics default values before the conversation is allocated and to assign a unique conversation_ID.

- The CPI Communications Accept_ Conversation (CMACCP) calls are used to accepts an incoming allocation request and set the conversation characteristics default values at the remote logical unit.

- CPI-C calls need to be entered in exact syntax (CMALLC, CMACCP, etc.).

The following is a list of CPI Communications calls and the corresponding APPC/LU 6.2 verbs:

CPI-C Calls	APPC/LU 6.2 Verbs
Initialize_Conversation (CMINIT) and Allocate (CMALLC)	[MC_]ALLOCATE
Deallocate (CMDEAL)	[MC_]DEALLOCATE
Send_Data (CMSEND)	[MC_]SEND_DATA
Receive_Data (CMRCV)	[MC_]RECEIVE_AND_WAIT [MC_]RECEIVE_IMMEDIATE
Confirm (CMCFM)	[MC_]CONFIRM
Confirmed (CMCFMD)	[MC_]CONFIRMED
Flush (CMFLUS)	[MC_]FLUSH
Prepare_To_Receive (CMPTR)	[MC_]PREPARE_TO_RECEIVE
Send_Error (CMSERR)	[MC_]SEND_ERROR
Request_To_Send (CMRTS)	[MC_]REQUEST_TO_SEND
Test_Request_To_Send_ Received (CMTRTS)	WAIT
commit	SYNC_POINT
backout	BACKOUT

8.7 CPI-C FLOW DIAGRAMS

In this section we are going to look at several examples of how CPI-C calls may be used in designing various types of distributed applications. The flow diagrams assume that the local and the remote resources have already been configured, started, and initialized as explained in Sec. 7.14 for the APPC environment.

8.7.1 Error Recovery in Send-Pending State

When the data and Send state are received on the same Receive call (the application program receives data and the status_received= CM_SEND_RECEIVED), then the program enters Send_Pending state. If there are no errors then the Send-Pending state should be treated exactly the same as the Send state. Usually in this state a program starts sending data by issuing a Send-Data call. However; if an error occurs, the programmer may want to distinguish between an error encountered because of the received data or an error encountered after the data was received and processed. The programmer may issue a Set_Error_Direction call to modify the error_direction characteristic and to indicate how the error occurred. The error_direction characteristic is significant only in the Send_Pending state and is ignored in other CPI-C states. It can be set to the following values:

- **CM_RECEIVE_ERROR** (the default value) — indicates that the error occurred in the received data. When Send_Erorr is issued, the partner program is notified of the error by means of the return_code (RC=CM_PROGRAM_ERROR_PURGING), which indicates that the data might have been purged.

- **CM_SEND_ERROR** — indicates that the error occurred after the data has been received and processed. The partner program is notified by means of the return_code (RC=CM_PROGRAM_ ERROR_NO_TRUNC), which implies that the error had nothing to do with the data sent to the remote program. The remote program detected some other error condition after it had successfully received and processed the data.

Figure 8.12 illustrates an error condition which was detected after the remote program had successfully received and processed all the data sent by the local program. The following are the steps:

Step 1.   The local program (program A) is currently in the Send or Send-Pending state and is sending data to the remote program (program B) by issuing Send_Data calls. The conversation characteristics are set to their default values for both programs.

Step 2.   Program A issues the CPI-C Receive call to flush LU A's send buffer. Program A is suspended until some information is received from program B.

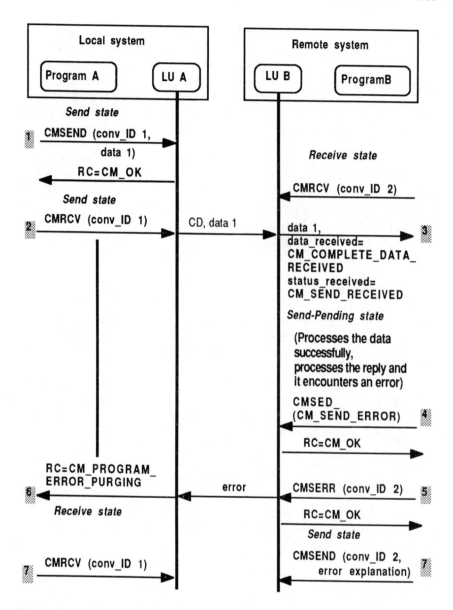

Figure 8.12 Error recovery in Send_Pending state.

Step 3.   Program B issues a Receive call in order to receive the data record sent by program A. The data_received parameter is set to CM_COMPLETE_DATA_RECEIVED indicating that a complete data record is received on this mapped conversation. The status_received parameter is set to CM_SEND_RECEIVED indicating that program B received the Send state on the same

CPI-C Receive call. Program B enters the Send-Pending state and processes the received data. The data is processed without any errors. Then, program B begins performing other processing (e.g., prepares a reply to be sent to program A), and it encounters an error condition. Notice that the error occurred after the data was received and processed by program B. Therefore, program B needs to notify program A that the error did not occur in the received data.

Step 4.   If program B issued a Send_Error call at this time, it would mean that the error occurred in the received data since the default error_direction characteristic is set to CM_RECEIVE_ERROR. Therefore, program B issues the Set_Error_Direction (CMSED) call to change the error_direction characteristic to CM_SEND_ERROR. This specifies that program B detected an error after it had successfully received and processed the data.

Step 5.   Program B issues the Send_Error call. Since the conversation is currently in the Send_Pending state, CPI-C examines the error_direction characteristic and sends the appropriate error notification to program A. Program B enters the Send state and should start a user-defined error recovery procedure.

Step 6.   The Receive call issued in Step 2 completes with RC=CM_PROGRAM_ERROR_NO_TRUNC, which indicates that the data was delivered successfully and that the remote program detected some other error condition.

Step 7.   Program A enters Receive state, and it must issue the Receive call to get an error explanation from program B. Program B initiates an error recovery procedure (e.g., by issuing the Send_Data call explaining the error). The user-defined error recovery must be agreed upon by the two communicating programs at the program's design phase.

8.7.2 Requester/Server Design

The most common types of a conversation is the requester/server model. This example was already discussed in Sec. 7.14.3 for the APPC environment (see Fig. 7.35). Figure 8.13 illustrates possible CPI-C design steps for the requester/server model. The reader should compare the APPC and CPI-C designs. The local program (the requester) sends a single request to a remote program (the server). The server receives and processes the request and sends back either the data that satisfies the request or a reason why the request was rejected. Once the requester receives the answer it can then issue another request to the server.

The following are the design steps:

Step 1.   The requester issues the Initialize_Conversation call to initialize local resources for the new conversation. Upon successful completion of this call the control is returned to the program with a new conversation_ID (conv_ID 1) that identifies the local end of this conversation.

Step 2.   The requester issues the Set_Send_Type (CMSST) call to set the send_type conversation characteristic to CM_SEND_AND_ PREP_TO_RECEIVE. This forces the local LU to flush its send buffer and to release the Send state each time a Send_Data call is issued. The server will receive the data and Send state as soon as the requester issues the Send_Data call. This will allow the server to start processing the request and also send the reply while the requester is performing some other processing. Combining multiple distributed functions on one Send_Data call improves performance of the communicating programs. Compare this design to the APPC design illustrated in Fig. 7.35.

Step 3.   The requester issues the CPI-C Allocate verb, requesting a conversation with the server. The conversation_type is set to the default value CM_MAPPED_CONVERSATION. The default sync_level is set to CM_NONE, which means that this conversation cannot issue Confirm or commit calls to perform confirmation or synchronization processing.

Step 4.   The requester issues the Send_Data call in order to send the request to the server. Since the send_type conversation characteristic is set to CM_SEND_AND_PREP_TO_RECEIVE, the local LU flushes its send buffer with change direction a this time. The requester may now perform local processing or issue a Receive call to wait for the reply from the server.

Step 5.   LU B receives the allocation request and starts a new instance of the server. The server issues the Accept_Conversation (CMACCP) call to accept the incoming allocation request. Upon successful completion of the call the remote LU returns control to the server. The RC is set to OK and the conversation_ID is set to conv_ID 2, which uniquely identifies this conversation at the remote end. The server issues the Set_Send_Type (CMSST) call to set the

send_type conversation characteristic to CM_SEND_AND_PREP_
TO_RECEIVE.

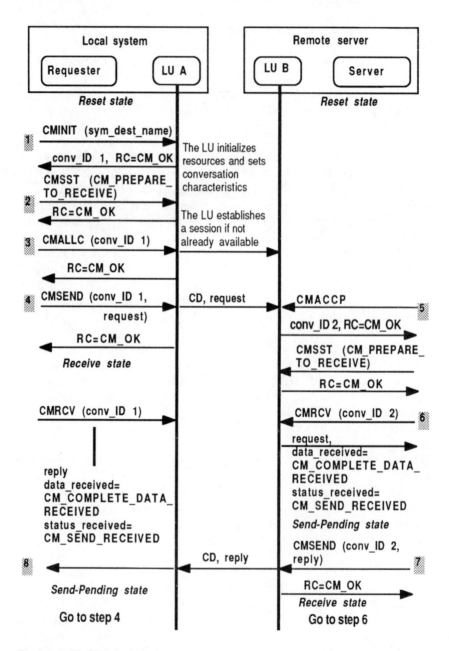

Figure 8.13 CPI-C requester/server flow.

Step 6. The server issues the Receive call to receive the request sent by the requester. The data_received parameter is set to CM_COMPLETE_DATA_RECEIVED indicating that a complete data record has been received. The status_received parameter is set to CM_SEND_RECEIVED indicating that the server received the Send state on the same Receive call. The server may now process the request and immediately send the reply back to the requester.

Step 7. The server issues the Send_Data call to send a reply back to the requester. Since the send_type conversation characteristic is set to CM_SEND_AND_PREP_TO_RECEIVE the Send call causes LU B to flush its send buffer with change direction. The server may now go to Step 6 to receive another request from the requester.

Step 8. The requester issues the Receive call in order to receive the reply from the server. The data_received parameter is set to CM_COMPLETE_DATA_RECEIVED indicating that a complete data record is received. The status_received parameter is set to CM_SEND_RECEIVED indicating that the requester received the Send state on the same Receive call. The requester enters the Send-Pending state and may end the conversation or send another request to the server by going to Step 4. This design is appropriate if the session is not shared by other TPs. The requester can use the session exclusively until it sends all the requests to the server and then it deallocates the conversation. If there are other TPs competing for the session resources, then the requester should immediately deallocate the conversation and release the session to other conversations. This was illustrated in Fig. 7.36 for the APPC environment.

The CPI-C requester/server design described above is more efficient than the APPC design illustrated in Fig. 7.35. Fewer CPI-C calls are required to perform the same distributed functions. The CPI-C Receive call is capable of receiving data and the Send state on the same call (see steps 6 and 8). Also by combining Send_Data with Prepare_To_Receive, in steps 4 and 7, the data and the Send state are flushed to the partner program when the Send_Data call is issued. This allows both programs to resume processing earlier than it would in the corresponding APPC design. An APPC program would have to issue an MC_SEND_DATA verb followed by an MC_PREPARE_TO_RECEIVE verb in order to perform the distributed functions carried out by the Send_Data call issued in steps 4 and 7. The CPI-C design described above, should improve the overall performance of the communicating programs.

8.7.3 CPI-C File Transfer Example

Let us look at the very common requirement of transferring files between a PC and a host. The CPI Communications call sequence shown in Fig. 8.14 may be used when a file needs to be copied between any two systems residing in an SNA/LU 6.2 distributed network. In our example the local program (program A) transfers a file to the remote program (program B). The APPC file transfer design was illustrated in Fig. 7.37. The following are the design steps that can be used by the two transaction programs:

Step 1.   The local program (program A) issues the Initialize_Conversation (CMINIT) call to initialize local resources for a new conversation. The sym_dest_name points to side information containing partner_LU_name, mode_name, and TP_name. Upon successful completion of this call the control is returned to the program with RC=CM_OK and the new conversation_ID (conv_ID 1). The conversation characteristics are set to the default values as shown in Fig. 8.1.

Step 2.   Program A issues the Set_Sync_Level (CMSSL) call to set the sync_level coversation characteristic to CM_CONFIRM. This will allow confirmation processing to be performed on this conversation.

Step 3.   Program A issues the Allocate call to start a mapped conversation with program B. The local LU (LU A) establishes a session with the remote LU (LU B) if the session was not already established. The LU buffers the allocation request and no information is sent to the partner program yet.

Step 4.   Program A reads n records from a disk file and issues Send_Data calls (one for each record). The data records are buffered locally by the logical unit until a sufficient amount of information is reached for transmission. Let us assume that the LU accumulated enough data for transmission and its send buffer is flushed. The resulting network message (BIU) is generated with the begin bracket (BB) indicator in the RH, and the ATTACH header (FMH-5) and the data in the RU.

Step 5.   The remote logical unit receives the allocation request and starts a new instance of program B. Program B issues the Accept_Conversation (CMACCP) call to accept the incoming allocation request. Upon successful completion of the call the remote

LU returns control to program B. The RC is set to CM_OK and the conversation_ID is set to conv_ID 2, which uniquely identifies this conversation.

Step 6.   Program B receives and processes the data by issuing Receive calls. The data_received is set to CM_COMPLETE_ DATA_RECEIVED indicating that a complete mapped conversation data record has been received. Program B then continues to issue Receive calls until all the data records and the confirmation requests are received. We are assuming that the requested_length is larger than the maximum data length to be received in order to ensure that only one Receive call is required for each Send_Data call issued by program A. If the maximum requested length that can be passed to the program's receive buffer is shorter than the received record length, program B would have to issue multiple Receive calls in order to receive one complete data record. This would decrease performance and should be avoided.

Step 7.   Program A issues the Confirm call to deliver the remaining records to program B and to perform confirmation processing. The local LU flushes its send buffer. The resulting network message (BIU) is generated with the RQD2 indicator in the RH and the remaining data records in the RU. The SNA request definite response 2 (RQD2) indicator requires successful confirmation processing before program A can resume its processing. Therefore, program A is suspended until confirmation processing is completed.

Step 8.   Program B issues a Receive call and receives the last data record sent by the local program. The data_received is set to CM_COMPLETE_DATA_RECEIVED indicating that a complete mapped conversation data record has been received. The status_received indicator is set to CM_CONFIRM_RECEIVED indicating that program A requested confirmation processing. Notice, that the corresponding APPC design illustrated in Fig. 7.37 required an additional receive call just to receive the confirmation request.

Step 9.   Program B issues a Confirmed call which acknowledges that the data was received and processed without errors. Upon successful completion of this call program B returns to the Receive state and should issue another Receive call. Alternatively, program B may issue a Send_Error call indicating an error condition. In this case program B would enter the Send state and should perform user-defined error recovery.

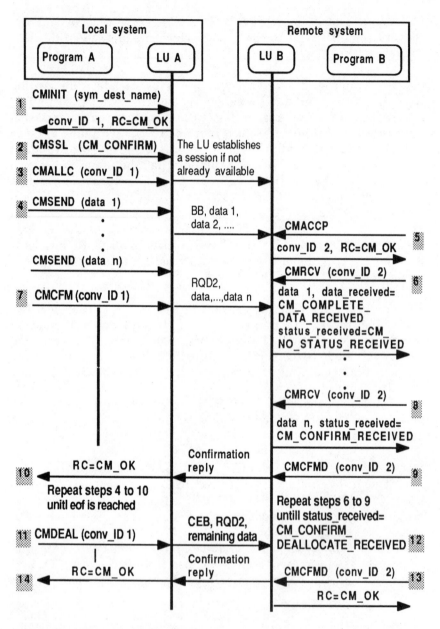

Figure 8.14 File copy example.

Step 10. The confirmation reply arrives at the local LU and the CM_OK return_code is sent to program A. Program A may now repeat steps 4 to 10 until the end of file (eof) is reached. Program B would have to repeat steps 6 to 9.

Step 11. The local program issues the Deallocate call. The default deallocate_type characteristic is set to CM_DEALLOCATE_ SYNC_LEVEL and the conversation was allocated with the sync_level set to CM_CONFIRM. Therefore, LU A will return the control to program A after successful confirmation processing. LU A flushes its send buffer and sends the remaining data, the confirmation request (RQD2) and the deallocation request (CEB) across the session to LU B.

Step 12. Program B receives the remaining data by issuing Receive calls. Then program B receives the confirmation and deallocation requests by means of a status_received parameter set to CM_CONFIRM_DEALLOC_RECEIVED.

Step 13. Program B issues a Confirmed call and the conversation deallocates without errors.

Step 14. The RC=CM_OK indicates that the two communicating programs have copied the file without errors and agreed to terminate the conversation.

The design described above assumes that there are no errors during the copy operation. If an error occurs, the program that detects an error issues the Send_Error call and enters the Send state. Then this program should start user-defined error-recovery procedures (e.g., the programs may agree to redo all the processing from the previous successful confirmation processing). The partner program is notified that an error occurred by means of the RC= Program_Error_Purging. The partner program is placed in the Receive state and should issue the Receive call to wait for the error explanation. Error recovery was discussed in Sec. 7.11 .

8.8 SUMMARY

In Chaps. 7 and 8 we learned the **Advanced Program-to-Program Communications (APPC)** and the SAA **Common Programming Interface-Communications (CPI-C),** distributed architectures. **CPI Communications** calls have been built on top of the LU 6.2 verbs. The major differences between the APPC level interface and CPI-C communications level interface is due to the fact that APPC was introduced in 1984, 3 years prior to the SAA announcement, and did not impose any syntax rules on the application programming interfaces. CPI-C was introduced to provide a consistent application programming interface for program-to-program communications in the SAA environments. Since the major difference between APPC and CPI-C is the syntax and not the functionality, the reader should be able to translate the APPC flow diagrams illustrated in this book to CPI-C flow diagrams. In Sec. 8.7 we have shown the CPI-C design flows for the APPC flow diagrams discussed in Sec. 7.14. Generally the CPI-C communications level interface is more efficient than the APPC level interface. CPI-C allows many APPC functions to be performed on one programming call. For example, sending data can be combined with flushing the LU's send buffer, changing the Send state to Receive, confirmation processing, or transaction termination. Also, data and control information can be received on one CPI-C Receive call rather than two separate APPC [MC_]RECEIVE_AND_WAIT verbs. In most cases the old existing APPC applications can communicate with CPI-C applications unless PIP data, MAP_NAME, or FMH_DATA options were used. Both APPC and CPI-C are based on the LU 6.2 architecture, which is a chosen logical unit for the SAA computer enterprise. SAA is IBM's strategic direction for the 1990s. Therefore, the standards based on the LU 6.2 architecture are going to play a very important role in developing a customer's SAA computer enterprise. LU 6.2 does have many advantages over any other SNA logical unit, and this is discussed in Sec. 3.8 of this book. Numerous APPC and CPI-C advantages were discussed in Sec. 4.6. Overall, APPC and CPI-C are the best available standards for developing distributed applications and they are an obvious, if not only choice, for SNA distributed networks of the 1990s.

3

LU 6.2 Networks and Implementations

9

Configuration and Performance Issues

In this chapter we will concentrate on configuration and performance issues of SNA/LU 6.2 distributed networks. In subsequent chapters, we will examine LU 6.2 network activation and message flows, along with IBM and third-party vendor's LU 6.2 implementations. The network resources such as lines, physical units (PUs), logical units (LUs), modes, and the transaction programs (TPs) must be configured prior to starting distributed transactions. Both the APPC and SAA/CPI-C are based on the logical unit 6.2, and they require the same underlying SNA/LU 6.2/PU 2.1 distributed network. Therefore, the configuration and performance issues described in this chapter apply to both APPC and CPI-C environments. We will examine configuration issues of the peer-to-peer Low Entry Networking (LEN) PU 2.1 nodes and the VTAM/NCP support of the PU 2.1 and APPN distributed networks. Prior to reading this chapter the reader is strongly advised to review the following sections:

- Section 3.2 describing the concepts of a PU 2.1 node, and LEN and APPN networks.

- Section 3.4 describing the logical unit type 6.2 distributed network components.

- Section 3.6 describing the contention winner/loser sessions and the LU-LU session limit.

- Section 4.3.4 describing the LU 6.2 control-operator verbs.

- Sections 7.1 and 8.1 describing APPC and CPI-C environments and configuration requirements.

After reading this section the reader should review the programming and configuration performing tips in Appendix A of this book.

9.1 NETWORK RESOURCES

As described earlier, Systems Network Architecture (SNA) consists of physical processors (**distributed nodes**) interconnected via **physical links**. Logically the SNA distributed network consists of **Logical Units (LU 6.2s)** interconnected via logical connections called **sessions**. A logical unit acts as a port between a transaction program (called an **SNA end user**) and the path control network. The communicating programs exchange messages over a **Conversation** which is assigned to a single session established between the local and the remote LUs. The operator defines the sessions for which the local LU is designated to win the allocation race as **conversation-winner** (also called a **conwinner or first-speaker**) sessions. The sessions for which the local LU is designated to lose the allocation race are called **conversation-loser** (also called a **conloser or bidder**) sessions. Conversation-winner and conversation-loser sessions were discussed in Sec. 3.6.3. The operator may regulate the number of sessions between LUs as well as the number of conversation-winner and conversation-loser sessions, by preconfiguring the session limit parameters or issuing the control-operator **CNOS** verbs. Figure 9.1 illustrates a typical example of an SNA/LU 6.2 distributed network consisting of two Virtual Telecommunications Access Methods (VTAMs) running in host A and host B and containing the System Services Control Points (**SSCPs**). There are also two Network Control Programs (NCPs), NCP A and NCP B that are connected to two **type 2.1 peripheral nodes** C and D. Each PU 2.1 or PU 5 node defines the local logical units and the list of remote logical units. The logical units are referred to by their network names, the **local (source) LU** and the **remote (target or partner) LU**. Most of implementations hide the true network names from the application programmers. Transaction programs and operators may use installation-specific names (called **alias names**) to refer to network resources rather than the actual network names or addresses. This allows the system programmers to change the network names without affecting the application programs. The following is a list of LU 6.2 resources and configuration parameters that need to be defined by system programmers:

- Physical links (e.g., SDLC, Token Ring, X.25, S/370 Channel, S/390 ESCON). Let us assume that the link connection between NCP A and the PU 2.1 node C is a leased line, and between NCP B and the PU 2.1 node D is a switched line.

- SNA physical nodes (PUs) that manage the node's resources (see Sec. 3.1 for a description of a PU 2.1 node).

- Local and remote logical unit names and their aliases.

- Control points (CPs) in type 2.1 nodes and SCCPs in type 5 nodes.

- Single or parallel sessions between the local and the remote logical units.

- Mode names describe the set of session parameters (such as priority, MAXRU sizes, routing). The SNASVCMG mode name is an LU 6.2 defined mode designated for the CNOS verbs that manage the number of parallel sessions between the local and the remote LUs.

- Transaction programs (TPs).

- The total LU-LU session limit is the maximum number of sessions that can be active at one time, from one LU to all of its partner LUs.

- The (LU, mode) session limit is the maximum number of active LU-LU sessions with a specific partner LU for a particular (partner LU, mode) pair. For example, Fig. 9.1 illustrates two modes, "Mode 1" and "Mode 2" defined between LU C and LU D. This allows a maximum of two parallel sessions to LU D with the session characteristics identified by the name "Mode 1" (e.g., for interactive-type applications) and two other parallel sessions with the session characteristics identified by the name "Mode 2" (e.g., for batch job applications).

- The automatic activation limit for a particular (LU, mode) pair the maximum number of LU-LU sessions that the LU will automatically activate and create the initial session pool.

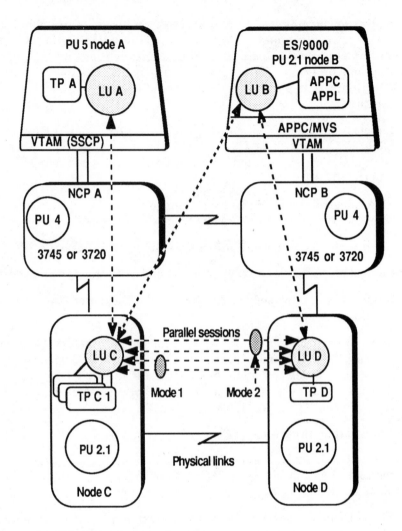

Figure 9.1 SNA/LU 6.2 network resources.

- The local-LU minimum contention winner for a particular (LU, mode) pair specifies the minimum number of sessions for which the local LU is allowed to be the contention winner. For example, if all the conversations initiate from LU C for "Mode 1'" it would be advantageous to configure two contention winner sessions for "Mode 1" at LU C.

- The partner LU minimum contention winner for a particular (LU, mode) pair, specifies the minimum number of sessions for which the partner LU is allowed to be the contention winner.

9.2 CONFIGURING PU 2.1 NETWORKS

The PU 2.1 nodes may be connected directly with each other, and in this case they do not require any connections to the host (see Fig. 9.2). Such PU 2.1 nodes are called Low Entry Networking (LEN) nodes. LEN requires adjacent PU 2.1-PU 2.1, peer-to-peer communications and was discussed in Sec. 3.2.1 in this book. Let us first look at the configuration issues of LEN nodes (e.g., two personal computers with APPC packages emulating LU 6.2 and PU 2.1). PU 2.1 nodes can also be connected to an SNA subarea network as illustrated in Fig. 9.1 and will be discussed in the following sections.

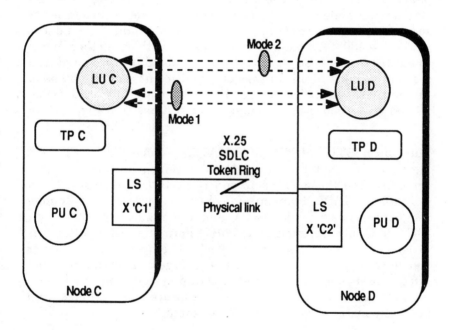

Figure 9.2 Configuration of LEN nodes.

The following are the typical steps performed by system programmers at each physical unit type 2.1 node to define the network resources required for peer-to-peer communications (e.g., between two PCs with APPC packages emulating LU 6.2 and PU 2.1; see Fig. 9.2):

I. Identifying the physical link. Typically physical unit type 2.1 nodes are connected using IBM Token Ring network, Ethernet local area network, X.25, PC network, or SDLC link. Some PU 2.1 nodes may support X.25 networks. The following are typical link level configuration parameters:

- **Link station address** — identifies the PU address of this PU 2.1 node in an SNA network (e.g., **X'C1'** for node C and **X'C2'** for node C). This is the address that is carried in the link level header (LH) address field.

- **Link station role (primary, secondary, or negotiable)** — for peer connections is recommended to configure the station role to **negotiable** in order to avoid the same link station roles. Then the link station role is determined during the XID-3 link negotiation phase discussed in Sec. 3.2.3 in this book. If both of the link stations (for node C and node D) were configured as primaries or secondaries, then the link establishment would fail and the stations would not be able to communicate with each other. When connected to the host, the PU 2.1 node should be configured as a secondary link station. In case of a multipoint connection one of the nodes should be configured as the primary link station and all the other nodes as secondary link stations (see Fig. 3.10 in Sec. 3.2.3).

- **Maximum BTU length (MAXDATA)** — identifies the largest message size that can be sent and received by the link level protocol. The Basic Transmission Unit (BTU) is composed of a 6-byte-long FID2 transmission header (TH), a 3-byte-long request/response header (RH), and the request/response unit (RU). BTU, also referred to as Path Information Unit (PIU), was discussed in Sec. 3.7.3 in this book. The system programmer should configure this parameter to the largest value that does not affect the memory requirements of the system and the level 2 adapter board. Larger buffers generate less frames and generally increase the network throughput.

- **Link level (level 2) modulus (8 or 128)** — implies the modulus to be used on this link connection. The most common modulus used on leased connections is **modulo 8**. Satellite communications use modulo 128.

- **Link level (level 2) window size (MAXOUT)** — identifies the maximum number of frames that the link station can send before receiving an acknowledgment. The maximum window size for modulo 8 is 7 and for modulo 128 is 127. It is not easy to determine the optimal window size. Usually the default values recommended by the products are satisfactory. Generally, if the line quality is good, the window size will be large resulting in improved performance. Let us use modulo 8 and a **window size equal to 7** for the example shown in Fig. 9.2.

- **Line mode (full-duplex or half-duplex)** — for peer-to-peer communications, such as shown in Fig. 9.2, configure the line for full-duplex operation to avoid the line turnaround delay. Generally the PUs should be configured for **full-duplex** operation for best performance. On a multipoint line though the secondary link stations must be configured for half-duplex operation.

II.   Identifying the node type 2.1 (e.g., node C in Fig. 9.2).

- **PU name** — **(PU C)** identifies this node in an SNA network. If the node is communicating with a PU 2.1 peer node (see Fig. 9.2, where node C communicates to an adjacent node D), this name can be set to any desired name without coordination with the partner node. If the PU 2.1 node is connected to a subarea network (see Fig. 9.1) then this name should be coordinated with the host name specified on the NCP PU definition. This name is used to log error messages in the error log files or to send alerts to a network management component residing on the mainframe such as NetView.

- **node ID** — is used in **XID-3** to determine which of the PU 2.1 nodes is to assume the **primary** link station role and **secondary** link station role. The PU 2.1 node with the higher XID-3 value becomes a primary link station. For example, let us assume that node C (OS/2 PC with APPC) is connected via an SDLC line to node D (another OS/2 PC with APPC). We can assign to node C (OS/2 with APPC) a node **ID=X'05D00002'** and to node D a node ID='05D00001'. Then, when an operator activates the line, XID-3 occurs and node C becomes the primary SDLC link station and it will issue the SNRM SDLC command to start the link level protocol. The node IDs do not have to be unique unless the PU 2.1 node is connected to the host. If node IDs are the same then random IDs are generated to determine the primary link station. Generally it is advantagous to configure node IDs to unique values to avoid additional XID-3 exchanges needed to resolve the link station role. The physical unit type 2.1 link initiation and the XID-3 link negotiation was discussed in Sec. 3.2.3.

III. Identifying the local logical units (LUs), for peer communications, requires only the independent logical units to be configured. The dependent and independent logical units were discussed in Sec. 3.3.

- **Local LU name** — the real local LU name, as it is known in the network (e.g., LU C is a local LU name for node C in Fig. 9.2). This name must be coordinated with the remote node configuration and must match the remote (partner LU) name configured at the remote node. For example, the remote LU name for **LU C** must be LU D in the configuration file at node C. The configuration file at node D should specify LU D as the local LU name which communicates with the remote LU name of LU C. The BIND command that establishes the session between the local and the remote LUs carries the real local and remote LU names.

- **Alias LU name** — transaction programs may use this name which is known only at the local node instead of the real LU name. The alias LU name is mapped by the LU into the real LU name. For example, the alias name for LU C can be **LU CA**. Programs at node C use LU CA to access the local LU C.

- **LU local address** — the address of the local LU. This value must be set to **X'00'** for independent LUs. Independent LUs use special Local-Form Session Identifiers (LFSIDs) to distinguish between different sessions (not the LU addresses which are used for dependent LUs). Therefore, the local address of LU C must be set to X'00' at node C and the local address of LU D must also be set to X'00' for the peer-to-peer environment shown in Fig. 9.2. Dependent LUs (for a host configuration only) should have a non-zero unique value discussed in Sec. 9.3

- **Total LU-LU session limit** — the maximum number of sessions that can be active at one time at an LU to all of its partner LUs. Let us configure this parameter to **6** for LU C. This will allow a maximum of six sessions to be active at the same time from LU C to all partner LUs (LU D, other LUs).

IV.   Identifying the remote (partner) logical units (LUs) for the local LU.

- **Partner LU name** — specifies the fully qualified partner LU name as it is known in the network (e.g., **LU D** is a remote LU name for node C in Fig. 9.2). This name must be coordinated with the remote node configuration and must match the local LU name configured at the remote node.

- **Partner alias LU name** — an alias name known only to transaction programs at the local node. For example, programs residing on node C may use the alias name **LU DA** in their allocation requests. LU C maps this name into the real network name LU D before sending it to the remote node. LU DA is known only at the local node C, and the real name LU D must be known and configured at both ends of the connection node C and node D.

- **Security** — specifies the session and/or the conversation level security with this partner LU. The **session level security** requires the same **LU-LU password to be configured** at the local LU and the partner LU for a successful session to be established. If the passwords are not the same, then the session initiation BIND command will fail and sessions cannot be started between the local and the remote LUs. The **conversation level security** requires a **user-id, password, and profile** to be checked on the incoming allocation requests. Session and conversation level security were discussed in Sec. 3.6.5 in this book.

V. Specify the Mode Table Entries; describing the session parameters for sessions from the local logical unit (LU C) to the remote logical unit (LU D).

- **Mode name** — specifies the name of a mode entry that describes the characteristics of a single session or a group of sessions from the local LU to the partner LU. Multiple modes can be specified for each partner LU that allow parallel sessions. For example, the mode name **Mode 1** in Fig. 9.2 may specify the session characteristics for interactive-type applications and **Mode 2** for batch job applications.When parallel sessions are used, the local LU uses a special mode name **SNASVCMG** to negotiate the number of parallel sessions between the local and the partner LUs.

- **Maximum RU size (MAXRU)** — specifies the largest request/response unit size allowed for this mode. This determines the maximum amount of data that the LU will place in the RU before building another RU. LU 6.2 flushes its send buffer when it accumulates MAXRU size of data. Generally larger RU sizes will generate less network messages and better performance, but they may require more system memory to be allocated for buffering data. When many LUs are competing for memory resources, large RU sizes may in actual fact decrease the overall performance of the system. IBM performance tests have shown that configuring the max RU size to **1920** performs well on a 4-Mbit/s Token Ring network.

- **Pacing window** — specifies the largest pacing window size. Pacing prevents a session from overloading the partner program. The sending application program may send data

384   Configuration and Performance Issues

much faster than the partner program can receive it. The partner LU buffers the data before passing it to the receiving program. The pacing window determines the number of RUs the sending LU can send to the remote LU without getting a pacing response back from the receiving LU. If the RUs are arriving too fast, the receiving LU will not allow the sending LU to send additional data until enough space is released in the receive buffer. Ideally, configuring a session for no pacing or a large pacing window produces optimal performance. Using no pacing or large pacing windows, though, may require a lot of system memory to be reserved for each session, which may have negative impact on the overall performance of the system. For this example, the pacing window should be configured equal to 8.

- **The (LU, mode) session limit** — the maximum number of sessions allowed for this mode. For example, in Fig. 9.2 LU C may be configured to have the (LU C, Mode 1) session limit=2 and (LU C, Mode 2) session limit=2. This allows a maximum of two parallel sessions to the remote logical unit LU D with the session characteristic identified by the mode name **Mode 1** and two additional parallel sessions with the session characteristic identified by the mode name **Mode 2**.

- **The local-LU minimum contention winner for a particular (LU, mode) pair** — specifies the minimum number of sessions for which the local LU is allowed to be the contention winner. It is advantageous to allocate the programs that initiate conversations (issue the allocation requests) to the contention winner sessions. For example, if all conversations are started from LU C for Mode 1, it is advantageous to configure two contention winner sessions for Mode 1 at LU C and none at LU D.

- **The partner-LU minimum contention winner for a particular (LU, mode) pair** — specifies the minimum number of sessions for which the partner LU is allowed to be the contention winner.

- **The automatic activation limit for a particular (LU, mode) pair** — the maximum number of contention winner sessions that the local LU will automatically activate to create the initial session pool. It is a good idea to automatically activate some sessions when the LU is started; then the allocation requests will not have to wait the time required to establish a session for this conversation. This may improve performance; however, the impact on resources should be taken into account because starting too many unused sessions reserves and holds system resources. We are going to configure this value to 1.

9.3 VTAM/NCP PU 2.1 SUPPORT

Figure 9.1 illustrates a typical example of VTAM/NCP type 2.1 node support. With the announcement of VTAM V3R2 and NCP V4R3/V5R2, a distributed node such as AS/400, S/36, OS/2 APPC, DOS APPC/PC, and other PU 2.1 nodes can communicate over the subarea network (the network of communications controllers 37XX and hosts) using peer-to-peer communications. A PU 2.1 node supports dependent and independent logical units (LUs). Dependent LUs require assistance from the System Services Control Point (SSCP) to activate an LU-LU session. Independent LUs, on the other hand, may have a SSCP-PU session for network management messages, but they do not have SSCP-LU sessions. Both the Low Entry Networking PU 2.1 nodes and the APPN network nodes can communicate over the subarea network. APPN network appears as an adjacent PU 2.1 node with multiple independent LUs. The SNA subarea network appears to a PU 2.1 node as an adjacent PU 2.1 node. For example, when LU C wants to establish a session with LU D (see Fig. 9.1), it issues a BIND command as if LU D resided directly in the adjacent NCP A. NCP A will route all the traffic via NCP B to node D. LU C and LU D will not know that the communication occurs over the subarea network. Notice that LU C acts as a primary logical unit that is capable of establishing peer-to-peer sessions by issuing BIND commands. Prior to VTAM/NCP PU 2.1 support BIND commands were always issued by the logical units residing in the host. The LUs residing in peripheral nodes were always secondary logical units not capable of issuing BIND commands and they were limited to host communications only. The following new PU 2.1 capabilities are supported by VTAM/NCP:

- **XID-3** used to exchange and negotiate the primary-secondary link station role and the PU 2.1 node capabilities.

- **Independent Logical Units** which can establish sessions by sending BIND from PU 2.1 nodes through subarea network, to other PU 2.1 nodes or host applications. There is no need for SSCP-PU (ACTPU), SSCP-LU (ACTLU) sessions or the INITSELF or CINIT flows. The SSCP-PU session may be activated, though, for network management flows. The PU 2.1 nodes can have primary and secondary logical units, and can have multiple sessions with the same partner (called the parallel sessions) or different partners in the network.

- **Dependent Logical Units,** which act as secondary logical units and work similarly to all the other SNA dependent logical units (e.g., LU 2). They are limited to a single session and they can accept BINDs only from the host . The SSCP-PU (ACTPU) and SSCP-LU (ACTLU) sessions are required prior to activating LU-LU sessions.

- The address field in the Format Identifier (FID2) carries a **Local-Form Session Identifier (LFSID)** that uniquely identifies each LU 6.2 session. LFSIDs and their assignment will be discussed later in this book.

- PU 2.1 nodes are supported over SDLC leased or switched lines, Token Ring LANs, and X.25 NPSI.

9.3.1 VTAM/NCP PU 2.1 Leased Configuration

Let us first look at PU 2.1 node VTAM/NCP definitions illustrated in Fig. 9.3 for **independent LUs** over a leased SDLC line.

The following is a list of relevant parameters:

1. The **network ID** (the network name of the host) of the NCP that connects to node C must be the same as the the network ID at node C.

2. The NCP PU definition statement, the **ADDR=X'C1'**, which specifies the address of the physical unit (PU), must be the same as the node C station address (e.g., the SDLC line address).

3. The **PUTYPE** specification for the PU has to be **2**. The new parameter **XID=YES** must be specified for PU 2.1 node. XID-3 is exchanged at CONTACT time to negotiate PU 2.1 node's parameters.

4. The LU name **LU C** in NCP definition must be the same as the **local LU name** in the node C configuration file (e.g., OS/2 APPC LU name or AS/400, S 36 local location name).

5. The **LOCADDR** must be equal to **zero** for independent LUs. Both the LU C in NCP and in node C must have the address set to zero.

6. The VTAM/NCP **DLOGMOD** (optional parameter) should point to a suggested parameters for LU 6.2 BIND in a logmode table. If this operant is not specified, then the first entry in the logmode table specified on **MODETAB** operant on a PU definition is used by default.

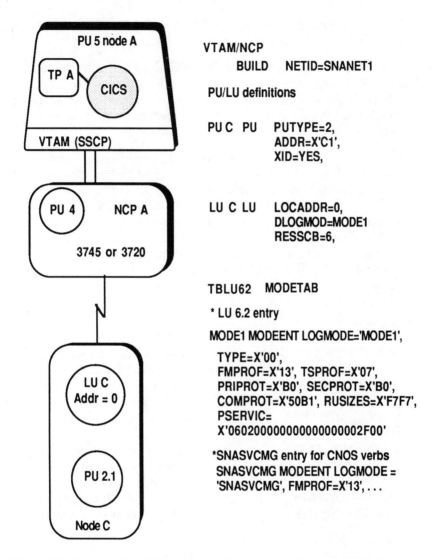

VTAM/NCP
    BUILD   NETID=SNANET1

PU/LU definitions

PU C PU   PUTYPE=2,
            ADDR=X'C1',
            XID=YES,

LU C LU   LOCADDR=0,
            DLOGMOD=MODE1
            RESSCB=6,

TBLU62   MODETAB

* LU 6.2 entry

MODE1 MODEENT LOGMODE='MODE1',
    TYPE=X'00',
    FMPROF=X'13', TSPROF=X'07',
    PRIPROT=X'B0', SECPROT=X'B0',
    COMPROT=X'50B1', RUSIZES=X'F7F7',
    PSERVIC=
    X'0602000000000000000002F00'

*SNASVCMG entry for CNOS verbs
SNASVCMG MODEENT LOGMODE =
'SNASVCMG', FMPROF=X'13', ...

Figure 9.3 Independent LU configuration across a leased SDLC line.

7. The new parameter **RESSCB** (optional parameter) specifies the number of the boundary session control blocks (BSBs) that are reserved for this LU. Each independent session needs a BSB. In addition to the user sessions we need to allocate two BSBs for the CNOS negotiation sessions which use the mode name SNASVCMG. If the sessions requested exceed the number specified in RESSCB, then additional sessions are obtained from the pool defined by the **ADDSESS** (specified on the NCP

BUILD macro) as long as the **MAXSESS** limit has not been exceeded by that independent LU.

8. The SNA defined name **SNASVCMG** should also be defined in the VTAM logmode table. When parallel sessions are used the **SNASVCMG** mode name is used for establishing sessions on which the CNOS exchange occurs to negotiate the session limit between the local and remote logical units.

9. In order to complete these definitions the resources need to be configured for the host application with which LU C will communicate. For example, for **CICS** the appropriate CICS tables need to be configured. The SIT table APPL id that CICS will employ to open an ACB, must match the label of VTAM APPL definition for this region. This name also need to be configured in the PU 2.1 node C as the remote LU name with which LU C will establish LU 6.2 sessions. The appropriate RDO definitions to support parallel sessions must be configured as well:

DEFINE

CONNECTION (LUCA)	!Sysidnt the local name for the !remote system
GROUP (REMNODE)	!The same as for DEFINE !SESSIONS
ACCESSMETHOD (VTAM)	!Must be VTAM for remote !system
NETNAME (LUC)	!The applid of the remote system !(the !partner LU name) as !known to VTAM
PROTOCOL (APPC)	!to define LU 6.2 type system
SINGLESESS (N)	!for parallel session support

DEFINE

SESSIONS (csdname)	
CONNECTION (LUCA)	!Sysidnt the local name for the !remote system
GROUP (REMNODE)	
MODENAME(MODE1)	!The LU 6.2 VTAM logmode !entry
MAXIMUM (m1,m2)	!m1 — maximum number of !sessions for MODE1, !m2 — maximum number !of !contention winners.

9.3.2 VTAM/NCP Switched Token Ring Definitions

Figure 9.4 illustrates relevant configuration parameters for a PU 2.1 switched Token Ring network.

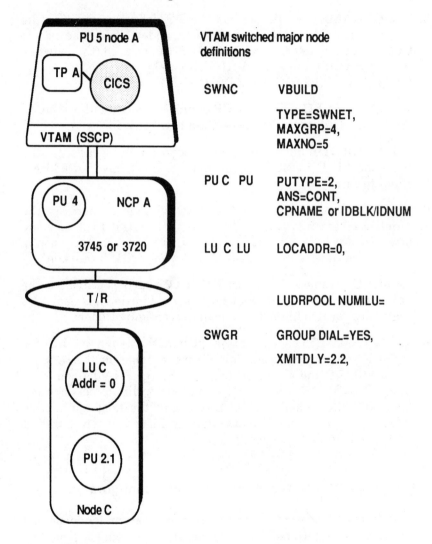

Figure 9.4 Switched PU 2.1 Token Ring configuration

The following is a list of relevant parameters:

1. Node C and its independent logical units are defined in the VTAM switched major node definitions.

2. The **PUTYPE** specification for the PU has to be **2**. The **XID=YES** is not coded for switched connections. XIDs are always exchanged at CONTACT time for switched connections to negotiate the PU 2.1 node parameters.

3. The **CPNAME** specification on the PU definition must be the same as the CPNAME configured at node C. Instead of the CPNAME parameter, **IDNUM/IDBLK** can be used (this must be the same as the the IDNUM/IDBLK configured on node C, e.g., for APPC on OS/2 IDBLK=05D0, IDNUM=A002).

4. The LU name **LU C** in the NCP definition must be the same as the **local LU name** in the node C configuration file.

5. The **LOCADDR** must be equal to **zero** for independent LUs. Both the LU C in NCP and in node C must have an address equal to zero.

6. **XMITDLY** parameter on the GROUP macro specifies the number of seconds that NCP delays its initial transmission, after it answers an incoming call. This gives the calling station the time to transmit first and avoids XID-3 collisions.

7. **NUMILU** parameter on the **LUDRPOOL** macro specifies the the number of control blocks that are reserved for independent LUs that have switched or dynamically reconfigured nodes.

8. The VTAM/NCP configuration parameters such as LU 6.2 logmode table entries containing a mode name for the sessions between LU C and a host LU (e.g., CICS), the SNA defined mode name **SNASVCMG** for negotiating session limits between the local and the remote logical units, and the host application (e.g., CICS, which matches the remote LU name configured at node C) should also be configured.

9.3.3 VTAM/NCP PU 2.1 Dependent LU Configuration

The PU 2.1 node supports both the SSCP dependent and independent logical units (LUs). Dependent LU requires assistance from the System Services Control Point (SSCP) to activate an LU-LU session. They do act similarly to all other SNA dependent LUs (e.g., LU type 2) and require ACTPU and ACTLU commands (SSCP - PU and SSCP-LU sessions) prior to LU-LU session establishment. Dependent logical units act as secondary LUs only and are not capable of establishing sessions. They always accepts BINDs from a host application such as CICS, which acts as the primary logical unit.

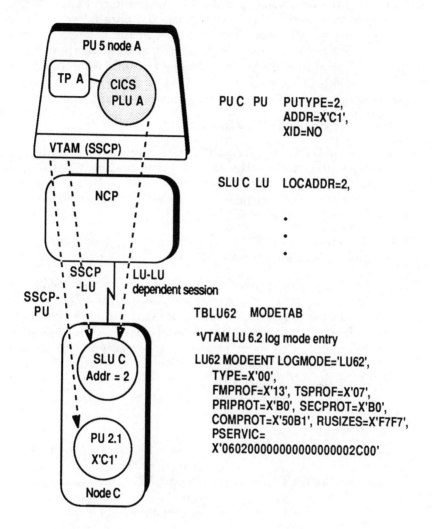

PU C PU   PUTYPE=2,
            ADDR=X'C1',
            XID=NO

SLU C LU   LOCADDR=2,

            .
            .
            .

TBLU62   MODETAB

*VTAM LU 6.2 log mode entry

LU62 MODEENT LOGMODE='LU62',
        TYPE=X'00',
        FMPROF=X'13', TSPROF=X'07',
        PRIPROT=X'B0', SECPROT=X'B0',
        COMPROT=X'50B1', RUSIZES=X'F7F7',
        PSERVIC=
        X'060200000000000000002C00'

Figure 9.5 Dependent LU configuration.

Figure 9.5 shows the CICS transaction program TPA communicating with a transaction program residing in the PU 2.1 node C. If the user requirements were for a single conversation, then the logical unit residing in the PC may be configured as a dependent LU. An operator must activate the logical and the physical units by issuing VTAM V, NET, ACT, ID=commands prior to starting the LU-LU sessions. In this case the PC is totally controlled by the host SSCP and the VTAM operator. If such control is required and there is no need for LU 6.2 parallel sessions or communications with other than host LUs in the network, then a dependent logical unit may be the right choice. Configuring a dependent logical unit 6.2 is very similar to configuring any other SNA dependent LU (e.g., LU type 2). The following is a list of relevant parameters when configuring the dependent logical units:

1. The **PUTYPE=2** and the **XID=NO**.

2. The **LOCADDR** in NCP configuration must match with the corresponding address in node C configuration file (SLU C address is equal to 2 in both NCP and node C). If more dependent LUs are required, they should be configured with nonzero addresses equal to 3, 4, 5, etc.

3. The **Logmode Table Entry** must contain suggested parameters for the LU 6.2 session between CICS and SLU C.

4. In order to complete these definitions the resources need to be configured for the host application with which LU C will communicate. The SIT table **APPL ID** that CICS will employ to open an ACB must match the label of VTAM APPL definition for this region. This name also need to be configured in the PU 2.1 node C as the remote LU name with which LU C will establish LU 6.2 sessions.The appropriate RDO definitions to support a single session must be configured as well:

DEFINE

CONNECTION (SLUA)	!Sysidnt the local name for the !remote system
NETNAME (SLUC)	!The applid of the remote system !(the !partner LU name) as !known to VTAM
SINGLESESS (Y)	!only single sessions is allowed !for !dependent LUs

DEFINE

SESSIONS(csdname)

MAXIMUM (1,1)	! maximum 1 session with 1 ! contention winner session.

The remaining parameters were discussed in Sec. 9.3.1.

Single-session APPC terminal can also be defined as a
TERMINAL with an associated TYPETERM. This method
supports the AUTOINSTALL facility.

DEFINE

TERMINAL (sysid)
  MODENAME (LU62)
  TYPETERM(DFHLU62T)

  DEFINE TYPETERM(DFHLU62T)
    DEVICE (APPC)

9.3.4 Additional VTAM/NCP PU 2.1 Definitions

The following is a list of additional VTAM/NCP parameters
relevant to a node type 2.1 configuration:

NCP   BUILD
      ADDSESS=n
      AUXADDR=n
      NAMTAB=n
      MAXSESS=n

- **ADDSESS=n** This parameter defines the number of the
  boundary session control blocks (**BSBs**) in a general pool.
  These control blocks can be used by any independent LU when
  the number of sessions exceed the value specified in **RESSCB**
  parameter but it is less than **MAXSESS** limit. One session
  control block is needed for each independent session.

- **MAXSESS=n** This parameter defines the maximum number of
  sessions that any independent LU can have. In order for LUs to
  support parallel sessions **n** should be greater than **two**. The first
  two sessions are needed for the **SNASVCMG** sessions to
  negotiate the session limit (execute the CNOS verbs).

- **AUXADDR=n** This parameter defines additional addresses
  for the independent LUs. A new primary logical unit (PLU)
  address is assigned each time an independent LU starts a
  session. Therefore, each session does have a unique session
  address even though the parallel sessions are established
  between the same LU partners (PLU/SLU).

- **NAMTAB=n** This parameter defines the maximum number of entries in the network name table. This table holds names of Networks, SSCPs and PU 2.1 nodes.

9.3.5 VTAM/NCP APPN Support

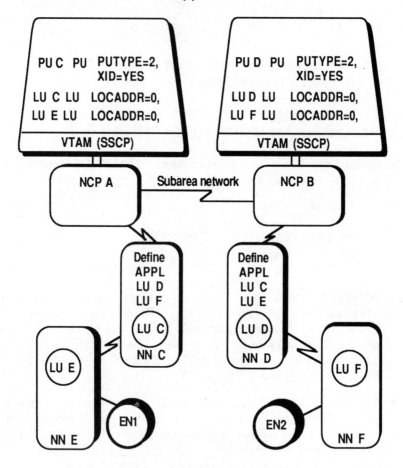

Figure 9.6 VTAM/NCP APPN configuration.

Advanced Peer-to-Peer Networking (APPN) architecture is a PU 2.1 Low Entry Networking (LEN) architecture with two major enhancements:

1. The PU 2.1 node has the ability to perform intermediate network routing. Such PU 2.1 node is called a **network node (NN)**.

The LEN PU 2.1 nodes are not capable of intermediate network routing and they are called **end nodes (ENs)**.

2. It allows dynamic network configuration.

APPN architecture was discussed in Sec. 3.2.2 in this book. Figure 9.6 illustrates VTAM/NCP configuration requirements of APPN nodes communicating over SNA subarea network. The network consists of two hosts running VTAMs (V3R2 or later). The APPN nodes are connected to communications controllers running NCPs (V4R3 or later). The APPN network consists of network nodes (AS/400s or S/36s) and end nodes (any PU 2.1 nodes). Any PU 2.1 node (EN or NN node) can communicate with any other PU 2.1 node attached to the APPN network or to VTAM/NCP subarea network. An APPN network node (e.g., NN C or NN D in Fig. 9.6) appears to VTAM/NCP subarea network as an adjacent PU 2.1 node with multiple independent LUs. VTAM/NCP subarea network appears as LEN node to APPN network. Therefore, the PU 2.1 VTAM/NCP leased and switched configuration discussed earlier (see Figs. 9.3, 9.4) apply as well to configuring APPN nodes attached to subarea network. The hosts are aware only of APPN nodes directly attached to a subarea network. Therefore, only the network nodes NN C and NN D must be configured in VTAM/NCP as PU 2.1 nodes. NCP A is aware only of its adjacent APPN nodes (Fig. 9.6 NN C). All the LUs in the APPN network are defined in the NCP as if they resided in NN C. The NCP A configuration shows one physical unit PU C (that corresponds to NN C) and the independent logical units (LU C residing in NN C and LU E residing in NN E). When a program residing on NN E requests a conversation with a host application (such as CICS), the independent logical unit LU E issues a BIND command which is routed by NN C to the host. The host is not aware of NN C routing and it considers LU E as an independent logical unit that resides in the adjacent PU 2.1 node NN C. NN C must also have configuration entries for NN D and NN E as well as the logical units residing in the APPN network.

9.3.6 Typical PU 2.1 Connection Failures

The following is a list of typical failures caused by incorrect configurations:

1. Both **link station roles** are configured as **primary** or **secondary**. For peer connections it is suggested that the link

station role be configured as **negotiable**. For host connections the PU 2.1 node should be configured as the secondary link station and the NCP, as the primary link station.

2. The **network ID** of the VTAM/NCP that connects to adjacent PU 2.1 node does not match the network ID of this node for switched connections.

3. The NCP PU address (**ADDR=**) does not match the physical unit address configured on the remote PU 2.1 node. For peer (nonhost PU 2.1-PU 2.1) connections the physical unit addresses do not have to match.

4. The **XID is not set to YES for leased** VTAM/NCP PU 2.1 connections.

5. The **fully qualified partner LU name** (Network_name.LU name) of the local physical unit type 2.1 node does not match the fully qualified **local LU name** configured on the remote PU 2.1 node.

6. **Mode mismatch.** This may mean one of the following: there is no entry in the SLU's mode table that matches the mode name in the PLU's mode table; there may be no LU 6.2 mode entry defined in VTAM **logmode table or the corresponding PU 2.1 node** or the **SNASVCMG** mode is not defined for parallel sessions (some PU 2.1 nodes, e.g., APPC on OS/2, may not required to configure SNASVCMG).

7. The **CPNAMEs** do not match for host switched Token Ring connections. The **CPNAME** specification on the PU definition must be the same as the CPNAME configured on the PU 2.1 node. In some cases **IDNUM/IDBLK** may be used instead of the CPNAME parameter. **VTAM/NCP** may require specific IDNUM/IDBLK for different peripheral nodes (e.g., for APPC on OS/2 IDBLK must be equal to 05D0).

8. Insufficient resources in NCP. The most common resources affected are: not enough session control blocks configured (check **RESSCB, ADDSESS** and **MAXSESS** parameters) for PU 2.1 host connections; the network name table (**NAMTAB**) is too small; not enough PLU addresses (**AUXADDR**).

9. The LU-LU passwords do not match for the session level security. The user-id and passwords do not match at the local and remote logical units if the conversation level session security is used.

9.4 PROGRAMMATIC CONFIGURATION

Many APPC implementations (e.g., APPC/PC on DOS) require programming calls to define or modify the local LUs operational parameters prior to a conversation initiation sequence. The APPC architecture defines control-operator verbs specifically for this purpose.

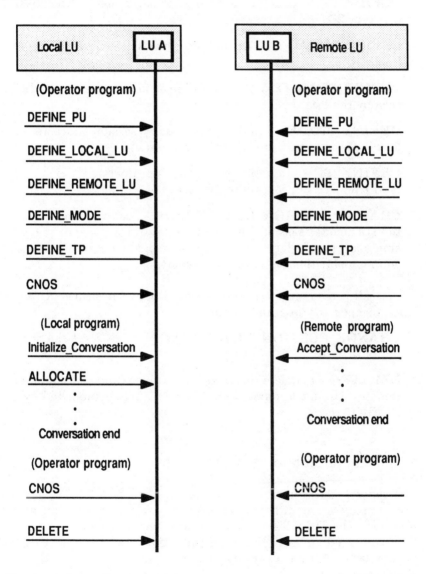

Figure 9.7 Programmatic configuration.

Figure 9.7 illustrates the control-operator verbs required prior to starting the first conversation and after all the conversations have been deallocated between the local and the remote logical units. The following is a typical sequence of configuration calls that an operator program may have to issue prior to the conversation initiation sequence:

- **DEFINE_PU** — to define or modify the parameters of the physical unit type 2.1.

- **DEFINE_LOCAL_LU** — to define or modify the parameters of the local LU 6.2.

- **DEFINE_REMOTE_LU** — to define or modify the remote LU as seen by the local LU.

- **DEFINE_MODE** — to define or modify session characteristics for all sessions with the specified mode name.

- **DEFINE_TP** — to define or modify parameters describing the local transaction program to the local LU.

- **CHANGE_SESSION_LIMIT (CNOS)** — to initialize or modify the (LU,mode) session limit from a zero to a nonzero value for single or parallel sessions. This also establishes contention winner polarities for parallel sessions.

Once all conversations are deallocated between local and remote LUs, the operator program should issue:

- **CHANGE_SESSION_LIMIT (CNOS)** — to reset the session limits to zero.

- **DELETE** — to delete the parameter values (for the local and the remote LUs, mode name, and TP) previously established by the DEFINE verbs.

9.4.1 DEFINE Control Operator Verbs

The control-operator verbs were discussed in Sec. 4.3.4. They are executed by an installation-specific control operator transaction program. The DEFINE control-operator verbs are local verbs and they are used to initialize or modify the local LU's operational parameters. As an example, we will examine the DEFINE_REMOTE_LU verb.

DEFINE_REMOTE_LU — initializes or modifies the parameters describing the remote LU as seen by the local LU.

FULLY_QUALIFIED_LU_NAME (Net_Id.LU X) — (referred to as **partner LU name**) specifies the **fully qualified** partner LU name (**network ID.LU name**) as it is known in the network. This name must be coordinated with the remote node configuration and must match the local LU name configured at the remote node. The network ID (e.g., the network name of the host) of the NCP that connects to node C must be the same as the network ID at node C.

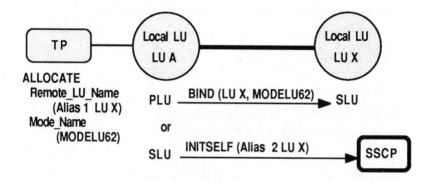

Figure 9.8 Network names and aliases.

Supplied parameters (see Fig. 9.8):

LOCALLY_KNOWN_LU_NAME (Alias 1 LU X) — (referred to as **partner alias LU name**) specifies an alias name known only to transaction programs at the local node. Figure 9.8 shows a TP issuing an ALLOCATE verb. The supplied parameters **Alias 1 LU X** is a local name and is mapped by LU A into the true network name LU X which is carried in the BIND.

UNINTERPRETED_LU_NAME (Alias 2 LU X) — this name is carried in INITSELF if the local LU (LU A) is a secondary logical unit connected to a host, and a session is not yet established when the TP issues an ALLOCATE verb.

INITIATE_TYPE   (INITIAL_ONLY I QUEUE) — specifies whether the SSCP will queue the initiation request (the INITSELF) received from SLU.

PARALLEL_SESSION_SUPPORT (YES | NO) — specifies whether parallel sessions are supported from the local to the remote logical units.

CNOS_SUPPORT (YES | NO) — specifies whether CNOS verbs are supported.

LU_LU_PASSWORD — specifies the password to be used for the session level security. The same password must be configured at the local and the remote LUs.

SECURITY_ACCEPTANCE   (NONE|CONVERSATION| ALREADY VERIFIED) — specifies what security information will be accepted by the local logical unit on allocation requests received from the remote LU.

- NONE — no conversation level security is required.

- CONVERSATION — specifies the user ID and password and which are required. An optional profile parameter may be specified to define different access rights (e.g., read/write/delete).

- ALREADY VERIFIED — specifies that the LU will accept the already-verified access security indicator which allows the use of the user ID and profile (if present) from the allocation request that started the local TP instance.

Similarly, **DEFINE_LOCAL_LU** control-operator verb defines, initializes, and changes parameters that control the operation of the local LU, and DEFINE_MODE initializes or changes the parameters that control a group of sessions with the same session characteristics from the local to the remote logical units.

9.4.2 CNOS Verbs

Change number of session (CNOS) verbs — allow an operator program for a specific (LU, mode) name to control:

- ° Contention winner polarities for LU 6.2 parallel session connections

- ° The number of parallel sessions between the local and the remote logical units for a specific mode name

° Selection of the LU that is responsible for activation or deactivation of LU-LU sessions required as a result of the imposed new limits

° Resetting of the (LU, mode) session limits to zero

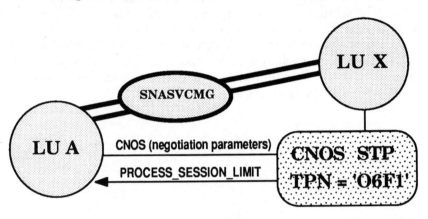

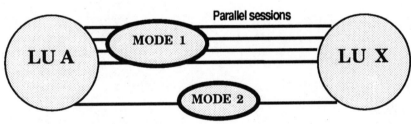

Figure 9.9 CNOS verb.

The CNOS verb below sets the session (LU A, Mode 1) to 4 for the number of parallel sessions. Two out of the four parallel sessions to LU X are the conversation winner sessions (first-speaker sessions) and the remaining are the two conversation loser (the bidder) sessions. The source LU is responsible for imposing the change.

```
CNOS
    LU_NAME                         LU X
    MODE_NAME                       MODE 1
    LU_MODE_SESSION_LIMIT           4
    MIN_CONWINNERS_SOURCE           2
```

MIN_CONWINNERS_TARGET   2
RESPONSIBLE   (SOURCE)

An operator transaction program issues **Change number of sessions (CNOS)** command to impose the new (LU, mode) session limit. The sessions may be activated or deactivated to conform to the new session limit and polarities. The LU may establish special LU 6.2 sessions using the SNA defined mode name=**SNASVCMG** over which the CNOS exchange occurs (see Fig. 9.9). The reader should also review the programming and configuration performing tips summarized in Appendix A of this book.

10

PU 2.1 and LU 6.2 Network Flows

In this chapter we will concentrate on SNA/LU 6.2 distributed network activation and the network message flows. Prior to reading this chapter the reader is strongly advised to review the following sections:

- Section 2.9 describing the hierarchical SNA sessions and the SNA network activation

- Section 3.2 describing the distributed node type 2.1

- Section 3.6 describing the logical unit 6.2 session protocols

- Section 3.7 describing the SNA message units

- Section 6.3.5 describing the mapped conversation message unit transformation

- Section 6.3.6 describing network message flow sequences and the mapping of different LU 6.2 distributed functions to the SNA network messages

After reading this section the reader should see Appendix C for the network message flows

10.1 PU 2.1 NETWORK ACTIVATION

Once all the resources have been configured, the operator needs to activate them. The **control point (CP)** residing in each physical unit type 2.1 node assists the operator in link and session activation. The link activation requires XID-3 to be exchanged between the control points to determine various characteristics of the communicating physical unit type 2.1 nodes. Low Entry Networking (LEN) LU-LU sessions can be activated by either one of the two participating logical units, or by an operator command, or automatically at system startup. Figure 10.1 shows an example of typical startup steps between two physical unit type 2.1 nodes. The following are the activation steps:

Step 1.   An operator issues an operator's **activate link command**. (START LINE). Since both nodes C and D were configured for negotiable roles, XID-3 is exchanged until one of the nodes assumes **the primary link station role**. The node with greater **node ID** (in our case node C) becomes the primary link station. Some nodes (e.g. NCP) at startup may send initially **a null XID** (an XID with an I-field of zero) which is used to poll an adjacent PU2.1 node. A null XID may also be used to find out if the adjacent node is a type 2.1 node. A PU 2.1 node always responds with XID-3 to a null XID. Once XID-3 has completed, the primary link station initiates the link by sending the mode-setting command SNRM for SDLC or SABM for X.25. The secondary link station responds to the mode-setting command with an unnumbered acknowledgment UA command. The link is established and ready for the session initiation command.

Step 2.   An operator issues a **Change number of sessions (CNOS)** command to activate sessions from local logical unit LU C to to the remote logical unit LU D for mode 1. LU C was configured to support two parallel sessions for mode 1, out of which one should be started automatically. Therefore, LU C performs the LU 6.2 defined change number of session (CNOS) exchange to negotiate session limits for mode 1. LU C establishes a special LU 6.2 defined session, using the SNA defined mode name=SNASVCMG over which the CNOS exchange occurs. Once CNOS negotiation is completed, LU C establishes one session for mode 1. This session is now available for access by conversations. The SNASVCMG session may be brought down after successful negotiation and the establishment of the initial session.

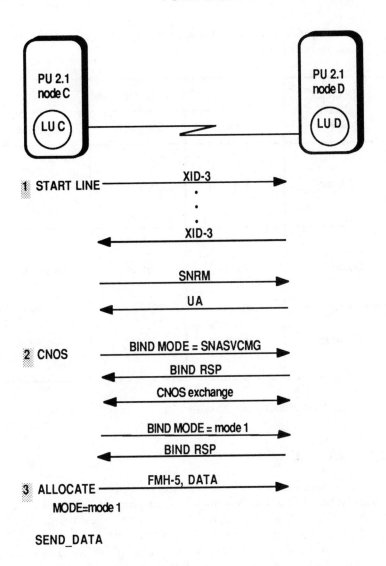

Figure 10.1 LEN network activation.

Step 3. A transaction program issues an ALLOCATE verb to establish a conversation over a session with mode 1 session characteristics. Since the first session for mode 1 was already started, the conversation can be immediately allocated to this session. If another ALLOCATE is issued for mode 1 while the first session is in use, then LU C will start another session up to the (LU C, mode 1) session limit, which in our example is 2. The following allocation requests for mode 1 would be queued by LU C until one of the sessions is released.

SDLC Link station role sent	Link station role received		
	Primary	Secondary	Negotiable
Primary	Error	Primary	Primary
Secondary	Secondary	Error	Secondary
Negotiable	Secondary	Primary	Negotiable

Figure 10.2 Link station role comparison.

10.1.1 XID-3 Exchanges

The link station role can be configured to be primary, secondary, or negotiable. PU 2.1 nodes support only a null XID and an XID-3. The primary or the negotiable link stations may initially send the null XID to the remote node, which must reply with the XID-3. An error will occur if both stations were configured to be primary or secondary link stations as shown in Fig. 10.2. To avoid collisions on point-to-point connections, both PU 2.1 nodes should be configured as **negotiable link stations**. Then the node with greater **node ID** becomes the primary link station. The link station uses the broadcast address X'FF' in the DLC header until the link station roles are determined. On a multipoint line, one of the nodes must be configured as a **primary link station** and all the other nodes as **secondary link stations**. In this case, the secondary link station address must be defined and the broadcast address cannot be used. Point-to-point and multipoint PU 2.1 link connectivity was discussed in Sec. 3.2.3 in this book. The primary and secondary link station roles have no relevance for **asynchronous balance mode (ABM)** connections used on X.25 and Token Ring networks. In those networks, the XID-3 is used to determine which link station will initiate the link, by sending the ABM or the Asynchronous Balance Mode Extended (ABME) command. XID-3 is also used to determine the setting of the Origin Destination Assignor Indicator (ODAI), which is used to assign unique Local-Form Session Identifiers (LFSIDs) discussed in Sec. 10.2.1. The following are the major fields of XID-3 that are used by the sending and receiving PU 2.1 nodes.

Node Identification Field

It is used to resolve the station role (primary or secondary) if the two PU 2.1 nodes are configured as **negotiable**. The node with the greater node identification number (**node ID**) becomes the primary link station. This field consists of block number (2 bytes) and ID number (3 bytes). If the node identification fields are equal, then configuration services (CS) randomizes its ID number and sets the block number to all 1s or 0s.

Generation and Receipt of BIND Segments

This indicates whether the PU 2.1 node can generate or accept BIND segments. Nodes that do not support segmentation check each received Basic Transmission Unit (BTU) and send a negative response if a segmented BTU is received.

ACTPU Suppression Indicator

It is set by PU 2.1 nodes that do not require support for dependent LUs, and that do not require the SCCP-PU session. This indicator is also used to determine the division of the Local-Form Session Identifier (LFSID) address space between dependent and independent logical units discussed in Sec. 10.2.1.

ABM Support Indicator

This will indicate whether the XID sender can be a combined asynchronous balanced mode (ABM) station. If both stations are

ABM-capable, then the mode-setting command is set Asynchronous Balance Mode (SABM) or set Asynchronous Balance Mode Extended (SABME) (used on X.25 and Token Ring connections). If both stations indicate that they are not ABM-capable, then the Set Normal Response Mode (SNRM) or Set Normal Response Mode Extended (SNRME) is used for the mode-setting command (used for SDLC connections).

Link Station Role

This field can be set to primary, secondary, or negotiable. The link station role is determined as illustrated in Fig. 10.2.

I-Frames Received before Acknowledgment

This implies the modulus for the send and receive sequence count (8 or 128). Modulus 128 is used only if both stations set this filed to 128; otherwise the modulus is set to 8. A modulus of 8 allows the frames to use sequence numbers ranging from 0 to 7 and a maximum level 2 window size of 7. A modulus of 128 allows the frames to use sequence numbers ranging from 0 to 127, and the maximum level 2 window size of 127. Modulus 8 is typically used on leased SDLC link connections. Token Ring networks and satellite connections use modulus 128.

Control Vectors

XID-3 contains control vectors representing the following information about the PU 2.1 node:

* Network name (X'0E', CP name) control vector — contains the control point name

* Product set IDs — information specific to a product ; i.e., specific hardware, microcode, or software

* XID negotiation error — present only if an error is detected in the received XID-3. It contains a pointer to the first byte of the field in error in the received XID-3

* Network name (X'0E', PU name) control vector — send in XID3 when the sender is a PU type 4 or type 5 node

10.2 PU 2.1 SESSION ASSIGNMENT

Once, XID-3 negotiation occurs, and the mode-setting command (SNRM, SNRME, SABM, or SABME) completes with no errors, the link stations are activated and the physical unit type 2.1 nodes may send BIND commands to initiate LU-LU sessions (see Fig. 10.1). A session can be activated as a result of an operator change number of sessions (CNOS) command, as shown in Fig. 10.1. A session can also be started when a transaction program (TP) issues a CPI-C Allocate call if there is no session currently available between the local and remote logical units to which this conversation can be allocated. The **control point (CP)** residing in each PU 2.1 node assists the LUs in initiating, terminating, routing, and managing LU-LU sessions.

10.2.1 Local-Form Session Identifiers (LFSIDs)

Each time a new session is initiated, the control point must assign a unique 17-bit **Local-Form Session Identifier (LFSID),** which is carried with all network messages associated with this session. The control point defines an address space consisting of 131,072 LFSIDs for each link attached to the PU 2.1 node. The **17-bit LFSID** is composed of (see Fig. 10.3):

• A 1-bit OAF'-DAF' assignor indicator **(ODAI)** dividing the address space into two partitions.

   0 The node with the primary link station role.

   1 The node with the secondary link station role.

• A 16-bit Session Identifier composed of:

   Session Identifier High **(SIDH)**

   Session Identifier Low **(SIDL)**

   The ODAI bit ensures that the communicating PU 2.1 nodes never assign the same session identifiers. All the sessions initiated from a PU 2.1 node with the primary link station node (the one that initiated the link with a mode-setting command) have ODAI set to 0, and those sessions initiated by the other node have ODAI set to 1. The following algorithm is used to assign the 16-bit Session Identifier (SIDH, SIDL):

• Set (SIDH, SIDL) to '0101' for the first session.

- Increment by 1 for each new session (the lowest unused value released by deactivated sessions should be reused first).

SIDH, SIDL	Usage
X'00', X'00'	SSCP—PU session
X'00', X'01' X'00', X'FF'	SSCP—LU sessions
X'01', X'00'	BIND flow control

X'01', X'01'
 	
X'01', X'FF'
	IF dependent LUs exist in the node
	    Dependent LU-LU sessions
	ELSE
	    Uused for independent LU-LU
	    sessions

X'02', X'00' X'FE', X'FF'	Independent LU-LU sessions
X'FF', X'00' X'FF', X'FF'	Reserved

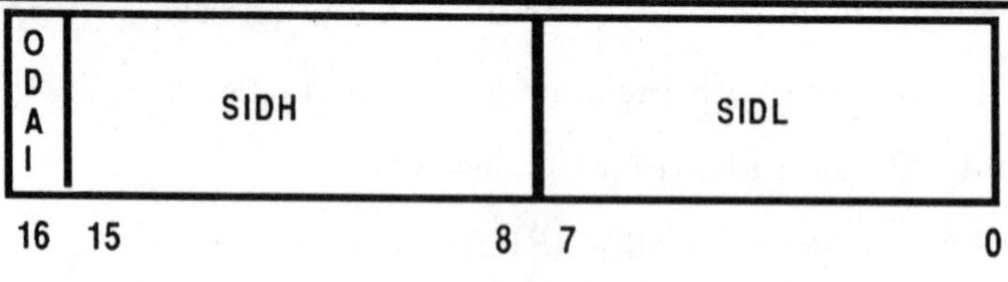

ODAI	SIDH	SIDL

16 15   8   7   0

Figure 10.3 Local-Form Session Identifier (LFSID).

10.2.2 Mapping between LFSID and TH

Each session is associated with a unique Local-Form Session Identifier. The LFSID is carried in the transmission header (TH) with each network message that carries information pertaining to this session. When a PU 2.1 node receives a network message, it uses the LFSID to determine the session and the conversation for which this message is destined. Figure 10.4 illustrates the LFSIDs and the corresponding fields in transmission header (TH).

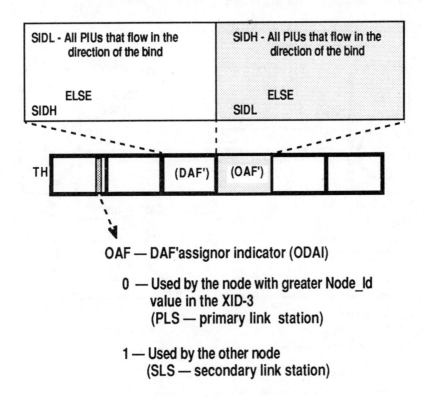

OAF — DAF'assignor indicator (ODAI)

0 — Used by the node with greater Node_Id value in the XID-3 (PLS — primary link station)

1 — Used by the other node (SLS — secondary link station)

Figure 10.4 Mapping between LFSID and TH.

10.2.3 Example of LFSID Assignment

Figure 10.5 illustrates how the control points assign the LFSIDs. Three parallel sessions are started between LU A and LU B.

The first BIND flows from the local logical unit LU A to the remote logical unit LU B. The transmission header carries the following LFSID:

- ODAI is set to 0 since PU 1 assumed the primary link station role after the XID-3 exchange.

- The (SIDH, SIDL) is set to 0101 for the first session.

The second BIND flows from LU A to LU B. The transmission header carries the following LFSID:

- ODAI is set to 0 for all sessions initiated from PU1.

- The (SIDH, SIDL) is set to 0102.

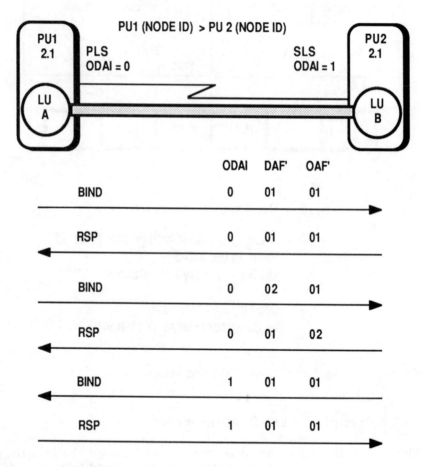

Figure 10.5 Example of LFSID assignment.

The third BIND flows from the remote logical unit LU B to LU A, starting the third parallel session. The transmission header carries the following LFSID:

- ODAI is set to 1 for all sessions initiated from the remote physical unit (PU2).

- The (SIDH, SIDL) is set to 0101 (this is the first session initiated by the PU2 node) which is the same as the first session initiated by PU1. The two 17-bit LFSIDs differ though, since the ODAI bits are different.

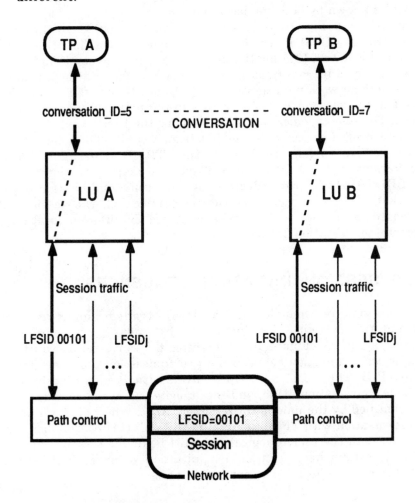

Figure 10.6 Conversation_ID and LFSID mapping.

10.2.4 Mapping between Conversation_ID and LFSID

A local transaction program (TP) communicates with its local LU by means of a unique **conversation_ID** which must be supplied on each APPC or CPI-C call. Each conversation is associated with one unique **conversation_ID**. The conversation ID is a local entity, and is not sent across the session to the partner program. The conversation is assigned to a single session for the duration of the conversation. The session is identified by a unique LFSID. This LFSID is a unique entity that is carried to the remote node, and it must be known by both the local and the remote control points. For example (see Fig 10.6), a conversation (identified by unique conversation_ID=5) is assigned to a single session (identified by unique LFSID=00101) for the duration of this conversation. TP A messages on this conversation are mapped by the local logical unit LU A into network messages with LFSID=00101, which is carried in the transmission header (TH) across to the network to the remote node. The remote logical unit (LU B) maps the LFSID=00101 to the remote program's conversation_ID (e.g., 7). All TP A messages with conversation_ID=5 and the TP B messages with conversation_ID=7 are carried on the same session with LFSID=00101 for the duration of this conversation (an SNA bracket). When this conversation is deallocated, the session is released to another conversation identified by different local and remote conversation_IDs.

10.3 SESSION INITIATION SEQUENCES

As previously mentioned, a local transaction program communicates with its local LU by means of a unique conversation_ID. Figure 10.6 illustrates the conversation which is the logical connection between the two transaction programs TP A and TP B. The local end of the conversation is identified by the unique conversation_ID=5, and the remote end of the conversation is identified by the unique conversation_ID=7. When TP A initiates a conversation with TP B, the local logical unit (LU A) establishes a session with the remote logical unit (LU B) (if the session was not already established). The session initiation sequence is different for dependent and independent logical units.

10.3.1 Dependent LU Session Activation

A dependent LU is limited to a single session, with the primary logical unit (PLU) always residing in a mainframe. Activating a same-domain LU-LU session for SNA dependent logical units was discussed in Sec. 2.9.2 (see Fig. 2.15). Since the activation sequence of dependent logical unit 6.2 is identical to the activation sequence of any other SNA dependent logical unit, the reader is advised to review Sec. 2.9. Figure 10.7 illustrates activating a cross-domain dependent LU-LU session:

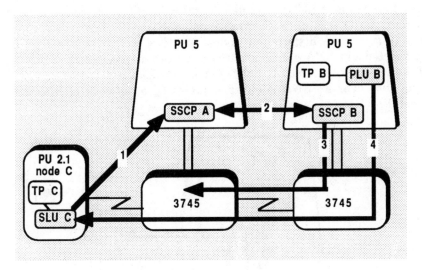

Figure 10.7 Dependent LU session activation.

1. A LU-LU session can be initiated from node C by an operator command or as a result of an Allocate call (a conversation initiation request) issued by TP C. LU C sends an **INITSELF (LU B, mode name)** command that carries the remote logical unit name (LU B) and the mode name, pointing to a suggested BIND in VTAM logmode table. The INITSELF commands always flow to owing VTAM on the previously started SSCP-LU session.

2. The owing SCCP A locates LU B and sends SSCP B session parameters, identified by the mode name carried in INITSELF. This is done by using the cross-domain protocol **CDINIT** and **CDCINIT**.

3. SSCP B tells LU B to activate a session with LU C and it **activates the virtual route (VR)** for the session.

4. LU B activates a session with LU C by sending an SNA **BIND** command. LU C replies with a positive response and the session is established. Once the session is established, an Allocate request may flow on the session from either side to establish a conversation between TP C and TP B. The session is then used exclusively by the conversation until one of the TPs issues a Deallocate call.

10.3.2 Independent LU Session Activation

The independent LU is capable of establishing LU-LU sessions with logical units residing in mainframes as well as logical units residing in SNA distributed nodes. The two PU 2.1 nodes may be connected via SNA subarea network or other networks (e.g., X.25, Token Ring, or an SDLC link). Let us look at a session initiation sequence over an SNA subarea network (the network of 37xx and hosts).

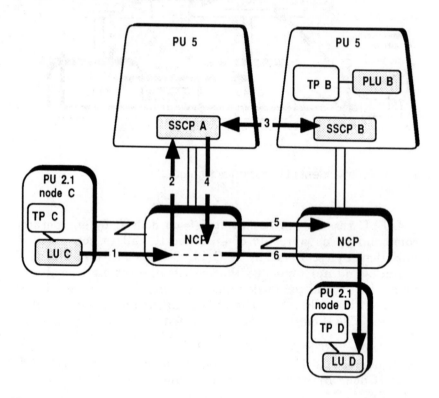

Figure 10.8 Independent LU session activation.

Figure 10.8 illustrates activation of a cross-domain independent LU-LU session:

1. A LU-LU session can be initiated from Node C by an operator command or as a result of an Allocate call (a conversation initiation request) issued by TP C. LU C assigns a unique (LFSID) for the new session and sends a **BIND (LU D, mode name) command** naming the partner LU and mode name to the adjacent NCP.

2. The NCP notifies the owing SSCP A of the BIND request by sending the boundary function initiation request **(BFINIT)** to SSCP A.

3. This step need be performed only if the remote LU resides in another domain. SSCP A uses normal cross domain protocol **(CDINIT and CDCINIT)** to locate the secondary logical units (SLUs).

4. SSCP A must have the configured SLU's mode name in the VTAM logmode table. SSCP A sends the suggested session rules [pacing window sizes, maximum request/response unit (RU) sizes, class of service (COS) name, and the virtual route (VR list) in the **BFCINIT** command].

5. The NCP **activates the virtual route (VR),** which must be coded during the NCP configuration.

6. The NCP **forwards the BIND** received in step 1, and modified with the parameters received in step 4, to the secondary logical unit (SLU). LU D returns a positive response and the session is established. Once the session is successfully established, an Allocate request may flow on the session from either side to establish a conversation between TP C and TP D. The session is then used exclusively by the conversation until one of the TPs issues a Deallocate call. LU D may also send a negative response to LU C rejecting the session. The following is a list of typical session failures:

   • BIND parameters are not configured properly

   • SLU's mode name is not coded in VTAM

   • Virtual routes (VRs) are not coded properly

   • Insufficient resources in NCP for (ADDSESS, RESSCB, AUXADDR, or NAMTAB) described in Chap. 9

Independent LUs are capable of establishing parallel sessions. A session can be initiated by either LU C or LU D, which means that for some sessions LU C assume the role of the primary logical unit (as shown in Figure 10.8), and for others LU D may act as PLU.

The session initiation for peer-to-peer PU 2.1 nodes connected directly (e.g., via X.25, Token Ring, Ethernet, or SDLC link) is much simpler. When a TP request (e.g., Allocate or CNOS) or an operator command requires a session initiation with a remote LU, the control point (CP) residing in the local node assigns a unique LFSID as shown in Fig. 10.5. Then the local LU sends a **BIND** command to the remote LU. If the BIND parameters are accepted, the remote LU responds positively and the session is established. Prior to session establishment, the PU 2.1 nodes need to be activated, as discussed in Sec. 10.1 (see Fig. 10.1). If parallel sessions are supported, the independent logical units require CNOS exchange to negotiate the session limit. This may require special LU 6.2 sessions to be started using the SNA defined mode name= SNASVCMG over which the CNOS exchange occurs (see Fig. 10.1).

10.3.3 BIND Negotiation

The BIND carries parameters describing the PLU session rules. LU 6.2 uses a negotiable BIND for session establishment. The following is a list of BIND parameters that can be modified by the secondary logical unit (SLU): Contention winner, pacing window sizes, maximum RU sizes, conversation level security, already-verified indicator support, maximum synchronization level support, responsibility for the session reinitiation after the session failure.

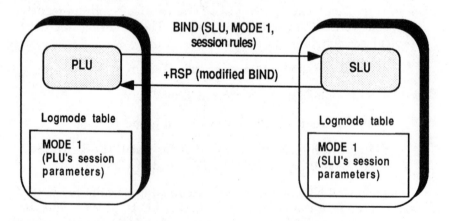

Figure 10.9 Negotiable BIND.

These parameters are configured during a system generation in a logmode table. Figure 10.9 illustrates a BIND negotiation process. The secondary logical unit (SLU) receives and negotiates the session rules using its own preconfigured values in a logmode table entry pointed by the mode name (MODE 1) carried in the BIND received from the PLU. The SLU sends a positive response containing the received BIND image modified with its own parameters. The SLU can change the BIND parameters only to "less powerful values." For example, the maximum RU, window, or pacing sizes can be changed only to smaller values (e.g., MAXRU 1024 can be changed to 512 but not to 1920). The SLU can request to be a conversation winner or it can request the PLU to take the responsibility for the session reinitiation. The negotiation process consists of a single BIND command generated by the PLU and a single BIND response generated by the SLU. If the LUs cannot agree on the session parameters, the session activation fails and the LUs must be reconfigured to session parameters acceptable by both sides.

10.3.4 Adaptive Session and BIND Pacings

Pacing is used to control:

1. The flow of BINDs between PU 2.1 nodes. It is called **adaptive BIND pacing**.

2. The normal-flow requests (mainly end-user data) exchanged between the local and the remote logical units on a particular session. This type of pacing is called **session level pacing**.

Pacing assures that the sending LU will not overflow the receiving LU, and also ensures that the sending LU will not generate more than a certain fixed number of messages at a time. The number of messages that can be sent depends on the **pacing window size**. There are two types of pacing: fixed and adaptive. In fixed pacing the window size is fixed to some number (N) agreed upon at BIND time. In an adaptive session or BIND pacing, the pacing window size varies depending on the buffer availability. The fixed session level pacing is also used for all other LU types in an SNA hierarchical network. LU 6.2 is capable of using both the session fixed and adaptive pacing. Adaptive pacing is the preferred mode of operation for the logical unit 6.2; fixed pacing is used only when the partner LU does not support adaptive pacing. The adaptive BIND pacing is also used to prevent the node from being overloaded with the incoming session initiation requests (BIND commands). The sending and receiving algorithms for LU 6.2 fixed and adaptive pacing is described in the *IBM LU 6.2 Reference Peer Protocols* manual.

10.4 LU 6.2 PROTOCOLS AND MESSAGE FLOWS

Once the session is established, the local and remote transaction programs use the session to exchange data. The APPC and CPI-C programming calls are translated by the local and remote logical units into SNA message units. In this section we will discuss SNA/LU 6.2 network messages exchanged between logical units and the protocols that govern the message exchange. A **Message Unit (MU)** is an SNA-defined bit string exchanged between SNA layers and sublayers. The SNA/LU 6.2 message units, such as General Data Stream (GDS) variables, logical records (LRs), request/response units (RUs), and the Path Information Units (PIUs) were discussed in Sec. 3.7.

10.4.1 LU 6.2 Message Unit Transformation

Figure 10.10 illustrates a typical transformation of programming calls into SNA network message units. The transaction program issues a mapped conversation **MC_SEND_DATA** verb followed by the MC_FLUSH verb, which forces the LU to flush its send buffer. Let us assume that the maximum **RU size was configured to 1024 bytes** and the maximum link level buffer size **(MAXDATA) to 265 bytes**. An RU size parameter limits the size of the request/response unit that can be exchanged between the local and remote LUs. The maximum link level buffer size limits the size of information that can be carried in a single frame sent from a local link station to an adjacent node. The presentation services (PS) layer of the local LU maps the MC_SEND_DATA verb into a **single GDS variable** containing the 2-byte LL field, the 2 byte ID='12FF' field (indicating that this is a single send data call), and the 1100 bytes of user data. In order to send the GDS variable to the remote LU, the half_session(s) consisting of the data flow control (DFC) layer and the transmission control (TC) layer must divide the 1104-byte GDS variable into a series of related requests called basic information units (BIUs — in our example BIU1 and BIU2). This series of related requests (called **chain elements**) is called a **chain**. A chain is the smallest error-recoverable unit in SNA network that is treated by the receiving LU as a single request. The begin chain indicator (BCI) and the end chain indicator (ECI) are set in the request/response header (RH). Each of the BIUs is passed to the path control layer (PC) for transmission over a communication line to the adjacent node.

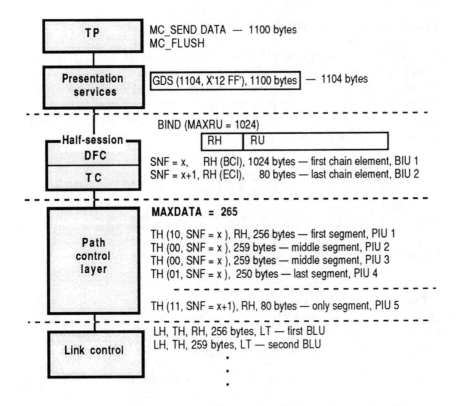

| TP | MC_SEND DATA — 1100 bytes
MC_FLUSH |

| Presentation services | GDS (1104, X'12 FF'), 1100 bytes — 1104 bytes |

Half-session

| DFC | BIND (MAXRU = 1024)
RH \| RU
SNF = x,   RH (BCI), 1024 bytes — first chain element, BIU 1 |
| TC | SNF = x+1, RH (ECI),   80 bytes — last chain element, BIU 2 |

| Path control layer | **MAXDATA = 265**
TH (10, SNF = x), RH, 256 bytes — first segment, PIU 1
TH (00, SNF = x), 259 bytes — middle segment, PIU 2
TH (00, SNF = x), 259 bytes — middle segment, PIU 3
TH (01, SNF = x), 250 bytes — last segment, PIU 4

TH (11, SNF = x+1), RH, 80 bytes — only segment, PIU 5 |

| Link control | LH, TH, RH, 256 bytes, LT — first BLU
LH, TH, 259 bytes, LT — second BLU |

Figure 10.10 Message unit transformation

The PC layer builds two PIUs by adding a 6-byte (for PU 2.1 nodes) transmission header header to each BIU. The first PIU is 1033 bytes long (TH — 6 bytes, RH — 3 bytes and 1024 bytes of data). Since the maximum link buffer size is limited to 265, the PC layer needs to divide the first PIU into **segments**. **Segmenting** is the division of a single PIU into multiple PIUs. In our example, the BIU1 will generate four PIUs and the BIU2 one PIU. Therefore, the single MC_SEND_DATA verb generated two chain elements, five PIUs, and five frames. Notice that the same MC_SEND_DATA would generate only one chain element, one PIU, and one frame if we reconfigured the MAXRU size to 1920 and the maximum frame size to 2048. Usually avoiding segmenting and chaining will generate better performance. The drawback in using large buffers is that more memory needs to be allocated for the incoming and outgoing RUs and frames. When many LUs are competing for memory resources, large buffer sizes may actually decrease the overall performance of the system.

10.4.2 LU 6.2 General Data Stream Variables

Logical units transform all mapped conversation data into the General Data Stream (GDS) variable (see Fig. 10.11) format discussed in Sec. 3.7 (see Fig. 3.24). A GDS variable consists of transaction program data preceded by a 2-byte prefix (LL) and a 2-byte ID format identifier describing the type of information contained in the variable.

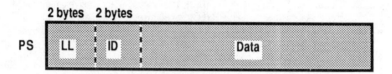

Figure 10.11 The General Data Stream (GDS) variable.

The following GDS variables are generated by service transaction programs (STPs), such as the LU 6.2 change number of sessions (CNOS), the LU 6.2 syncpoint resynchronization (RESYNC), or the LU services manager:

- ID=X'1210'   change number of sessions (CNOS)

- ID=X'1211'   exchange log name

- ID=X'1213'   compare states

- ID=X'12A0'   workstation display passthrough

- ID=X'12E1'   error log (conveys to an LU implementation specific errors, follows FMH-7, and is not passed to the receiving TPs)

The following GDS variables can be generated as a result of mapped conversation calls issued by an application transaction program:

- ID=X'12F1'   null data (The programmer issued MC_CONFIRM, and there was no data in the LU send buffer.)

- ID=X'12F2'   user control data (The programmer issued MC_SEND_DATA with FMH=yes, the user data contains function management headers.)

- ID=X'12F3'   map name [The programmer issued (MC_SEND_DATA with MAP_NAME=yes).]

- ID=X'12F4'   error data [The LU detected an error in the data being received from a partner LU. The LU issues SEND_DATA following SEND_ERROR to convey the error to the partner LU (e.g., mapping error information).]

- ID=X'12F5'   PIP data (The programmer issued an ALLOCATE call supplying program initiation parameters. The parameters are carried in a special GDS variable following the ATTACH header.)

- ID=X'12FF'   application data (The programmer issued an MC_SEND_DATA verb. The logical unit builds one GDS variable per single issuance of the MC_SEND_DATA verb.)

Programs that use mapped conversations do not have to be concerned with these GDS variables, as they are handled by the presentation service of the logical units. The programs may be notified of different types of GDS variables by means of return codes or other return parameters. The basic conversation program may be required to build the appropriate GDS variables if they communicate, for example, with service transaction programs.

10.4.3 LU 6.2 Headers

SNA headers are message units that carry certain control information to the remote LU. The following function management headers (FMHs) are generated by the logical unit 6.2 (see also Fig. 10.12):

- **FMH TYPE 5** (ATTACH header) — carries the Allocate parameters such as conversation type, remote TP name, and security).

- **FMH TYPE 7** — describes a transaction program error. It informs the remote LU of an application error [a TP-issued SEND_ERORR or DEALLOCATE TYPE (ABEND) verb].

- **FMH TYPE 12** — carries the enciphered version of random data for LU-LU session level security.

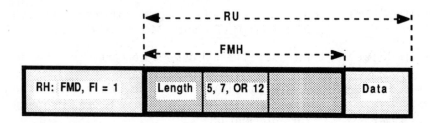

Figure 10.12 Function management headers.

In addition to FMH headers, the LU 6.2 uses a presentation services header to perform AN SNA two-phase commit to synchronize all protected resources (e.g., databases) throughout the distributed transaction. This header would be generated as a result of SYNCPT or BACKOUT calls. The presentation services header has the format of a logical record with the LL field set to 1 (LL=X'01', the length of the header and the PS header related data).

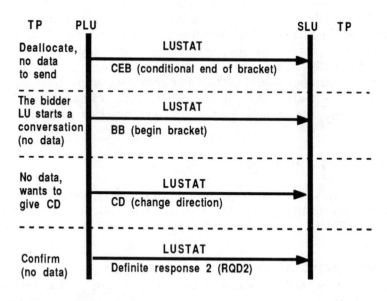

Figure 10.13 DFC LUSTAT command.

10.4.4 LUSTAT and SIG Commands

The programming calls are mapped by the LU into appropriate GDS variables or bits in the request header. **LUSTAT** is a data flow control (DFC) command that sends 4 bytes of status information used in LU 6.2 as no-op. It is generated when there is no data in the LU's send buffer and the TP issues a call that requires sending some control information to the partner TP (e.g., confirmation processing (RQD2 set in RH), change direction (CD set in RH), begin bracket (BB set in RH), or conditional end of bracket (CEB set in RH) as illustrated in Fig. 10.13

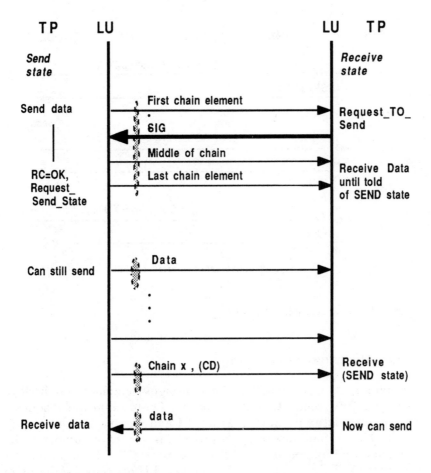

Figure 10.14 DFC SIG command.

SIG is a DFC expedited command that can be sent between LUs regardless of the send/receive mode status of the normal flow. SIG is generated when a TP issues a Request_To_Send call in the Receive state to ask the partner TP for the Send state as illustrated in Fig. 10.14.

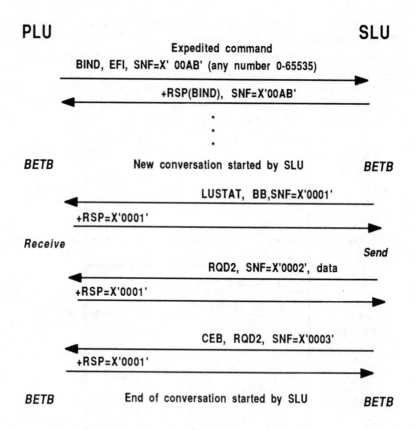

PLU   **SLU**

Expedited command
BIND, EFI, SNF=X' 00AB' (any number 0-65535)

+RSP(BIND), SNF=X'00AB'

BETB   New conversation started by SLU   *BETB*

LUSTAT, BB,SNF=X'0001'

+RSP=X'0001'

Receive

Send

RQD2, SNF=X'0002', data

+RSP=X'0001'

CEB, RQD2, SNF=X'0003'

+RSP=X'0001'

BETB   End of conversation started by SLU   *BETB*

Figure 10.15 Sequence numbering.

10.4.5 Message Sequencing

The data Flow Control (DFC) layer assigns sequence numbers to
FMD and DFC requests and responses. The normal flow requests
(mainly user data) are numbered from 1 and incremented by 1 up to
65,535. The normal flow responses carry the sequence number of the
corresponding begin-bracket (BB) request. The high order bit
identifies the LU that started the bracket (LU 6.2 conversation) and
is set to 0 if the bracket was started by the SLU; to 1, if the bracket was
started by the PLU. Expedited requests such as the BIND command
use label instead of sequence numbers. Figure 10.15 illustrates a
session started by a BIND with SNF='00AB'. The response to the
expedited request carries the sequence number of the corresponding
request. In Fig. 10.15 the SLU starts a bracket and requires
confirmation processing (RQD2). Notice that all the responses in

this bracket (this conversation) carry the sequence number of the corresponding BB request (in our example 1). Normally the Send_Data calls are buffered by the LU, and they are sent as exception response chains in a conversation that does not require positive responses. The only time a positive reponse is required is when the TP performs confirmation or synchronization processing by issuing, for example the Confirm call.The confirmation processing applies to all Send_Data calls sent so far on this conversation(a single SNA bracket). A positive response implies that all data was received and processed by the remote TP. Therefore, the normal flow responses checkpoint all processing in this bracket, rather than just acknowledge the receipt of the last message.

10.4.6 Half-Duplex, Flip-Flop Protocol

The LU 6.2 uses **half-duplex, flip-flop protocol** for normal flows, in which only one side can send and the other must receive until a change direction occurs. The half-duplex, flip-flop protocol imposes on transaction programs (TPs) strict rules regarding when data may be sent and received. These rules (referred to as the send/receive modes) were discussed in Sec. 3.6.4 of this book. Figure 10.16 illustrates the half-duplex, flip-flop protocol. A source TP issues an Allocate in the Reset state to start a new conversation. The session is currently in between-bracket state (BETB), which means that there is no conversation (bracket) using the session. Therefore, the session is available for a new conversation. Allocate puts the source TP in Send state. When Allocate is sent to the partner LU, the session enters in-bracket state (INB). This session is now used exclusively by the conversation (no new bracket can be started in INB state) until one of the programs issues a Deallocate call, which ends the conversation and the bracket. The TP enters the Receive state and the session enters BETB. The session can now accept new conversations (start new brackets). When the session is INB, the two communicating programs must follow the send/receive mode protocol. The Receive call releases the Send state and the LU sends a change direction indicator in the RU to the remote LU. The CDI flip-flops the TP that was in Receive state to Send state so that it can then start sending data. The conditional end bracket (CEB) indicator is used to indicate bracket (conversation) termination. The bracket is terminated unconditionally in all cases except when a negative response is received (-RSP) to a (CEB, RDQ2, or RDQ3) chain, which is generated when a TP issues the Deallocate Type

(Confirm). In this case the session stays in the INB state, the conversation does not end, and the TPs may start user-defined error recovery.

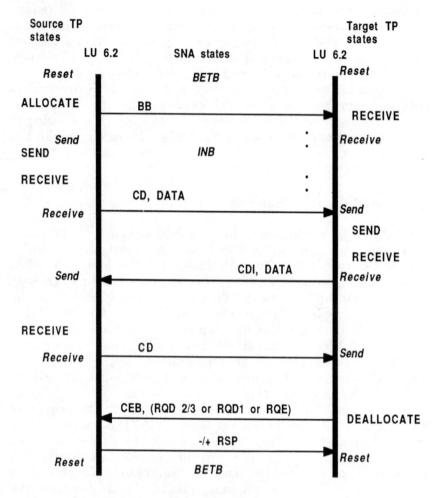

Figure 10.16 Half-duplex, flip-flop protocol.

The LU 6.2 programming verbs are carried as GDS variables, bits in the RH, FMH headers, PS headers, or some SNA commands. The mapping of the LU 6.2 verbs to the appropriate network message flows is discussed in Appendix C in this book.

11

APPC and CPI-C Implementations

IBM and other vendors have already brought to market a lot of products that are an integral part of building an SAA computer enterprise. This chapter summarizes the major LU 6.2 functions and capabilities of IBM and third party vendor SAA/CPI-C and APPC/LU 6.2 implementations. The reader should refer to specific implementation manuals for detailed information on these products.

11.1 APPC/MVS SERVICES

APPC/MVS is a VTAM application that provides **APPC and SAA/CPI-C interfaces** to MVS/ESA programs. The SAA/CPI-C interface is available in HLL (COBOL, C, PL/1, FORTRAN, and REXX). The APPC MVS-specific interface is available in HLL and in assembler language. APPC/MVS offloads programmers from having to code directly to VTAM/LU 6.2 assembler low-level interface. It also enables development of MVS applications that can communicate with CPI-C or APPC programs which reside in the same or other MVS systems, including CMS, CICS, IMS, OS/2 EE,

OS/400, or any other system that implements the SNA logical unit 6.2 (see Fig. 11.1).

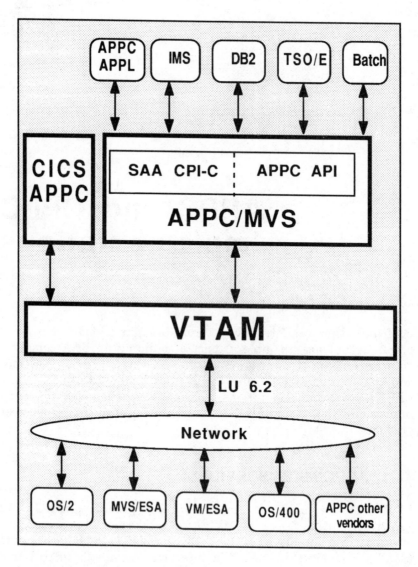

Figure 11.1 APPC/MVS services.

An APPC/MVS transaction program (TP) can be any program in any address space on MVS that issues calls to APPC/MVS services. The TP can run in task or SRB mode and can use any other

MVS/ESA services. The following is a list of major capabilities of APPC/MVS applications:

- TPs can be scheduled by the **APPC/MVS transaction scheduler** or by an installation-defined scheduler, in response to an incoming allocation request. The APPC/MVS transaction scheduler maintains a pool of address spaces, called **subordinate address spaces**, for scheduling TPs.

- A TP can be scheduled in two ways:

  Standard scheduling — allocates new resources for each conversation (for each incoming Allocate) and deallocates the resources when the conversation is deallocated. TPs with low resource overhead, that are not invoked frequently, are good candidates for standard scheduling.

  Multi-trans scheduling — allocates the resources once. When the conversation terminates, the TP remains active with its resources available. The next incoming conversation (transaction) may reuse the same resources. Multi-trans scheduling may be appropriate for short transactions that require a lot of resources to be initialized and allocated at conversation startup.

- TPs are capable of initiating multiple, concurrent, and asynchronous processing.

- TPs may use the SAA CPI-C calls or an API unique to MVS on both mapped and basic conversations.

- TPs can use JES SYSOUT and job submit facilities.

- TPs can use certain TSO/E programming services and TSO/E command facilities.

- TPs can create or access the following type of data:

  VSAM, sequential, or partitioned data sets can be updated or read through dynamic allocation or the TP profile(containing the TP capabilities, status, and scheduling information). **CICS VSAM** data may be extracted using only dynamic allocation, assuming a data disposition of SHR and the possibility of updates are in progress. In order to update CICS VSAM data, a conversation to CICS TP is required.

  IMS DL/1 data may be updated and accessed directly if the APPC application follows the IMS BMP rules.

DB2 data can be accessed directly via HLL call-attach facilities provided by DB2.

TPs can access MVS/ESA **shared data spaces** or **hiperspace data spaces** to share data and improve performance.

- APPC/MVS TPs support the LU 6.2 **conversation level security**. The **Resource Access Control Facility (RACF)** and VTAM security may limit access to the logical unit and the TPs.

11.1.1 CPI-C and APPC/MVS API

APPC/MVS services provides the TPs with APPC and CPI-C interfaces.

CPI-C Interface

The MVS **SAA/CPI-C interface** is available in HLL (COBOL, C, PL/1, FORTRAN, and REXX). MVS programers should use CPI-C calls in cases where **portability** of programs to other than an MVS environment is an important issue. Programs written using the CPI Communications interface can be moved between different SAA systems (e.g., mainframes, AS/400s, or OS/2 EEs). The syntax (CMALLC, CMSEND, CMRCV, ..., CMDALLC) and the functionality of the MVS CPI Communications calls comply with the SAA architecture discussed in Chap. 8 in this book, with the following exceptions:

- Synchronization processing (CPI-C **commit** function) is not supported. The highest synchronization level is Confirm.

- CMRTS is only supported within the same MVS system.

- Data logging (error logging) caused by the Deallocate or Send_Error call is accepted but ignored.

- The allowable character set for LU, mode, and TP names differ from the SAA/CPI-C character set.

The remaining SAA/CPI Communications calls (CMALLC, CMSEND, CMDEAL) are supported by APPC/MVS services. The reader should review Chap. 7 for detailed information on CPI-C calls and various design flows.

MVS-Specific APPC Interface

The **APPC interface** is available through the MVS-specific Application Programming Interface (API) available in high level languages (COBOL, C, PL/1, FORTRAN, and REXX) and in assembler. It supports all the LU 6.2 functions provided by the MVS CPI-C interface and, in addition, it supports functions that make use of the MVS/ESA architecture, including data spaces, asynchronous processing, scheduling, and test services. If the transaction program needs to use the **MVS data spaces or to initiate multiple, concurrent, and asynchronous requests, or use the multi-trans scheduling**, then the APPC/MVS specific interface should be used. The MVS-specific interface implements the LU 6.2 verbs and it functionally complies with the APPC/LU 6.2 architecture discussed in Chap. 7. The reader should refer to Chap. 7 for the functionality of the APPC verbs, keeping in mind the syntax differences between the APPC/MVS calls and the APPC/LU 6.2 verbs ([MC_]ALLOCATE, [MC_]SEND_DATA,...,[MC_]DEALLOCATE). The syntax of MVS-specific calls is similar to CPI-C syntax other than the MVS calls which start with ATB instead of CM (ATBALLC — for the Allocate function, ATBSEND — for the Send_Data function, ATBDEAL — for the Deallocate function, etc.). TPs using MVS-specific calls may specify security (None, Same, PGM) as described in Chap. 7. TPs may also specify an ECB (event control block) on the Notify_Type parameter of MVS-specific calls if asynchronous processing is required. Then, the APPC/MVS returns a return code of zero and the program may immediately resume processing. When the services are completed, APPC/MVS notifies the TP by posting the ECB. Only one outstanding asynchronous call is possible for each conversation, with the exception of ATBDEAL type ABEND, which can be issued for the same conversation even though a previously issued call has not completed yet.

11.1.2 Mapping of APPC/MVS Calls to LU 6.2 Verbs

APPC and CPI-C architectures were discussed in detail in Chaps. 7 and 8. The CPI-C calls and design diagrams, discussed in Chap. 8, apply directly to the APPC/MVS CPI-C calls and designs, since the calls must comply with the SAA architecture. The APPC verbs and design flows discussed in Chap. 7 are functionally equivalent to the APPC/MVS-specific calls. The TP design diagrams discussed in Chap. 7 would have to be slightly modified to comply with the MVS-

specific syntax shown below. The following list shows APPC/LU 6.2
verbs and the corresponding MVS APPC and CPI-C calls.

APPC/LU 6.2 verbs	APPC/MVS calls	MVS/CPI-C calls
[MC_]ALLOCATE	ATBALLC	CMINIT, CMALLC
[MC_]CONFIRM	ATBCFM	CMCFM
[MC_]CONFIRMED	ATBCFMD	CMCFM
[MC_]DEALLOCATE	ATBDEAL	CMDEAL
[MC_]FLUSH	ATBFLUS	CMFLUS
[MC_]GET_ATTRIBUTES	ATBGETA	CMEMN, CMESL, CMEPLN
[MC_]FLUSH	ATBFLUS	CMFLUS
(Incoming Allocate)	ATBGETC	CMACCP
MC_]GET_TP_PROPERTIES	ATBGETP	(no CPI-C call)
[MC_]GET_TYPE	ATBGETT	CMECT
MC_]PREPARE_TO_RECEIVE	ATBPTR	CMPTR
[MC_]RECEIVE_IMMEDIATE	ATBRCVI	CMRCV
[MC_]RECEIVE_AND_WAIT	ATBRCVW	CMRCV
[MC_]REQUEST_TO_SEND	ATBRTS	CMRTS
[MC_]SEND	ATBSEND	CMSEND
[MC_]SEND_ERROR	[MC_]SEND_ERROR	CMSERR

11.2 CICS/ESA APPC

CICS supports both APPC/LU 6.2 and SAA/CPI-C interfaces. The CPI-C interface is available under CICS/ESA Version 3 Release 2. CICS/ESA CPI-C transaction programs may be written in COBOL, PL/I, C and in 370 assembler. CICS transaction programs may use both CPI-C and APPC interfaces in the same program, but not in the same conversation. The CICS CPI-C interface complies with the CPI Communications architecture described in detail in Chap. 8. The reader should refer to Chap 8 for detail information on the CPI Communications calls and CPI-C application design issues.

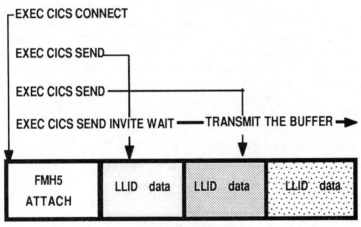

Figure 11.2 CICS APPC command level interface.

Figure 11-2 illustrates the CICS/APPC command level interface. A CICS APPC transaction program may communicate with any other LU 6.2 transaction program residing in another address space (e.g., another CICS or APPC/MVS) or with a TP residing on a remote system, such as a mainframe, AS/400, OS/2 EE, or DOS/APPC. The communication protocol between any of the systems is the same; therefore the CICS transaction program does not have to be concerned with the different environments it communicates with. The same CICS/LU 6.2 code can communicate with all the different machines without any changes to the programs. CICS offers a set of LU 6.2 commands that allow a CICS transaction to establish **mapped** or **basic conversations**. The

following is a syntax for mapped and basic conversation CICS
APPC command-level services:

* Mapped conversation LU 6.2 ALLOCATE verb

  EXEC CICS ALLOCATE
  EXEC CICS CONNECT PROCESS

* Basic conversation LU 6.2 ALLOCATE verb

  EXEC CICS **GDS** ALLOCATE
  EXEC CICS **GDS** CONNECT PROCESS

The CICS program does not have to be concerned with the physical
connections or the SNA sessions, but only with the exchange of
application data. CICS itself takes the responsibility for
establishing LU 6.2 sessions and negotiating session parameters
(MAXRU sizes, conversation winners, etc.). In order for CICS
transaction to use LU 6.2 resources, they must be defined in CICS ,
VTAM, and the remote system. CICS configuration issues for
dependent and independent logical units were discussed in Sec. 9.3
(see Fig. 9.3 and Fig. 9.5). CICS buffers the programming calls in
its internal buffers (see Fig 11.2). The advantages of LU 6.2 data
buffering were discussed in Sec. 3.8 in this book. The actual
transmission may not occur when a send operation is performed.
The following steps are performed by CICS for a typical APPC
transaction initiated from CICS:

Step 1.   CICS transaction program issues EXEC CICS ALLOCATE
command. CICS establishes an SNA LU 6.2 with the remote logical
unit if a session has not already been started by an operator or
another transaction program.

Step 2.   CICS transaction program issues the EXEC CICS
CONNECT PROCESS command. CICS builds the ATTACH header
(containing the values of the APPC/LU 6.2 ALLOCATE verb
parameters such as remote transaction program name) and buffers
the allocation request in its send buffer.

Step 3.   CICS transaction program issues EXEC CICS SEND
command. CICS builds the appropriate GDS variables and adds the
data to its send buffer. Further EXEC CICS SEND commands add
more data to the CICS send buffer and no information is transmitted
yet.

Step 4.   CICS transaction program issues the EXEC CICS SEND INVITE WAIT command. WAIT flushes the CICS buffers to the remote LU. The INVITE releases the Send state to the partner's program. The CICS transaction enters the Receive state and should issue the EXEC CICS RECEIVE command to receive data from the partner program.

11.2.1 Mapping of CICS APPC Interface to LU 6.2 Verbs

CICS implements the APPC/LU 6.2 architecture discussed in detail in Chap. 7. The APPC/LU 6.2 verbs and design flows discussed in Chap. 7 are functionally equivalent to CICS APPC. The transaction program design diagrams discussed in Chap. 7 would have to be slightly modified to comply with the CICS command level syntax shown below. The following list shows APPC/LU 6.2 verbs and the corresponding CICS commands:

LU 6.2 Architecture	CICS Implementation
MC_ALLOCATE	EXEC CICS ALLOCATE +EXEC CICS CONNECT PROCESS
BACKOUT	EXEC CICS SYNCPOINT ROLLBACK
MC_CONFIRM	EXEC CICS SEND CONFIRM
MC_CONFIRMED	EXEC CICS ISSUE CONFIRMATION
MC_DEALLOCATE	EXEC CICS SEND LAST [CONFIRM] +EXEC CICS SYNCPOINT +EXEC CICS FREE
MC_FLUSH	EXEC CICS WAIT OR EXEC CICS SEND WAIT
MC_GET_ATTRIBUTES	EXEC CICS EXTRACT PROCESS OR EXEC CICS ASSIGN
MC_PREPARE_TO_RECEIVE	EXEC CICS SEND INVITE

MC_RECEIVE_AND_WAIT	EXEC CICS RECEIVE [NOTRUNCATE]
MC_REQUEST_TO_SEND	EXEC CICS RECEIVE [NOTRUNCATE]
MC_REQUEST_TO_SEND	EXEC CICS ISSUE SIGNAL
MC_SEND_DATA	EXEC CICS SEND
MC_SEND_ERROR	EXEC CICS ISSUE ERROR
SYNCPOINT	EXEC CICS SYNCPOINT

In addition, the CICS EXEC CICS CONVERSE command is equivalent to an EXEC CICS SEND command followed by an EXEC CICS RECEIVE command. This command is well suited to partners exchanging one block of data at a time (e.g., requester/server transactions). The reader should refer to Chap. 7 for a detailed explanation of the LU 6.2 functions shown above.

11.2.2 The EXEC Interface Block (EIB)

The EXEC Interface Block is used with CICS mapped conversations to convey return codes and status information (see Fig. 11.3).

- **EIBERR** — indicates that an abnormal condition has occurred. Check EIBERR after every command, and if its set, then the error code can be obtained from EIBERRCD.

- **EIBERRCD** — contains the reason for the error. If EIBERRCD= X'0889' (Issue Error command), the TP enters the Receive state and should issue the RECEIVE command. EIBERRCD=X='0864' indicates that the partner TP aborted the conversation (issued DEALLOCATE TYPE(ABEND).

- **EIBRSRCE** — contains the conversation id (CONVID) that must be acquired after an ALLOCATE verb.

- **EIBTRMID** — contains the name of the principal facility (the conversation id CONVID for the back-end transaction).

- **EIBSIG** — indicates that the conversation partner has issued an ISSUE SIGNAL command.

11.2.3 CICS APPC Command and States

The following is a short description of the major CICS/LU 6.2 commands:

ALLOCATE

Initial state — state 1 (session not allocated)

```
EXEC CICS ALLOCATE SYSID (ALLU)
              [PROFILE (profile_name)]
              [NOQUEUE]
```

ALLU is the SYSIDNT name of the remote LU

CONVID returned in EIBRSRCE of the EXEC interface block

Enter state 2 — session allocated

The ALLOCATE command acquires a session with a remote system. If no session is currently free, CICS will wait for one, unless NOQUEUE was specified, in which case the SYSBUSY condition will be raised. SYSIDERR and SYSBUSY should be checked for CICS errors and EIBERR for LU 6.2 errors. The EIB should be checked after each command level operation and prior to issuing another command, because a subsequent operation will re-use the EIB and may overwrite fields set by the previous operation. Particulary the error conditions should be checked if the **RESP or NOHANDLE** parameter is used. If there are no errors, the session is allocated, and the program should retrieve the conversation ID from EIBRSRCE (e.g., MVC CONVID, EIBRSRCE).

CONNECT PROCESS

```
EXEC CICS CONNECT PROCESS
              CONVID (CONVID)
              SYNCLEVEL (0, 1 or 2)
              PROCNAME ('PCTP') !the name of the back-end
                              !(remote) transaction program
              PROCLENGTH (4)
              [PIP]
```

Enter state 3 — send state

The CONNECT PROCESS command completes the conversation allocation process by designating the remote TP name and the synchronization level (0-NONE, 1-CONFIRM, 2-SYNCPT). The

PIP parameter allows the parameters to be passed to the remote TP. Upon successful completion of this command the conversation is allocated, although the partner program may not yet be attached. The actual flow will happen when a CICS command is issued and flushes the send buffer (e.g., EXEC CICS SEND WAIT).

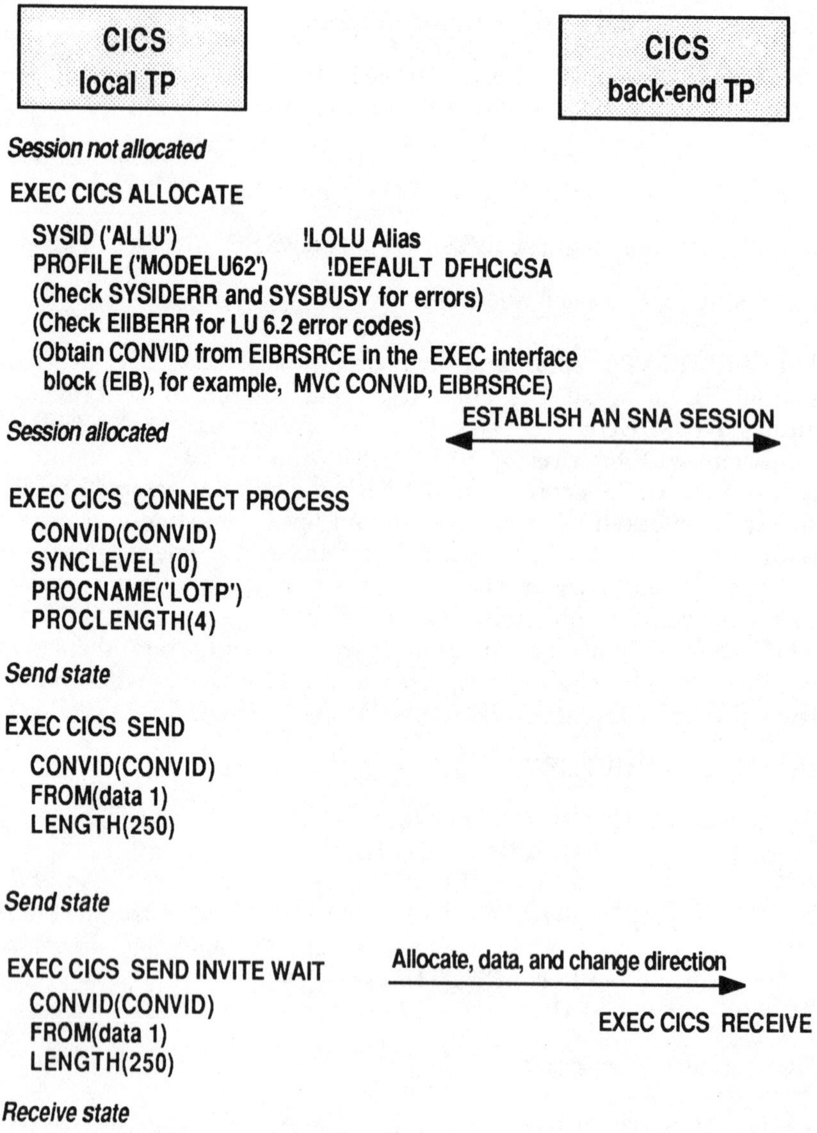

```
┌─────────────────┐          ┌─────────────────┐
│      CICS       │          │      CICS       │
│    local TP     │          │   back-end TP   │
└─────────────────┘          └─────────────────┘
```

Session not allocated

EXEC CICS ALLOCATE

    SYSID ('ALLU')   !LOLU Alias
    PROFILE ('MODELU62')   !DEFAULT DFHCICSA
    (Check SYSIDERR and SYSBUSY for errors)
    (Check EIIBERR for LU 6.2 error codes)
    (Obtain CONVID from EIBRSRCE in the EXEC interface
    block (EIB), for example, MVC CONVID, EIBRSRCE)

Session allocated   ESTABLISH AN SNA SESSION
                            ◄───────────────────►

EXEC CICS CONNECT PROCESS
    CONVID(CONVID)
    SYNCLEVEL (0)
    PROCNAME('LOTP')
    PROCLENGTH(4)

Send state

EXEC CICS SEND

    CONVID(CONVID)
    FROM(data 1)
    LENGTH(250)

Send state

EXEC CICS SEND INVITE WAIT   Allocate, data, and change direction
    CONVID(CONVID)   ─────────────────────►
    FROM(data 1)   EXEC CICS RECEIVE
    LENGTH(250)

Receive state

Figure 11.3 CICS mapped conversation verbs.

A CICS transaction can be started by an incoming allocation request from a back-end (remote) transaction program. Such conversation is the principal facility of the transaction. In this case the conversation ID is stored in EIBTRMID, but the CICS transaction can omit the CONVID parameter for its principal facility. The CONVID must be supplied on all CICS/LU 6.2 commands for all other conversations (alternate facilities). The CICS transaction enters the Receive state and can get retrieve information through the EXTRACT PROCESS command.

SEND

```
EXEC CICS SEND
         [CONVID (CONVID)]
         [FROM (data)]
         [Length(value)]
         [INVITE I LAST I CONFIRM I WAIT]
```

     Enter state 3 — Send state

The CICS SEND command performs the function of LU 6.2 MC_SEND_DATA verb discussed in Sec. 7.8 in this book. The [INVITE I LAST I CONFIRM and WAIT] optional parameters allow the combination of the SEND function with PREPARE_TO_ RECEIVE, DEALLOCATE, CONFIRM or FLUSH on the same call, which is similar to the CPI-C Send_Data call discussed in Sec. 8.4. The CONVID id parameter is a required parameter for alternate-facility conversation, but it is optional for the principal-facility conversation.

RECEIVE

```
EXEC CICS RECEIVE
         CONVID (CONVID)
         INTO (inrec)
         Length(outlen)
         [NOTRUNCATE]
         [MAXLENGTH]
```

The RECEIVE command performs the function of MC_RECEIVE_AND_WAIT discussed in Sec. 7.10. This command can be the first command issued if the CICS transaction was allocated by a back-end transaction program. If the actual amount of data is greater than MAXLENGH and NOTRUNCATE is specified, then EIBCOMPL=X'00', indicating that the incomplete mapped conversation data record has been received. The TP must issue EXEC CICS RECEIVE until EIBCOMPL is set to X'FF', indicating that the last portion of the data record has been received. If NOTRUNCATE was not specified and the TP receives an incomplete data record, then CICS truncates the remaining data and raises the LENGERR condition.

What fields to test in the Exec Interface Block (EIB):

- **EIBRECV** — if it is 'OFF' the partner TP invites the local TP to send, otherwise an EXEC CICS RECEIVE command should be issued.

- **EIBFREE** — the remote program has deallocated the conversation and the local TP must issue a FREE command

- **EIBCOMPL** — used only when the NOTRUNCATE parameter is set to X'FF' to indicate that a complete data record has been received. The program should know the maximum length to be received and the NOTRUNCATE parameter should be avoided (then the EIBCOMPL do not have to be checked).

- **EIBCONF** — indicates that the remote program has sent a SEND CONFIRM which combines the send and confirm functions.

- **EIBSYNC** — indicates that the remote program has sent a SYNC-POINT command. The local TP should issue a SYNCPOINT command

- **EIBSYNRB** — the remote program has sent the SYNCPOINT ROLLBACK command. The local TP should issue a SYNC-POINT ROLLBACK command.

ISSUE SIGNAL

EXEC CICS ISSUE SIGNAL CONVID (CONVID)

The EXEC CICS ISSUE SIGNAL performs the function of a MC_REQUEST TO SEND verb discussed in Sec. 7.12. The partner TP EIBSIG is set to a nonzero value and the RESP variable will be set to DFHRESP(SIGNAL).

ISSUE ERROR

EXEC CICS ISSUE ERROR CONVID (CONVID)

The EXEC CICS ISSUE ERROR command performs the function of the MC_SEND_ERROR verb discussed in Sec. 7.11. The local TP (the issuer of this verb) enters the Send state and should perform a user-defined error-recovery procedure. The partner TP's EIBERRCD is set to X'0889' (Issue Error Command) and is placed in the Receive state. The local TP should check for error race condition by checking EIBERR. If EIBERR=X'FF' and EIBERRCD is set to X'0889', then the remote TP also has issued the ERROR command and has won the race condition. In this case the local TP is placed in the Receive state and should issue the EXEC CICS RECEIVE command. The local TP should also check if EIBFREE is set to a nonzero value. If it is, then the partner TP has already deallocated the conversation and the conversation ends.

ISSUE ABEND

EXEC CICS ISSUE ABEND CONVID (CONVID)

The EXEC CICS ISSUE ABEND command performs the function of the MC_DEALLOCATE TYPE (ABEND) verb discussed in Sec. 7.7. The partner TP's EIBERRCD is set to X='0864', and the conversation is placed in Free state. This verb should be issued only when an urecoverable erorr condition occurs.

SYNCPOINT

EXEC CICS SYNCPOINT

The EXEC CICS SYNCPOINT and EXEC CICS SYNCPOINT ROLLBACK commands perform the function of the syncpoint processing discussed in Sec. 7.5. This command can be issued by either party if the conversation is in the Send state. The partner program enters the Receiver_Take_Syncpoint state and the EIBSYNC field is set to a non-zero value. The partner should reply with its own EXEC CICS SYNCPOINT (to commit all the resources to the next synchronization point) or EXEC CICS SYNCPOINT ROLLBACK (to backout all the resources to the previous synchronization point). The conversation can be deallocated with synchronization processing by issuing the sequence of SEND LAST, SYNCPOINT, and FREE.

11.2.4 CICS Basic Conversations

CICS transaction should use basic conversations when the partner program is not capable of mapped conversations. Otherwise mapped conversations should be used since they were designed for high level application programs and are much easier to use. The main difference between basic and mapped conversations are listed below:

- The TP is responsible for building GDS variables (LL, ID=X'12FF').

- The Exec Interface Block is not used. The error and state conditions are returned in two additional parameters used on basic conversations RETCODE (6-byte area that indicates an error condition) CONVDATA (24-byte area containing state information).

- The EXEC CICS HANDLE CONDITION cannot be used for error conditions indicated by RETCODE or CDBERR.

- The basic conversation calls must be issued in assembler.

- Both parties must use basic conversations.

- The INVITE and WAIT must be explicit (otherwise the EXEC CICS GDS RECEIVE after EXEC CICS GDS SEND will cause invalid state condition).

- EXEC CICS GDS FREE can be issued only in the Free state (after EXEC CICS GDS SEND LAST or SEND LAST CONFIRM or SEND LAST WAIT).

- The GDS commands, unlike those for mapped conversations, require the CONVID parameter even for the principal facility.

11.3 OS/2 EE LU 6.2 IMPLEMENTATION

The IBM OS/2 EE is the chosen programmable workstation for the SAA computer enterprise. The OS/2 EE Version 1.3 or lower implement only the APPC architecture discussed in Chap 7. This APPC interface has been significantly improved with the introduction of IBM SAA **Networking Services/2** product running under OS/2 EE. Network Services/2 provides both the **APPC** and **SAA/CPI-C** interfaces to the OS/2 application programmers.

11.3.1 IBM SAA Networking Services/2

Networking Services/2 provides OS/2 EE workstations with **Advanced Peer-to-Peer Networking (APPN)** capability. It provides end node (EN) and network node (NN) support in a distributed

APPN network. The APPN network was discussed in Sec. 3.2.2. The APPN support on OS/2 EE significantly enhances the capabilities and performance of the the APPC OS/2 EE (the older LU 6.2 implementation on OS/2). Figure 11.4 illustrates the OS/2 APPN network node, which is capable of any-to-any routing. For example, the messages received from CPI-C and APPC requesters can be routed to any PU2.1/LU 6.2 partner residing on a local or a remote Token Ring network or to any partner attached to a SNA wide area network. The OS/2 workstation can communicate using peer-to-peer LU 6.2 protocols with other workstations, midrange computers, and mainframes.

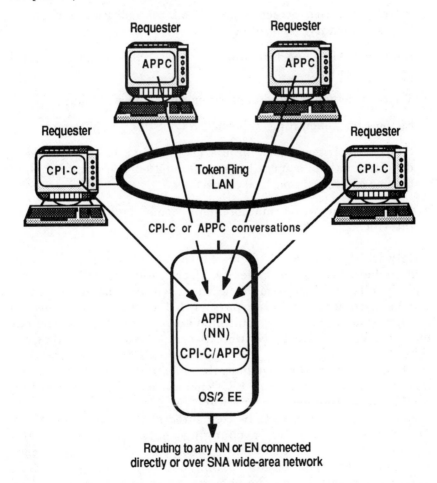

Figure 11.4 OS/2 EE APPN network node.

The IBM SAA **Network Services/2** enhances significantly the Communication Manager/APPC OS/2 EE implementation with:

- Advanced Peer-to-Peer Networking (APPN). OS/2 EE can act both as APPN network node (NN) or end node (EN).

- Physical Unit type 2.1 Low Entry Networking (LEN) node in non-APPN environments.

- Common Programming Interface-Communications (CPI-C).

- Advanced Program-to-Program Communications (APPC).

- PM configuration Screens. The LU 6.2 configuration is dynamic and significantly simplified.

- Improved APPC performance (at least twice as fast in LAN environment).

- Tools for debugging and application development tools.

- Support for Token Ring, Ethernet, X.25, SDLC, and Twinax.

- Support for tramsmission groups (TGs) at link level. This allows definition of two or more links to an adjacent node and enabling the use of alternate paths if a link fails.

- Improved network management tools and programming interfaces.

Networking Services/2 significantly simplifies configuration and reduces network complexity. Users need not define partner logical units and modes multiple times within a node. Wildcards can be used when defining partner LU names which allow to configure single entry for multiple-partner logical units. Default mode names provided by Network Services/2 can be used that are consistent throughout an APPN network. System managers can reconfigure the network dynamically which implies that there is no need to take down the OS/2 EE Communications Manager during configuration changes. The network resources configured at the remote node do not have to be configured at the local node. APPN nodes are capable of exchanging network topology and dynamically locating the remote resources. The network nodes maintain a database of the current network topology, which is updated dynamically as the changes occur in the network. The network nodes will calculate the optimum route between any two nodes in the network. In addition to these capabilities, Network Services/2 provides network management tools for forwarding alerts to the focal point residing in an APPN network or NetView residing on the host.

11.3.2 APPC and CPI-C Interfaces

Network Services/2 supports both the **APPC/LU 6.2** and **SAA/CPI-C** interfaces. The existing OS/2 EE APPC applications do not have to be changed to take advantage of the new functionality provided by the Network Services/2. New applications can be written using the SAA/CPI-C interface (CMALLC, CMSEND,...,CMDEAL), which was discussed in detail in Chap. 8. The reader should refer to Chap 8 for detail information on the CPI Communications calls and CPI-C application design issues. SAA/CPI-C allows programmers to develop portable applications across SAA Enterprise Information System (EIS). The programs may be written in high level programming languages such as C, COBOL, or REXX, which are the SAA high level programming languages. OS/2 EE provides additional extensions to the CPI-C interface, for example, an additional call to set the conversation level security. The following calls can be issued to set conversation level security:

- XCSCST (Set_Conversation_Security_Type)

- XCSCSP (Set_Conversation_Security_Password)

- XCMSSI (Set_CPIC_Side_Information)

In addition to the CPI-C interface an OS/2 EE LU 6.2 application program can now issue one verb for the entire conversation to send and block data to the conversation partner. This reduces the number of calls and increases performance. Sample programs, debugging, and application development tools are also provided to improve application development and implementation. In addition to this, Network Services/2 provides a programmer with an application programming interface for dynamic configuration and network management resulting in dynamic temporary changes to the network without operator intervention.

11.4 OS/400 LU 6.2 INTERFACE

The IBM AS/400 mid-range computers with OS/400 operating system are an integral part of the SAA enterprise. OS/400 supports the **Advanced Peer-to-Peer Networking (APPN)**. APPN provides the user with advanced functions such as dynamic configuration, dynamic route selection, and distributed directory searches. AS/400 can be configured as an APPN end node (EN) and a network node (NN). If the node does not require to perform intermediate network routing for other APPN nodes it should be configured as an end node. The end node uses a network node server to communicate with other APPN nodes in the network.

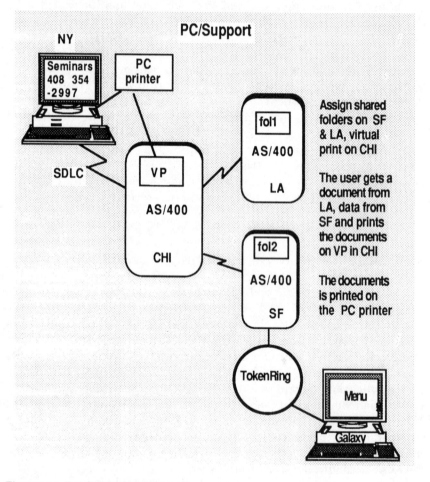

Figure 11.5 AS/400 PC/support.

The distributed capability of AS/400 APPN network is illustrated in Fig. 11.5. The PC/Support product allows PC users connected to AS/400 to define shared folders and virtual printers. For example, a PC user can assigned disk D to a shared folder (fol 2) residing on an

AS/400 in San Francisco (SF) and disk E to shared folder (fol 1) residing on an AS/400 in Los Angeles (LA). Then, the PC users can issue local commands as if disks D and E existed locally on the PC. Similarly, the user may assign LPT2 to a virtual printer residing on AS/400 in Chicago (CHI). The user may then read documents for SF and LA, modify them, and print the output on LPT2. The output is going to be printed to a virtual printer in Chicago. The virtual printer in Chicago may be configured to point to a real printer attached to a PC in New York (NY). Therefore, the output will be printed on the PC's printer in New York. PC support uses the APPC programming interface to establish conversations between various nodes, and it takes advantages of the APPN dynamic routing capabilities.

11.4.1 APPC and CPI-C Programming Interfaces

OS/400 provides both the **CPI-C and APPC** interfaces to the application programmers. The APPC conversation verbs are implemented via the OS/400 Intersystem Communication Function (ICF). The LU 6.2 verbs can be implemented by Data Description Specification (DDS) or by appropriate language operations. The CPI-C interface is available in SAA high level languages C, COBOL, FORTRAN, REXX, RPG and the AS/400 Application Generator. AS/400 CPI-C interface implements all the CPI Communications functions described in detail in Chap. 8 with the exception of the synchronization processing. The reader should refer to Chap 8 for detail information on the CPI Communications calls and CPI-C application design issues. The SAA/CPI-C programming interface allows developing applications on AS/400 that are portable across SAA environments (e.g., OS/2 EE or APPC/MVS). AS/400 APPC interface implements all the APPC/LU 6.2 functions described in detail in Chap. 7 with the exception of the following options:

- Synchronization processing

- Function management headers (FMHs)

- Profile verification

- Long locks on [MC_]PREPARE_TO_RECEIVE

- [MC_]RECEIVE_IMMEDIATE

- TEST TEST(POSTED)

- [MC_]ALLOCATE LU_NAME (OWN)

- [MC_]ALLOCATE LU_NAME
        RETURN_CONTROL (IMMEDIATE)

11.5 OTHER IBM LU 6.2 IMPLEMENTATIONS

The logical unit 6.2 is implemented on all IBM major platforms. This section give a very short desribtion of many of these implementations.

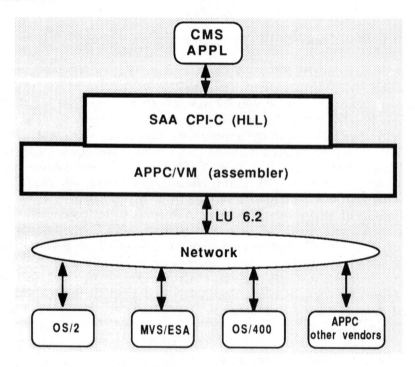

Figure 11.6 VM LU 6.2 interface.

11.5.1 CM/SP LU 6.2 Interface

VM/SP implements both the APPC and CPI-C architectures discussed in Chaps. 7 and 8. Figure 11.6 illustrates the VM LU 6.2 interface. The application programs may be written in the

SAA/CPI-Communications interface and the **APPC/VM** assembler programming interface. VM LU 6.2 transaction programs can communicate with programs residing on the same or a different VM system, and to any other system that supports either the CPI-C or APPC interface. The application programs residing in SNA/LU 6.2 network view VM/SP as one or many LUs. The APPC/VM interface is provided in the assembler language. The VM/SP CPI-C interface runs on top of APPC/VM, which implies that the CPI-C calls are mapped to APPC/VM calls. CMS programmers can use the CPI-C interface to develop portable applications across SAA enterprise. The applications can be written in the SAA procedure language REXX and all SAA high-level languages except RPG. The CPI-C interface supports both basic and mapped conversations. VM/SP provides additional extensions to the CPI-C interface, for example, an additional call to set the conversation level security. The reader should refer to Chap 8 for detail information on the CPI Communications calls and CPI-C application design issues.

11.5.2 VTAM LU 6.2 Interface

VTAM V3R2 or later implements the APPC architecture, and it provides programmers with **Application Programming Interface (VTAM-API)** for developing LU 6.2 transaction programs. VTAM automatically manages session establishment and terminations for those APPC applications which specify APPC=YES in their VTAM APPL definition. Therefore, APPC applications do not have to be concerned with session management, as was the case in the earlier session types. Notice that VTAM manages only the LU 6.2 sessions for which APPC=YES was specified. It is still possible for VTAM programmers to implement LU 6.2 functions entirely on their own (those application do not code APPC=YES on their APPL statement. VTAM implements the LU 6.2 verbs via **APPCCMD** macroinstructions (APPCCMD CONTROL=ALLOC,..., APPCCMD CONTROL=DEALLOC). The APPCCMD macro uses a **request parameter list (RPL)** to describe its requests to VTAM. The RPL includes an extension specifically used by the LU 6.2. VTAM supports only basic conversation verbs. Mapped conversations may be implemented by building the appropriate GDS variables. There are no APPCCMD macroinstructions for synchronization processing, but VTAM supports presentation services (PS) headers which allow programmers to implement the synchronization processing in the applications themselves. VTAM supports both the session and conversation level security.

11.5.3 DB2 LU 6.2 Interface

DB2 V2R2 distributed database uses **Distributed Database Facility (DDF)** to communicate with remote databases. DDF provides three major services:

1. **Distributed Transaction Management (DTM)** — manages the structures for distributed transaction.

2. **Distributed Relational Database Services (DRDS)** — communicates with DRDS residing on the remote system to executes SQL requests that require remote access.

3. **Communications Services** — interacts with VTAM/APPC and manages LU 6.2 conversations to remote systems.

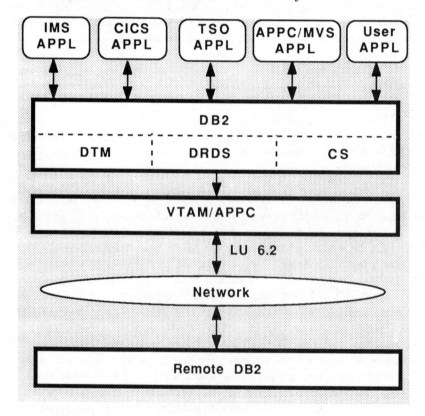

Figure 11.7 DB2 LU 6.2 interface.

Figure 11.7 illustrates various applications issuing SQL request to the DB2 database. When a DB2 receives an SQL request from an application program, it   creates a service transaction program (STP) which establishes one or more conversations to the remote DB2 system. The STP communicates with the STP at the remote DB2 system to perform the SQL request. The application programmer issuing the SQL statements is not aware of the underlying LU 6.2 conversations.

11.5.4 IMS LU 6.2 Interface

IMS applications can communicate with LU 6.2 applications residing on remote systems. The current **APPC   IMS** implementation converts the LU 6.1 protocol [which uses the Intersystem Communication (ISC) half session] to LU 6.2 functions and vice versa. IMS supports both basic and mapped conversations. Since the ISC and LU 6.2 are two separate protocols, IMS LU 6.2 implementation does have many limitation, some of which are listed below:

- IMS applications can not issue directly LU 6.2 verbs. APPC Verbs such as CONFIRM and CONFIRMED are handled by the IMS queue manager rather then the application.

- PIP is not supported.

- Data mapping is not supported.

- Only the password, can be passed to IMS from received allocation requests that carry conversation level security (user_id, password, and profile).

- DEALLOCATE will complete when transaction is placed on IMS queue which does not provide any indication of the transaction execution.

- The remote APPC programs must strictly issue verb sequences that are supported by IMS. For example, issuing SEND_ERROR or CONFIRM will cause immediate session termination. REQUEST_TO_SEND issued by the remote program is ignored by IMS.

Application programs running under **IMS/ESA** may use APPC/MVS **CPI-C** calls as long as the CPI-C libraries are accessible to IMS programs at compilation time. Because of the limitations listed above, IMS application programmers may consider using CICS or APPC/MVS LU 6.2 interfaces that can access the IMS database for writing more complicated LU6.2 transaction programs.

   IBM has announced a new IMS/DC LU 6.2 implementation that will allow IMS programmers to issue CPI-C calls directly from IMS transaction programs. The reader should refer to Chap. 8 for detail information on the SAA/CPI Communications calls and CPI-C application design issues.

11.5.5 PC/DOS APPC Implementation

APPC/PC is an implementation of SNA logical unit type 6.2 and the physical unit type 2.1 architectures on a DOS personal computer. APPC/PC implementation of LU 6.2 architecture can emulate a distributed node type 2.1 when communicating other PU2.1 nodes as well as a PU 2.0 node when communicating with mainframes. Figure 11.8 illustrates APPC/PC transaction program (TPPC) communicating with a host CICS or APPC/MVS or IMS LU 6.2 transaction (RETP). APPC/PC implements the base set of verbs and various options. the following is a list of major futures of APPC/PC implementation:

* Basic and mapped conversation are supported.

* APPC/PC verbs must be issued in assembler.

* Program initiation parameter (PIP) is supported.

* Synchronization level None and Confirm.

* Conversation and session level security.

* Parallel sessions are supported.

* Network Management Vectors (NMVTs) can be forwarded from APPC applications to the host.

* The user must write an application subsystem that will configure the LU 6.2 resources (LUs, PUs, partners, modes), manage multiple transaction programs and the incoming allocates.

   Since DOS is not a multi tasking operating system it is no easy to design a applications that would allow multiple concurrent conversations from the DOS PC to one or multiple partners. The APPC/PC implementation does not provide tools for handling multiple conversations, staring TPs, or configuring the LU 6.2

resources. The user is responsible for writing an application subsystem that will configure the APPC/LU 6.2 resources (LUs, PUs, partners, modes), and manage multiple transaction programs (TPs) and the incoming allocates.

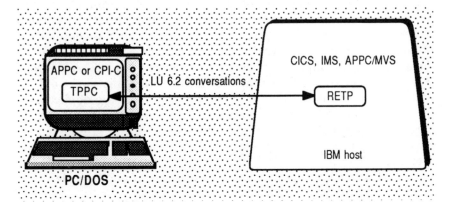

Figure 11.8 PC/DOS LU 6.2 interface.

IBM has announced a new PC/DOS LU 6.2 implementation which significantly enhances the older APPC/PC version with:

- Common Programming Interface-Communications (CPI-C).

- Improved Advanced Program-to-Program Communications (APPC) interface.

- Advanced Peer-to-Peer Networking (APPN) end node (EN) support..

- Half a memory requirement (about 110 kbytes).

- Improved LU 6.2 performance .

11.5.6 Other Vendor LU 6.2 Implementations

The SNA logical unit 6.2 is implemented by most hardware and software vendors. Figure 11.9 illustrates connections between application programs residing in other vendor networks (e.g., requesters on LANs or DEC applications on DECNET network communicating via LU 6.2 gateways with IBM enterprise network). Applications access the gateway via APPC or CPI-C programming interfaces. The LU 6.2 gateway enables other vendor transaction programs and remote IBM transaction programs to take part in a distributed and cooperative processing environments. The gateway provides a set of procedures (called LU 6.2 verbs) that programmers use to communicate with the SAA enterprise. A transaction involves two participants: a requester of processing operation and the server. Applications issue requests to the LU 6.2 gateway, which routes them to the remote transaction programs residing in an SAA enterprise. The remote programs return replies to the gateway, which passes them back to the application that issues the request. The advantage of the gateway approach is that the IBM enterprise is aware only of the gateway and is not aware of the requesters or the applications residing in the other vendor network. The communication between non-IBM applications and the gateway uses other vendor networking protocols (e.g., DECNET protocols or Novell LAN protocols). The gateway in turn establishes and manages LU 6.2 conversations with remote IBM transaction programs residing in the SAA enterprise.

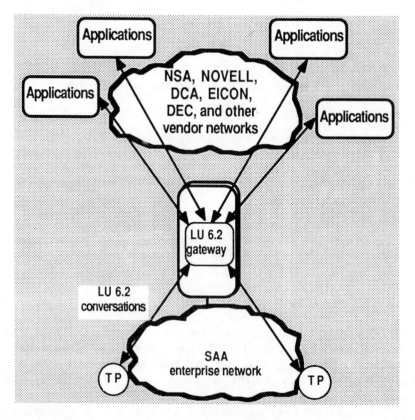

Figure 11.9 Other vendor LU 6.2 implementations.

11.6 SUMMARY

The chosen IBM connectivity method for SAA enterprise networks
in the 1990s is the SNA logical unit 6.2 (LU 6.2) and OSI/RM. The
logical unit 6.2 makes SNA a modern distributed architecture
comparable to the Open Systems Interconnection (OSI) Reference
Model. IBM's strategy for the 1990s is to build a computer enterprise
with distributed applications and data that looks, to the end user,
like a single system.

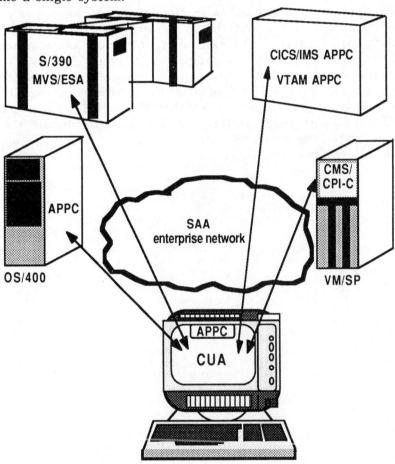

Figure 11.10 SAA Enterprise Information System (EIS).

Figure 11.10 illustrates an IBM computer enterprise consisting of
IBM mainframes, AS/400 midrange computers, and OS/2 PCs

interconnected via LU 6.2s. OS/2 CUA gives an end user a single log on interface to the computer enterprise. The computer enterprise looks to the user as a single system. The resources, such as applications or data, are distributed throughout the computer enterprise, but the user accesses all the resources as if they were local. Whenever remote access is required, CPI-C or APPC peer-to-peer cooperative processing is used to access the resources as if they were residing on the local system.

The SNA logical unit 6.2 is gaining wider acceptance among computer users and product implementors. With the addition of LU6.2, APPC and SAA/CPI-C SNA becomes an advanced distributed and cooperative processing standard that will tie together the world of mainframes, minicomputers, and personal computers into a single SAA **Enterprise Information System (EIS)**. The truly heterogeneous networks of the 1990s will play a large part in the information age as third parties begin to migrate their products into these networks and the utilization of computers once again enters a new era.

A

Performance Tips

This appendix describes programming performance tips as well as how to configure various LU 6.2 network parameters for optimal network efficiency. The following is a list of suggested configuration and programming tips that may improve performance and network efficiency.

CONFIGURATION TIPS

- **Configure optimal max DLC frame sizes**. If the line quality is good, then using **large transmit buffers** will reduce network traffic and therefore improve the overall performance of the communication LU 6.2 programs. The tradeoff in using large buffers is that more memory needs to be allocated for the incoming and outgoing frames. The system programmer should configure this parameter to the largest value possible. The tradeoff in using large buffers is that more system memory needs to be allocated for each of the incoming and outgoing frames. For example, on a 4-Mbit/s Token Ring using APPC large BTUs (e.g., RU size 1920 bytes, the frame buffer size 2048 bytes) produces much better performance than smaller BTUs. If the line quality is low (a lot of noise), then the optimal buffer size depends on the error rate of the link. Generally, if the error rate is high, the large transmit buffers will decrease performance. Also the probability of an error while transmitting large frames is higher than when transmitting smaller frames. When an error occurs, more data has to be retransmitted for large frames. In this case the best performance is usually determined by performing tests that use different buffer sizes.

- **Configure optimal level 2 window sizes and the modules.** Generally for high-quality connections the larger the window and modulus, the better the performance. The tradeoff in using large window sizes is that **more system memory** needs to be used. When many resources are competing for the system memory, large window sizes may actually decrease the overall performance of the system. Usually the default values suggested by manufactures are satisfactory. The most common modulus used on leased or switched connections is **modulo 8**. Satellite communications should use modulo 128.

- **The node identification field in the XID-3 should be configured to unique values.** This will decrease the amount of time during the link negotiation phase to determine the primary and secondary link station roles.

- **Configure the line for full-duplex operation.** This will provide best performance by transmitting frames in both directions at the same time. When using a **multipoint** line, only the secondary link stations should be configured for **half-duplex** operation.

- **Configure optimal maximum SNA request/response unit size** (referred to as **maximum RU size** or MAXRU size). This value should be configured as large as possible to minimize data exchanges on a session and to avoid chaining. The maximum RU size should be less than the maximum frame size (**MAXRU size < max DLC frame size**) to avoid segmentation. The tradeoff in using large RU sizes is that more system memory needs to be allocated for each session. If only a small percentage of messages are large, then chaining and segmenting may be appropriate for these messages.

- **Configure optimal session pacing windows.** Ideally, no pacing or a large pacing window produces the best performance. Using no pacing may overflow the LU's buffers, and it may overflow the buffers of intermediate routing nodes. However, large pacing windows require a lot of memory to be reserved for each session. Generally the default values suggested by manufactures should be used or values derived from statistical information gathered by trying different sizes in a production environment.

- **Avoid session and allocation contentions**. Define the number of contention winners (allocation winner sessions) and losers on each side of the connection, in such a way that the number of contentions of minimized. For best performance the programs that initiate conversations (issue the ALLOCATE verb) should always get the contention winner sessions.

- **Keep sessions and links up**. When a conversation is deallocated, it releases the session to other conversations. The sessions and links should be kept up. Sessions and link initiation is time consuming and requires initializing many control structures. It is also advantageous to automatically start some sessions initially at the LU's startup time. This can be done by configuring the automatic activation limit for a particular (LU, mode) pair to a nonzero value. The LU will automatically activate sessions to create the initial session pool. The initial conversations can use the sessions immediately. When all the sessions from the initial session pool are started, then the subsequent allocation requests will initiate new sessions up to the preconfigured maximum (LU, mode) session limit.

- **Minimize the number of modes, LUs, and PUs**. This reduces the number of resources that need to be configured and maintained in a distributed network. Network management of a network with fewer resources is easier as well. Usually one local LU is satisfactory to handle multiple transaction programs (TPs). Also, one partner LU should be satisfactory for each remote system. The number of modes between local and remote LUs should be minimized as well (e.g., one mode for interactive sessions and one mode for batch access).

PROGRAMMING TIPS

- **Minimize the number of programming Receive calls**. Generally transaction programs should allocate a large memory block for incoming data and receive as much data as possible on one Receive call. When designing applications the local TP's send buffer should be set up to be equal to the remote program's receive buffer to avoid the DATA_INCOMPLETE indication on Receive calls. Then there would be only one Receive call needed for each corresponding Send call. This would require fewer programming calls to be issued and less processing power. Basic conversation programs should use the Fill (Buffer) option to receive as much data as possible on one Receive call. However, a large requested length requires a large memory block to be reserved for the incoming data each time a Receive call is issued. If many applications are competing for memory resources, the overall system performance may decrease significantly if the memory is not available.

- **Minimize the number of programming Send calls.** A program may reduce the number of SEND_DATA calls by packing as much data records (for mapped conversations) or logical records (for basic conversations) into the one send buffer.

- **Minimize the Send/Receive state changes.** The LU 6.2 half-duplex, flip-flop protocol requires that the two communicating transaction programs follow the send/receive mode protocol. The send/receive mode protocol is enforced by the LU for each conversation. This means that the local and remote logical units exchange data in one direction at a time on a single session. Each time a local program issues a Receive call, it suspends until the partner receives and processes the data and releases the Send state. This may decrease performance if the communicating programs change the conversation Send and Receive states too often. The programs should send as much data as possible before issuing a Receive call and any other call that requires a reply from the partner program. The communicating programs may also use a full-duplex data exchange by establishing two half-duplex conversations as discussed in Sec. 6.2.3 in this book.

- **Minimize the number of CONFIRM and SYNCPOINT calls.** Confirmation and synchronization processing should be used very carefully. The local transaction program is suspended for the duration of the confirmation and synchronization processing until an explicit acknowledgment is received from the partner program. The synchronization processing also requires logging of the Logical Unit of Work (LUW) throughout the distributed transaction and high usage of system resources. The SNA/LU 6.2 two-phase commit processing is also time-consuming. All of this may cause performance degradation. Therefore, APPC or CPI-C programmers should not issue SYNCPT or CONFIRM LU 6.2 verbs after each send. Transaction programs should send as much data as possible before asking for confirmation or synchronization processing.

- **Avoid the use of the FLUSH verb.** The FLUSH verb forces the LU's send buffer to be sent to the partner LU. Therefore, each time a FLUSH is issued a network message is generated. Unless the partner program needs the data immediately, the TP should allow the LU to decide when to flush the data. LU 6.2 buffers the data for optimal network performance.

- **Reuse sessions**. Session establishment is time consuming and requires building a lot of control blocks. Programs should try to reuse the same session. A session can carry many LU 6.2 conversations in a serial manner.

- **Do not mix long transactions with short transactions on the same session**. A conversation uses a session exclusively until a programmer issues a Deallocate call. Then, the session is released to other programs and conversations. A long lived transaction (such as a batch job application) should not be using the same session as a short transaction (such as an interactive application) that will need a fast response time. In the requester/server model the conversation should be deallocated as soon as a reply is received by the server. This will release the session to other requests issued by the same or other requesters. Also the server can release the resources such as buffer space and control blocks to other requesters.

- **Consider processing delays**. Programs should avoid performing a lot of processing when the partner program is suspended and waiting for a reply. When programs receive a confirmation request, a synchronization request, or any other request that requires a reply, then the programs should issue a reply as soon as possible. This will allow the partner to resume processing.

- **Combine the LU 6.2 functions**. CPI-C and many APPC implementations allow programmers to combine LU 6.2 functions. Combining multiple distributed functions is very efficient and improves the overall performance of CPI-C and APPC distributed transactions. It saves on extra programming calls and often generates less network messages. In addition, less processing and fewer network messages improves performance and network efficiency. The following LU 6.2 functions can and should be combined together:

  - Send and flush data in the LU's send buffer.

  - Send, flush data, and release the Send state.

  - Send data and perform confirmation processing.

  - Send data, perform confirmation processing, and release the Send state.

- Send data, perform synchronization processing, and release the Send state.

- Send data and perform synchronization processing.

- Send data and deallocate a conversation.

- Receive data and states on one call.

- Deallocate with confirmation or syncpoint processing

- Change direction with confirmation or synchronization processing.

- **Use Deallocate type (FLUSH).** Deallocate type (FLUSH) flushes the LU's send buffer and deallocates the conversation unconditionally without a need for an acknowledgment from the partner TP. This allows the local TP to immediately resume processing on other conversations or initiate new conversations. This type of deallocate is very fast, but it should be issued only if all data sent thus far on this conversation was already checked and acknowledged by the communicating transaction programs; otherwise the data sent with the deallocation request may be lost. In these cases the Deallocate type (CONFIRM) should be used.

B

LU 6.2 Programming Examples

The COBOL sample programs illustrated in this appendix are for tutorial purposes only. The purpose of these sample programs is to illustrate a cooperative processing design using the SAA/CPI-C interface. The programs main processing and error recovery is largely simplified. The details and complexity of such processing and distributed error recovery depend on specific implementation and should be added to the sample codes below.

Example 1: Client/Server model

The sample programs below use the client/server model and the SAA/CPI-C interface for a typical banking application. A PC user enters a customer account number and in response gets the current information on the account.

Program 1 (CUSTREQ) — (initiator of the conversation) is the requester side of the design that performs the following steps:

1. Establishes a conversation with the CPI-C server (**CUSTSVR)** residing on the host.

2. Sends a customer's account number to the server and waits for the reply.

3. Receives a current customer record and displays it to the user. The requester is capable of receiving multiple records from the server. It receives data from the server by issuing the CPI-C Receive_Data call. The data is received until the server transmits all of the records and deallocates the conversation normally.

```
IDENTIFICATION DIVISION.
PROGRAM-ID. CUSTREQ.

*    This is the CUSTREQ program that establishes a conversation *
*    with a server on the host, retrieves a requested customer record *
*    (or multiple records) and displays them to the PC user          *

ENVIRONMENT DIVISION.
DATA DIVISION.
WORKING-STORAGE SECTION.

*    Copy the CPI-Communications pseudonym file CMCOBOL, *
*    which defines the CPI-C return codes, conversation states,*
*    data received indicators, and other variables, e.g.:         *
*    01 CM-RETCODE                        PIC 9(9) COMP-4.*
*      88 CM-OK                           VALUE 0.          *
*      88 CM-DEALLOCATE-ABEND             VALUE 17.         *
*      88 CM-DEALLOCATE-NORMAL            VALUE 18.         *
COPY CMCOBOL.

01  ERROR-MSG              PIC X(40) VALUE SPACES.
01  REMOTE-SYSTEM          PIC X(8)   VALUE "REMNODE".

* * * * * * * * * * * * * * * *
* Customer Record   *
* * * * * * * * * * * * * * * *

01  CUST-RECORD.
      02  CUST-NUM          PIC X(4)     VALUE "0025".
      02  CUST-NAME         PIC X(20)    VALUE SPACES.
      02  TRANSACTIONS      PIC X(56)    VALUE SPACES.

* * * * * * * * * * * * * * * * * * * * * * * * * * * * * * * * * * * * * * * * * * * * * * * * * *
*    Notice that the customer account number and the remote system*
*    are hard coded. These values should be entered by the user to *
*    to allow conversations with servers residing at different     *
```

```
*   geographic locations. Error recovery  has been omitted for *
*   simplicity.                                                 *
***************************************************************

PROCEDURE DIVISION.
    PERFORM CPI-C-INITIALIZE
        THRU CPI-C-INITIALIZE-EXIT.

    PERFORM CPI-C-ALLOCATE
        THRU CPI-C-ALLOCATE-EXIT.

* Send the customer account number to the server.              *
    MOVE LENGTH OF CUST-NUM TO SEND-LENGTH.
    MOVE CUST-NUM  TO BUFFER.
    PERFORM CPI-C-SEND
        THRU CPI-C-SEND-EXIT.

    MOVE LENGTH OF CUST-RECORD TO
                    REQUESTED-LENGTH.
    PERFORM CPI-C-RECEIVE
        THRU CPI-C-RECEIVE-EXIT
        UNTIL NOT CM-OK.

    DISPLAY "All transactions processed successfully — Program
    End!!!".
    STOP RUN.
***************************************************************

CPI-C-INITIALIZE.
*       Initialize conversation characteristic default values.  *
*       The symbolic destination name REMOTE-SYSTEM points      *
*       to the actual REMOTE LU, MODE and REMOTE TP names. *
CALL "CMINIT" USING   CONVERSATION-ID
                      REMOTE-SYSTEM
                      CM-RETCODE.
    IF NOT CM-OK
    MOVE "Invalid REMOTE-SYSTEM name"
        TO ERROR-MSG
        PERFORM PROGRAM-ERROR.
CPI-C-INITIALIZE-EXIT. EXIT.
***************************************************************

CPI-C-ALLOCATE.
*       Allocate the conversation.                              *
```

```
        CALL "CMALLC"   USING  CONVERSATION-ID
                                CM-RETCODE.
        IF NOT CM-OK
           MOVE "Conversation Allocation failed:"
              TO ERROR-MSG
           PERFORM  PROGRAM-ERROR.
  CPI-C-ALLOCATE-EXIT.  EXIT.
  *************************************************************

     CPI-C-SEND.
  * Send an account number to the server.                          *
        CALL "CMSEND" USING CONVERSATION-ID
                            BUFFER
                            SEND-LENGTH
                            REQUEST-TO-SEND-RECEIVED
                            CM-RETCODE.
        IF NOT CM-OK
           MOVE "Send to the Server failed:"
              TO ERROR-MSG
           PERFORM  PROGRAM-ERROR.
  CPI-C-SEND-EXIT.  EXIT.
  *************************************************************

  CPI-C-RECEIVE.
  *************************************************************
  *   Receive data records from the server until the RC is equal to   *
  *   CM-DEALLOCATE-NORMAL which indicates  that                  *
  *   the transaction completed without any errors.                 *
  *************************************************************
        CALL "CMRCV" USING CONVERSATION-ID
                           CUST-RECORD
                           REQUESTED-LENGTH
                           DATA-RECEIVED
                           RECEIVED-LENGTH
                           STATUS-RECEIVED
                           REQUEST-TO-SEND-RECEIVED
                           CM-RETCODE.

     IF CM-COMPLETE-DATA-RECEIVED
        DISPLAY CUST-RECORD.

     IF CM-OK OR CM-DEALLOCATED-NORMAL
        NEXT SENTENCE
     ELSE
```

```
        MOVE "Receive data processing failed"
            TO ERROR-MSG
        PERFORM PROGRAM-ERROR.
 CPI-C-RECEIVE-EXIT. EXIT.
 *****************************************************

 PROGRAM-ERROR.
 * Display the error and stop the program                *
        DISPLAY "Program Failure CUSTREQ — ",
            ERROR-MSG,"RC=", CM-RETCODE
        STOP RUN.
 *****************************************************
```

Program 2 (CUSTSVR) — (acceptor of the conversation) is the
server side of the design that performs the following steps:

```
IDENTIFICATION DIVISION.
PROGRAM-ID. CUSTSVR.

*************************************************************
*   This is the CUSTSVR program that accepts a conversation   *
*   from CUSTREQ, receives a customer account number,         *
*   retrieves the customer record for the account number, and *
*   sends it to the requester. The server can be easily modified *
*   to be able  retrieve  and to send back multiple customer records. *
*************************************************************

ENVIRONMENT DIVISION.
DATA DIVISION.
WORKING-STORAGE SECTION.

*   Copy the CPI-Communications pseudonym file CMCOBOL *
*   which defines  the CPI-C return codes, conversation states,*
*   data received indicators, and other variables, e.g.:      *
*   01 CM-RETCODE                         PIC 9(9) COMP-4.*
*     88 CM-OK                            VALUE 0.        *
*     88 CM-DEALLOCATE-ABEND              VALUE 17.       *
*     88 CM-DEALLOCATE-NORMAL             VALUE 18.       *

COPY CMCOBOL.
```

```
01  ERROR-MSG                    PIC X(40)    VALUE SPACES.

*   Customer Record                                              *
01  CUST-RECORD.
        02  CUST-NUM         PIC X(4)     VALUE  SPACES.
        02  CUST-NAME        PIC X(20)    VALUE  SPACES.
        02  TRANSACTIONS     PIC X(56)    VALUE  SPACES.

*   Error recovery has been omitted for  simplicity.             *
PROCEDURE DIVISION.

*   Accept the conversation.                                     *
    PERFORM CPI-C-ACCEPT
        THRU CPI-C-ACCEPT-EXIT.

*   Receive an account number from the requester until           *
*   CM-SEND-RECEIVED, which indicates a state change             *
*   from Receive to Send or Send-Pending state.                  *
    MOVE LENGTH OF CUST-NUM TO
                    REQUESTED-LENGTH.
    PERFORM CPI-C-RECEIVE
        THRU CPI-C-RECEIVE-EXIT
        UNTIL CM-SEND-RECEIVED.

*   Query the customer account database.                         *
    PERFORM QUERY-ACCOUNT.

*   Send the retrieved customer record to the requester.         *
    MOVE LENGTH OF CUST-RECORD TO
                    SEND-LENGTH.
    PERFORM CPI-C-SEND
        THRU CPI-C-SEND-EXIT.

    PERFORM PROGRAM-END.

CPI-C-ACCEPT.
*   Accept incoming ALLOCATE from the requester and initialize*
*   the conversation characteristics to the default values.    *
    CALL "CMACCP" USING    CONVERSATION-ID
                           CM-RETCODE.
    IF   NOT CM-OK
        MOVE "Accepting Conversation failed:"
            TO ERROR-MSG
        PERFORM PROGRAM-ERROR THRU PROGRAM-END.
```

```
CPI-C-ACCEPT-EXIT. EXIT.
************************************************************

CPI-C-RECEIVE.
    CALL "CMRCV" USING CONVERSATION-ID
                       CUST-NUM
                       REQUESTED-LENGTH
                       DATA-RECEIVED
                       RECEIVED-LENGTH
                       STATUS-RECEIVED
                       REQUEST-TO-SEND-RECEIVED
                       CM-RETCODE.

    IF   NOT CM-OK
      MOVE "Receive_Data failed:"
        TO ERROR-MSG
      PERFORM PROGRAM-ERROR THRU PROGRAM-END.
    CPI-C-RECEIVE-EXIT. EXIT.
************************************************************

QUERY-ACCOUNT.
*    Write the code to query the customer account database for the    *
*    current account information and move it to CUST-RECORD.          *
************************************************************

CPI-C-SEND.
        CALL "CMSEND" USING CONVERSATION-ID
                            CUST-RECORD
                            SEND-LENGTH
                            REQUEST-TO-SEND-RECEIVED
                            CM-RETCODE.
        IF NOT CM-OK
            MOVE "Send_Data failed:"
                TO ERROR-MSG
            PERFORM PROGRAM-ERROR
            THRU PROGRAM-END.
    CPI-C-SEND-EXIT. EXIT.
************************************************************

PROGRAM-ERROR.
* Display the error and stop the program.                             *
        DISPLAY "Program Failure CUSTSVR — ",
            ERROR-MSG,"RC=", CM-RETCODE.
        SET CM-DEALLOCATE-ABEND TO TRUE
```

```
        CALL "CMSDT" USING  CONVERSATION-ID
                            DEALLOCATE-TYPE
                            CM-RETCODE.

PROGRAM-END.
        CALL "CMDEAL"USING   CONVERSATION-ID
                             CM-RETCODE.
        STOP RUN.
*****************************************************
```

Example 2: Remote Procedure Call

The COBOL sample programs below illustrate an example of a Remote Procedure Call (RPC) design using the SAA/CPI-C interface. A remote procedure with one parameter can be invoked by any calling program with the following COBOL statements:

```
MOVE "REMNODE" TO REMOTE-SYSTEM.
MOVE "REMPROC" TO REM-PROC.
MOVE LENGTH OF PARAM TO PARAM-LEN.
CALL "RPCREQ" USING REMOTE-SYSTEM REM-PROC
              PARAM-LEN PARAM RETCODE.
```

Upon successful completion of the above call the PARAM contains the returned parameter data and the RETCODE contains a return code set to zero (or a nonzero CPI-C CM-RETCODE value if an error condition occurred). RPCREQ is a CPI-C requester that establishes a conversation with a CPI-C server (RPCSVR) residing on a remote system (REMNODE) in order to execute the remote procedure (REMPROC).

Program 1 (RPCREQ) — (initiator of the conversation) is the requester side of the RPC design that performs the following steps:

1. Establishes a conversation with the server (RPCSVR) .

2. Sends a remote procedure name and one parameter to the server (the program can easily be modified to pass multiple parameters).

3. The server calls the remote procedure and returns a reply to the requester.

4. Upon successful receipt of the reply, the requester receives Deallocate_Normal and exits to the calling program returning a reply in PARAM and a return code in RETCODE.

```
IDENTIFICATION DIVISION.
PROGRAM-ID. RPCREQ.

ENVIRONMENT DIVISION.
DATA DIVISION.
WORKING-STORAGE SECTION.

*    Copy the CPI-Communications pseudonym file CMCOBOL *
*    which defines  the CPI-C return codes, conversation states,*
```

```
*    data received indicators, and other variables, e.g.:           *
*    01 CM-RETCODE                         PIC 9(9) COMP-4.*
*        88 CM-OK                          VALUE 0.          *
*        88 CM-DEALLOCATE-ABEND            VALUE 17.         *
*        88 CM-DEALLOCATE-NORMAL           VALUE 18.         *
COPY CMCOBOL.


01  ERROR-MSG              PIC X(40)    VALUE SPACES.
01  BUFFER                PIC X(256)   VALUE SPACES.


LINKAGE SECTION.


01  REMOTE-SYSTEM    PIC  X(8).
01  REM-PROC         PIC  X(8).
01  PARAM-LEN        PIC  9(9) COMP-4.
01  PARAM            PIC  X(256)
01  RETCODE          PIC  9(9) COMP-4 VALUE 0.


*    Error recovery  has been omitted for simplicity.              *
PROCEDURE DIVISION USING REMOTE-SYSTEM REM-PROC
PARAM-LEN PARAM RETCODE.


*    Initialize the conversation default values.*
     PERFORM CPI-C-INITIALIZE
         THRU CPI-C-INIALIZE-EXIT.


*    Allocate the conversation with the server.*
     PERFORM CPI-C-ALLOCATE
         THRU CPI-C-ALLOCATE-EXIT.


*    Send the remote procedure name to the server.*
     MOVE LENGTH OF REM-PROC TO SEND-LENGTH.
     MOVE REM-PROC  TO BUFFER.
     PERFORM CPI-C-SEND
         THRU CPI-C-SEND-EXIT.


*    Send the parameter data to the server.*
     MOVE PARAM-LEN TO SEND-LENGTH.
     MOVE PARAM TO BUFFER.
     PERFORM CPI-C-SEND
         THRU CPI-C-SEND-EXIT.


*    Receive the reply from the server.*
     MOVE PARAM-LEN TO REQUESTED-LENGTH.
```

```
    PERFORM CPI-C-RECEIVE
       THRU CPI-C-RECEIVE-EXIT
    UNTIL NOT CM-OK.


    DISPLAY "The remote procedure call was  successful!!!"
            UPON CONSOLE.
    GOBACK.
**************************************************************

CPI-C-INITIALIZE.
*       Initialize conversation characteristic default values.      *
*       The symbolic destination name REMOTE-SYSTEM points     *
*       to the actual REMOTE LU, MODE, and REMOTE TP names.
*
CALL "CMINIT" USING      CONVERSATION-ID
                         REMOTE-SYSTEM
                         CM-RETCODE.
    IF   NOT CM-OK
       MOVE "Invalid REMOTE-SYSTEM name"
          TO ERROR-MSG
       PERFORM  PROGRAM-ERROR.
CPI-C-INITIALIZE-EXIT.  EXIT.
**************************************************************

CPI-C-ALLOCATE.
*       Allocate the conversation.                                  *
       CALL "CMALLC"   USING  CONVERSATION-ID
                              CM-RETCODE.
       IF NOT CM-OK
          MOVE "Conversation Allocation failed:"
              TO ERROR-MSG
          PERFORM  PROGRAM-ERROR.
CPI-C-ALLOCATE-EXIT.  EXIT.
**************************************************************

 CPI-C-SEND.
*   Send the remote procedure name or the parameter to the server. *
       CALL "CMSEND" USING CONVERSATION-ID
                           BUFFER
                           SEND-LENGTH
                           REQUEST-TO-SEND-RECEIVED
                           CM-RETCODE.
       IF NOT CM-OK
          MOVE "Send to the Server failed:"
```

```
                    TO ERROR-MSG
              PERFORM PROGRAM-ERROR.
       CPI-C-SEND-EXIT. EXIT.
       **********************************************************

       CPI-C-RECEIVE.
       *    Receive the reply in PARAM from the server.              *
       *    RC= CM-DEALLOCATE-NORMAL indicates that the             *
       *    remote procedure was executed without any errors.       *
              CALL "CMRCV" USING CONVERSATION-ID
                            PARAM
                            REQUESTED-LENGTH
                            DATA-RECEIVED
                            PARAM-LEN
                            STATUS-RECEIVED
                            REQUEST-TO-SEND-RECEIVED
                            CM-RETCODE.

              IF NOT CM-DEALLOCATED-NORMAL
                 MOVE "Receive data processing failed"
                            TO ERROR-MSG
                      PERFORM PROGRAM-ERROR.
       CPI-C-RECEIVE-EXIT. EXIT.
       **********************************************************

          PROGRAM-ERROR.
       *    Display the error and stop the program                  *
                 DISPLAY "Program Failure RPCREQ — ",
                      ERROR-MSG,"RC=", CM-RETCODE
                      UPON CONSOLE
                 MOVE CM-RETCODE TO RETCODE
                 GOBACK.
       **********************************************************
```

Program 2 (RPCSVR) — (acceptor of the conversation) is the server side of the RPC design that performs the following steps:

1. Accepts a conversation from the requester

2. Receives a remote procedure name and one parameter

3. Invokes the remote procedure

4. Sends a reply to the requester

4. Deallocates the conversation

```
IDENTIFICATION  DIVISION.
PROGRAM-ID.  RPCSVR.

ENVIRONMENT  DIVISION.
DATA  DIVISION.
WORKING-STORAGE  SECTION.

*    Copy the CPI-Communications pseudonym file CMCOBOL      *
*    which defines  the CPI-C return codes, conversation states,   *
*    data received indicators, and other variables, e.g.:          *
*    01 CM-RETCODE                      PIC 9(9) COMP-4.*
*        88 CM-OK                        VALUE 0.           *
*        88 CM-DEALLOCATE-ABEND          VALUE 17.          *
*        88 CM-DEALLOCATE-NORMAL         VALUE 18.          *
COPY CMCOBOL.

01  BUFFER                  PIC X(256)    VALUE  SPACES.
01  REM-PROC                PIC  X(8).
01  PARAM-LEN               PIC  9(9) COMP-4.
01  PARAM                   PIC  X(256)

*    Error recovery  has been omitted for simplicity.                *
PROCEDURE DIVISION.
*    Accept the conversation.                                         *
    PERFORM CPI-C-ACCEPT
        THRU  CPI-C-ACCEPT-EXIT.

*    Receive the procedure name in REM-PROC from the requester.*
    MOVE LENGTH OF REM-PROC TO REQUESTED-LENGTH.
    PERFORM CPI-C-RECEIVE
        THRU  CPI-C-RECEIVE-EXIT.
    MOVE BUFFER TO REM-PROC.
```

```
*    Receive the parameter data in PARAM  from the requester.        *
     MOVE LENGTH OF PARAM TO REQUESTED-LENGTH.
     PERFORM CPI-C-RECEIVE
        THRU CPI-C-RECEIVE-EXIT.
     MOVE BUFFER TO PARAM.
     MOVE RECEIVED-LENGTH TO PARAM-LEN.


*    Invoke the procedure.                                           *
     CALL REM-PROC USING PARAM.


*    Send the the reply to the requester.*
     PERFORM CPI-C-SEND
        THRU CPI-C-SEND-EXIT.


     PERFORM  PROGRAM-END.
*********************************************************************

CPI-C-ACCEPT.
*    Accept incoming ALLOCATE from the requester and initialize *
*    the conversation characteristics to default values.        *
     CALL "CMACCP" USING      CONVERSATION-ID
                              CM-RETCODE.
     IF   NOT CM-OK
        PERFORM PROGRAM-ERROR THRU PROGRAM-END.
CPI-C-ACCEPT-EXIT. EXIT.
*********************************************************************

CPI-C-RECEIVE.
*    Receive  a procedure name or a parameter from the requester.   *
     CALL "CMRCV" USING CONVERSATION-ID
                        BUFFER
                        REQUESTED-LENGTH
                        DATA-RECEIVED
                        RECEIVED-LENGTH
                        STATUS-RECEIVED
                        REQUEST-TO-SEND-RECEIVED
                        CM-RETCODE.

     IF   NOT CM-OK
        PERFORM PROGRAM-ERROR THRU PROGRAM-END.
CPI-C-RECEIVE-EXIT. EXIT.
*********************************************************************
```

```
CPI-C-SEND.
*    Send the reply to the requester.                              *
     MOVE PARAM TO BUFFER.
     MOVE PARAM-LEN TO SEND-LENGTH.
     CALL "CMSEND" USING CONVERSATION-ID
                         BUFFER
                         SEND-LENGTH
                         REQUEST-TO-SEND-RECEIVED
                         CM-RETCODE.

     IF NOT CM-OK
        PERFORM  PROGRAM-ERROR
              THRU  PROGRAM-END.
CPI-C-SEND-EXIT.  EXIT.
*******************************************************

PROGRAM-ERROR.
*    Set the deallocate_type characteristic to an abend condition.   *
     SET CM-DEALLOCATE-ABEND TO TRUE.
     CALL "CMSDT" USING  CONVERSATION-ID
                         DEALLOCATE-TYPE
                         CM-RETCODE.

PROGRAM-END.
     CALL "CMDEAL"USING        CONVERSATION-ID
                               CM-RETCODE
     STOP RUN.
*******************************************************
```

C

LU 6.2 Network Flows

This appendix describes LU 6.2 network flows in terms of the verb sequences and the corresponding Basic Information Units (BIUs). the following is the SNA notation used in the figures describing the network message flows:

RH —request/response header indicators

BB — begin bracket indicator

CEB — conditional end of bracket indicator

CD — change direction indicator

RQD1 — definite response indicator 1

RQD2 — definite response indicator 2

RQE1 — exception response indicator 1

RQE2 — exception response indicator 2

BC — begin chain

EC — end chain

+DR2 — positive response to RDD2

-RSP(0846) — Negative response with a sense-data 0846

RU — request/response unit contents

   FMH-5 — function management header type 5, an ATTACH
            header

   FMH-7   — function management header type 7, error
              description header

The sense-data

   0846 — abnormal deallocation

   0889 — program-detected error

   data — refers to mapped conversation DGS variables or
          basic conversation logical records

The sequences below are valid for both mapped and basic
conversation since every mapped conversation verb is mapped by
the LU into a corresponding basic conversation verb.

LU 6.2 VERB SEQUENCES

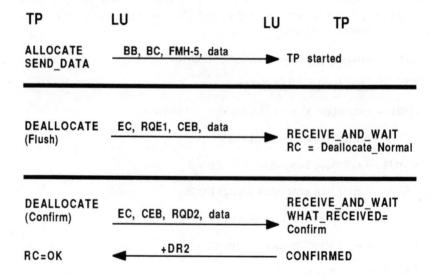

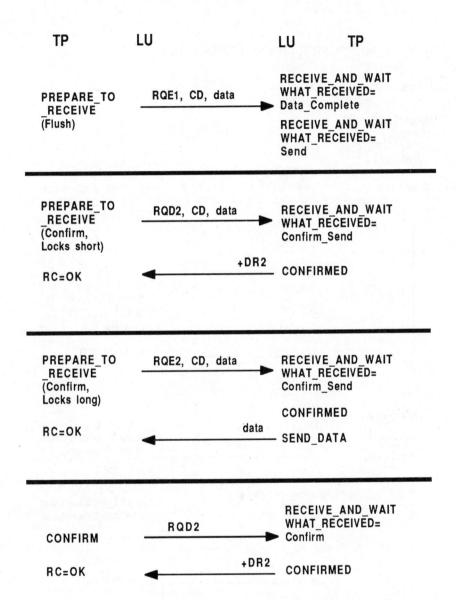

Allocate with Confirmation Processing

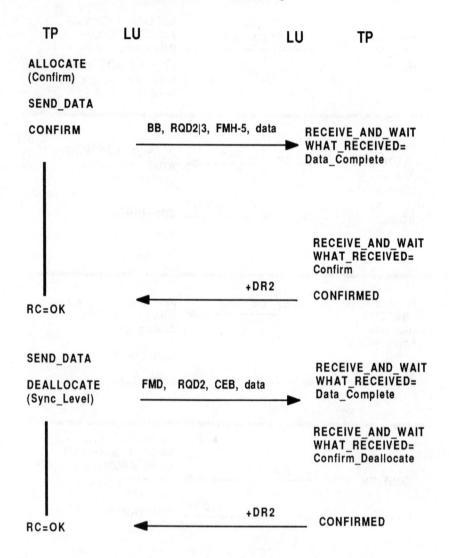

ALLOCATE (None)

T P	LU		LU	T P

ALLOCATE
(None)

SEND_DATA

RECEIVE_
AND_WAIT   FMH-5, BBI, CD, RQE1, data   RECEIVE_AND_WAIT
WHAT_RECEIVED=
Data_Complete

RECEIVE_AND_WAIT
WHAT_RECEIVED=
SEND

RECEIVE_AND
WAIT
WHAT_RECEIVED=
Data_Complete   FMD, RQE1, CEB, data   SEND_DATA

DEALLOCATE
RECEIVE_AND_WAIT   (FLUSH)
RC=Deallocate_Normal

ALLOCATE (Immediate)

T P	LU		LU	T P

ALLOCATE
(Immediate)

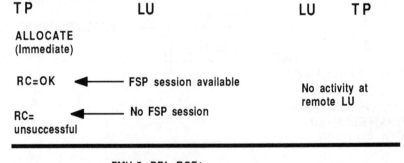

RC=OK ◄——— FSP session available

No activity at
remote LU

RC= ◄——— No FSP session
unsuccessful

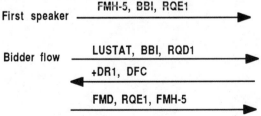

First speaker ——— FMH-5, BBI, RQE1 ———►

Bidder flow ——— LUSTAT, BBI, RQD1 ———►

◄——— +DR1, DFC ———

——— FMD, RQE1, FMH-5 ———►

SEND_ERROR in Receive State

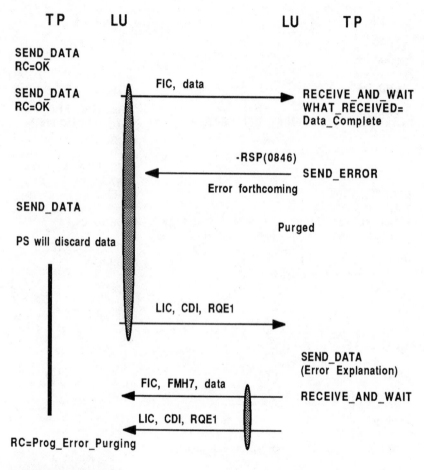

TP   LU   LU   TP

SEND_DATA
RC=OK

SEND_DATA   FIC, data   RECEIVE_AND_WAIT
RC=OK   WHAT_RECEIVED=
                                                         Data_Complete

                              -RSP(0846)
                                                         SEND_ERROR
                            Error forthcoming

SEND_DATA
                                                         Purged

PS will discard data

                            LIC, CDI, RQE1

                                                         SEND_DATA
                                                         (Error Explanation)

                          FIC, FMH7, data   RECEIVE_AND_WAIT

                          LIC, CDI, RQE1

RC=Prog_Error_Purging

RECEIVE_AND_WAIT
WHAT_RECEIVED=
Error Explanation

SEND_ERROR in Send State

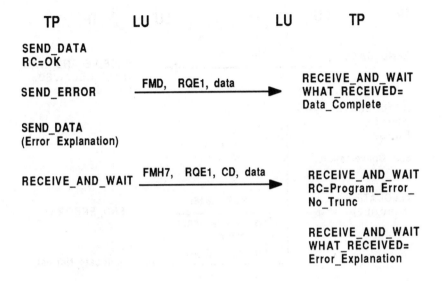

REQUEST_TO_SEND Processing

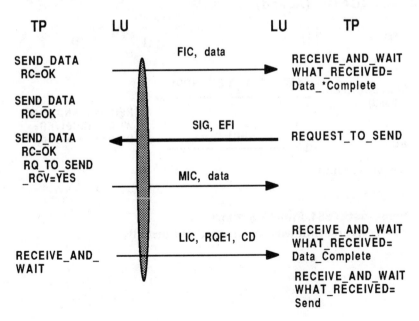

DEALLOCATE (Flush), SEND_ERROR

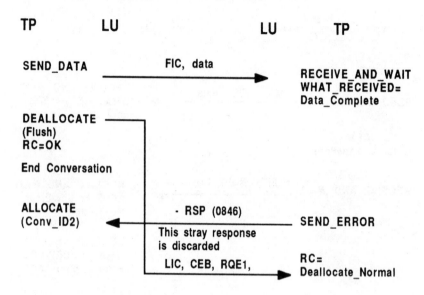

TP   LU   LU   TP

SEND_DATA ——————→ FIC, data ——————→ RECEIVE_AND_WAIT
WHAT_RECEIVED=
Data_Complete

DEALLOCATE
(Flush)
RC=OK

End Conversation

ALLOCATE   - RSP (0846)   SEND_ERROR
(Conv_ID2) ←——————
This stray response
is discarded
LIC, CEB, RQE1, ——————→ RC=
Deallocate_Normal

DEALLOCATE (Abend)

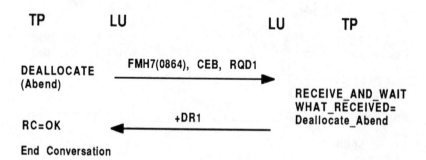

TP   LU   LU   TP

DEALLOCATE   FMH7(0864), CEB, RQD1 ——————→
(Abend)
RECEIVE_AND_WAIT
WHAT_RECEIVED=
RC=OK   +DR1 ←——————   Deallocate_Abend

End Conversation

Sense-data 0864, Function Abort
The conversation was terminated abnormally

Glossary and Acronyms

ABM — asynchronous balance mode; link level protocol in X.25 networks

ABME — asynchronous balance mode extended; link level protocol in X.25 networks

ACB in VTAM — access method control block, which is the name specified in the ACBNAME parameter of VTAM's APPL statement

ACF — advanced communications function; a group of SNA-compliant IBM program products such as ACF/VTAM, ACF/TCAM, ACF/SSP, and ACF/NCP

ACF/NCP — ACF for the network control program

ALLOCATE — a LU6.2 application program interface verb used to assign a session to a conversation

ANSI — American National Standards Institute; an organization sponsored by the Computer and Business Equipment Manufacturers Association for establishing voluntary industry standards

API — application program interface

APPC — Advanced Program-to-Program Communications

APPN — Advanced Peer-to-Peer Networking

ASCII — American Standard Code for Information Exchange; the code developed by ANSI for information exchange between data-processing systems, data communication systems, and associated equipment; ASCII character set consists of 7-bit characters plus one bit for parity check

AS/400 — Application System/400; a family of IBM's midrange computers

ASM — address space manager

Attach Manager — in OS/2, the component of APPC that managers incoming ALLOCATE requests

BB — begin bracket; in SNA, the value of the begin-bracket indicator in the request header (binary 1) in the first chain of a bracket

BETB — between brackets (indicator)

BF — boundary function; in SNA (1) a capability of a subarea node to provide protocol support for adjacent peripheral nodes, such as transforming network addresses to local addresses, performing session sequence numbering, providing session level pacing support; (2) a component that provides these capabilities

Bidder — in SNA, the LU-LU half session defined at session activation as having to request and receive permission from the other LU-LU half session to begin a bracket; contrast with first speaker

BIND — a request to activate a session between two logical units

BIU — Basic Information Unit; in SNA, the unit of data and control information that is passed between half sessions; consists of a request/response header (RH) followed by a request/response unit (RU)

BLU — Basic Link Unit

BSC — Binary Synchronous Communication; a line protocol that uses a standard set of transmission control characters and control character sequences to send binary-coded frames over a communication line; contrast with synchronous data link control (SDLC)

BTU — Basic Transmission Unit; in SNA, the unit of data and control information passed between path control network components; BTU can consist of one or more Path Information Units (PIU)

CASE — Computer-Aided Software Engineering

CBX — Computerized Branch Exchange

CCITT — International Telegraph and Telephone Consultive Committee

CCP — Configuration Control Program Facility

CCS — SAA/Common Communications Support

CD — change direction (indicator)

CDRM — cross-domain resource manager

CEB — conditional end bracket (indicator)

CICS — Customer Information Control System; teleprocessing and transaction management system which runs as a VTAM application

CMS — Conversation Monitor System (on VM/SP)

CNM — Communication Network Management

CNOS — change number of sessions

COS — class of service

Commit — a process that causes the changes to the protected resources to become permanent

Communications Manager — in OS/2, a component of OS/2 Extended Edition that lets a workstation connect to a host computer and use host services as well as resources of other personal computers to which the workstation is attached

Conversation — the logical connection between a pair of transaction programs for serially sharing a session between two type 6.2 logical units; conversations are delimited by brackets to gain exclusive use of a session

CP — Control Point or Control Program; a System Services Control Point (SSCP) which provides hierarchical control of a group of nodes in the network; a control point local to a specific node that provides control of that node

CPI — SAA Common Programming Interface

CPI-C — SAA Common Programming Interface-Communications

CUA — SAA Common User Access

DAF — Destination Address Field

DBCS — double-byte character set

DCA — Document Content Architecture

DCE — data circuit-terminating equipment

DDF — Distributed Data Facility

DDM — Distributed Data Management

DES — Data Encryption Standard

DFC — data flow control; the SNA layer within a half-session that controls whether the half-session can send, receive, or concurrently send and receive RUs; groups related RUs into RU chains; delimits transactions through the use of brackets; controls the interlocking of the requests and responses; generates sequence numbers; and associates requests with responses

DIA — Document Interchange Architecture

DISOSS — Distributed Office Support System

DLC — data link control layer; the SNA layer that consists of the link stations that schedule data transfer over a link between two nodes and performs error control for the link

DR1 — definite response 1 (indicator)

DR2 — definite response 2 (indicator)

DTE — data terminal equipment

Domain — a System Services Control Point (SSCP) and physical units (PU), logical units (LU), links, link stations, and all associated resources that the SSCP can control

EB — end bracket (indicator)

EBCDIC — Extended Binary-Coded Decimal Interchange Code

EC — end chain

EIA — Electronic Industries Association

EN — end node; synonym for type 2.1 end node

EP — emulation program.

ER — explicit route that defines the physical path from the origin subarea node to the destination subarea node

ERI — exception response indicator

ERP — error-recovery processing

FDX — full duplex

FI — format indicator

FID — format identification

FID2 — format identifier 2

FMH — function management header; in SNA, one or more headers, optionally presented in the leading RUs of an RU chain, that allow one half session in the LU-LU session to carry a conversation establishment request, a session and conversation error-related information, or an LU-LU password verification data; which select, change, or transmit a destination at a session partner

GDS — General Data Stream (variable); data and commands that are defined by length (LL) and identification (ID) bytes

HS — half session

I-FIELD — information field

IMS — Information Management System

INB — in bracket (indicator)

ISO — International Standards Organization

LAN — local area network; the physical connection that allows information

LEN — Low Entry Networking

LFSID — Local-Form Session Identifier

LH — link header

LS — link station

LT — link trailer

LU — logical unit; a port through which an end user accesses an SNA network in order to communicate with another end user (transaction program)

LU-LU — session between two logical units in SNA network

LUW — Logical Unit of Work

LUWID — Logical Unit-of-Work identifier

MCR — Mapped Conversation Record

MSA — Management Services Architecture

MVS — Multiple Virtual Storage

MVS/370 — MVS for IBM S/370

MVS/ESA — Multiple Virtual Storage/Enterprise Systems Architecture

MVS/XA — Multiple Virtual Storage/Extended Architecture

NAU — Network Addressable Unit; a logical unit (LU), a physical unit (PU), or a System Services Control Point (SSCP) which is the origin or the destination of the data transmitted by a path control network

NCP — Network Control Program; an IBM-licensed program that runs on a communications controller and supports single-domain, multiple-domain, and interconnected network capabilities of the controller

NN — network node; synonym for APPN network node

NetView/PC — CNM PC applications (Token Ring or LAN managers)

NMVT — Network Management Vector Transport

NPDA — Network Problem Determination Application

NPSI — X.25 NCP Packet Switching Interface

OAF — Origin Address Field

ODAI — OAF/DAF Assignor Indicator or Origin Destination Assignor Indicator

OSI — open systems interconnection; a layered architecture that is designed to allow for interconnection between heterogeneous systems

PBX — Private Branch Exchange

PC — path control

PIP — program initialization parameter

PIU — Path Information Unit; a message unit that consists of a transmission header (TH) alone or TH followed by BIU or BIU segment

PLU — primary logical unit; the logical unit that sends the BIND request for a particular LU-LU session

PU — physical unit

PU 2.1 — physical unit type 2.1

RESYNC — resynchronization (syncpoint function)

RH — request/response header; in SNA, control information preceding a request/response unit (RU)

RRI — request/response indicator

RSP — SNA response unit

RU — request unit or response unit; in SNA, a generic term for a message unit that can contain a request, control information, or a response to a request.

SAA — System Application Architecture; a set of software interfaces, protocols, and conventions that provides a framework for designing and developing consistent, portable applications across various computer environments

SC — session control

SDLC — synchronous data link control

SLU — secondary logical unit; in SNA, the logical unit that contains the secondary half session for a particular LU-LU session, i.e., the LU that receives the session activation request

SNA — Systems Network Architecture; the description of the logical structure, formats, protocols, and operational sequences for transmitting information through and controlling configuration and operation of networks

SNADS — SNA Distribution Services; an IBM architecture that defines a set of rules to receive, route, and send electronic mail across networks

SON — session outage notification

SQL — Structured Query Language

SSCP — System Service Control Point

TC — transmission control layer; in SNA, the layer within a half session that synchronizes and paces session-level data traffic, checks session sequence numbers of requests, and enciphers or deciphers user data

TG — transmission group

TH — transmission header; in SNA, control information, optionally followed by a Basic Information Unit segment, that is created and used by the path control for message routing

TP — transaction program; application program written by a user that is an end user of a type 6.2 logical unit

TPN — transaction program name

TS — transmission services

TSO — time sharing option (MVS/SP); a feature of an operating system (i.e., MVS) that provides conversational time sharing of system resources from remote stations

USS — Unformatted System Service

VM — virtual machine

VM/SP — Virtual Machine/System Product; an IBM-licensed program, which is an operating system that manages the resources of a mainframe

VR — virtual route; in SNA, a logical connection between two subarea nodes that is physically realized as a particular explicit route

VSAM — Virtual Storage Access Method

VSE — virtual storage extended (synonymous with VSE/AF)

VTAM — Virtual Telecommunication Access Method; an IBM-licensed program that controls communication and data flow in an SNA network

XID — Exchange Identification

XID-3 — XID with format 3 I-field

ABOUT THE AUTHOR

John J. Edmunds (Los Gatos, Calif.), a principal of Galaxy
Consultants, is a widely quoted expert on IBM Enterprise
Computing. He is a leading developer and presenter of IBM
Networking Seminars on SNA, LU 6.2, SAA, and APPC,
both in the United States and Pacific Rim for corporations
such as IBM, Hewlett-Packard, Xerox, NEC, TRW, Boeing,
etc. He earned a B.S. in mathematics and computer science
from Monash University in Melbourne, Australia.